THE WARSHIP
MARY ROSE

THE WARSHIP MARY ROSE

The Life and Times of King Henry VIII's Flagship

DAVID CHILDS

CHATHAM PUBLISHING
LONDON

In association with the Mary Rose Trust

TO ALL WHO SERVED IN

Mary Rose

AND THOSE WHO HAVE WORKED

TO PRESERVE THEIR MEMORY

First published in Great Britain in 2007 by
Chatham Publishing,
Lionel Leventhal Ltd,
Park House, 1 Russell Gardens,
London NW11 9NN
www.chathampublishing.com

In association with the Mary Rose Trust, Portsmouth
www.maryrose.org

Distributed in the United States of America by
MBI Publishing Company,
Galtier Plaza, Suite 200, 380 Jackson Street,
St Paul, MN 55101-3885, USA

British Library Cataloguing in Publication Data
Childs, David
The warship Mary Rose : the life and times of King Henry's VIII's flagship
1. Mary Rose (Ship) 2. Warships - England - History - 16th century
I. Title
623.8 225 0942
ISBN-13: 9781861762672
ISBN 978 1 86176 267 2

Designed and Typeset by Roger Daniels
Printed and bound in Singapore by Kyodo Printing Company

Contents

Picture Credits

Illustrations sources for the pages listed are as follows:

By courtesy of the Mary Rose Trust – 11, 18, 19, 21, 23, 27, 28, 30-34 (all), 37, 38, 42-47 (all), 50 (both), 52-56 (all), 65, 68, 70-72, 73 (top), 74-78 (all), 80-87 (all), 89, 91, 93 (both), 94, 96, 98-100 (all), 107, 108, 149, 152 (bottom), 154, 155, 179, 181-183 (all), 185, 187, 190, 193, 194, 196, 198, 202-204 (all), 206, 207, 209-212 (all), 213 (top)

© 2007 www.artistsharbour.com www.artistsharbour.com from whom prints are available –12-13, 164-165, 167, 169

Courtesy of Portsmouth Museums & Record Office – 16, 152 (top), 162

Southampton City Council Heritage Services – 24

Author – 35, 104, 109, 110, 111, 113, 114, 118, 139, 141-146 (all), 172, 213 (bottom)

The *Matthew* of Bristol – 40

British Library – 41, 123, 130-131, 157, 159

Magdalene College, Cambridge – 58, 103, 121

The National Archives, Public Record Office – 61, 132, 147

The Bridgeman Art Library – 62, 63, 136-137, 165 (top), 188-189

Christopher Dobbs – 73 (bottom), 200, 201 (both)

The Trustees of the National Museums of Scotland – 101

Scala Archives – 119, 176-177

History Today – 152

Remaining illustrations from out-of-copyright sources in the public domain.

Acknowledgements

THE WRITING OF THIS BOOK has been a joy compounded by the fact that its composition has enabled me to meet, debate and correspond with wonderful people to whom I owe a debt of gratitude. First, I must give grateful thanks to John Lippiett who invited me to join him at The Mary Rose Trust to develop their ideas for a museum worthy of the *Mary Rose* and the many objects recovered from the ship. My interest in the Tudor navy was rekindled through the enthusiasm and knowledge of the many members of staff and volunteers who care for the ship and the museum and who were a joy to be with. They all gave me their time and patience in equal measure, and I would only single out Christopher Dobbs and Dr. Doug McElvogue for particular mention as I worked most closely with them and made full use of their detailed knowledge, experience and ideas. Doug McElvogue has acted as my archaeological advisor and made me look with fresh eyes at some areas where the conventional interpretation needed further study: without his analytical mind I would have been hesitant in proposing much of what seems to me to be logical.

Nick Braddock, the Chairman of The Mary Rose Society, read the book and provided essential recommendations as to its structure, which it would have been foolish to ignore. He also very kindly gave me permission to reproduce many of the drawings and diagrams that the society has produced over the years. I was extremely lucky that many of those who were involved with the raising of *Mary Rose* were available to tell their stories. Principal amongst these were Christopher Dobbs and Maurice Young, both of whom have a continuing enthusiasm for the project which is infectious. Peter Crossman at the Trust took and processed many photographs and drawings, and Simon Ware made available many artefacts from the reserve collection.

The nature of this book has meant that each chapter has examined specialised areas relating to *Mary Rose*. I am an expert in none of these and, if my inexpertise is cloaked successfully, it is due to the contributions, advice and guidance of many whose knowledge far exceeds my own. As well as the Mary Rose Trust, the research that I needed to undertake was made possible through the helpful support of many centres, including Portsmouth City Library, The Royal Naval Museum, the Admiralty Library (and Jeannie Wright in particular), the National Archive at Kew and the National Library. All I called upon took pity on my ignorance and naivety and pointed me in the right direction. The Chart Depot at Portsmouth Dockyard gave whatever support I asked of them and thus enabled me to examine closely the time that *Mary Rose* spent at sea. Sara Rodger and the archive team at Arundel Castle provided me with insights into the life, actions and motivations of the Howard brothers that I would otherwise have missed. My woeful lack of French was redeemed by the support of Michelle Chapman-Andrews who acted as a translator in England and my wife, Jane, who acted as an interpreter abroad. To Jane, I owe the greatest debt for her patience, encouragement, suggestions and support.

Finally, I would like to thank the team at Chatham Publishing for agreeing to undertake this work, in particular, Rob Gardiner, my publisher, and Naomi Waters, my editor, who overcame conflicts between incompatible software.

CLARENCE HOUSE

I was one of those present in the Solent when, in 1982, the hull of the *Mary Rose* appeared above the waves for the first time in 450 years. Many millions more watched the event on television around the world and still remember that extraordinary moment. The magic remains, and since that October morning twenty-five years ago some seven million visitors have been thrilled by tours of the ship and its wonderful artefacts. Now, at last, the prospect of reuniting those objects from the hull is on the horizon and a museum is being built to display these artefacts and tell the story of the ship.

Contrary to the view held commonly, the *Mary Rose* did not sink on her maiden voyage. She served in Henry VIII's Navy Royal for thirty-six years, many of which she spent as the flagship on active service. She took part in three wars against the French and one against the Scottish and it was during this time that the principles of our naval strategy and tactics were honed. Her first two admirals, brothers Sir Edward and Lord Thomas Howard, can claim to be Britain's first modern admirals and the loss of Sir Edward in battle is a story of heroism as exciting today as it was at the time. The struggle for the mastery of the Channel, especially against the threat of French galleys, was one that England needed to win if it was to become a successful maritime nation. The *Mary Rose* played a full part in this struggle.

The search for the wreck of the *Mary Rose,* led by Alexander McKee, and her recovery by Margaret Rule's team, was so exciting and received so much publicity that the history of the ship herself tended to be forgotten. The information available often concentrated on her last day, 19th July 1545, and not her earlier career. Yet to ignore this is to do injustice to the *Mary Rose* as an important and still present representative of the Tudor Navy. It disregards the vital role she played in the creation of the standing navy, for she was present at the birth of greatness that became the Royal Navy. Her story is seminal and a joy to read.

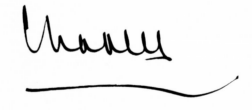

Introduction

IN 2005 I WAS MANNING A *Mary Rose* stand at the London Boat Show, courtesy of one of our sponsors, Lewmar, and was surprised by the number of people who came up and either enquired whether, or told me that, the ship had sunk on her maiden voyage. When I raised this strange fact at a Trustees' meeting one of those present, very bravely, confessed that he too had thought that *Mary Rose* had been lost on her first voyage. In fact she had been a part of Henry VIII's navy royal for thirty-six years. So why was there this universal feeling that her career could be measured in days rather than decades?

Primarily it is because the wonder of the raising of *Mary Rose* led people to look no further back in her history than that marvellous moment in October 1982 when her hull broke the surface for the first time in 437 years. A worldwide television audience watched spellbound as the great crane lifted her precious cargo out of the choppy Solent. And who, of those who remember that day, would ever forget that heart-stopping moment when the rig jerked and slipped, luckily without damaging the ship's timbers. That indelible memory marks people's earliest awareness of the ship; they had enough wonderment from that moment on without needing to travel back further through history. Those early witnesses who flocked to Portsmouth Historic Dockyard to see the hull, and later the objects in the temporary exhibition, came to see the hulk that they had witnessed being salvaged.

The two people most closely, and most indelibly linked to that event, and the years of patient exploration and uncovering that preceded it, Alexander McKee[1] and Margaret Rule,[2] both wrote books about the ship but these, quite naturally, concentrated on their endeavours, while Ernle Bradford's book[3] is almost entirely devoted to the ship's last moments, the search for her and her recovery and raising. Add to this the fact that the first information board that greets the visitor to the *Mary Rose* exhibition asks, 'Why did the *Mary Rose* sink?' and is followed by an introductory film about diving and salvage, then it is not surprising that the story of the career of this major Tudor warship has failed to attract attention.

The search for *Mary Rose* and her recovery, along with some 20,000 ship-borne objects is a tale of human perseverance, determination, endurance, endeavour, skill, cunning and achievement. But, magnificent as it was, it is not the story of the ship herself, but the account of those who found and raised her. It is, essentially, the story of a ground-breaking archaeological enterprise that set new standards in recording and recovery that the world would not have dreamed possible until that time. As such, the ship buried beneath the Solent could have been any of the other wrecks that have sunk in those waters, such as *Royal George* or *Edgar*. It could have been any other Tudor ship, or even a vessel of earlier or later date; it could have been a ship whose name or fate had previously been unknown. It happened to be *Mary Rose*, and she had sunk under the watchful eye of the king who had commissioned her and whose favourite warship she had been. But the tragedy of her high-profile loss was incidental to the romance of her recovery. The story of the Tudor warship named *Mary Rose* was not considered that important an aspect of the great endeavour that brought her back home to Portsmouth.

Now, some twenty-five years after her recovery – when the end of the long and painstaking process of conservation is in sight and the vision of a purpose-built museum in which the objects can be re-united with the hull from which they came is nearing reality – now is the time to restore the historiographical balance between the living ship and an archaeological object. Now, with the publication of a very detailed report of the archaeological discoveries,[4] is the time to tell the story of the warship *Mary Rose* herself. Not to do so would be rather like having a thirty-six-year-old friend who, heaven forbid, is killed in a plane crash and doing nothing in his memory afterwards but to talk about the day of the accident and sifting through the wreckage. In the same way, *Mary Rose*'s remains help to support but do not tell the full story of her life as it was lived.

Mary Rose was a flagship. For this reason we have a collection of correspondence from her admirals to both the king and the Master Almoner, Thomas Wolsey. These provide a wonderful window on personal relationships at the time and are an excellent record about the birth of a standing navy and the demands imposed and the potential conferred on the crown by such a force. The letters[5] and objects and the vessel itself come together only in the retelling of the career of the ship whose creation represents the beginnings of the Royal Navy. For this reason the story of the warship *Mary Rose* tells of the birth of greatness. Those who wish to study the Tudor navy go fishing in a shallow, well-trawled sea, where few new and exciting catches can be made. This means that, when their wares are laid out on the slab to be surveyed by the would-be purchaser, they can appear pretty unvaried. Some have taken the detailed documentation to be of value in itself and presented it accurately but unappetisingly. Others skim the whole sea's surface without looking for information at a greater depth. Those who wish to enter the waters in search of something new have either to present startling new recipes or sail into the headwaters that feed the sea and add ingredients from these peripheral ponds to their main course. The problem then becomes one of balance.

In understanding Tudor shipbuilding techniques how far back is it logical to go? In studying the armament of Tudor warships how much of the history of ordnance should be described? Too much, and the garnish overwhelms the main dish. Too much, and it would appear that the peripheral is being deployed to support a lack of substance in the centre. 'Probable', 'possible', 'perhaps' and their hesitant companion, 'may be', could legitimately escort many a statement in a book based around certain evidence and much assumption. Their presence can, however, be stultifying, and I would ask the readers' indulgence in support of my belief that their role is best recognised in acknowledging them in their absence rather than having them constantly present. Where I have made assumptions without authority I have done so, where possible after discussions, by taking what seems to me a logical position.

The nature of this book has meant that each chapter has examined specialised areas relating to *Mary Rose*. I am an expert in none of these and, if my inexpertise is cloaked successfully, it is due to the contributions, advice and guidance of many colleagues whose knowledge far exceeds my own.

CHAPTER 1

The Birth of Greatness

HENRY WANTED WAR. Whatever his other aims and ambitions on ascending to the English throne none was more obvious to observers than this. Henry VIII was not overly concerned about whom his enemy might be as long as he had one, but there were certain parameters even his youthful hot head had to take into account. His cautious father, Henry VII, founder of the Tudor dynasty, had ensured that England was neither a threat to or in danger from her enemies. The new king's elder sister, Margaret, was married to James IV of Scotland, which put that traditional enemy of the English in check for the time being. Henry himself was married to the king of Spain's daughter, Katherine of Aragon, which precluded Iberia from any direct conflict; the Holy Roman Empire was too amorphous; and the Turks were at too great a distance for England to undertake a crusade in that direction. This left France – another traditional enemy – as the likely candidate for war. Henry just needed an excuse, and the opportunity. The Venetian ambassador to England, Andrea Badoer, recognised this, writing to his masters on 25 April 1509, just three days after Henry had been proclaimed King: 'The King is magnificent, liberal and a great enemy of the French. He will be the signory's friend.'[1] While on the next day another Venetian stated in a letter quite clearly that: 'The King swore, *de more*, immediately after his coronation to make war on the King of France. Soon we shall hear that he has invaded France.'[2]

Henry was even reported to have retained some Venetian trading galleys at Southampton for the express purpose of using them to load troops for a French invasion. But why? England was not threatened. In continental Europe, the current cockpit of confrontation was northern Italy, not the Channel coast and the Low Countries – areas in which Henry would have had a legitimate interest. The motivation for this bellicose stance was a personal desire for the prestige of success in arms. In taking to the field of battle, sixteenth-century princes gauged their self-esteem and gained respect from other monarchs. Henry believed that the time he spent in the tilt yard and hunting, as well as his many suits of mail, were very much a part of his kingly duties and regalia. Coupled with this was the young king's loathing of the elderly Louis XII of France, whose gout-ridden feebleness Henry saw as an affront to the very idea of kingly virtue. Moreover, in 1509 Henry VIII had much to prove if he were to be counted among the great princes of Europe.

A model of Henry VIII in his prime, based on the well-known Holbein portraiture.

Had Henry VIII wed five fewer wives, sired two fewer children and defended only one faith he would probably be remembered as an insignificant, unpleasant Catholic king of a backward peripheral nation, which he bankrupted in pursuit of unrealised foreign fame. His European peer group were far more significant individuals. In the last decade of the fifteenth century, along with Henry, three other princes were born who were to play major roles in the future of Europe once, in their teens or early twenties they had ascended to their inheritance. Süleyman became the Ottoman sultan at the age of twenty-five in 1520; Francis I, king of France at nineteen in 1515; Charles I of Spain and V of the Holy Roman Empire (longhand for the German states) was only fifteen when he became the Spanish king in 1515; while Henry himself was just seventeen when he inherited the throne of England. Of the four, Süleyman's rightfully earned sobriquet 'the Magnificent' sets him apart from his peers who spent a large part of their reigns warring both against him but, principally, amongst themselves. These latter wars were largely centered around lands in Italy where Francis was to achieve one glorious victory, at Marignano in 1515, and one catastrophic defeat, at the hands of Charles, at Pavia in 1525.

During these turbulent times the English king was to remain a secondary player, rather like a child clinging on to the legs of two struggling adults in an attempt to influence the outcome. As a military leader Henry laid siege to a Flemish town, Tournai, and a French village, Thérouanne; fought one battle, The Spurs, in which the sides scarcely clashed; seized one French ferry port, Boulogne, and retained a tenuous hold over another, Calais. Although Henry was paid handsomely to return his gains these forays, which bankrupted England, are scarcely more than a footnote in contemporary European history. This was minor stuff indeed compared with the dynastic struggle between the houses of Hapsburg and Valois to establish hegemony over the whole of western Europe. After the deaths of those four rulers, (Henry and Francis in 1547, Charles in 1558 and Sulyeman in 1566), contemporaries would have ranked Henry as the least significant of the four. The contempt with which the English were held by the European super powers is best summed up in the words of the Holy Roman Emperor, Maximilian, to his grandson and successor, Charles, in the spring of 1517 when he remarked about the terms of the recent Treaty of Noyon, 'My child, you are about to cheat the French and I the English.'

At the end of his life Henry VIII bequeathed to the nation four things of lasting significance: a national Church; a countryside of romantic ruins,[3] a daughter, Elizabeth, who was to achieve for the nation the greatness that Henry could only dream about; and, in the navy royal, a legacy greater and more

The capture of Boulogne was one of Henry's most positive military achievements, although it led Francis I to attempt the invasion of England in 1545. The original from which this engraving was made in 1788 was commissioned by the same man as the better known panorama of the Mary Rose's last battle, the so-called Cowdray engraving.
© 2007 www.artistsharbour.com www.artistsharbour.com from whom prints are available.

lasting than any left by his contemporary dynastic rivals. It was not a legacy easily or rapidly created given the international position that England occupied throughout his reign and her lack of ocean-going ships and sailors. The limitations of England's sphere of influence can be seen by studying the imperial and maritime achievements of other European powers during Henry's lifetime. In 1492 Columbus discovered America for Spain; in 1499 the Portuguese navigator Vasco da Gama returned from the East Indies; in 1500 Brazil was discovered; between 1514 and 1517 the Turks seized Egypt and Syria; in 1520 the Spaniard

Cortes conquered Mexico; in 1529 the Turks besieged Vienna; in 1533 Pizarro overthrew the Incas. The list goes on, and it is one of extraordinary achievement in this one sphere of endeavour alone. Add to it developments in art, architecture, religion and philosophy, and the minuteness of the English contribution becomes starkly clear.

At the beginning of Henry's reign, England had a long way to go before she could contribute to this list of seminal events or join the ranks of the great players. By the end of the Tudor century, she was

The best-known image of a late fourteenth-century merchant ship, this depicts a Flemish 'Kraek' (or carrack).

poised to dominate them. Henry, without understanding its potential, laid the foundation for England's greatness through the creation of the standing navy royal, and was blessed that, in Elizabeth, he had an heir able to build magnificently upon this foundation. Henry's treatment of his own inheritance demonstrated all the characteristics of a second-generation heir to a thriving business thriftly assembled. He blew it. Whereas his father had fought to establish the family firm and had taken no chances with its fortune, which was significant at the time of his death,[4] Henry was to show little interest in how the business was run, preferring to spend his inheritance in courtly delights such as the joust and chase at which he excelled. Standing at over six foot and possessing an athletic build the king could match any man in the tilt yard, archery butts, or other knightly venues, the pursuit of which often occupied his whole day leaving little time for tedious matters of state. Henry would thus not be a model ruler along the lines laid down by Renaissance philosophers. He was a man of action, not contemplation, but his willingness to delegate, idle though its origins may have been, was a key element in the transition of the English state from an autocratic kingdom to a constitutional monarchy and parliamentary democracy, well ahead of its European counterparts.

Henry was fortunate in finding, first in Thomas Wolsey, then in Thomas Cromwell, two men to whom he could entrust those matters of state that he himself found too boring. They would serve him well. Not that, in the end, their service would count for much when they let their monarch down. For Henry, among his many virtues was also a cruel and calculating bully, whose sleep was not disturbed by signing the death warrants – often on trumped-up evidence – of those who, having served him well, had become an inconvenience. Indeed, if one were to seek a modern equivalent of Henry VIII, one could find many similarities in the behaviour of an Idi Amin or Sadaam Hussein, bullying, pompous leaders of less significant nations. But, however uneasily rested the heads that advised the crown, Henry was establishing the necessary domestic conditions and relationships for a modern state.

Internationally it was a different story. Here Henry was personally active in pursuing an aggressive foreign policy, but he lacked an army or commanders who could achieve his goals. England, a land so frequently at war with itself, did not trust standing armies. It was also protected from all but the Scots by the Channel, which served it like a fortress moat. Henry's foreign policy would depend, not for its success, but rather for its avoidance of failure, on the existence of a standing navy that was, towards the end of his reign, able to repel an invasion by a foreign force greater than that of the more famous Spanish Armada of his daughter Elizabeth's reign. Henry was the first English ruler to appreciate that the state would be better served if war ships were a permanent part of the king's armoury.

English monarchs required war ships for five reasons. These were to (i) transport an army; (ii) raid enemy coasts and towns; (iii) defend against invasion; (iv) protect trade and curb piracy, and (v) display the king's prestige. It had always been possible to achieve these aims, for a limited period, with ships hired for the occasion from the nation's merchant fleet and fitting them with pre-fabricated castles to hold soldiers. Even where such castles were not available they were easy to construct. Fir poles were lashed together to form a lattice cage which was fitted onto the ship's deck. Upon this was secured a plank floor enclosed with a crenelated breast-work to protect those mustered inside and to give them a raised platform from which to pour down arrows and gun fire onto an enemy's decks. That these castles were light meant that they had minimum effect on the ship's stability. Later, when a permanent naval force was desired, the castles were built as part of the main structure, creating a purpose-built warship with limited use as a merchant vessel. The potentially hazardous disadvantage of this was that the resulting heavier structure might be considered capable of carrying weapons whose weight, located high up, could adversely affect the ship's stability.

To facilitate his commandeering of merchant ships the king paid a bounty to merchantmen that entitled him to take up their vessels when he needed to transport his forces abroad. The amount payable varied, but was generally agreed at five shillings per ton; which indicates that it was a very expensive option for the sovereign, not lightly undertaken. In addition, the king was a shipowner in his own right, and able to use his few vessels either for his own trading or by leasing them to merchants. So, although the need for and concept of a permanent navy royal with a paid crew was recognised, it was a responsibility which earlier sovereigns chose to avoid. Henry VIII made it a reality in a reign in which all five reasons cited earlier for the possession of a fleet were to be evident.

The creation of a standing navy carried with it responsibilities over and above that of the manning, maintenance, and arming of the ships and the payment of their crews. Foremost among these was that of victualling, and Henry's 'naval staff' were constantly being harassed by the sea-going admirals to provide the food and drink necessary to keep the fleet active and healthy. But a cadre of sailors dependent on the king for their well-being created other responsibilities as the Act for Maintenance of the Navy of 1540 made clear:

> The maintenance of my master mariners making them expert and cunning in the art and science of shipmen and sailing, and they, their wives and children have had their living of and by the same...and have also been the chief maintenance and support of the cities, towns, villages, havens, and creeks near adjoining the sea coasts; and the King's subjects, bakers, brewers, butchers, smiths, ropers, shipwrights, tailors (shoemakers) and other victuallers and handicraftsmen inhabiting and dwelling near the said coasts have also had by the same a great part of their living...[5]

This gives some idea of the dependence of a small town like Portsmouth – established primarily for the purpose of supporting the fleet – on the navy royal, and how many skills and trades were needed. If policy decided upon in London set the scene, shipwrights in Portsmouth would create the scenery and, right at the beginning of his reign, it was to Portsmouth that Henry turned to build the set.

The king was aware that his relationship with

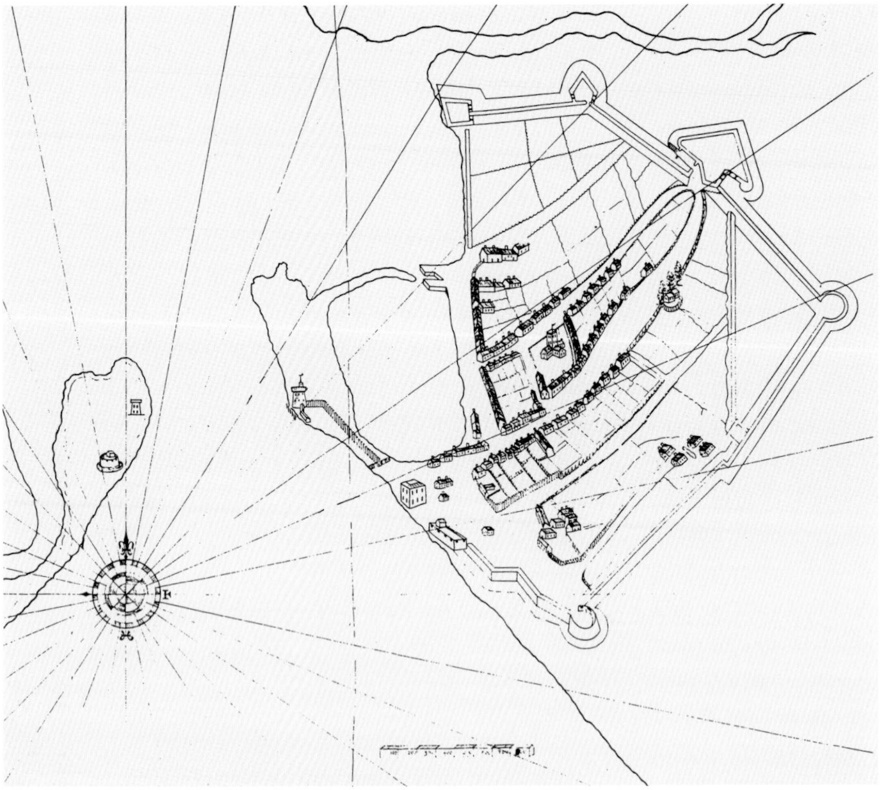

Based on the earliest map of Portsmouth, dating from around 1540, this map clearly shows the four breweries grouped around the pond.

France was not going to be an easy one. His decision to marry his brother's widow, Katherine of Aragon, linked, dynastically, two kingdoms located on either side of France – never a comfortable position for the one in the middle. Moreover, in recent decades England had lorded it over vast tracts of France, and Henry VII had even gone to war in support of Breton independence in 1494. By Henry VIII's time England retained only the well-defended town of Calais and its pale of just 120 square miles, yet its very occupation by the English was an irritation to the French out of all proportion to its geographical significance – similar to the irritation currently felt by the Spanish due to Britain's possession of Gibraltar.[6]

Tudor monarchs were always aware of the danger of fighting a war on two fronts, for the ever-troublesome Scots were the natural and traditional allies of the French. Placing two armies in the field, one in the north and one in the south of England would have been a logistical nightmare; it could also, given the Catholic leanings of the north, have created an internal threat to the throne. The major question was a complicated one; how could the king guarantee security at one extreme of the country while his forces were fully occupied either at the other or abroad and, at the same time, avoid having a standing army that might become a threat to the Crown itself?

The answer lay in the creation of a Channel force, a standing navy. This Henry VII had cautiously begun. His son was to complete its development. If a navy could be employed in the Channel as a selective filter, allowing English forces to pass through unimpeded in either direction, but preventing free passage to any would-be invader attempting to offer succour to an ally moving south from Scotland, the integrity of the southern frontiers could be guaranteed, thus enabling the full force of an English army to be directed north. For the first time in English history the nation was developing two military arms with separate priorities. Although for Henry VIII there was to be no glorious Agincourt to gild his name for posterity, his legacy was to be much more far-reaching and influential. For it was he who would lay the foundations for an English nation that we can recognise as the modern state, both civil, military and sacred. Among those legacies would be a standing, professional Royal Navy, for whom the earliest purpose-built warship would be *Mary Rose.*

It is popularly believed that *Mary Rose* was named for the king's thirteen-year-old sister, Mary. Were this true it would have been a fine coupling, for the feisty and beautiful youngster was a fitting match for the fine and frisky warship. Sadly, there is little evidence to support this romantic idea. There was a Europe-wide tradition throughout the fifteenth and sixteenth centuries to give naval vessels biblical names. The most famous class of ships so named was the 'Apostles' of the Spanish fleet, four of whom were to take part in the last fight of *Revenge* in 1591, and the English followed a similar pattern of nomenclature. Thus, Henry V's great ships included *Holigost, Jesus* and *Grace Dieu,* the largest of them all, whose outline can still be seen in the River Hamble at low water Springs. Significantly there was also *Trinity Royal,* which combined within its name reference to both Church and State. In 1464 *John Evangelist* and in 1470 *St Peter* joined the fleet. Henry VII, however, also introduced two major vessels with purely temporal names, *Sovereign* and *Regent.* Henry VIII's most significant indication of the natural alliance between church and state embodied in his warships was to be the 1500-ton *Henri Grace à Dieu,* popularly known as *Great Harry.*

This name alone indicates both the king's view that he governed 'by the Grace of God' and the manner of his relationship with the divine, a view made manifest in his dissolution of the monasteries and assumption of the role of Head of the Church in England. There is no reason to suppose that Henry would have felt emboldened to carry out these moves were it not for his belief that he was *rex et sacerdos* – a ruler who derived his powers from God. His fleet would be instruments of that divine authority; it was essential that their names reflected their sacred role.

In 1512 Henry purchased the 700-ton *Mary Lovet* and renamed her *Gabriel Royal,* while also acquiring the 400-ton *John Baptist* and the 300-ton *Christ* in the same year: *Trinity Henry* was built in 1519 and *Jesus of Lubeck* purchased in 1544. The two ships that Henry ordered at the start of his reign were *Peter Pomegranate* and *Mary Rose.* The former combined the symbol of the House of Aragon, a fetching tribute to the new Queen Katherine, with Peter. Peter who? There appears to be no-one significant of that name in either the Aragonese or Tudor families. The indication must be that the Peter referred to is the senior Apostle. There is then a logic that suggests that the other ship to be built at the same time was in fact named after the Virgin Mary. The link with the Tudor Rose contains a clever pun as the Virgin Mary was often referred to as the 'Mystic Rose'.

The hypothesis that *Mary Rose* might have been

A modern painting based on the ships of the Warwick Roll, which probably represent the biggest ships of Henry VII's navy, the *Regent* and the *Sovereign.*

named in honour of the Virgin is supported by the fact that it was to the shrine of Our Lady of Walsingham that the king went to pay homage following the birth of his son, the short-lived Henry, in January 1511. It was no casual journey, for the round trip would have taken at least fourteen days. Obviously, at this stage of his life, the king was a great respecter of the cult of the Virgin Mary. His naming of *Mary Rose* gives every indication that it was after her, rather than his sister, that his favourite vessel was named. In addition, naming a ship after his sister but not for his wife might not have been the most tactful step taken by the young and newly wed monarch who was very much in love with his spouse. In July 1509 he was to write about himself to Ferdinand of Aragon: 'The love he bears to Katherine is such that, if he were still free he would choose her in preference to all others.'[7] Certainly, naming a ship after such a love would seem a natural thing to do and there was a precedent for this. In 1505, James IV of Scotland had named his latest warship after his wife, Henry's eldest sister, Margaret. She was a large vessel of some 700 tons and King James was delighted with her, using every significant milestone in her development

A model of the *Mary Rose*, based on the Anthony Roll illustration.

as an excuse for a party with himself presiding wearing the internationally recognised badge of office of an admiral, a gold chain and boatswain's call or whistle. Queen Katherine had to wait until 1518 for the delightfully named *Katherine Pleasance* to be named for her and to be fitted out for royal pleasure.

It would be pleasing to think that Henry's two sisters both had much beloved ships named after them by their sovereign lords, but this would appear not to be so. One final piece of evidence would seem to tip the balance. In 1556, Queen Mary was to name one of the vessels that she had built while married to Philip of Spain, *Mary Rose*. There is no reason to suppose that she had any great affection for her dead aunt whose granddaughter Lady Jane Grey had been an unsuccessful (and reluctant) rival for her throne, but the Virgin Mary would certainly have been very close to her heart. Neither was the naming of a ship for the Virgin Mary a new idea at the start of Henry's reign. Fifty years earlier Bristol Customs accounts show, in 1466, the following ships trading just from that port: *Seynt Marye Grace de Luxbon*, *Marye Grace de Bristoll* and *Marrye de Rosse*. The significance of the latter name is obvious. Ships were, of course, also named after other Marys. In 1620, the 85-year-old Mrs Throckmorton wrote about her husband and brother-in-law, who built ships:

> I do well remember, one goodly ship they builded at their own charge, which they named the *Mary Rose*, being the name of their wives, for my brother's wife's name was Mary, and mine Rose.[8]

Whichever Mary the ship was named after, there is no doubt as to what the rose made reference. In 1546 Anthony Anthony, a Clerk of the Ordnance, presented to Henry an early version of *Janes' Fighting Ships*: a complete record of the English fleet showing pictures of the individual ships and listing their armament.[9] The work probably had a propaganda purpose for it is inclined to show, as in the case of *Mary Rose*, additional decks on some ships. However, just forward of the bowcastle of *Mary Rose* in the illustration is a circular

The recovered 'lollipop' timber, clearly showing the markings indicating that this might be the ship's crest.

structure on which is painted a Tudor Rose. Only one other ship in the Anthony Roll displays a crest, *Henry Grace à Dieu*, which had a golden orb at the forward end of the bowsprit on a short spritmast. Possibly, if these are crests, only the flagships carried such devices. They could certainly be indicators of their sovereign's love for these two particular ships which so much symbolised his creation of a standing navy royal.

On 2 October 2005, divers working to prepare the stem and an anchor of *Mary Rose* for raising from the Solent came across a strange piece of wood. Some four foot long it was shaped like a lollipop with the rounded section carved on both sides with what appears to be an embossed Tudor Rose. It seems that something resembling a ship's crest has been discovered; there certainly appears to be no other use for this large timber.

The policy of relying on taking ships up from

trade to conduct the state's business meant that on coming to the throne Henry VIII inherited just six warships. Two of these were the great ships, *Regent* and *Sovereign*, which were over twenty years old and in need of modernisation, as was the carvel *Mary and John*. The other three vessels were a Scottish prize, *Michael*, seized in 1488, and the galleasses *Mary Fortune* and *Sweepstake*. At the end of his reign in 1547 Henry was to leave to his son, Edward VI, a navy royal of eighteen ships, fifteen galleasses, nine pinnaces, two galleys and thirteen row barges – fifty-seven vessels in all. In his long reign 106 ships, at some time or other, served in Henry's fleet. The enormous building and refitting programme that this represents is quite staggering, and the economy buckled under the strain.

Henry had begun something of great importance to the survival and development of his nation. A man whose passion, instincts and skills were attuned to the chase, the joust, the archery butt and the practice of land warfare was to entrust the safety of his nation to an arm of warfare about which he knew little, and of which he would never exercise personal command. Nevertheless, the creation of England's wooden walls places Henry VIII in the same historic league as that occupied by Themistocles in ancient Athens when he created the fleet that defeated the Persians at Salamis in 480 BC.

Henry was also responsible for the creation of both the Board of Admiralty which would manage his fleet and Trinity House which would try to stop it running aground, through training his pilots and erecting lights around the coast, in an endeavour to mitigate the ever-present risks of seafaring in an age of navigational inaccuracy. Although Henry came to the throne determined to go to war with France, it was Scotland and the growth of that nation's naval forces that probably inspired and drove Henry to begin a programme of naval building at the earliest opportunity. Scotland had problems in building big ships. It was a country devoid of suitable timber in the necessary quantity and it did not have a deep exchequer. King James IV dealt with the first shortfall by importing both timber and shipbuilding expertise from France, and simply ignored the financial deficit.

In 1506, the year in which *Margaret* was launched work began in Scotland to create the even bigger warship, the 1000-ton *Michael*. It was not size alone that made *Michael* special. She was revolutionary. *Michael* represented the change from the medieval concept of the warship as a moving platform for soldiers, fitted with some light guns in support, to a ship which was a gun carrier in her own right. In military terms it marked a change from being a troop carrier to a tank. Rodger suggests that it was James's need to bombard errant Scottish lords secure in their inaccessible castles that led to the introduction of heavy guns into warships, and that it was thus Scotland, rather than England, where the revolution in ship construction and fitting out began.[10] Over two dozen large guns were cast for *Michael* and these were created in Scottish foundries mainly by the king's Master Smelter in Edinburgh. They were also probably fitted to fire through gun-ports, an innovation that would be introduced in England with *Mary Rose*. Henry would have been informed about this mighty vessel by Lord Dacre, his eyes and ears north of the Border.

South of the border work began in Portsmouth on the ships that could challenge both Scotland and France, even if those nations were to unite against England. Henry, with all his love of pomp and conspicuous display, could easily have ordered just one great vessel and ended up like James IV, with the unaffordable *Michael*, or Francis I of France, with the unfloatable *Grand François*. Henry waited until 1514 when he built the 1500-ton *Henry Grace à Dieu* for prestige. On his accession, however, he exercised restraint and sensibly ordered two medium-size warships, thus avoiding the temptation to create a ship too large to be of practical use and too prestigious to risk losing in major engagements. *Mary Rose* and *Peter Pomegranate* were built for a purpose: to defeat the king's enemies at sea.

CHAPTER 2

From Tree to Sea

England's most famous king may have ordered the building of *Mary Rose*, but it was a civil servant, Robert Brygandyne – of whom we know little apart from his name – who, as Clerk of Ships, was responsible for making the king's vision a reality. From the time of King John until the reign of Henry VIII, the Clerk of the King's Ships had been an insignificant and minor functionary who only came to the fore if a new vessel, such as Henry V's *Grace Dieu*, was commissioned. Even the title of Clerk of Ships disappeared during the second half of the fifteenth century. However, in 1480, Thomas Roger was nominated as Clerk of the Ships, in anticipation of an invasion of Scotland that would need maritime support. Whatever Roger's value as a Clerk, he was adept at keeping his job, for he held it not only during the reign of Edward IV, but also under both Richard III and Henry VII. Thomas Roger died in 1488 and was succeeded by William Comersall, of whom little is known apart from the suspicion that he may have been dismissed for the embezzlement of benefits accruing from his office. He was succeeded by Robert Brygandyne, who was appointed in 1495 and remained in office until 1523, thereby supervising the major refits, building and rebuilding programmes initiated by both the Tudor Henrys. There is a curious poem in *Reward and Fairies* by Rudyard Kipling about Henry VII and his shipbuilders and the general practice of them 'benefiting' from their duties. It is entitled 'King Henry VII and the Shipwrights – 1487', which is some eight years before Brygandyne was issued with his Letters Patent:

artist's impression of a sixteenth-century shipwright at work.

> Harry, our King of England, from London is
>   gone
> And come to Hamull on the Hoke in the
>   Countie of Southampton
> For there lay the Mary of the Tower, his ship
>   of war so strong
> And he would discover, certaynly, if his
>   shipwrights did him wrong.
> They heaved the mainmast overboard, that
>   was of trusty tree
> And they wrote down it was spent and lost by
>   force of weather at sea.
> But they sawn it into planks and stakes as far
>   as it might go
> To make beds for their own wives and little
>   children also.[1]

The poem makes it clear that Brygandyne wants none of this, or rather, only what he deems his fair share;

> 'I have taken a plank and rope and nail,
>   without the king, his leave,

After the custom of Portsmouth, but I will not
suffer a thief.'
Nay, never lift up thy hand at me – there's no
clean hand in the trade.
'Steal in measure,' quoth Brygandyne. 'There's
measure in all things made.'
When they had beaten Slingawai, out of his
own lips
Our King appointed Brygandyne to be Clerk
of all his ships.
'Nay, never lift up thy hands to me – there's
no clean hands in the trade,
But steal in measure,' said Harry our King.
'There's measure in all that's made.'[2]

Brygandyne hailed from Kent where he was a minor landowner who, prior to becoming Clerk of Ships had been rewarded for services to the crown with the payment of £10 a year for life. His appointment necessitated a move from the comforts of Kent to the fortress town of Portsmouth, which had a rough and rowdy reputation. In 1450, the Bishop of Chichester, who had been sent to the town to pay the soldiers and sailors their (reduced) wages, was set upon by a mob and stoned to death. The citizens of the town, both the guilty and innocent, were excommunicated. The imposition was not lifted until 1508. In that period marriages, baptisms and burial in sacred ground would not have been allowed for excommunicants. Portsmouth's slow population growth could be attributed to this violent incident. The Brygandynes would certainly have known of the town's reputation, so Robert probably moved there on his own, for it was not the sort of town to which he would have wished to take his young family.

Brygandyne's activities would be the making of the town for, if Henry was *Mary Rose*'s patron and Brygandyne her producer, then Portsmouth was the stage on which she would first perform and with whom she, and the ships that followed her, would be for ever associated, transforming the settlement from a small and insignificant town into the world's greatest naval base. The Cowdray engraving[3], which depicts the Battle of the Solent in July 1545, gives us the first picture of the town, and its accuracy is confirmed by a map of *c.*1540. The first clear written description we have of the town was written by John Leland a year or so later:

> The land here on the east side of Portsmouth Haven, runneth further by a great way straight into the sea by south-east from the haven mouth, than it doth at the west point. There is, at the point of the haven, Portsmouth town, and a great round tower, almost double in quantity and strength to that which is on the west side of the haven, right against it; and here is a mighty chain of iron to draw from tower to tower. About a quarter mile above this tower is a great dock for ships.... The town of Portsmouth is fended from the east tower... with a mud wall armed with timber, whereon are great pieces of iron and brass ordnance, and this piece of the wall, having a ditch without it, runneth so far flat south south east, and is the most apt to defend the town there open to the haven. There runneth a ditch almost flat east for a space, and without it a wall of mud like to the other, and so there goeth round about the town to the circuit of a mile. There is a gate of timber at the north east end of the town and by it is cast up a hill of earth ditched, whereon are guns to defend entry to the town by land. There is much vacant ground within the town wall. There is one fair street in the town, from west to north east.[4]

Portsmouth had many of the natural advantages that make for an ideal naval port. Its wonderful natural harbour is protected by its narrow entrance from winds from any direction, with the additional bulwark of the Isle of Wight giving a more open, but still sheltered fleet anchorage, at Spithead. The approach to the harbour mouth, which can be well defended even with short-range weapons, is complicated with extensive shallow patches, but these only serve to provide additional hazards to any approaching enemies who do not know the waters well. Entry could be made, for most sailing vessels, at all states of the tide, and extensive mud flats gave the opportunity, in future years, to build quay sides and docks with some ease or, more easily, to haul ships clear of the water for re-caulking and other maintenance. However, these drying mud banks could mean that at low water ships, with the rounded hulls of the time, would have lolled over on the mud, in which position the rising tide could have flooded them before sufficient water was available for them to refloat. This potential hazard was overcome by the establishment of mooring chains for which there were two locations. For refitting vessels and those in ordinary (in reserve) one set of chains was laid on the Gosport side of the harbour near to the village of Elson. Operational vessels were secured at a second line of chains that ran between the dry dock and the Round Tower. Other problems, such as trying to leave harbour with an incoming tide and an easterly wind would have been addressed by the use of boats to haul them through the harbour entrance, or ensuring that, in times of emergency or operational necessity, vessels anchored at Spithead.

The immediate hinterland of Portsea Island could be both well defended and easily settled by sufficient numbers of people to service a busy dockyard. Flat and fertile land provided space for both

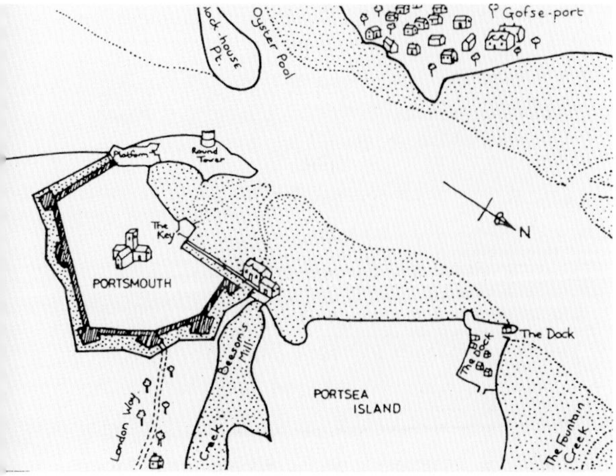

map of Portsmouth showing the location of Henry VII's dry dock.

market gardening and dairy herds, while the Hampshire fields beyond Portsdown Hill grew wheat in abundance. As far as shipbuilding was concerned, large forests of oak stretched across the countryside enabling local ship builders, with their practised eyes, to identify their major timbers as they strolled from tree to tree. Into this small town at the south-western end of this small island came the tradesmen to establish an industrial enterprise that would build the vessels that would establish England as the supreme maritime nation for centuries to come. A plethora of skills were needed, over two dozen in all, including: bricklayers, block-makers, braziers, caulkers, carpenters, coopers, carters, hatchellers, joiners, oakum boys, plumbers, pitch makers, riggers, rope-makers, shipwrights, smiths, sawyers, spinners, sail-makers, trenail mooters, wheelwrights and labourers. They would need to be supported by bakers, butchers, brewers, clergymen, farmers, fishermen and the usual shopkeepers that a town of this size would require. There were, quite possibly, also representatives of other crafts such as bowyers, fletchers and comb makers.

The civil authority would have required officers to keep law and order, and magistrates and jailors to become acquainted with those who failed so to do. The town authorities were also responsible for guarding the harbour and keeping it clean as well as providing boats for handling the larger vessels and for ferrying stores. On occasions the civil and military authorities almost came to blows, mainly over dues and taxes. Brygandyne and his successors needed a management structure that could bring these disparate groups together and focus them on a shared goal – to build, repair, maintain and refit the king's ships.

Brygadyne's first task on taking up his appointment in 1495 had been to build a permanent dry dock within which the great ships of Henry VII, the now elderly *Regent* and *Sovereign* could be refitted.[5] The importance of the dry dock in the development of Portsmouth cannot be exaggerated. The town's strategic position, now that the French had acquired the Duchy of Brittany, was obvious, but why Henry VII should have sited his dry dock here rather than keep

The Merchant House, Southampton, a fine property built by John Dawtry from profits made from supplying the navy royal.

his shipbuilding infrastructure in the Thames is not known. But, had he not done so, then *Mary Rose* and *Peter Pomegranate* might have been built elsewhere and Portsmouth's beginnings as a naval dockyard much delayed. Until the building of this dry dock, such docks as there had been were often just temporary scrapes dug out of the mud-banks and, occasionally, protected by brushwood, although more substantial ones were built, such as the one uncovered at Oyster Street in Portsmouth.[6] Once work on the permanent dry dock was completed these occasional docks were abandoned, often to the detriment and danger of future foreshore users.

The dock at Portsmouth was a permanent structure, with gates that allowed a vessel to be worked on whatever the state of tide outside. By modern standards it was basic, lacking the removable caisson that modern dry docks have to allow ships to be moved in at any state of tide, nor was a proper pumping out facility available. Nevertheless, it would have been recognisable for what it was and a definite improvement upon refitting ships on the shoreline.

Whether or not *Mary Rose* was built in this dry dock is not known. Both *Regent* and *Sovereign* were being overhauled in the same period, the latter, to judge by the cost, quite extensively. The time available to complete the work – which would have had to have been done in the dry dock – on these two vessels, as well as build the two new ships within the same dock, would have put considerable pressure on the work force. It is, therefore, more likely that both *Mary Rose* and *Peter Pomegranate* were constructed on adjacent slipways. This method would also have been more practical. Lowering timber and other bulky items into a dock bottom with primitive windlasses would have created unnecessary extra work and delays, besides giving the workers an unpleasant climb both up and down.

The records of the building of the dock show, along with all the other meticulous paperwork, what good value this one-man naval-department called Brygandyne offered. We can, therefore, be fairly certain, even without the accounts, that the two ships represented value for money and that Brygandyne was not pilfering more than his measure. A privy-seal warrant to the Exchequer of 29 January 1510, summarises the expenses that were to be paid to Brygandyne through an intermediary, John Dawtry,[7] a wealthy Southampton businessman, who built the still extant Merchant's House in that city:

> John Dawtry by our like commandment hath delivered and paid unto the said Robert Brygandyne, Clerk of our said ships, for timbers, ironwork, and workmanship of two new ships to be made for us £700, and the

> one ship to be of the burthen of 400 tons and the other ship to be of the burthen of 300 tons; and also the said Robert Brygandyne, Clerk of our said Ships three hundred and sixteen pounds thirteen shillings and four pence for all manner of implements and necessaries to the same two ships belonging as particularly hereafter ensueth, first for sails, twine, marline, ropes, cables, cablets, shrouds, hawsers, buoy ropes, stays, sheets, buoy lines, tacks, lifts, top armours, streamers, standards, compasses, running glasses, tankards, bowls, dishes, lanterns, shivers of brass and pulleys for the said two new ships, victual and wages of men for setting up of their masts, shrouds and all other tacklings for the said two new ships, which said several sums will extend in the whole to the sum of two thousand three hundred threescore and twelve pounds eleven shillings and eleven pence, for the which sum our servant John Dawtry as yet hath not had of us any matter of discharge.[8]

Late payment for services rendered is not a modern problem; in June of the same year Robert was writing to Richard Palshide, a partner of Dawtry's in the following terms:

> Right worshipful, sir, I heartily recommend me unto you, daily desiring to hear of your good welfare, furthermore desiring your mastership that for the indenture of parchment that I delivered unto you there may be made another new, extending to the whole sum of money as it specifieth of bearing the date and time according: but whereas it specifieth several sums of money, so much to the *Sovereign* spent and so much to the *Mary Rose* and *Peter Pomegranate*, I would not have it so, but the said whole sum of the indenture delivered by Master Dawtry and by you unto me in general, as well for the repairing of the *Sovereign* as for the new making of the *Mary Rose* and *Peter Pomegranate* jointly together, and moreover that it will please you I may be recommended unto Master Dawtry, desiring his mastership and you both that I may have the copy of the warrant whereby I received money of you for the keeping and for certain reparations done on the *Regent* in Ludovic de La Fava his time, and in as goodly haste as may be possible you would vouchsafe that the said indenture, and also copy of the warrant may be delivered unto the bringer hereof...for the expedition of my account.[9]

This document is the first to include reference to *Mary Rose* by name. John Dawtry prevaricated, again not an unknown ploy by those holding monies due to others. The letter was minuted by him:

> Master Brygandyne, the indenture you write for is in my coffer of iron at London, where no man can see it till my coming thither by no means, but I shall always be ready to follow and to fulfil your desire therein as for it is all one to me.[10]

By 30 June Brygandyne had received his money and Dawtry had witness of it. Creating a wooden warship was the most sophisticated industry of its day, requiring greater skills than those needed to build a royal palace or great church. To create a vessel as complicated as *Mary Rose* was the equivalent of space-shuttle engineering today, and the talents and training needed may have required just as long an apprenticeship.

There is a tradition that refers to *Mary Rose* as a revolutionary ship. In a way she was, but this adjective can only be justified if accompanied by a few caveats and an understanding of the developments in naval warfare and shipbuilding techniques that were taking place during the reigns of the first two Tudor monarchs. At the beginning of the sixteenth century the trade of the shipwright was neither well established nor widely spread throughout England. If new large vessels were required, then the country had to be trawled to find the expertise to deliver what was needed. Nor was the profession highly regarded; the scarcity of practitioners was not reflected in a healthy wage packet. As late as 1711, William Sutherland, in his essay *The Shipbuilder's Assistant* wrote:

> ...the proper business of a Shipwright is counted a very vulgar Imploy; and which a Man of very indifferent Qualifications may be Master of. Many have as mean an Option of it as a certain Gentleman, who told one of our former Master Builders, that he had a Blockhead of a Son uncapable to attain any other trade unless that of a Ship-carpenter, for which he designed him.[11]

A Guild of Shipwrights was not established until 1605, which would also indicate that this profession, undifferentiated, it would seem, from carpentry, was not held in high regard during the sixteenth century. The lack of an obvious wage differential would also demonstrate that the carpenter and basic shipwright's skills were not considered exceptional. They received between four pence and sixpence a day plus their food, and lodgings – a good rate, but not an exceptional one. However, the master shipwright, John Haster, was paid eighteen pence a day in 1485 to supervise the removal of the *Grace Dieu*'s masts at Bursledon on the Hamble.

The gathering of a handful of shipwrights would not have been sufficient to produce the vessels that the king desired. These were ships still wedded to the medieval principle of taking 'castles' to sea. *Mary Rose* was to be a 'carrack', that is, a four-masted vessel with a high forecastle and after-castle and low waist, which would equip her well for a fight alongside an opponent. As far as can be ascertained, there was no equivalent of a blueprint for a 'carrack', nor did the shipwrights produce a scale model, as became the accepted practice some hundred years later. In part this is due to the fact that shipwrights did not trust each other. Matthew Baker, the principal royal shipwright, who was the first to commit his ideas to paper in his 1586, *Fragments of Ancient Shipwrightry*, stated in his prologue: 'Our author thought not good our uses to disclose. Within his head he keeps the same from all his filching foes.'[12]

The term 'carrack' is a confusing one. It was first used in the 1370s to define a round-stemmed,

An engraving by Breugel of a four-masted Portuguese carrack, one of the largest ships of her day.

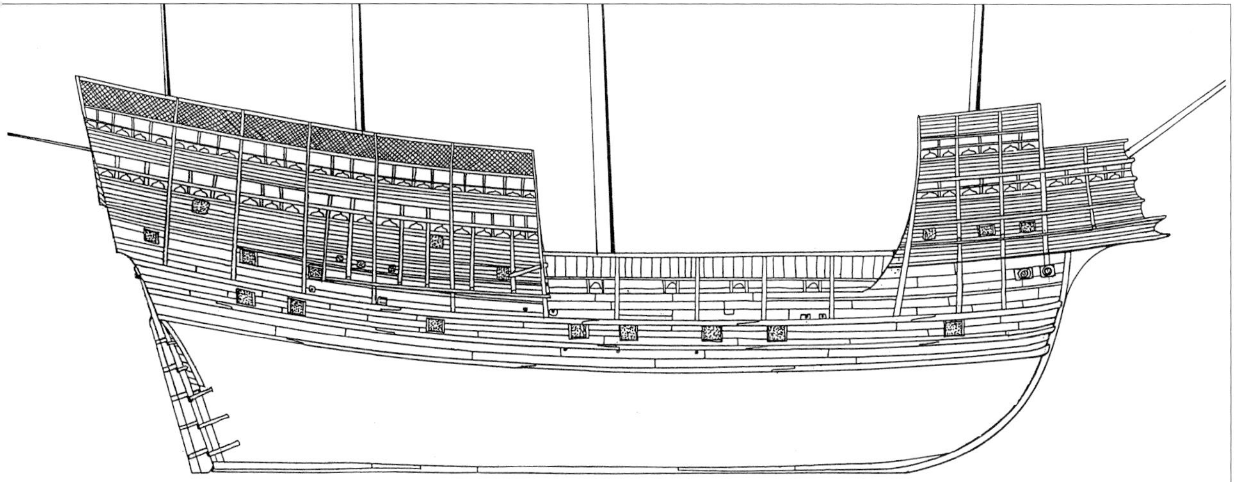

Reconstructed elevation of the *Mary Rose* hull and superstructure.

carvel-built, Mediterranean merchant ship, possibly with a stern-rudder, square sail and a mizzen. One hundred years later the type seems to have moved on to encompass the three-masted Flemish 'kraeck' which had a two-decked forecastle and a long, single-decked after-castle above the quarterdeck on which guns were mounted. Further indications of her warship status are indicated by spears being present in her mast tops, while the mizzen top has a swivel gun mounted which is very similar to the ones raised with *Mary Rose*. That boarding remained the main objective is shown by the large grapnel attached to the bowsprit, which would have been dropped on to the enemy deck to hold the two ships together. Thirty years later a print of a Venetian carrack shows that an extra mizzen, with a lateen sail, to aid manoeuverability and sailing close to the wind, had been added to the general design of the carrack. Then, from 1520 we have a painting at the National Maritime Museum in Greenwich that represents a truly enormous carrack. It has been identified as the Portuguese warship *Santa Catarina do Monte Sinai*, a vessel with a vast main sail, a newly introduced fore topsail, six decks and some 150 guns. Dating from about 1540, another painting which was thought to depict Henry departing from Dover to meet Francis at the Field of the Cloth of Gold shows a fleet review with a group of six large carracks including *Henry Grace à Dieu*, *Mary Rose*, *Peter Pomegranate* and *Katherine Fortileza*.[13] They represent a powerful fleet and a clear indication of the king's might at sea.

Brygandyne's team would have worked out what proportions and ratios they needed to build a carrack and applied these to the frames, length and beam. To do this they used a sophisticated system of arcs to ensure that the lines of the ship's hull were both smooth and efficient, so it is likely that they spent some time discussing the vision before agreeing how best to proceed. Dr. Douglas McElvogue, an archaeologist at the Mary Rose Trust who has spent several years studying, measuring and drawing the timbers of *Mary Rose*, has produced a list (*see* Appendix 1) that indicates the factors requiring consideration by the shipwright. The result, in the mind's eye of the shipwright would have been a drawing much as shown above.

Once agreement was reached as to the concept, the creation would have involved the master shipwright in a three-step process. First, he would have defined the overall dimensions and the ratios of beam to keel length. In the case of *Mary Rose* this would be 1:2.75 which made her, proportionally, longer and thinner than was the norm in continental Europe – her shipwright was not following slavishly the ideas of others, but producing a vessel that would sail well in English waters. Secondly, he would have designed the hull's 'master frame', the central cross section from which the shape both fore and aft would have been derived. Thirdly, he would have designed the frames fore and aft of the master to give the ship her lines; this was certainly not a task that could have been done 'by eye', and the secret of how best to do it would have been closely guarded.

To turn these lines into reality would have involved drawing the timber shapes as required using moulds – thin strips of wood cut to shape from drawings – either chalked or pegged out on the floor of what would have been some sort of covered shed, although we have no evidence of such a structure. The master shipwright could not, of course, achieve all this without a bureaucratic structure to ensure the necessary supplies were delivered and wages paid to him and his carpenters. In this area, and in the offices of Clerk Comptroller and the Clerk of the Ships, Henry created one of the most efficient arms of the civil service: lean on manpower and broad on responsibility, initiative and delivery.

Re-enactors at the Mary Rose Museum demonstrating how timbers were prepared for the ship's planks.

Brygandyne had to supervise what was by now a momentous transformation in English shipbuilding techniques. So much so that it can be asserted with confidence that it was he who oversaw the final transition from medieval methods to a form that would remain recognisable until the days of wooden ships passed away. Up to this time, many vessels built in northern Europe had been clinker built, with overlapping planks nailed together to form a skin, which was strengthened by an internal frame that could be fitted afterwards. Southern Europe had a different tradition, whereby a ship's frame or skeleton was built first before boards were laid butt-ended along it to give a smooth hull. These boards were attached to the frame by trennals, which gave a better, and probably cheaper, bond. This method of skeleton construction is popularly called 'carvel' after the Portuguese 'caravels' that were built in this fashion.

If the maritime nations of northern Europe were to compete on the high seas in trade, exploration and warfare with their southern rivals they needed to change from clinker to carvel construction, for there was a limit to the dimensions at which a clinker-built vessel could be built successfully. Above a certain size the shipwright would be trying to support a structure of planks that had no bonding frame. He would be trying to create a skin without a skeleton. The carvel method gave him that rigid skeleton. The change of method is as significant as that which took place when twentieth-century shipbuilders moved away from riveted iron plates to welded ones for their ships' sides, and a similar redundancy of skills took place now.

The clinker building team included 'berders', who fitted the planks together; clenchers who bent the clench-nails over a metal washer, called a rove, on the inside of the hull, and holders, who steadied the nail head on the outside while the clencher did his work. A laborious process. And costly. Thousands of clench-nails were needed for even the smallest of ships; large vessels such as *Grace Dieu*, needed tons. Brygandyne's meticulous accounts for the refitting of both *Regent* and *Soverign* during the reign of Henry VII do not include payments to clenchers, berders and holders; the old trades had gone. Carvel-built vessels needed no such ironmongery.[14] Instead the ship's sides were secured to the frame by the use of trenails – cheaper wooden dowels – whose location could be rapidly augered out and that, once fixed, gave a more lasting and secure joint.

What carvel construction did demand was skilled caulkers. These tradesmen were responsible for filling the gaps along the end-butted timbers to make them waterproof in such a way that the movement of the ship, the pressure of the sea and the swelling and drying of the timbers did not cause leaks to appear. This caulking was achieved by forcing fibre (either oakum or flax) into the seams and sealing them with pitch, tar or rosin, which was imported from Scandinavia. The ship's hull was given additional protection by the placing of thicker planks, called 'wales', at intervals along the ship's side, which also served to secure rigging and to assist anyone clambering on board.

Mary Rose's keel was built from three large timbers, two of elm and one of oak. As with all the choices in the age of wood there was a very good reason for this combination. Elm is a solid, stable wood, which, as long as it stays wet, is virtually rot-proof, unlike oak. It is, therefore, an ideal wood for the keel of a warship destined to spend most of its life afloat. Elm was also a very common timber in the south of England until Dutch elm disease wiped out this magnificent dark and stately tree. But, of course, it was oak with which the forests of the south were identified, and oak was the major wood needed for the king's ships.

Once the decision to build the ships had been made then the master shipwright and his carpenters would have moved out into the woods to select the trees that would serve their purpose. This was not merely a matter of finding straight-bowled timber that could be felled, transported and sawn up easily into timbers. The shipwright needed to see the vessel in the wood in the same way that Michelangelo could look at a block of Carrera marble and see his David. The major shapes needed for frames and knees had to be identified in the tree, its forks and boughs had to be seen as potential fittings, and any flaw or weakness had to be spotted before felling took place.

Moving through the woods individual trees would have been marked and the fellers would set to work. A practiced eye could make a very reasonable estimate of the cubic content of a tree. This was done by measuring the circumference at the level of sawing and estimating it at the height of usable timber. These measurements were averaged and one quarter of this mean multiplied against itself and the height to give a volume. The amount needed was then divided into loads. A contract would then have been drawn up for the acreage to be felled, lopped and transported to the dockyard at Portsmouth.

An organised shipbuilding programme allows for timbers to be felled in the correct season, to be hauled, hewn or stored until needed, and thus seasoned and available in the quantity required well ahead of the commencement of building, but such arrangements did not come into being in England until the seventeenth century. Henry ordered his handful of great ships and wanted them delivered expeditiously. The trees were, therefore, felled and sawn in the green, and the ships built of unseasoned planks and frames. So, although a log pond was built at Portsmouth, it was not a part of the dockyard set-up until well after Henry's reign. The main purpose of such a pond was to wash out the sap and to get the wood into such a condition that it was less likely to split than if it dried out on land. In practice, every shipwright had his own ideas as to the efficacy of seasoning and most vessels, like *Mary Rose*, would have been built with unseasoned frames.

The timber, once felled and lopped had to be carted out of the woods. This was done by a pair, or even three horses, pulling a tug. In its simplest form this was a wagon consisting of a pair of wheels joined by a curved bolster which could be driven over the timber to the place of attachment. Chains were then used to raise one end of the timber up while the other was allowed to drag on the track. More sophisticated four-wheel wagons required the team of horses to drag the timber onto the wagon at right angles before moving to the front of the wagon to haul the load. Movement would have been slow on the level, snail-like up hill and dangerous in the descent. Most carts could only drag about fifty cubic feet in one load. This would have entailed about 20,000 deliveries for *Mary Rose*, which alone required about 600 trees to be felled over some thirty-six acres. Brygandyne was also building the slightly smaller *Peter Pomegranate* at this time.

Far better for him would have been the option to move the timber by water, for there was no other port or potential dockyard in the south that had as many advantages of location as did Portsmouth in relation to the raw materials needed to build wooden ships. Behind the bulwark of the Isle of Wight existed a sheltered waterway, the Solent, into which many rivers, the Itchen, Test, Hamble, Beaulieu, Meon and Lymington flowed, their banks lined with oaks, many of which stood in royal forests making them readily available for their royal master to exploit. Road transport between Southampton and Portsmouth was not as bad in the sixteenth century as it was around many other ports of the country because the old Roman roads in southern Hampshire were still in reasonable condition. Nevertheless, water transport, utilising the unique double tide of the Solent and Southampton Water meant that great timbers could also be rafted or towed down to Portsmouth expeditiously and cheaply. Throughout his period in office Brygadyne's accounts are full of payments being made for both methods of transport:

> Also paid in likewise for the hire and wages of five cartmen each of them with his eleven horses carrying stuff to the said dock…[15]

> Also paid in likewise for the hire of two boats which carried and conveyed certain masts from Hampton to Portsmouth for the use of the said ship [*Regent*] that is to say to John Carpenter of Poole for the hire of his boat 10s. And to William Purcer of Southampton for like hire of his boat 6s 9d.[16]

> Also paid to William Purcer and his company by covenant in great made at Hampton as well for carriage of certain masts to the waterside and there to be made in a raft and so to be conveyed to Portsmouth – 14s.[17]

That raft, it would appear, reached Lymington where it was forced to take shelter from inclement weather and Brygandyne, in need of the masts, had to send John Carpenter to help bring the cargo into Portsmouth.

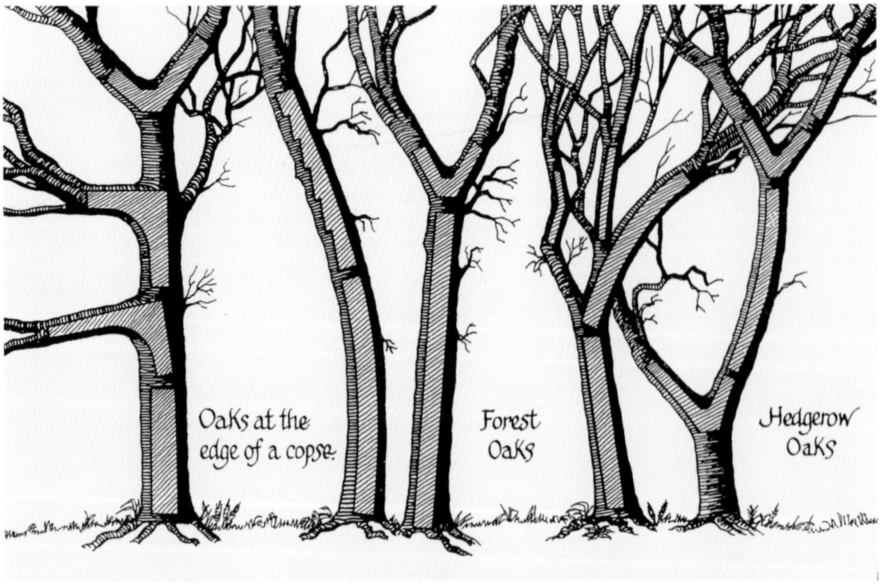

The parts of trees used for shipbuilding. There are straight and naturally curved timbers for frames, but the most valuable (because of their scarcity) were the crooked joints of trunk and branches that became the massive knees (brackets) that bound the deck beams to the frames.

The shipwright and his carpenters would have divided their requirements into five main categories of timber. These were:

(i) Great Timbers: over twenty feet long and almost two feet across, used for the keelson and the stern post.
(ii) Compass Timbers: large curved logs used for frames and the stem.
(iii) Straight Timbers: large straight logs used for the deck beams, wales and stringers.
(iv) Planks and Boards: thinner pieces of straight wood cut to about one to six inches thick.
(v) Knee timbers: angular logs used for knees and similar positions.

To work fallen trees into these categories of timber would have required busy saw-pits and timber yards. The iconographic picture is of a saw pit with the viewers' sympathy always going to the fellow below the timber into whose eyes it would seem sawdust would continually fall. It is no wonder that, based on the name for the spikes that held the log in place, the top sawyer was referred to as the 'top dog' – a much better position to be in than the unfortunate 'underdog'. Reconstruction of this method of sawing planks, however, has shown that a perfectly satisfactory regime can be introduced that does not cause unnecessary discomfort. But it was thirsty work. John Horsley tells the story of two itinerant sawyers:

> The top sawyer was the headman and he started by sharpening the saw, leaving the pitman or bottom sawyer to his own devices – in this case searching out the local inn. By the time the saw was ready the pitman was too drunk to work. While he sobered up, the top sawyer sampled the local brew until he, too, was in no condition to work. This might very easily go on for two or three days.[18]

Before the building of *Mary Rose* could begin a row of carefully aligned wooden blocks was laid in position, onto which the keel was laid, thus guaranteeing that this primary timber was straight and true, while also allowing space for the carpenters and caulkers to work underneath the vessel. These three timbers that would form *Mary Rose*'s 32m-long keel were then joined with scarf joints, after which the stem and stern posts were secured in place. Then followed the floor timbers and keelson, which was secured with long iron bolts to the keel. A number of futtocks, shaped to form the ribs of the frame were then attached to the floor timbers. As the frame rose from the keel it would have been supported by timber shoring. Internal wooden braces ran from just below the waterline into the hold to strengthen the structure, which was further reinforced by stringers and knees.

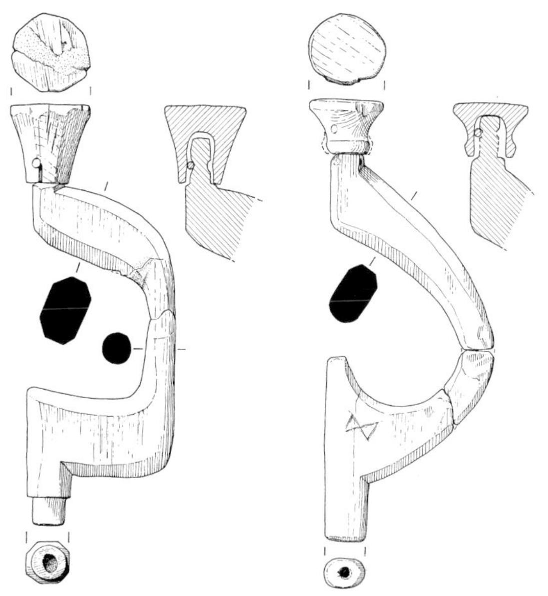

Carpenter's tools recovered from the *Mary Rose*: brace handles.

The end result was a ship of great strength with a total length of 45m, a breadth of 11.6m, and a draught of 4.6m. Yet the seaworthiness of the vessel would depend on the skill and thoroughness of the caulkers whose job it was to make every seam watertight. If the shipwrights, caulkers and carpenters did not do their job properly then there could be major problems. Writing to Wolsey on 5 April 1513 Edward Howard the Lord Admiral remarked:

> Sir, the *Katherine Fortileza* has so many leaks by reason of Bedell the carpenter that worked her at Woolwich that we have had much to do to keep her above water. He hath bored an 100 auger holes in her and left it unstopped, that the water came in as it were in a sieve. Sir, this day I have all the caulkers of the army on her: I trust by tomorrow she shall be more staunch.[19]

And so she proved to be, but the passage for the ship's company of *Katherine Fortileza* from the Thames to Plymouth, from where Howard was writing, must have been a worrying one, especially as victualling was also a problem on board. Two paragraphs earlier, in the same letter to Wolsey, Howard had written:

> Sir, the *Katherine Fortileza* hath troubled me beyond reason; she brought out of the Thames but for 14 days' victual, and no victualler is come to help her. And so have I victualled her ever since.[20]

A few weeks earlier Howard had praised *Katherine Fortileza* for sailing well, but also expressed his concerns over her condition after her refit being, in his opinion, 'overladen with ordnance beside her heavy tops, which are big enough for a ship of 8 or 900 [tons].'[21] This overburdening was the hidden danger that could capsize even the best-built carrack. The value of skilled shipwrights was no more in evidence than when the work of unskilled ones became obvious. *Katherine Fortileza* is last recorded after being damaged in a storm in 1521; perhaps her defects, exposed by the weather, could no longer be addressed adequately by a team of shipwrights and caulkers trying to make good the mistakes made by their less competent colleagues ten years earlier. Her captain at the time of her battering by the weather in 1521 was none other than Robert Brygandyne; he must have felt sorely tried by being palced in command of a vessel that was clearly not built to his own exacting standards.

Mary Rose and *Peter Pomegranate* were carvel built, but so too was the earlier *Regent* (but not *Sovereign*), which is referred to as being of 'novel' construction and for whom the records show 'carvel' nails were ordered. However, *Sovereign* may have been converted to a carvel hull during a refit which took place in Portsmouth. Both were massive, purpose-built warships, with *Regent* having 225 guns and *Sovereign* a double-tiered forecastle and a three-tiered after-castle. The Edwardian historian Sir Geoffrey Callender considered '*Regent* better compared with Nelson's ships than any predecessor'.[22]

So, if a revolution in English warship design is sought for in this period, it probably began with *Regent* and continued with *Mary Rose.* English native woodland, although providing excellent timber to be shaped into frames and planks, has never been capable of growing the long straight timbers needed for the masts of great ships. The introduction of multi-masted vessels emphasised this shortcoming, and mast timber had frequently to be imported from Scandinavia or eastern Europe, a practice made clear by the fact that the English word 'spruce' derives from the word 'Prussia'. In some cases, masts were made up from a number of narrower, shorter trees bonded together with bands of iron or rope. In these cases the mast

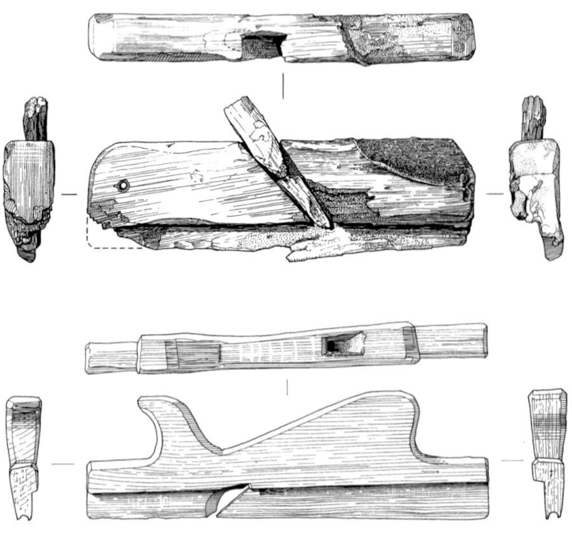

Carpenter's tools recovered from the *Mary Rose*: two planes.

often consisted of a central spindle of spruce or pine surrounded by oak.[23] Although *Mary Rose* was to all appearances a four-masted ship, at least two of her masts were made from several masts joined together so that her true fit, as recorded in an inventory of 1514 was eight, as shown in the illustration below.

She would also have been fitted with a bowsprit and, possibly, a bonaventure mizzen topmast. The lengths of timber needed were extraordinary. Records indicate that *Regent* had a mainmast of at least 114ft, and a mizzenmast of 105ft; *Mary Rose*'s requirements would not have been very different. Where the lower mast joined the next one up a structure known as a trestle tree was formed to hold the two structures together. Once the masts were raised – a development that was a major event in the ship's construction – they needed to be held firmly in place. To achieve this they were well bedded into a mast step, preferably at keelson level, but if their position forward or aft made this impossible then they were secured to either the stem or deck beams. They were further reinforced wherever they passed between decks by the use of mast partners, firmly secured to the deck beams in such a way as to absorb and distribute the forces that endeavoured to bend the mast sideways.

Above deck the masts were steadied by the use of standing rigging: fore and back stays and shrouds, which, through the creation of ratlines, also gave the crew access to the uppermast and yards. Miles of rope, of many different dimensions, were needed for both standing and running rigging and hawsers. The yards from which the sail hung would have been simpler, probably single, pieces of wood; nevertheless, they

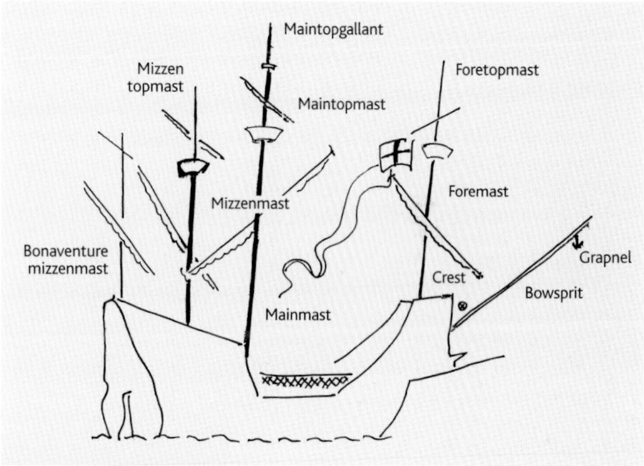

ABOVE The masts of the *Mary Rose* based on the Anthony Roll illustration.

LEFT A model of the *Mary Rose*, built to recreate the moment of her sinking for Channel 4's 2000 television programme *Secrets of the Dead*.

would have been heavy. Manpower alone would have had to haul the yards up, and adjusting their angle while hoisted would have been a slow and exhausting process, as friction and gravity exerted their debilitating influence. To ease the task a roller block consisting of seven sets of wooden rollers, called a parrel, was used as an early ball-bearing race. The balls were made from walnut, a very durable hard wood that exudes oils, thus making the parrel self-lubricating. It was a good system and lasted throughout the age of sail, and is still in use on some modern yachts.

At the end of the foremast and main mast yards the Anthony Roll[24] shows large, sickle-like objects. These were shear hooks placed so as to rip through an enemy's rigging as *Mary Rose* came alongside prior to boarding. Another piece of ironmongery linked to boarding was the grapnel situated at the end of the bowsprit. From this position it could be dropped onto an enemy deck to secure the vessels firmly together. In order that the securing line could not be cut through easily its first 2.25m were made from iron chain.[25]

The rope for Tudor ships was made from hemp. At the start of the sixteenth century Bridport in Dorset was the centre of the English rope-making industry, for the rich, damp soil of the region produced a high-quality fibre. The introduction of the tackle board which allowed several yarns to be turned together all at the same tension led to Bridport's expansion and a reputation for providing the best yarn in Europe. At one stage the town had forty ropewalks, but competition from Europe was fierce, and Bridport's fortunes and position in the market waxed and waned and required state-intervention to keep it going.

Once again, parallels with more recent times are very obvious.[26] The type of rope cordage needed ranged from heavy, hefty hawsers for the anchors, which were up to 16in in circumference, to thin yarn for sailmaking and repairing. In between, cordage of varying dimensions served as standing and running rigging. Rope, like timber, was transported to Portsmouth by both road and water. Brygandyne paid

Specimens of rope from the *Mary Rose*, preserved because it was well tarred. Most of the rope would have been made at Bridport in Dorset.

Locronan, Brittany. The wealth generated by the sail cloth trade can still be seen today in the fine merchants' houses built around the square.

John Miller of Erith for several voyages by his ship *Trinity of Erith*, with a cargo of cordage:

> The said vessel first freight at London with cordage sailing from thence unto Portsmouth and there discharging then from thence to Southampton and there recharged with the new cordage appointed for our sovereign lord the King' ships and so sailed again to Portsmouth and there discharged. Then after again to Hampton which there recharged the great anchor a carrack anchor with two other anchors bought of Philipp Lockyer one of the Customers of Southampton and brought these anchors aboard the *Regent* at Stokes Bay.[27]

Later it is recorded that:

> Robert Brygandyne...paid certain foreign cost and necessary expenses concerning the provision of the said tackle and apparell that is to say first to John Easton of Portsmouth for his costs sent unto Lynne there to provide and see the best stuff that could be had...to be put into the making of cordage.[28]

The hawsers required to secure and work the ship's anchors needed to be massive. The great ships had up to eight large anchors. The starboard anchor of *Mary Rose*, raised in 2005, measures just under five metres and probably weighs over 1000 kilograms. Such fittings were expensive to make as they required good-quality iron and casting if they were to prove reliable and long lasting during a lifetime of immersion in salt water and being dragged across the seabed. The 13in-circumference hawsers and the winding gear to raise them would have been expensive as well. But ships could not go to sea without a secure method of holding their ground. A sailing ship on a lee shore, unable to raise sail to move out of danger, is in very present danger if her anchors start to drag. Tudor anchor design, although recognisable as built for purpose, could not necessarily guarantee to hold when wind and tide threatened. An insurance was to use several anchors, trusting in their combined holding power. Anchors were also needed to warp ships out of harbour when wind or tide were not favourable. For this purpose smaller kedge-anchors were carried. These were taken away from the ship by boat in the direction it was required to move in and then dropped. The ship then hauled herself to the anchor and the process was repeated: a cumbersome but effective method of movement when none other was available. The rope for the standing rigging was secured to the ship's side through the use of dead-eyes and chains arranged in such a way that they could be tensioned to make allowance for wear or the natural stretching and slackening caused by the ropes getting wet and then drying out.

Yet, with all these fixtures and fittings having been delivered to Portsmouth there was one main item without which the ship would have remained a dull hulk with no character or drive – her sails. Hemp was also the raw material used for making these sails, but there seems to have been little native industry dedicated to the production of sail cloth, although Bridport, quite naturally, produced some material. The cloth was named after its place of origin and the appearance in inventories of names such as Olron (Isle of Oléron), Vitery (Vitre) and Poldavys (so called because the canvas made at Locronan was exported from Pouldavid, now a suburb of Douarnenez) would indicate that France, especially Brittany was the main source. The output of the town of Locronan was especially favoured because it produced a wider strip than its rivals.[29] Thus the canvas under which *Mary Rose* sailed into battle may well have come from the same source as that unfurled by her foes.

The sail cloth was delivered as bolts of material consisting of forty yards of canvas about two foot wide. These were then sewn together locally with a reasonable overlap to ensure the sail did not split along its seams. Here also, the multi-masted ship had an advantage, being able to lose a sail without having the whole vessel placed at the mercy of the elements. The sailmaker's dues were properly recorded: '...paid unto John Stedeham of Portsmouth for the sewing and making of the sails of the said ship [*Sweepstake*]... 20s 8d.'[30] Sailmaking appears, therefore, to have been a task that Brygandyne could have carried out in Portsmouth although he also employed workers from elsewhere along the coast:

> Robert Brygandyne hath paid to eight workmen labouring and working upon making and sewing of the sails of the said ship [*Mary Fortune*] by the space of two weeks each of them at 12d by the week – sixteen shillings. Also for the hire of a boat and two men that conveyed the canvas for the said sails from Shoreham to Winchelsea.[31]

The edges of the sails were sown with bolt-ropes to prevent fraying, give tautness to the sail and to enable attachment points for eyes and lines. A major problem for the ship's master was where to stow his sails when they were not in use. Putting them away wet would rapidly lead to rot and weakness, but such large canvases could not be left to hang unattended. The lowered sails were then another bulky item that reduced the area available for the crew to make themselves comfortable onboard.

In strong winds the sails would have been reefed by a series of lines sewn into the canvas but in fine conditions extra studding sails, called bonnets, were laced to the foot of the sail to increase the surface area. Indeed, bonnets themselves could be added to by the use of even smaller additional sails called drablers. With all her canvas spread a four-masted, multi-sailed vessel, such as *Mary Rose*, would have been a beautiful sight to behold.

To work masts, yards and sails by rope required the support of blocks and tackles, and a practical knowledge of the principles of mechanics to ensure that these pulleys were roved to advantage to give maximum help to the sailors straining upon them. The blocks were, for the most part, made of ash with a grooved wooden wheel or wheels running inside. Experimental metal blocks were also being introduced, with designs endeavouring to create strength without the problems caused by the use of the heavier metal. The majority of the blocks and pulleys were designed to work the rigging and cables but other, massive blocks were stowed in the hold for occasional major work, such as raising a spare mast for, when away from Portsmouth, the ship's company would have been expected to carry out any such evolution using their own resources. Keeping the ropes, especially the standing rigging, well maintained would have been a major task onboard, and to achieve this barrel loads

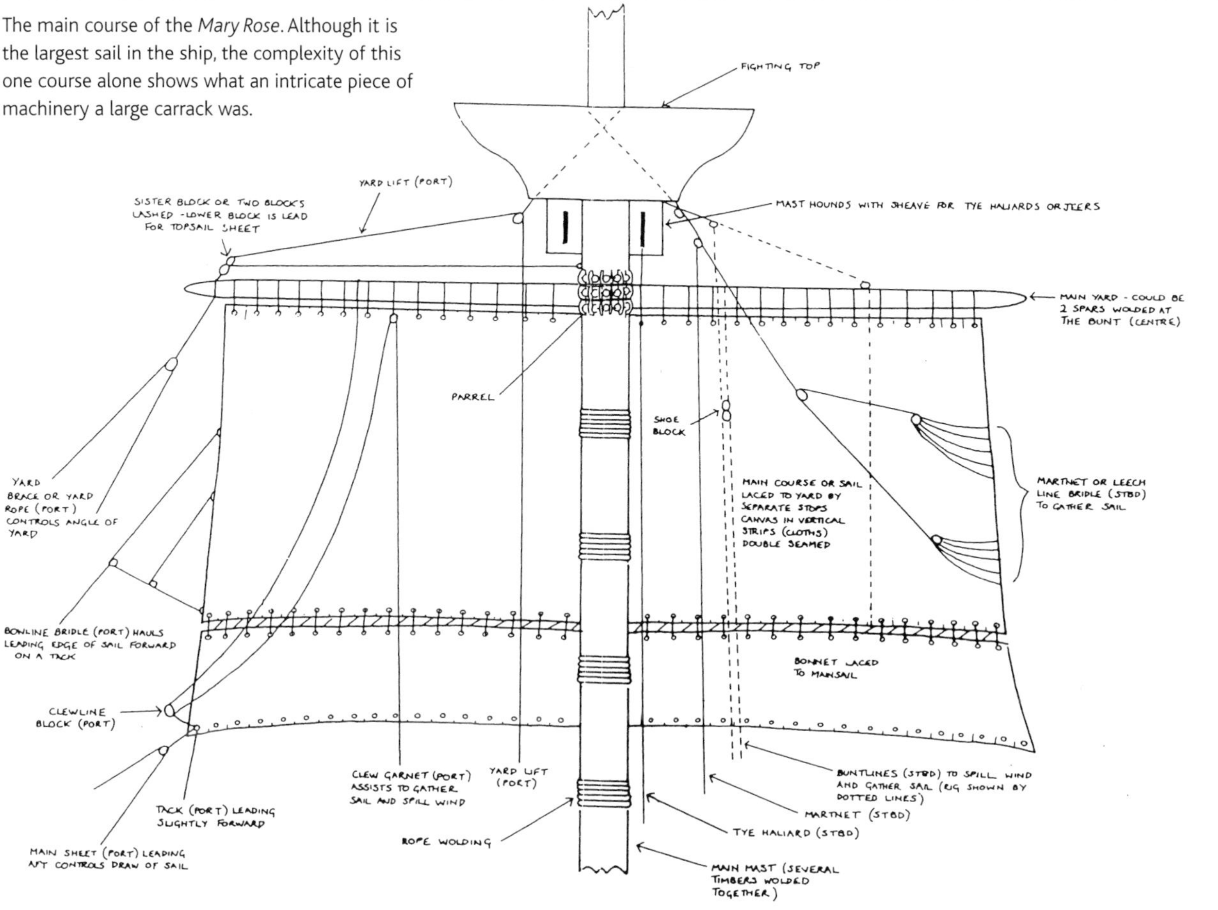

The main course of the *Mary Rose*. Although it is the largest sail in the ship, the complexity of this one course alone shows what an intricate piece of machinery a large carrack was.

of pitch and tar were required: 'Twenty barrels tar spent upon tarring of certain new cables and new tackle at Portsmouth with all the shrouds that belong unto the *Sovereign*.'[32] The efficacy of tarring needs no better evidence than the great amount of well-preserved rope lifted with *Mary Rose*, which still retains its smell and, in certain cases, its stickiness.

There was one other massive piece of timber that needed to be fitted to the ship – her rudder. The design of the ship meant that, unlike earlier clinker-built ships, she had both a squared-off and a flat, transom stern with a straight stern post. This meant that a rudder, with a straight leading edge could be fitted neatly to the stem post, which was an improvement on earlier design. This long piece of timber came up as high as the upper deck where it was moved by means of a tiller, or helm, connected directly to the rudder head.

Mary Rose and *Peter Pomegranate* appear to have been completed by early July 1510. They were still not warships, however, for their weaponry was not available in the Portsmouth dockyard. Instead it was necessary for them to be taken around to the Thames for the final part of their construction – arming. But, before they were ready for this first sea voyage one further essential delivery was needed to ensure their stability – ballast. When the ships had been in the water a sufficient length of time for the water tightness of all their joints to have been checked and any necessary leaks stopped up, Brygandyne would have called for ballast to be delivered. This consisted of about one hundred tons of shingle, of which Portsmouth had local supplies a plenty. As any one who has walked the beaches of Southsea knows its

ABOVE A selection of the wide range of blocks from the ship. Hundreds of these were needed for the handling of running rigging, sails, and anchors.

RIGHT The pulley wheels from the blocks, called sheaves, survive in large numbers from the ship. Unlike the later use of lignum vitae for this purpose the *Mary Rose* examples are made from single pieces of ash or elm.

main constituent is rounded pebbles which are very easy to shovel up. What is more they are already well washed and, on a summer's day at low water, well dried. The easiest task in the whole of the building programme would have been for boats to be hauled up on the beach just outside the harbour, to be loaded with shingle, and then sailed back alongside the ships.

Mary Rose's ballast weight would have been increased by the building, directly on top of the shingle, of the ship's two galleys, which Christopher Dobbs, a maritime archaeologist at the Mary Rose Trust estimates would have added another eight tons of weight in the bottom of the ship, a not-insignificant amount to offset the potential turning moment contributed by heavy weapons higher up and on the ship's side. The importance of placing the correct amount of ballast onboard needs no better illustration than the fate of *Vasa*. This incredibly ornate and expensive flagship of the Swedish navy sailed from her builder's yard in Stockholm on 10 August 1628, and capsized forty-five minutes later as she made her first major course alteration. An enquiry concluded that she had not carried enough ballast (just some 120 tons) for a ship much larger than *Mary Rose*.

Lying in the bilges the ballast could become foul smelling and saturated so chain pumps were fitted to keep those spaces reasonably dry. These pumps were a marvel of Tudor craftsmanship for their twenty foot or more channel was bored out of one piece of timber.

The weaponry for Brygandyne's two ship's awaited them in London where the king's arsenal was housed and where many of the guns were made. The ship fitters in London were in for a surprise because it was in the positions prepared for these guns that

Mary Rose was, for the English, a revolutionary ship. Prior to her construction all ships' great guns had been carried on the upper deck or in the fore- and after castles, which limited the size of weapon that could be safely deployed at sea. Now, the smooth carvel sides of *Mary Rose* had enabled her shipwrights to cut lidded gun-ports into her sides at main-deck level. These could be closed snugly and watertightly with wooden lids against the ship's side, something which could not be achieved with the serrated sides of a clinker-built ship. *Mary Rose* sailing up the Thames in 1511 was the harbinger of the age of the great-gunned sailing ship, for after her fitting out the English would make use of gun-ports by introducing more and heavier weapons low down in their fighting ships and even, by lowering the headroom, create a second gun deck.

Brygandyne's shipwrights did not invent the gun-port, however. The credit for that must go to the Breton, presumaly nicknamed, Descharges, who had built a ship with this feature at Brest at the end of the fifteenth century. The French flagship *Grand Louise* and Breton carrack *Cordelière,* which fought against *Mary Rose* in 1512, were both considered to have had gun-ports, making the battle off Saint Matthew's Point near Brest the first occasion when ships so fitted came up against each other. They would continue to do so until the mid-nineteenth century; the gun-ports of *Mary Rose* introduced a design that was to last until the relegation of HMS *Warrior* to the Reserve Fleet in 1883.

Brygadyne's final task was to recruit the sailors needed for the Channel voyage and to equip the ships for their passage to the Thames. On 29 July he was paid £120 for his expenses related to the movement of the two ships and in September he receieved an additional £50. At the same time Richard Palshide (John Dawtry's partner) at Southampton was paid for the provision of twenty-four coats in the Tudor colours of green and white to be worn by the soldiers who formed the onboard defenders of *Mary Rose* for this short voyage. The mariners were issued with six similar coats to be worn by the master, the four quartermasters and the boatswain. Each coat cost 6s 10d. Palshide himself received a 'reward' of forty shillings for sailing with the ship while, John Clerke, who was appointed master for this one trip was paid 20s.

Obviously it was intended that their arrival in London should be a proud moment for the crew. We can take the liberty of assuming that as the two ships slipped out of Portsmouth on that late July day another group of proud men, led by Brygandyne, gathered on the shore and watched them depart. Their chests must have swelled along with the ships' sails as the breeze filled them for the first time and the vessels moved through the narrow gap between Portsea and Gosport and into the Solent. That pride would have been justified. The yacht designer Colin Mudie, who was to design the reconstruction of *Matthew,* a near contemporary of *Mary Rose,* thought that the hull of the latter was far more sophisticated than he would have imagined possible for the period. Of the many admirable qualities in her design he found:

> ...the main eye-opener is that the shape of the hull is such as to positively enhance the possibility of the establishment of laminar flow to be produced around the hull at low water speeds. Laminar, or smooth flow, markedly reduced the skin friction and thereby importantly reduces the drag of the hull. *Mary Rose* ought to have been excellent in steering and manoeuvering.[33]

He considered her below-water lines to be, '...very close to what scientists have developed to optimise laminar flow and create lift.'[34] Peter Firstbrook reiterates Mudie's view claiming that: 'Here was a ship which could be sailed efficiently in all conditions including the lightest winds'[35] – and that *Mary Rose*'s builders could be likened to NASA space technicians in the way they pushed their ideas and technologies to the limit.

Contemporary accounts of her sailing qualities would support this view. However, the exact lines of the ship that sailed out of the Solent in July 1511 are not known. The contemporary Anthony Roll shows a carrack with high castles fore and aft as might be expected, but also shows a totally erroneous second gun deck. Since the ship was raised, artists and model makers have produced recreations, based on the archaeological evidence, that resemble a transition between a carrack and a galleon. Doug McElvogue is not convinced by these later renditions and has, after careful study, proposed an outline much closer to that indicated in the Anthony Roll and the paintings of the period. Whatever the truth may be, there is no doubt that she would prove to be a good seakeeping craft. Perhaps Brygandyne and his men kept pace with their ship as she passed the Square Tower and the Round Tower. Maybe they stood and watched long enough to see the dwindling shape of *Mary Rose* sail proudly over the spot where, in another thirty-four years, she would disappear beneath the waves for the next 437 years.

Based on the best available sources of information, this is a recreation of the *Matthew*, the 50-ton, three-masted, carvel-constructed vessel in which John Cabot reached North America from Bristol in 1497. Under sail the ship gives a good impression of a vessel roughly contemporary with the *Mary Rose*.

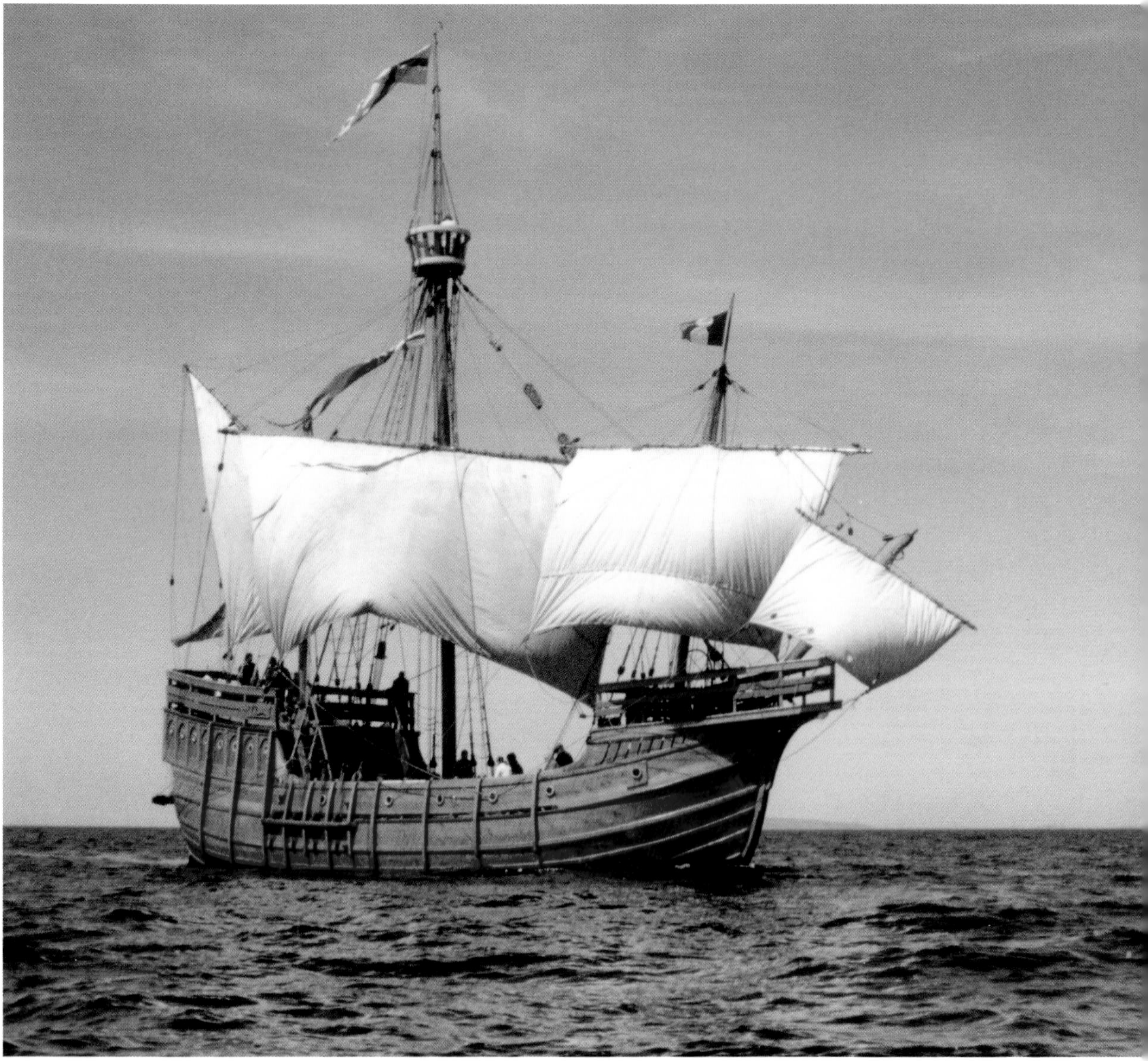

The galleasse *Jennet* from the Anthony Roll, built at Portsmouth in 1539.

These men would not have been able to foretell that event, nor would they have considered their sturdy vessel capable of such a catastrophic failure. They would have considered whether or not further orders would follow. This would depend on what the king in London would think of the quality of their workmanship, and whether or not his bellicose intentions required more vessels of war to achieve his aims. The records show no other vessels being built in Portsmouth until *Jennet* in 1539, many years after Brygandyne had retired. Most others, including the massive 1500-ton *Henry Grace à Dieu*, were to be constructed in the Thames. This may well have disappointed Brygandyne himself, but when he retired in early 1523 he would have known that he had done his duty well. And, although he was granted the usual pardons for undiscovered embezzlements, he would also have known that he had nothing to fear as long as he had 'stolen in measure'. What he would not have known was that he had been responsible for building one of the most famous and best-loved of all British naval vessels.

As for the building of future vessels on the Thames the preference for this location had more to do with Henry's interest in every aspect of his fleet and the fact that his emerging Navy Board was based in London than it did with the relative merits of the shipwrights of the two cities. From his beloved palace at Greenwich the king had very little distance to travel either east to his shipyards at Woolwich or west to his reserve fleet base and depots at Dartford while, across the river, and close to the arsenal at the Tower of London, he based his master gunsmiths. No clearer demonstration of the king's interest in every detail of his navy exists than this close geographical proximity to his main residences of the key elements of his new fleet.

Portsmouth, although it was where the majority of the fleet overwintered, languished. No master shipwright was ordered to reside here until Elizabeth's time and few buildings were erected to support dockyard activities, although the dockyard itself was enlarged and enclosed in 1527. Its fortifications improved and decayed according to the present danger and the funding available to carry out repairs and improvements. Eventually, pure logic and improvements in transport and communications, ensured that it became and retained its position as Britain's and the Commonwealth's premier naval port, long after Thames-side activities silted up.

CHAPTER 3

Ballocks, Bows and Bastards

ONCE IN THE THAMES the fitting out of *Mary Rose* continued apace. In addition to her ordnance the items delivered included: eight loads of elm for the gun carriages, additional rigging and tackle and banners and streamers. Expensive although these latter items were, Henry deemed it would be money well spent. He required his new ships to impress foreign ambassadors and heads of state, and money spent on a lick of paint and a decorative streamer was, for him, worth every penny. The principal flag to be flown was the banner of the English coat of arms, quartering the three gold lions of England on a red field and the three gold *fleur de lis* of France on a blue field. There were also flags of the red cross of St George and long streamers with St George at the hoist, and the green and white Tudor livery colours over the rest of their length. The Anthony Roll depicts *Mary Rose* with an immense pennant unfurled. This is no exaggeration. Records show that streamers up to fifty yards long were often deployed. This would indeed have been an impressive site for any visiting dignitary[1].

The bronze muzzle-loading bastard demi-culverin from the ship mounted on a reconstructed carriage. Cast in 1537, the extensive decoration of this gun indicates the pride that casting such guns held for gunsmiths like the Owen brothers.

However, the main reason for the two ships (*Mary Rose* had been accompanied by *Peter Pomegranate*) to be brought from Portsmouth to London was for them to be fitted out as full-time warships. The guns delivered to *Mary Rose* were many and varied and were referred to by a variety of names. There were, however, eight distinctive types of straightforward single-bored muzzle-loading guns which, in ascending order of size, were; falconets, falcons, minions, sakers, demi-culverins, culverins, demi-cannons and cannons. These weighed between 300lbs and 6,000lbs, with the largest recovered from *Mary Rose* being a 4873-pounder bronze cannon made by Peter Baude. These types could be further divided according to their calibre into:

(i) Legitimate Pieces – a gun of a standard bore-to-length ratio.
(ii) Bastard Pieces – a gun with a larger bore and shorter length than standard.
(iii) Extraordinary Pieces – a gun with a smaller bore and a longer length than standard.

These names were added to the description of the weapon so that the most ornate weapon on *Mary Rose* was a bronze demi-culverin bastard. Weapons could be further sub-divided depending on the thickness of the metal at breech and bore. Iron breech-loaders had their own names of which the most important were the long, hooped port-pieces. Smaller guns were referred to either by traditional names, such as 'serpentine' or by their role, such as 'murderers', 'hail shot pieces' and 'swivel pieces'. The material with which

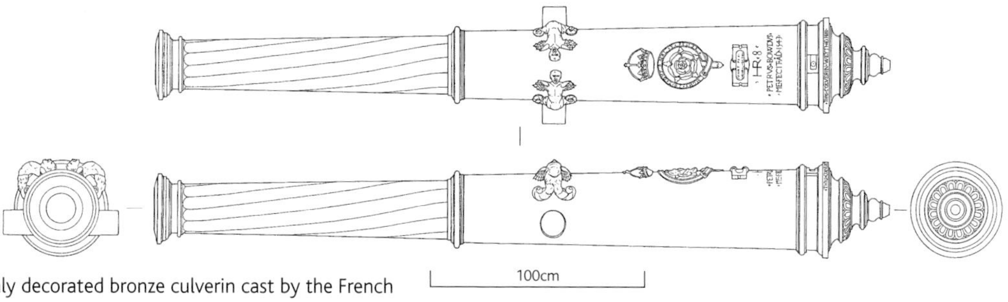

A highly decorated bronze culverin cast by the French gun founder Peter Baude at Houndsditch in 1543.

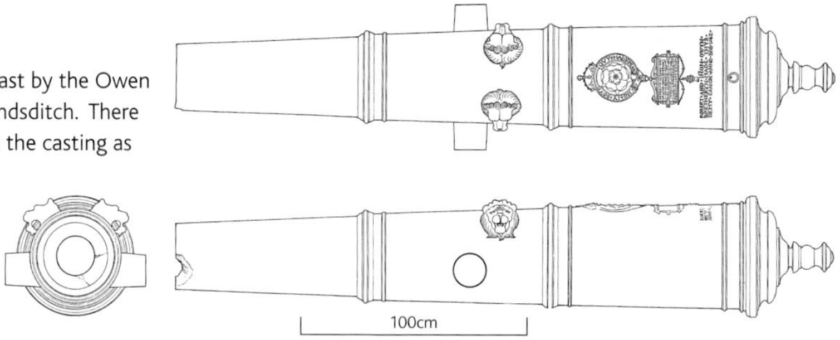

A bronze demi-cannon cast by the Owen brothers in 1542 at Houndsditch. There may have been a fault in the casting as the muzzle end has been cut away.

the gun was made – bronze or iron – and whether or not it was cast or forged provides yet more diversity as did the method of loading, either breech or muzzle.[2]

All this diversity indicates a science and an industry in a period of both innovation and transition. *Mary Rose* was armed and re-armed during these years of development, and the range of her weapons provides a wonderful record of a time of change. It also shows quite clearly the move away from fitting warships with guns originally designed and mounted for land warfare to those built and put on carriages expressly to serve at sea. This diversity also reflected the way the ship was fought and handled. Long-range weapons, such as culverin with, of necessity, smaller shot were required both to soften up an enemy during an approach or to warn an assailant to keep his distance. As the range closed, larger shot was fired to inflict material damage on the opponent. This was followed by chaotic fire to cow the defenders and, finally, as the ships came together, by a barrage of anti-personnel shot such as diced, hail, cannister or grape-shot, all supported by archery. Thus a continuing fire could first disable a ship by damaging its masts and sails and then maim and kill those members of its crew exposed to fire. With the close quarters addition of smoke, noise and flame this weaponry could cause shock and awe.

The armament of fifty-eight of the king's ships, galleys, pinnaces and row-barges was recorded in the Anthony Roll in 1546, along with the number of crew, weapons and ammunition: comparison with similar inventories, dated 1514 and 1540, provides an exceptionally detailed account of how *Mary Rose* was armed throughout her career (*see* page 46). Before the accession of the Tudors, England was not a major producer of heavy weaponry, which was often purchased from abroad, particularly from the Low Countries, with Malines, Ghent and Bruges being the notable manufacturing centres, along with Venice, whose Arsenale was a world leader. Thanks to the efforts of the two Tudor Henrys this all changed: England became, first of all, self-sufficient, and then an exporter of arms, a trade she has conducted ever since.

Early wrought-iron breech-loaders had weak barrels and insecure detachable breech-blocks that could blow up in the face of the gunners. Cast-iron guns offered greater strength, shorter and tapered barrels, and thus a lighter weapon that could be deployed at sea, but casting such guns in iron was

Henry and his gun founders. Henry was determined to create his own gun-manufacturing industry and established a major foundry at Houndsditch within easy reach of his palaces.

not feasible at the start of Henry VIII's reign. Bronze was the alternative, being strong, workable and malleable, so that graciously ornate weapons could be produced. But bronze guns were heavy, so placing them on ships without causing instability was a problem. The innovative solution was the gun-port, which allowed guns to be positioned between decks. Thus *Mary Rose*'s artillery was able to occupy three decks, with the heaviest guns lowest down on the main deck. As far as efficiency was concerned, the power of breech-loading port pieces was restricted by the failure to develop a totally air-tight and secure breech; the brass muzzle loaders were thus more efficient as well as being safer. The fourteen guns that were eventually to be placed on *Mary Rose*'s main deck were a mix of bronze cannons, demi-cannons and culverins and wrought-iron port pieces. The upper deck had six wrought-iron guns and four bronze guns, four port-pieces, two sakers and a falcon, while the castle deck held two demi-culverins that could fire forward.

The quality of this artillery clearly reflects the importance that the king placed on fitting his vessels with the most modern armaments. Bronze was expensive, however, and an expanding navy would need cheap guns. These could only be produced from iron but there had to be a transition from wrought- to cast-iron manufacture before reliable muzzle-loading iron guns could be made. The transition took time, but by the end of the Tudor century cast-iron guns were in the ascendancy and the way was clear for mass production and standardisation. *Mary Rose* had twenty-nine large guns, all different types; the 100-gun HMS *Victory* had three classes of cannon. The short period when bronze was best left a beautiful legacy, and this latter age of bronze was an age of pride. To cast these guns the king had to recruit gun founders, at first from the continent but later, once he had established his own foundries, using native craftsmen who proved as skilled as their continental rivals. So, in 1510, with the completion of his first two warships in sight, the king ordered from the famous gun founder, Hans Poppenreuter of Malines in Flanders, a dozen heavy brass curtows, a dozen lighter brass curtows and two dozen brass serpentines. Then, in September 1511, he paid a blacksmith, John Blewberry, to provide anvils, bellows, shears, hammers, pincers, troughs and other necessities for a new forge at Greenwich to be made for the 'armourers of Brussels'. Two months later, Cornelius Johnson, an Englishman, was paid for mending and re-stocking guns for *Mary Rose*: home manufacture was growing.

The production of a large bronze gun was a complicated procedure, which resulted in the mould having to be destroyed so that no two guns were ever the same – a fact that the casters relished, as can be seen from the ornate decorations on their weapons.

Once cast the guns were tested by firing and those that had not 'failed proof' were sent to the fleet. Given the opportunity for embellishment and the fact that each weapon was unique it is not surprising that the makers chose to record their details on the weapons themselves. One can imagine the pride with which the Owen brothers recorded on their wonderful brass bastard demi-culverin, with its fine lion heads and acanthus columns, the following inscription:

> ROBERT AND JOHN OWYN BRETHERYN BORNE IN THE CYTE OF LONDON THE SOMNNES OF AN INGLISH MADE THYS BASTARD ANNO DNI 1537

– while the pride of their king was made manifest on the same weapon by the presence of the Tudor Rose crowned and within the Garter, supported with the additional inscription:

> HENRY EIGHT BY THE GRACE KING OF ENGLAND AND FRANCE, DEFENDER OF THE FAITH, LORD OF IRELAND AND ON EARTH SUPREME HEAD OF THE ENGLISH CHURCH

In those few words, in that location, can be summed up the aspirations and illusions of a spendthrift king. The king of Calais still considered himself, by divine right, ruler of France, and he was prepared to melt down both the treasury and monastery bells to cast bronze guns to support his claim. As a result, Henry VIII's reign was an arms race from beginning to end and, although this gave birth to the modern navy the immediate effect was bankruptcy.

Until the Tudor century the engagement of an enemy fleet at sea was an accidental occurrence, for it was difficult both to seek out the enemy and, once found, to report his position and movements in a timely manner. Nor, with such dependence on the wind, was open-seas manoeuvring an option that could be undertaken with any certainty that it would end with a close-enough encounter. In consequence many medieval and early modern sea battles took place just offshore and close by an enemy port where the presence of the opposition could be assumed with some certainty. These geographical constraints, and the fact that war at sea was regarded as a peculiar, but nevertheless related, way of fighting a land battle were reflected in the design and armament of the main warships themselves. Thus Henry VII's two major warships, *Regent* and *Sovereign*, were fitted with a great number and variety of guns, but all useful only at close quarters for clearing an opponent's decks prior to boarding. Gun casting was too imprecise and gunpowder too variable for these weapons to be expected to do otherwise.

The requirements for *Mary Rose* and *Peter Pomegranate* were different, and new skills and ship designs would enable improvements to be made. The newer naval ships were also fitted with stern-chasers, guns placed in the stern facing aft where they could be brought to bear on an enemy without exposing one's own ship's side to enemy fire. There was also a need to bring these guns down closer to the waterline where the effect of penetration of an enemy hull could cause sufficient damage to sink the ship. This was especially important in engagements with galleys, whose low-lying form could, at close and effective range, mean that shot could pass harmlessly overhead

Detail of the decoration on the Owen brothers' demi-cannon.

and, even if it damaged mast and rigging, still leave the galley able to make its get away under oars. In 1574, a Spaniard wrote that:

> The ordnance flush with the water should be at once discharged broadside on, and so damage their hull and confuse them with smoke. This is the English way of fighting and I have many times seen them do it to the French 30 years ago.[3]

Apart from a possible failure in recollection – for broadsides do not appear to have been used against the French in 1545 – the text indicates the close-quarters encounters that were the norm for, if smoke was to be an important factor in confusion, the ships would have had to be very close indeed. The advantage would lie with the ship to windward, hence the need to achieve this position and follow it up with boarding the enemy vessel. Anti-boarding nets rigged over the ship's waist would not have deterred an enemy bent on seizing a ship. Rather, it would have limited the boarders' options and placed them in some danger if they leapt upon this netted trampoline. As they swung over or cut their way through the soldiers below would have been able to thrust upwards with pike and bill hook. In fact the practical use of a twenty-foot-long pike on board ship would only seem to arise in such circumstances; there would have been no room to hold it in anything other than the almost vertical position. Other soldiers would have had the task of destroying the sails and rigging of their opponent thus removing its ability, once grappled, to break away. Long pole weapons would have been swung into the standing rigging, while others tried to set fire to the sails through hurling primitive missiles with blazing tar nose-cones into them. Even if unsuccessful, the latter could cause smoke and confusion, very necessary ingredients in this mayhem.

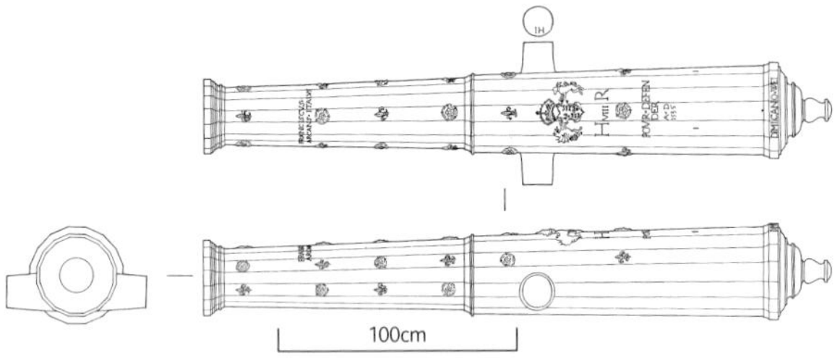

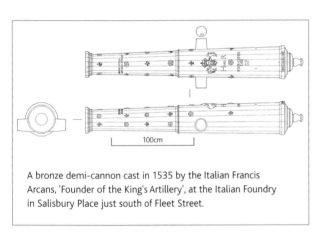

A bronze demi-cannon cast in 1535 by the Italian Francis Arcans, 'Founder of the King's Artillery', at the Italian Foundry in Salisbury Place just south of Fleet Street.

An Inventory of the Guns of *Mary Rose*

	1514	1541	1546	Brass guns recovered
BRASS GUNS				
Great curtows	5			
Murderers	2			
Falcons	2	2	1	
Falconets	3			
Chamber-less brass gun	1			
Cannons			2	2
Demi-cannons		4	2	3
Culverins		2	2	3
Demi-culverins		2	6	2
Sakers		5	2	
Total Brass Guns	**13**	**15**	**15**	**10**
IRON GUNS				
Great murderers	1			
Murderers	2			
Cast pieces	2			
Murderer	1			
Demi-slings	2		3	
Stone guns	26			
Top guns	3			
Serpentines	28			
Port pieces		9	12	
Slings		6	2	
Quarter slings		6	1	
Fowlers			6	
Bases		60	30	
Top pieces			2	
Hail shot pieces			20	
Total Iron Guns	**65**	**81**	**76**	
TOTAL GUNS	**78**	**96**	**91**	

Along with the positioning of the main armament the range and effectiveness of the weapons was of equal importance. This would have varied quite considerably depending on the quality of the gunpowder, the air-tightness of the combustion chamber and the movement of the ship itself. Aiming at anything other than at close range through the small gun-ports of *Mary Rose*, was not an option so, in practice, there would have been a great difference between the potential maximum range of a gun and the maximum effective range – that distance at which a telling hit could be achieved on the enemy with a degree of certainty. A reconstructed weapon based on one from *Mary Rose* would suggest that 200 metres might have been considered the maximum effective range of her guns.

The introduction of the gun-deck has led to much speculation about whether or not these ships ever fired broadsides. This is unlikely. The guns themselves were canted at an angle so that their barrels lay perpendicular to the hull from which they extruded. This would mean that few guns could be brought to bear on an enemy vessel simultaneously unless the two ships were lying almost side by side. To fire each gun at the enemy would require the Master to con his own ship along a gently curving course so that each gun could be brought to bear sequentially. If, at the end of the turn, he was left stern on to the foe then his final riposte, before reloading, would be delivered from his heaviest guns in the gunroom.

Additionally, firing all weapons on one side at the same time would have caused enormous forces to exert themselves on the ship's structure as the power of the recoil took effect, even if this was less noticeable in guns which were far from airtight on firing. As a tactic a ripple delivery had much to recommend it as it kept the attacking vessel with headway on and out of grappling range while allowing a much more constant rate of fire to be kept up. N A M Rodger suggests another reason why a broadside was impractical was that there were not enough professional gunners on board to deliver such a discharge:

Re-enactors demonstrating the firing of a muzzle-loader. The accurate effective range of these weapons was greatly reduced by a number of problems, such as ship movement, aiming, inconsistencies in powder, and excessive windage around the shot.

> The conclusion seems to be inescapable that however the guns were being reloaded, there were not enough men available to load all of them at once. We have to imagine teams of men moving from gun to gun. Reloading the whole armament, by whatever method, must have taken a long time, and there was no advantage in lingering within range of the enemy while one did so.[4]

A ship's captain could, therefore, either aim to get alongside his enemy as fast as possible, or bear down on him and haul away firing his guns in succession as his angle allowed. But it was not possible to stand off inside range and deliver blast after blast in a broadside fashion, for Rodger estimates that it could have taken up to one and a half hours to reload and fire each gun.[5]

However, one needs to exercise some caution here. To be fitted with offensive weapons that could not be used with anything approaching the speed with which a captain needed to bring them to bear because of a dearth of professional gunners would have been anathema to any commander. The obvious solution was to train up sailors to fill the subordinate roles of the guns' crew so that each gunner was allocated to one weapon. It would then have been his responsibility to train his own crew while the Master Gunner was in overall control. *Mary Rose* certainly had more seamen than she could accommodate on her upper deck at anyone time; what better use for the surplus than to man the guns?

Nevertheless, whatever the constraint, from the moment *Mary Rose* sailed from the Thames in 1512, the navy royal had a ship capable of firing a broadside with guns of significant power. In fact, the rippled broadside, the mastery of which was to give Britain dominance in future fleet engagements, was the best answer to the insurmountable problem that a combination of the sailing ship and the carriage-mounted gun gave the navy for some 400 years. Its existence meant that ships had to fight in lines, beam on, presenting their greatest profile to the enemy when common sense dictated that the smallest profile was the best position from which to fight, if only the weaponry allowed. The broadside was the maritime equivalent of trench warfare and it lasted for 400 years at sea as opposed to the much deprecated four years during which trench warfare was conducted upon the Western Front.

If this seems too sweeping and critical a statement, one has only to look at the greatest engagement in the age of sail, the Battle of Trafalgar, in which Nelson threw away the rule book and hurried through the gun gap in line ahead presenting the smallest profile to his opponents until his ships were able to sweep their decks from aft to fore with devastating discharge after discharge. After Trafalgar nothing could be the same again, but it took the introduction of both the steam turbine and the gun turret to change a fighting tradition that began with *Mary Rose.*

Training would have been all important, for not only was the artillery idiosyncratic but they were one of the few weapons that required teamwork to make them function. Estimates of the size of gun crew vary enormously, but Nicholas Hall, Keeper of Artillery at the Royal Armouries, believes that the space available around the great guns in *Mary Rose* would have made a team of six the most efficacious. In the case of a port piece, the crew would have consisted of: a Captain of the Gun who primed, aimed and fired; four assistants to lift and place the breech chamber, and one assistant who loaded the shot and inserted and removed the elevating peg and breech wedge.

Training with non-firing drills would have been an essential part of creating an efficient crew, and it is noteworthy that the Tudor age produced several manuals on gun drills and advice on the use of artillery.[6] Yet there is no evidence that the drills themselves were practised in order to ensure both gun-crew safety and reasonably accurate fire, although achieving the latter often lay outside the skill of the Captain of the Gun. Drills, based on the recreation and firing of a weapon by Nicholas Hall can be seen opposite.

Reconstructed gun drill for breech-loading port piece

1. Elevate gun by lowering back of sledge on to ground, remove elevating post, check barrel-retaining ropes.
2. Remove forelock, wedge and chamber.
3. Place chamber to rear of gun (left).
4. Clean chamber.
5. Load with cartridge wadding.
6. Ram.
7. Insert tampion and hammer flush with chamber mouth.
8. Lay down chamber, insert handspikes.
9. Load projectile into breech end of barrel and hold.
10. Lay chamber in sledge, remove handspikes.
11. Use handpikes to drive chamber forward; insert forelock and wedge.
12. Drive home chamber by striking wedge.
13. Check alignment and fit of chamber to barrel.
14. Place elevating post in socket.
15. Depress the gun by raising the trail.
16. Lay for line.
17. Elevate or depress as required and postion retaining peg at position requested by gun-captain's sighting.
18. Check recoil ropes and barrel-retaining ropes.
19. GIVE FIRE.
20. Knock out forelock and remove wedge.
21. Insert handspikes and remove chamber.
22. Elevate and remove post.
23. Up-end chamber and sponge.
24. Examine for any residue.
25. Clear vent.

Reconstructed gun drill for breech-loading port piece

1. Elevate gun by lowering back of sledge on to ground, remove elevating post, check barrel-retaining ropes.
2. Remove forelock, wedge and chamber.
3. Place chamber to rear of gun (left).
4. Clean chamber.
5. Load with cartridge wadding.
6. Ram.
7. Insert tampion and hammer flush with chamber mouth.
8. Lay down chamber, insert handspikes.
9. Load projectile into breech end of barrel and hold.
10. Lay chamber in sledge, remove handspikes.
11. Use handpikes to drive chamber forward; insert forelock and wedge.
12. Drive home chamber by striking wedge.
13. Check alignment and fit of chamber to barrel.
14. Place elevating post in socket.
15. Depress the gun by raising the trail.
16. Lay for line.
17. Elevate or depress as required and postion retaining peg at position requested by gun-captain's sighting.
18. Check recoil ropes and barrel-retaining ropes.
19. GIVE FIRE.
20. Knock out forelock and remove wedge.
21. Insert handspikes and remove chamber.
22. Elevate and remove post.
23. Up-end chamber and sponge.
24. Examine for any residue.
25. Clear vent.

The great variety of guns and ammunition meant that few men would have been trained in the use of more than one type of weapon. The greatest difference, as far as the main armament was concerned, would have been between breech loaders and muzzle loaders. Whereas the former were loaded by the placing of a charged chamber wedged into the breech, the latter had to be run in board, sponged out and loaded through the muzzle. Breech loaders were potentially the most efficient weapon and the most capable of a rapid rate of fire, but the technical difficulties of manufacturing a safe and reliable weapon was to occupy the centuries from their disappearance under the Tudors to their re-emergence at the end of the nineteenth century.

In the intervening centuries warships were limited to having short-range weapons requiring large gun crews. The number of guns carried rather than their range defined the class of ship, and would do so as long as weapons had to recoil inboard to be loaded

Re-enactors demonstrating the drill for breech-loading. The main danger from these weapons was that the breech might blow out, causing severe injury to the gun crew.

Gunner's tools: few of these survive from other locations so their recovery greatly increases our knowledge about Tudor gunnery.

through the muzzle. The presence of such weapons occupying limited deck space dictated the quality of life onboard. Given the inconsistencies in the weapons, ammunition and powder, the Master Gunner's main skill was not based upon the laying and training of his weapon for long-range accuracy. Indeed, the phrase, 'a long shot' indicating an option with limited chance of success reinforces this fact. The gunner's professionalism was best employed, therefore, in ensuring that his weapon was loaded and fired safely, so that it neither blew up nor ejected its wedge with lethal velocity. The latter danger was specifically referred to by Cyprian Lucar in 1588 when he wrote:

> ...and when a Gunner will give fire to a chamber piece, he ought not to stand upon that side of the piece where a wedge of iron is put to lock the chamber in the piece, because the said wedge may through the discharge of the piece fly out and kill the Gunner.[7]

Sponging out, placing the right amount of charge and standing clear of the weapon on firing were all parts of the drills essential to protect the crew – not to give precision delivery at range. If they failed then guns would explode, as in *Mary John*, where Jacques Berenghier may have been made a scapegoat to save the Master Gunner,[8] or in *Less Galley* where an exploding saker blew up and fatally injured Sir John Berkeley[9]. So, when the enemy was engaged it was inevitably at close quarters and invariably bloody. *The Complaynt of Scotland* written in 1548 gives a vivid contemporary account:

> Then where I sat I heard the cannon and gun make many hideous crack – duf, duf, duf, duf, duf. The basilisks and falcons cried tirduf, tirduf, tirduf, tirduf, tirduf, tirduf. Then the small artillery cried tik, tik, tik, tik, tik. The reek, smoke, and the stink of the gunpowder filled the air…burning in one bad fire which generated such murkiness and mist that I could not see my length from me.[10]

After which, of course, followed the frenzy of hand-to-hand fighting, as each ship tried either to board or repel its opponent. It was a form of warfare that required both strong leadership and firm fellowship.

The type of shot that would have been fired in such engagements would have been broadly either stone or iron, with its size and shape varying according to its purpose. Iron guns usually fired stone shot, while muzzle loaders fired iron 'cannon balls'. Both had inherent inaccuracies in flight and it would be wrong to assume that Kentish ragstone was any less effective, pound for pound, than its iron counterpart. It certainly did not shatter on impact. Captain Rainsborrow in *Mary Sampson* in 1628 is quoted as stating that a 25-pound stone shot, unlike the smaller iron projectiles that did less damage:

> …staved on our lower deck two barrels of beef, two of pease, a Butt of Wine; some of the shot passing through nineteen inches of planke and timber…and made us leakie.[11]

Stone shot did fall out of favour, but for reasons of pure economics: it could cost about 2s and 6d to stone cut a shot which made one about ten times more expensive than an iron equivalent.

Fighting a land battle at sea was to be a principle of English maritime warfare until developments in the Mediterranean demanded a response. In that tide-

A medieval depiction of a typical sea fight, like Sluys, featuring archery and boarding.

less, and often calm sea, a new type of ship, or rather the resurrection of an ancient form, was being built – the galley. This was the successor to the triremes that had defeated the Persians at Salamis, and they were now being used in an attempt to hold back a newer threat from the East, the Turks. The galley of the sixteenth century was a long narrow, oared vessel that also carried a sail. It could thus get underway in flat calm or even row into a slight headwind. The long narrow form with its lines of oarsmen meant that it could be slow to turn but, with a forward facing gun, the galley was the motor torpedo boat of its time and was feared just as much,[12] especially in coastal waters. Its major drawback was that it needed to be lightly built to assist with its motive power, so it was of little use in choppy seas and that, however strong the oarsmen were, it could make little headway against an adverse tide or current. A low hull also meant that it could be swamped easily and that, when sailing in a stiff breeze, the leeside would be under water. Finally, with a high crew-to-storage-capacity ratio, the galley needed to replenish frequently, especially with water, thus making them impractical for long sea voyages away from land.

The typical galley was about 50m long with a 7m beam. A single deck gave access to the hold above which sat the oarsmen numbering up to 150 manning about twenty-five oars on either side. Forward was a platform that carried the main gun battery. This could consist of five guns: a 'cannon serpentine' amidships, a 'demi-cannon serpentine' on either side and two 12-pounders. The three large guns were fixed so that the only way that they could be brought to bear was through the helmsman steering towards an opponent. The remaining guns were located so that the could be used at close range or, in the case of the ones mounted on the poop, also to control the slaves should this prove necessary.

By the beginning of the sixteenth century, galley design was reaching its apogee. It had been realised that limiting the number of oars but increasing the number of men per oar by up to five, made the boat both easier to construct and more efficient to propel.

A hail shot piece, used in an anti-personnel role. Although many were produced this was not an effective weapon.

A greater beam made the vessel more seaworthy and also allowed for more forward pointing guns to be carried; in a painting by Pieter Breugel the Elder seven such guns are shown.

Of primary significance to the English was the fact that galleys were operating in the Channel – southern fighting machines were being utilised in northern waters. At Rouen the French created a shipyard expressly for the purpose of building such vessels. When the first of these gun galleys appeared in the Channel is not known, but the French kings, with a Mediterranean, Atlantic and Channel coast to patrol and defend, were well able to move these vessels from north to south and apply lessons learned on one coast to support operations on another. They also introduced professional sea warriors into the Channel theatre with over a century of collective wisdom on which to base their tactics. The amateur English ship commanders whom they would be opposing were still at the stage of adapting military land tactics for use at sea. Galleys would be formidable opponents to any force attempting to land on the coast of France or to bring the French fleet in to action. To defend themselves the English would need a mixed armoury, including not only their own rowed vessels, but also larger, stronger ships of war.

Although *Mary Rose*, a carrack, was part of the fleet that Henry built to challenge the French, the latter's possession of galleys meant that the English fleet would be most vulnerable while they were being operationally most effective, stationed off the enemy coast. For sailing ships had one major problem when coming up against the more manoeuvrable and low-lying galleys, in that, unlike the latter, they could not fire with forward-pointing guns. Instead they had to turn beam on to use their major armament and thus expose themselves to their opponent, when tactics indicated that as small a profile as possible had to be the favoured aspect. This problem endured into modern times. Faced with a fast-approaching small opponent, such as a motor gun boat, or a weapon such as a torpedo, the larger, slower warship needs to present itself bow on to offer the smallest target while still being able to engage the enemy. With the introduction of the gun turret this could be achieved, but before this revolutionary invention the sailing ship had a major problem of which their builders were well aware. *Mary Rose* was therefore built with two forward-facing guns positioned on the after castle. This, in a ship with masts and sails obscuring the gunners' view could not have been a satisfactory arrangement. Guns needed clear arcs of fire, including dead ahead from where, while manoeuvring for position, the approaching threat from a galley attack was likely to come. Indeed, *Mary Rose* did have two such guns mounted in the forecastle but they had to be of a light weight; heavier guns would have made the ship too heavy in the bow.

Eventually the problem of the galley was solved by a combination of design and strategy. The design was the galleon, the true predecessor of the ship of the line, which, by doing away with the tall forecastle allowed heavier forward-facing armament to be positioned in the bows. The long-term strategy was to take naval warfare into the open seas where the flimsy galleys could not be used to effect. In coastal waters and ports ship's boats and landing parties took on the role of the galley – not always successfully. Henry produced a fleet which was to have a mixture of ships, galleys and the hybrid galleass so that his admirals could deal with an enemy whatever the weather conditions and proximity of the shore. Given these demands the crew would have needed a fluency in many weapons other than just heavy artillery.

A young sailor going to sea for the first time onboard *Mary Rose* in 1512 would not have come across such gun armament before, and he would have been awe struck by what he saw. He would, however, have been well acquainted with two of the personal weapons that he might be expected to handle: the knife and the bow. In the wooden world that was Tudor England he would have learned from an early age how to carve and whittle. He would have been taught how to skin rabbits or fillet fish and to make little whistles from reeds and to carve spinning tops and other childhood toys. Like his father before him he would one day have been given a knife of his own, which he would wear proudly at his side. He would also have learned how to keep his knife sharp and had his own whetstone for this purpose. Handling and using a knife skilfully would have become second nature, an important attribute in a wooden sailing vessel where ropes and rigging could tauten in seconds or whip around the ankles of the unwary. A sharp knife was often all that lay between death and disfigurement. It is, therefore, ironic that the water that finally overwhelmed *Mary Rose* did so with such speed that few could use their blades to escape from beneath the anti-boarding netting.

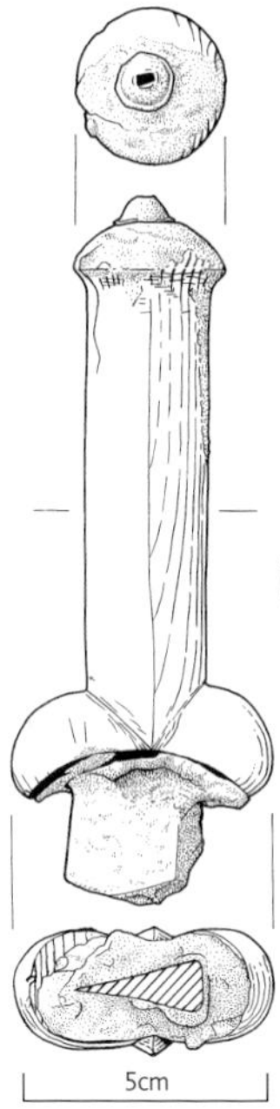

A ballock-knife handle.

At home on land the young sailor would have worn the most common type of knife found on board *Mary Rose*, the ballock knife. These knives were so named because of the two rounded shapes that formed the guard and the fact that, in many cases, the hilt was shaped like an erect penis. It seems strange that this form of knife should be so dominant onboard, and the possibility offers itself that the seamen in *Mary Rose* may have carried them as a machismo badge of identification that singled them out as the crew of that particular vessel.

Whatever the reason there would have been plenty of opportunities for knives to be used both for work and recreation. The best example of this was the carving of linstocks for use by the gunners. A linstock is a 0.75m-long carved pole along which is wrapped a slow fuse thus enabling the gunner to ignite the gunpowder at the touch-hole of his gun from a safe distance. The basic design consists of a stylised dragon's head or fist that grips the lit fuse; a shaft around which the remainder of the fuse cord is wrapped, and a handle. They are carved from a single piece of wood, usually ash, and very few are the same. Of the forty-four belonging to *Mary Rose* a few are masterpieces of the woodcarvers' craft, while most are very basic indeed. The variety would suggest that each was carved by an individual for his own use, and whittling them may well have been an enjoyable activity during quiet moments at sea. A number of the linstocks display burn marks indicating that they had been used.

The other weapon with which the young seaman would have had experience was the longbow. Shortly after he came to the throne Henry VIII reintroduced the law that required all fit males in the country below the age of 60 (except clergy and judges) to practice with the longbow. From the age of seven a boy had to be provided with a bow and two arrows until the age of seventeen when he became responsible for providing his own bow and four arrows. Buttes were required to be set up at every town and bowyers were obliged to sell bows to youths at the reduced rate of 12d while the maximum charge for a bow was set at 3s 4d. By the age of twenty-four every man in the kingdom was expected to be accurate with a bow at a range of a furlong. Moreover, archery was the one sport that could be practised on a Sunday. Most youngsters would have relished this opportunity. Neither was this a law more honoured in the breech than the observance. In 1554 the constable at Portsmouth was summoned for:

> ...not having inspected once a month the houses of their neighbours to see if every man and every boy from seven to sixty years of age have bows and arrows in their custody according to statute...[13]

– while the chamberlain was punished for not making up the butts where, on every holy day everyone had to turn out to shoot or face a penalty of a halfpence for each omission. Traditionally considered as a land weapon used by people from a fixed

Linstocks, probably carved by each gunner for his own use during the quieter moments at sea.

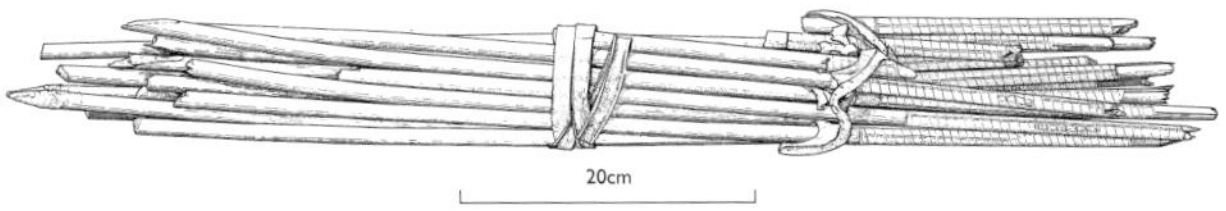

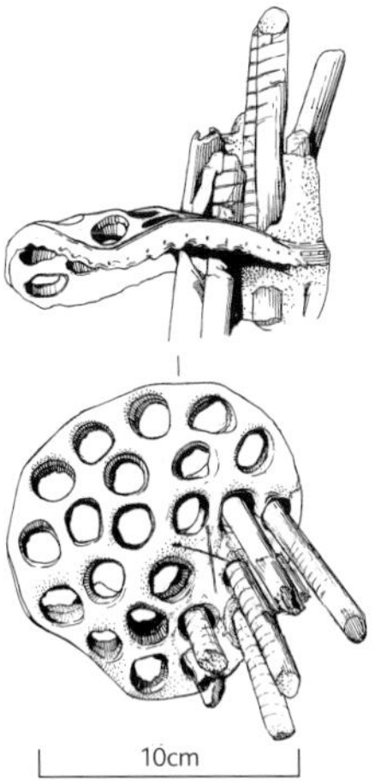

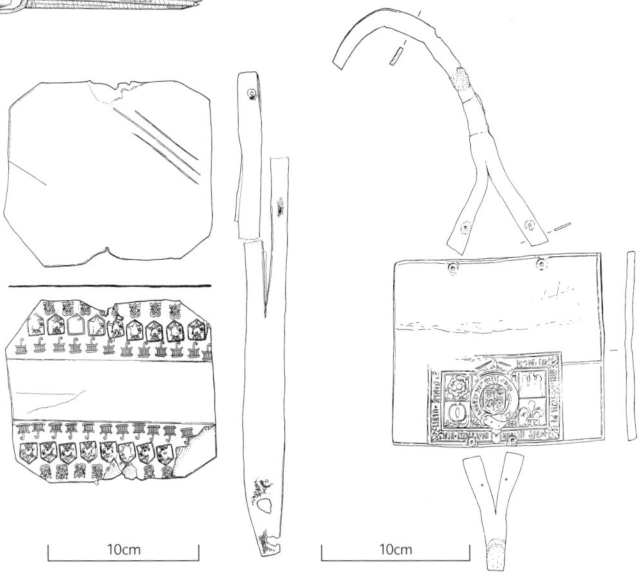

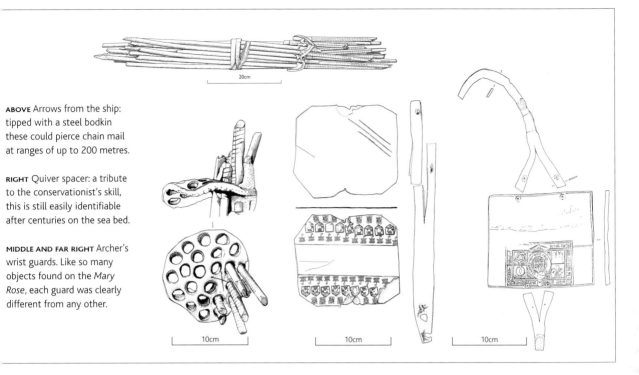

ABOVE Arrows from the ship: tipped with a steel bodkin these could pierce chain mail at ranges of up to 200 metres.

RIGHT Quiver spacer: a tribute to the conservationist's skill, this is still easily identifiable after centuries on the sea bed.

MIDDLE AND FAR RIGHT Archer's wrist guards. Like so many objects found on the *Mary Rose*, each guard was clearly different from any other.

position, the use of a bow and arrow from an unstable and moving platform at sea might appear to be a difficult skill to master, but for the English it had proved a success. At the Battle of Sluys in 1340, the longbowmen of Edward III's fleet sent down such a hail of arrows onto the upper deck of their anchored French adversaries that the English soldiers were able to board with little opposition. Only the Genoese, who had refused to anchor, escaped to sea. The admiration that was undoubtedly due to the archers for their deadly skill was enhanced by the gratitude of the soldiers. For as well as taking life the bow was also a weapon that saved lives. Time and again the enemy troops waiting with their swords and pikes to slice the English foe were destroyed – disheartened – by the deadly rain that fell on them well before they could come close enough for hand-to-hand fighting. Many a soldier swinging on board the ship to which his own vessel had become grappled would have seen that all that was left for him to do was a mopping-up operation, cut a few throats, disembowel a few seamen, 'liberate' a few items of property, and return to enjoy the glories of victory.

The archers also provided defence for another group on board – the gunners. On the upper deck each gun was ranged behind a series of removable blinds that the archers could take out to give themselves a sighting line while protecting their bodies from return fire. The gunners, if they were to get any decent sight of their target, had also to remove the blind directly above their gun. This left them exposed, especially as the range reduced rapidly to the point of impact. To give them protection an archer stood on either side of the gun barrel keeping an eye open for any enemy who might be aiming at the gun crew.

Although each sailor would have owned his own bow from childhood, there is no indication that he would have owned or been issued with his own bow once on board ship, for none of the those recovered bear any personal markings. Indeed, of all the numerous items raised from the ship the 172 longbows show the most homogeneity. The yew from which they were made was often imported as staves from Spain or Portugal where a finer-grained wood was available. This was important in the production of a sturdy bow, for each finished stave represented

Re-enactors demonstrating the role of shipboard archers: the many archers on board could deliver a 'sting' well before the range closed to a distance when the ship's guns could pound the enemy.

about 150 years of tree growth. The complete trunk or branch of the yew was not used in the making of a bow, for it had been discovered that if the junction between heart wood and sap wood was used then it added a greater springiness and suppleness to the weapon giving it a far greater range. So, what the poet Michael Drayton wrote of Agincourt would have held true of Sluys and the early Tudor navy as well:

> With Spanish yew and strong
> Arrows a cloth-yard long
> That like to serpent stung,
> Piercing the weather;...[14]

Northern Italy was another source of good bow staves, and a law of 1472 required every merchant landing goods into England to deliver four bow staves for every ton of goods landed, or risk a fine. In 1510, contrary to their own regulations, the Venetians sold 40,000 bow staves to Henry. A quarter of a century later the king was ordering 30,000 bows to be made and stored in the Tower.

The arrows, made from poplar, were probably English in origin, with iron bodkins at their point and goose-feather fletchings glued and tied at the other. They would also have had the addition of a small horn knock to protect the notched end for, with the draw weight of the bow at full stretch, the bowstring could easily split the arrow on release were it not so guarded. Knocks would also have been present at the ends of the bow to take the bowstring.[15]

Yet, despite the encouragement to keep the archer's skills well honed and to maintain a nation of bowmen, the days of the longbow were numbered. Its replacement, the arquebus and then the musket, was already present in *Mary Rose* but had little to recommend it as a substitute. A skilled bowman could release six or more arrows a minute with an accurate lethal range of up to 200 metres. The musketeer was probably limited to firing one round every two minutes with a lethal range of about twenty metres. Comparison between the two weapons all favour the longbow, until centuries later when handgun technology advanced sufficiently to be able to outshine its predecessor. It is probably true to say that a skilled longbowman would have been a more effective soldier than a musketeer until the end of the Napoleonic wars.

So, why the early demise of the longbow? Two things determined its fall from grace: first, the long period of training thought necessary to produce a skilled bowman in comparison with the few hours needed to train a musketeer and, secondly, the fact that musketry was the new technology and part of the rejection of wood for metal as the medium of warfare. Influencing the first of these was the fact that the old yeoman stock of England was also changing. A series of plagues had killed about a third of the population, and those that were left no longer seemed to possess the strength of their forefathers. The young sailors would not have had much personal experience with the musket, or 'hagbussh' (arquebus). In his endeavours to prevent the introduction of such weapons the king had issued, in 1528, a long proclamation that stated:

> No manner of person or persons must from henceforth have, or shoot in, or use any crossbow or handgun, nor keep any in their houses or any other places.[16]

Informers were encouraged to report anyone they suspected of harbouring these weapons, and those who refused to hand them over could suffer the death penalty.

There was one other personal weapon with which the young sailor was unlikely to have had any personal experience: the sword, then, as now, a weapon for the officers. In 1982 a nearly complete iron sword was excavated from beneath the stern castle of *Mary Rose* and brought to land for years of careful conservation. The chances of such a ferrous item surviving at all would not have been great, a point illustrated by the fact that it was the only such weapon recovered from the ship. It is a basket-hilted sword pre-dating by 100 years the only other two swords with firm dates attached to them, which both date to the civil war. The 88.5cm blade was forged from a piece of iron and a smaller part of carbon steel that was used to strengthen the edge of the double-edged blade. The basket-hilt itself is in the form of a saltire and indicates that the owner was a man with small hands.

None of the above would have been immediately obvious to the new member of the ship's company. What he would have noticed, on climbing on board, would have been her heavy weapons. And what he saw would have swelled his chest with pride. In his time on board he would have learned how to fight with these weapons as a member of a gun crew, and also how to wield the more traditional pike and bill which labourers had for centuries taken with them from their villages when called upon to fight. In the close-quarters environment in which he would be called upon to wield these weapons he would need to be both well trained and well led. And there was less than a year after *Mary Rose*'s arrival in the Thames in 1511 to get the ship and her company worked up and fit for purpose. And that purpose was to fight the French.

Armament other than guns carried by *Mary Rose* as described in the Anthony Roll

Gunpowder			
Serpentine powder in barrels	2 last		
Cornpowder in barrels	2 last		
Shot of Iron		**Shot of Stone and Lead**	
For cannon	50	For port pieces	200
For demi-cannon	60	For fowlers	170
For culverin	140	For top pieces	20
For sakers	80	For bases	
For falcons	60	Shot of lead	400
For sling	40	For handguns	
For demi-sling	40	Shot of lead	1000
For quarter sling	50		
Bows, bowstrings, arrows, Morris pikes, bills, and darts for tops			
Bows of yew			250
Bowstrings			6 gross
Lynere arrows in sheaves			400
Morris pikes			150
Bills			150
Darts for tops in dozens			40
Munitions		**Equipment for War**	
Pickhammers	12	Ropes of hemp	100 coils
Sledges of iron	8	Nails	1000
Crowes of iron	12	Bags of lead	8
Comanders	12	Fyrkins with pinsys	6
Tampions	14	Irine pots	10 dozen
Canvas for cartridges	20 ells	Spare wheels	4 pairs
Paper for cartridges	1 quire	Spare axel trees	6
Formers for cartridges	6	Sheepskins for sponges	12
		Timber for fordocks	100 feet

CHAPTER 4

Captains and Commanders

HENRY WAS A MAN for whom the time lapse between decision and action could be great. In the case of war against France it was to be two years, but this intervening period gave him sufficient time not only to have *Mary Rose* and *Peter Pomegranate* built and launched ready for the forthcoming campaign, but also to find men to appoint as his captains and commanders.

For peacetime passages it was sufficient for *Mary Rose* to have one man, an experienced seaman, to serve as both her master and commander, but with the approach of war Henry was obliged to appoint aristocrats to command his ships so that there would be no argument, especially from the embarked soldiers, as to who was giving the orders and on whose authority they acted. Henry's ability to appoint these men was handicapped by both a lack of experience and an absence of talent among the small group from whom he felt able to draw his senior maritime officers. The nobility who provided his military leaders had, through years of falling off horses in the chase and tiltyard, developed muscles that extended upwards from their necks as well as downwards. The Duke of Suffolk who, along with the blue-blooded Norfolks, was to be Henry's favoured military commander was said to possess; 'Of all the qualifications required in the leader of a great campaign...only one – the indomitable courage and big bones and Herculean muscles.'[1] It was easier, therefore, for Henry to order ships to be built to form his navy royal than it was for him to conjure up experienced officers to command them.

In later centuries command of a warship was to be considered so demanding a role that young men

The famous Anthony Roll illustration of *Mary Rose*: note the ship's crest of the Tudor Rose just forward of the bow. The ship's usual status as a flagship is exemplified by the profusion of flags, banners and pennants.

would be sent to sea from the age of twelve to gain sufficient experience in seamanship and leadership to enable them to serve their country well. That was the age at which both Nelson – the apotheosis of the fighting commander – and Fitzroy, among the finest of the navy's explorer-navigators, first went to sea. Henry had few men available to him with such experience, or rather, he had few who combined both the necessary status and the experience. The nation had a number of skilled seamen who could be appointed as masters of the king's ships but they lacked the social status required for command of a major warship. A skilled master and a respected, aristocratic captain was the ideal team that Henry desired.

Lacking men with the practical experience of serving at sea, Henry looked around the court, and nominated his 'Spears', his trusted friends from the tiltyard and the hunt, to take command of his ships. These were 'young gentlemen of noble blood which have none exercise in the feat of arms' who were to be trained in the arts of war and chivalry.[2] They were not seamen. A typical product of this system was Thomas Wyndham, who went to sea for the first time in 1510 and became second-in-command of *Mary Rose* in 1512, in which post he was knighted by his relative Edward Howard for services performed at Crozon. He went on to be captain of *John Baptist* in 1513, by which time he was also the Fleet Treasurer; from that post he was elevated to serve in the same year as Vice Admiral, becoming the first captain of *Henry Grace à Dieu* a year later. His son, also Thomas, continued in his father's footsteps, commanding the squadron that attacked the Firth of Forth in 1544 as part of the 'rough wooing' of Scotland and, while in command of *Great Galley*, was present at the Battle of the Solent the following year.

By Elizabeth's time things had changed. Her sea-dogs were men like Hawkins, Frobisher and Drake, born to the sea on which they served from an early age and with little other occupation. Henry may have commissioned sufficient ships to create a standing navy but until it was officered at a senior level by those who had been weaned on salt water it would not have the capacity to grow to dominate the oceans of the world. So, as befitted the ship that was the king's favourite and flagship, the masters and captains of *Mary Rose* were men of either experience or substance. Their names are listed below.

Mary Rose was the flagship of the fleet so, in addition to her captain, she carried the Lord Admiral, a post so important that Henry looked to the most senior families of the realm to provide the right man

Officers of the *Mary Rose*

Date	Position/rank	Name
September 1511	Master	John Clerke
Oct 1511–Jan 1512	Master	Thomas Spert
	Purser	David Boner
Nov 1511–Jan 1512	Master	Thomas Spert
	Purser	John Lawden
April–July 1512	Chief Captain and Admiral of the Fleet	Sir Edward Howard
	Captain	Thomas Wyndham*
	Master	Thomas Spert
early May 1513	Chief Captain and Admiral of the Fleet	Sir Edward Howard
May–August 1513	Admiral	Lord Thomas Howard
	Captain	Edward Braye**
	Surgeon	Robert Symson
	Purser	John Brerely
	Gunner	Andrew Fysche
	Master	Thomas Spert***
January 1514	Captain	Edward Braye
February 1514	Captain	Sir Henry Sherburn
March 1514	Master	John Brown
June 1522	Lord High Admiral	Thomas Howard, Earl of Surrey
	Master	John Brown
1524	Shipkeeper	Fadere Connor
1545	Vice Admiral	Sir George Carew
	Captain	Roger Grenville

*Knighted by Edward Howard in Crozon Bay in June 1512.

**Knighted October 1513 by Henry VIII at Tournai.

***Knighted in 1535 as Master of the King's Ships. Captain of Portsmouth 1538–40.

Note: For the period April 1514–May 1522 *Mary Rose* was in ordinary, that is, in reserve.

for the role. And there was none more noble than the Howard family, the family of the Earl Marshal and the Dukes of Norfolk, two of whom, the brothers Edward and Thomas, were to be Henry's first fighting admirals. They were also members of one of the few noble families who could claim links with and an understanding of the sea and the business conducted in great waters. Lord John Howard, the first Duke of Norfolk, had seen active sea service as Edward IV's Lord Admiral, and had provided escort services for merchantmen, many of whom were sailing in ships he himself owned.[3] However, the first duke did his family's fortune no good when he died fighting for Richard III at the Battle of Bosworth, leaving his son, Thomas, Earl of Surrey, who had fought at his side, to be attainted by Henry VII.

The Howard brothers, thus, grew to maturity under their father's cloud. Although their father rapidly returned to favour, the straitened circumstances in which his actions had placed his sons meant that they became involved in maritime activities from the East Anglian ports: ventures that combined legitimate trading with the occasional act of piracy when circumstances were favourable. Edward, the younger son, was to lead almost the traditional medieval life of a knight of arms. In 1492, at the age of fifteen he was serving under Sir Edward Poynings in a raid on Sluys, and in 1497 he was with his by-then pardoned father fighting the Scots. By 1509 he had so distinguished himself as a warrior that he was appointed the king's standard bearer, which meant that in 1511 he was in a position to volunteer to fit out two ships to take on convoy duties escorting merchantmen between London and Antwerp through waters threatened by the Scottish 'pirate' Sir Andrew Barton.

The full story is told with an acceptable degree of accuracy in the contemporary *Ballad of Andrew Barton*[4] which does, however, get the name of one of the Howards involved, wrong. The piracy and threat posed by Barton was brought to the king's attention by the merchants, possibly using the Earl of Surrey as an intermediary. Surrey, who would have seen this as an opportunity to ingratiate himself further with the king and regain his lost title of Duke of Norfolk is quoted as stating that: 'The narrow seas should not be so infected, while he had estate enough to furnish a ship, or a son capable of commanding it.'[5]

Henry responded by ordering the Howard brothers to escort the merchantmen and to seek out and destroy Barton. They came across the Scotsman in The Downs, off the East Kent coast, while he was returning from the Netherlands to Scotland in his ship *Lion*. The ensuing chase was made difficult by a sea mist but Thomas Howard was still able to close and board *Lion*. In a fierce fight Barton was struck by an arrow and died on the deck of an English ship. *Lion* and her surviving crew were brought to London along with her escorting pinnace, *Jenny Pirwyn*, which Edward had captured.

Returning from his fight with Barton, Edward Howard became immediately involved with *Mary Rose*, which would indicate that the king saw his potential as a naval commander. The accounts of Sir John Daunce, a teller to the Exchequer, record that in 1511 Howard was approving payments for material to make bunting for the ship as well as for the paints and dyes necessary to embellish her for her commissioning.[6] The victory against Barton was also sufficient for Edward to be promoted to vice admiral in 1512 and to be placed in command of the Channel fleet. His actions in the following years, until his death in 1513, qualify him for the position as England's first modern admiral. John Campbell, writing in an age not unafraid to extol heroes states:

> There never, certainly, was a braver man of his, or consequently of any family...and yet we are assured, that he was very far from being either a mere soldier, or a mere seaman, though so eminent in other characters: but he was what it became an English gentleman of so high a quality to be; an able statesman, a faithful counsellor, and a free speaker.[7]

Edward Howard had also been a favourite of the queen, Katherine of Aragon, whom he had represented as her champion in jousts. The closeness of their relationship can be seen in that the admiral left her, in his will, a wonderful relic of Thomas à Becket, the 'St Thomas Cup', an ivory bowl which, after later embellishments, was to be renamed 'The Howard Grace Cup'.[8] However, Howard also entrusted one of his two bastard sons to the king's care so the degree of closeness in his relationship with Katherine remains a matter of speculation, but it might have aroused suspicion in a later, crueler Henry. Suffice to say that Edward was a great favourite of both king and queen and a major presence at court. It is significant that a man of such stature was appointed Lord Admiral and that he must have been over thirty years of age before he first exercised command at sea. As such, he could not be expected to possess either the strategic or tactical sense that was to be shown by future seagoing admirals. His final days off Brest are a clear indicator of this inexperience, but there is no denying his bravery and endearing personality. This emerges as clearly in his written words as his deeds, for we are lucky in being able to lay alongside the accounts of his actions off Brest his correspondence with the king and Wolsey,[9] in order to gauge whether or not Campbell wrote with accuracy as well as adulation. John Hume saw in his brave impetuosity both his strength and his weakness:

> It was a maxim of Howard, that no admiral was good for anything that was not brave to a degree of madness. As the sea service requires much less plan and contrivance and capacity than the land, this maxim has a great plausibility and appearance of truth; though the fate of Howard himself may serve as a proof that even there courage ought to be tempered with discretion.[10]

It may seem strange that Edward was appointed Lord Admiral before his elder brother, Thomas, who succeeded him in the post, but there are indicators that the younger possessed more of what would now be referred to as 'officer-like qualities'. He seems to have been more energetic, more resourceful, more caring, more approachable than his aloof elder brother. Thomas was to command both at sea and on land but he was also much involved in proceedings at court. In 1495 he married Anne Plantagenet, a surviving daughter of Edward IV, and Henry VII's sister-in-law. Later, to feed his vanity and ambition, he encouraged the marriage of two of his nieces, Anne Boleyn and Catherine Howard, to Henry. The resultant scandals were the start of his own downfall. In 1497 Thomas was sent to quell rebellion in Cornwall before also joining his father in the war against Scotland, serving with such distinction that he was knighted by his father.

While his brother went to sea in 1512, Thomas, as a Lieutenant General, served with the Earl of Dorset in the debacle that was the army's campaign in Spain that year. The following year he replaced his dead brother as Lord Admiral. Alison Weir provides an

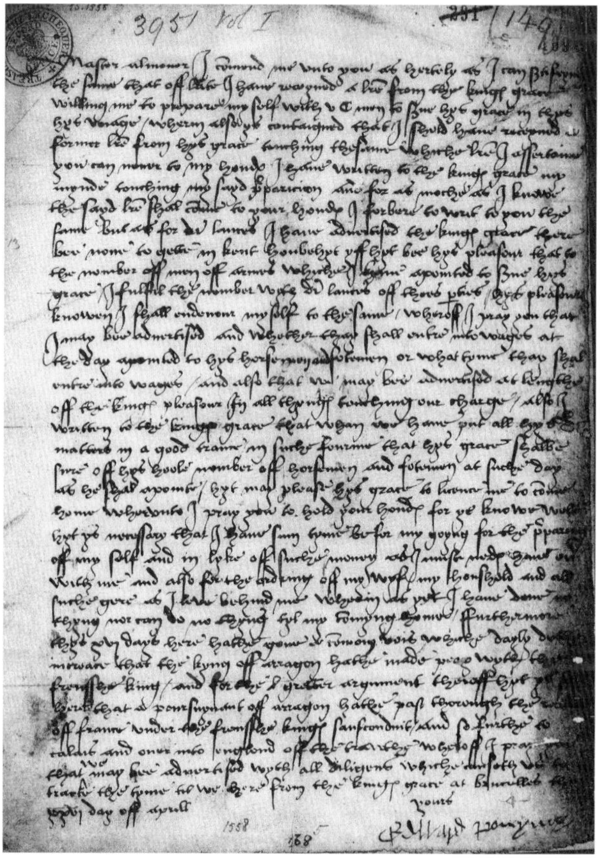

A letter from Edward Howard asking Wolsey to deliver an enclosed letter to his wife, 5 April 1513.

excellent summary of Thomas Howard's character from the time when he had left the sea with rheumatism as his only lasting memento:

> The third Duke of Norfolk was short, spare and black-haired, and a dour, pragmatic,

Thomas Howard (1473–1547), third Duke of Norfolk. The stern, haughty look of a senior courtier is well captured in this engraving.

> sometimes brutal man whose portrait by Holbein shows a face like granite with thin lips and a high-bridged, aristocratic nose. A martyr to rheumatism and indigestion, he was constantly grumbling or sighing, but was also an efficient and often ruthless military commander, and an able and polished courtier who could be liberal and affable but who had a nose for danger and a talent for survival. The guiding factor of his life was self interest.[11]
>
> ...he regarded himself as the chief representative of the older nobility at court. He was fiercely anti-clerical, and hated Wolsey...typical of his caste in that he despised book learning, loved hunting.[12]

That loathing for the butchers son, Wolsey, is subtly evident in the letters that Thomas Howard wrote to the cardinal, on whom he had to rely for both supplies and information while he was at sea. Howard was was well aware that Wolsey had the king's ear, and therefore needed to be treated with caution. So, instead of criticising the minister he exuded unctuous insincerity:

> Master Almoner, with all my heart I recommend me unto you. Good Master Almoner, I have found you so kind unto me that methink I can do no less than to write unto you from time to time of all my causes. So it is, though I be unable therof, it hath pleased the King's grace to give me this great room and authority more meet for a wise, expert man than me. But since it hath pleased his grace to admit me thereunto, as far as my poor wit can extend, I shall endeavour myself from time to time to do all manner of service.... And, good Master Almoner, as my most singular trust is in you, send me both now and at all times your advice and counsel, assuring you that never poor gentleman was in greater fear to take rebuke and ill report than I am...[13]

– and later, in the same letter:

> Which enterprises [going to Brittany] being debated before his grace, and such dangers as I thought might thereof ensue by me declared before his grace, I showed his grace I durst not enterprise the same feats unless his grace would discharge me if any misfortune fell by the same. And then his grace bade me not to spare to adventure the same, and to go with his army into the great water of Brest.[14]

The 'your graces' drip like grease from an oily joint to lard with justification the platter of Howard's self-preservation. The letter ends:

> Master Almoner, all the premises and all other causes I remit to your wisdom, fully trusting that you will not only from time to time give me your good advice and counsel, but also with your friendly words withstand all ill reports undeserved made, as my singular trust is in you. And thus Our Lord have you in his tuition.[15]

One cannot imagine Wolsey being deceived for a moment; besides which, the loathing was mutual. Wolsey was locked in a power struggle with the Howards, and

Thomas Howard was to be victorious, conspiring and delighting in the cardinal's fall from grace.

So the successful survival of the standing navy was based on the ability of a blue-blooded autocrat and an ambitious butcher's son to maintain a working relationship, despite a mutual loathing, until the job was done. It is an irony of literature that the philistine character of Howard was to feature in two major ballads and a Shakespeare play while, for all his own detestation of book-learning, he was to produce a son who was to be a more than adequate and innovative poet, producing the first sonnet and blank verse to be written in English. Sadly, Henry Howard inherited his father's overweening ambition, but neither his military talent nor his courtier's tact. When he incorporated the royal coat of arms into his own, his fate was settled. Lacking also his father's survival skills he went to the block. Had King Henry lived just one day longer Thomas would have followed him. The king's death spared his life.

When the nation went to war with France again in 1522 another admiral, with only limited sea experience was appointed in support of Howard. William Fitzwilliam, a close friend of the king, had sailed in Edward Howard's fleet in 1513 and been badly injured by an arrow. He recovered sufficiently to be active at the siege of Tournai, being knighted for his services on 25 September the same year. After active service he spent some time in Wolsey's household where he served with distinction and would, no doubt, have gained an inkling as to how the supply chain was managed. When war was declared in 1522 he was ideally placed to be appointed as Thomas Howard's vice admiral, with special responsibility for escorting merchant convoys.

Service with Wolsey left Fitzwilliam with no great loyalty to his old master, for he was one of the number who was closely involved in engineering the cardinal's downfall. Senior appointments were to follow this particularly unpleasant, but not untypical behaviour, and in 1537 Fitzwilliam was ennobled as the Earl of Southampton. Two years later he was sent to Portsmouth to take command of the town's defence in preparation for a French attack that never took place. That same year he was to escort the unfortunate Anne of Cleves from Calais to England for her brief marriage to Henry, which was to herald Thomas Cromwell's downfall. Once again, Fitzwilliam demonstrated the fickleness of friendship in high places when he personally stripped Cromwell of his Garter thus showing, as recounted by nineteenth-century historian James Froude: '...he was as much an enemy in adversity as in prosperity he had pretended to be his friend'.[16].

Sea ferrying and escort duties continued but in 1542 Fitzwilliam died at Newcastle-upon-Tyne while marching with the English land forces, commanded by his old admiral, Thomas Howard, against the Scots. In his honour his standard remained raised in the vanguard throughout the campaign. Fitzwilliam's death provided him with one posthumous link with *Mary Rose*. He had been the owner of the Cowdray estate near Midhurst in Sussex. On his death this passed to his half-brother, Sir Anthony Browne, Master of the King's Horse, who was to commission the painting that has become known as the Cowdray engraving showing the loss of *Mary Rose* off Portsmouth in July 1545.

William Fitzwilliam, Earl of Southampton, painting after Holbein.

The occasional student of Tudor history can easily become confused by the names of the *dramatis personae* as their titles change with their social and political advancement. Thus Thomas Howard in 1514 became the Earl of Surrey and then, in 1524, the Duke of Norfolk, in succession to his father who had had his title restored to him following his defeat of the Scots at Flodden Edge. Fortunately his illustrious career – which reached its apotheosis with his appointment as Earl Marshal in 1533 and its nadir with his attainment and near execution in 1547 – impinged but little on *Mary Rose* after 1523 so that there is just one name change to contend with.

Henry enjoyed playing pass the parcel with titles, no more so than with that of Viscount Lisle, several of whom became involved, in a minor way, with *Mary Rose*, but in a greater way with the English fleet a whole. The first Viscount Lisle whose life brought him into contact with *Mary Rose* was Charles Brandon, Mary Tudor's husband, who held the position for a few years. In 1545 he was, as Duke of Suffolk, in the final year of his life, to command the land forces at Portsmouth at the time that *Mary Rose* was lost. Then it was the turn of Arthur Plantagenet, another of Henry's seagoing 'Spears of Honour', who wrecked his command, *Nicholas of Hampton*, at the entrance to Brest in 1513 and was sent home by Howard with a kind note proposing that no further action be taken against him. Although he was to become a Vice Admiral of England in 1525 there is no record of his ever commanding at sea in this capacity. Created Lord Lisle in 1523, he was appointed to be Lord Deputy of Calais in 1533, at the age of seventy. He was to stay here until accused of treason in 1540 and bundled off to the Tower. A pardon was issued in 1542 but the emotional turmoil was too much for the old man. As Francis Sandford records:

> …the King sent him his Ring from off his own Finger, with such comfortable Expressions, that he immoderately receiving so great a Joy, his Heart was overcharged therewith, and the Night following he yielded up the ghost; which makes it observable that this King's Mercy was as fatal as his Judgements.[17]

With the death of Arthur Plantagenet the title passed to his step-son, John Dudley, who was appointed Lord Admiral the following year in time to command, with distinction, the fleet for the French wars of 1543–46. He flew his flag in *Henry Grace à Dieu*, with Sir George Carew, his vice admiral, on board *Mary Rose*.

Sir George Carew came from a family of sea-goers rather than seafarers. He, himself, appears to have been an adventurer, offering his services to the French in 1526 but being pardoned for what could have been construed as treasonable activity, as could have been his involvement with the Maid of Kent affair a few years later.[18] In 1536 he was knighted, and the following year went to sea under Sir John Dudley to patrol against pirates. In 1539 he succeeded his disgraced relative, Nicholas Carew, as the Captain of Rysbank, the castle that defended the entrance to the harbour at Calais. Here he could have found himself drawn greedily but unwittingly into the Botolf Conspiracy of 1540,[19] when it was suggested that he was more than willing to sell for 1000 crowns his captaincy to one of the conspirators. Yet again Carew appears to have emerged untainted for, although he had to go with Lisle to the Tower he was not imprisoned. In 1543, he was back across the Channel as Lieutenant General of Horse under Sir John Wallop in Flanders, where he took part in the sieges of both Thérouanne and Landrecy, narrowly avoiding death at the first and capture by the French at the second. In response to a personal request by Henry himself he was released in time to be appointed to *Mary Rose* to sail against his past captors in 1545. He would be the third Carew to die for Henry in combat, Sir John Carew having been blown up off Brest in *Regent* in 1513, while Edmund Carew was killed by a musket ball in the same year while campaigning south of Calais with the king.

Henry's admirals took up appointments in a navy that had yet to establish its capabilities, limi-

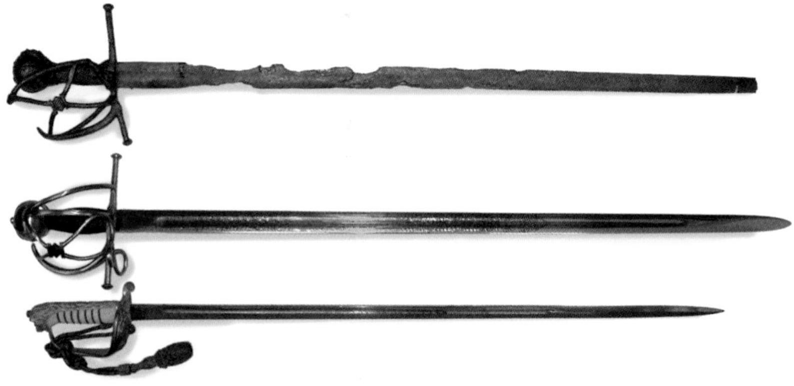

The one officer's sword recovered from the *Mary Rose* (top) and its replica (centre) compared with a modern equivalent (bottom). The longer and heavier Tudor sword suggests that the notion that the people of the time were smaller and punier than today is misplaced.

tations and strategy. It was their task to develop all these concepts and to endeavour to put them into practice. In the busy years at sea between 1512 and 1514 *Mary Rose* with her two brother admirals achieved a great deal that would lay the foundations of English naval strategy. They struggled for – and but for the threat of the French galleys, would have achieved for England – the domination of the Channel that was to become a reality during Elizabeth's reign. The careers of Henry's captains before they arrived on board *Mary Rose* and her sister warships, emphasises their lack of the relevant experience necessary to take command of such a prestigious vessel. Time at sea appeared not to have been an essential prerequisite.

What does seem to be apparent is that these commanders knew one another and could form what was to become known, later, as a Band of Brothers. Thomas Knyvet, the captain of *Regent*, was Edward Howard's brother-in-law; Thomas Wyndham was another relative by marriage. George Carew and Roger Grenville, vice admiral and captain on board *Mary Rose* in 1545, would have been acquainted in the West Country, and may even have known each other in Calais where Roger's father had held office (as High Marshall). Placing an admiral on board a ship commanded by an acquaintance would have been a good way to avoid that trouble which can arise when those who know less than they should are in positions of command. Roger Grenville, the last captain of *Mary Rose*, may also have been at lunch with the king and Carew in Portsmouth the day before his own ship sank. Of him little is known but his father, Sir Richard, had been High Marshal of Calais at the time that his aunt, Lady Lisle, was married to the Lord Deputy, Arthur Plantagenet, who had served with Edward Howard off Brest. Of his seagoing experience and campaigns history is silent.

It is assumed that his son, another Richard Grenville, was born in June 1542, which meant that he was just three years old when his father drowned. If his father's fate encouraged his mother to persuade her son not to follow his father's footsteps there is no record; if she did, she was unsuccessful. Hot headed, intemperate, poet and dreamer, it would be Sir Richard Grenville's lot to be in command of *Revenge* in 1591 when the might of Spain descended on the English fleet at Flores in the Azores. His decision to fight rather than flee gave rise to one of the great epic battles on which the most important traditions of the Royal Navy are based. The fight of the one against fifty-three is England's Thermopylae, and one of those rare engagements that are more important in their legacy than in their significance at the time.

The fact that the same names and families occur again and again in Henry's sea appointments is indicative of the personnel problem. Professional seamen had to earn their living by trade and could not be expected to train from their youth for the king's service unless the king was prepared to pay them to do so. He wasn't. He needed trained professional naval officers but, unlike the system of knights and squires under which his warrior class learned their trade ashore, no such apprenticeship existed at sea. The recurrence of names is indication more of limited choice rather than the genius of those selected.

The captains had, of course, not only to fight but also to maintain discipline on board what was always an overcrowded vessel when at sea on a war footing. Acts of indiscipline could range from serious incidents such as mutiny, sabotage, murder and theft to frictions between various elements of the ship's company. Mutiny does not seem to have cast its dreaded spectre over *Mary Rose* or the other ships in the fleet, but there was a suspected incident of sabotage in Edward Howard's fleet over which the Admiral had to arbitrate in 1512. A trader from Lille, named Jacques Berenghier, was impressed while in England and forced to serve as a gunner on board *Mary John*. Here, he was charged that he:

> ...falsely, wickedly, maliciously and fraudulently placed in certain of the said guns then in his custody two stones wrapped in thick cord, where it was not necessary or suitable to place more than one, so that many of the guns of these gunners in the said ship called the *Mary John,* being in battle with the enemies, were broken and fractured in such a way that they could not harm the said enemies, and even some guns not committed to the said Jacques were charged with similar stones, to their destruction.... he had in his shoes certain gunpowder, very fine and light, with a certain little stone and an iron for striking light, notwithstanding the powder which he had in a horn hung from his neck...[20]

Berenghier was seized and sent before the Lord Admiral in *Mary Rose.* Howard interrogated him and ordered him to be returned to his ship so that his own captain might, '...strictly examine and detain him and furthermore enquire by torture or otherwise if he had any companions or followers in the said

The command structure aboard the *Mary Rose*.

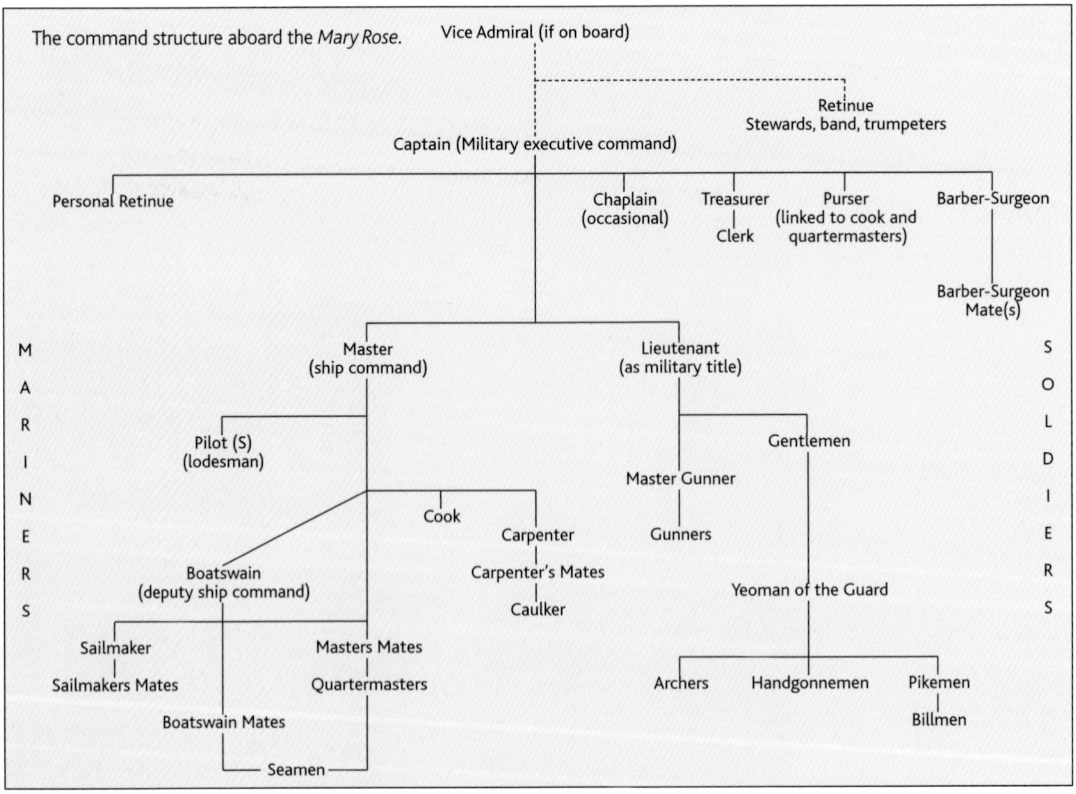

transgression.'[21] The end was unpleasant with Berenghier, following his torture, having both his ears cut off, a punishment that was broadcast throughout the fleet. We might not have a record of the incident today had not the formidable Margaret of Savoy to whom, as Regent of the Netherlands, Berenghier was subject, taken up the case and protested to Henry in September 1512 on her subject's behalf, claiming also that he had lost a foot as a result of being racked by Sir Griffith Don, the captain of *Mary John*. Margaret of Savoy was not a lady whom Henry would have wished to upset. He had asked her to sponsor his short-lived son, Henry, in 1511 and Margaret, the daughter of the Emperor Maximilian, had sent some lavish presents to mark the christening. Such treatment as Berenghier had received could have caused a major diplomatic incident. In 1739 representation to parliament about a similar incident seven years earlier led to the aptly named War of Jenkins' Ear. Henry, however, was able to smooth his way through the matter which, with the war against France in progress, he would not have wanted to upset his plans for glory.

The treatment of Berenghier may seem inhumane to modern sensibilities, but he might be considered lucky to have survived with his life had he had been found guilty of an act of sabotage that endangered his ship and shipmates in the face of the enemy. His fate does indicate that punishment was not arbitrary, but based on codes of conduct that might otherwise have been regarded as fanciful and menacing, rather than actual guidelines to be carried out to the letter.

The earliest extant code on which discipline at sea was based was the thirteenth-century French Laws of Oléron, which were adopted by English ships that sailed past that Breton Island on the way to Gascony for wine and incorporated into English law by King Richard. The code laid down that a master was not able to administer physical punishment of his crew but had to, as in the case of Berenghier, bring the accused before his admiral. The law even allowed a seaman, if struck twice by his master, to retaliate. Henry VIII ordered a modernisation of these old laws and a codification of regulations for discipline at sea. The new regulations were written by Thomas Audley and published in his *Book of Orders for the War both by Sea and Land* in 1530. As in the example above, it is based on the Laws of Oléron and it seems obvious that Audley rather gratefully incorporated these in order to save himself, as a landsman with no sea experience, the trouble of coming up with new ideas. The result was a thoroughly medieval system of punishment that sits uncomfortably within a modernising navy. For example, Audley ordered that:

> If any man kill another within the ship, he that doeth the deed shall be bound quick to the dead man, and so be cast into the sea, and a piece of ordnance shot off after they be thrown into the sea.[22]
>
> If any man within the ship draws a weapon, or causes tumult, or likelihood of murder or bloodshed within the ship he shall lose his right hand...[23]
>
> If any man within the ship steal or pick money, or clothes within the ship duly proved, he shall be three times dipped at the bowsprit, and let down two fathoms within the water, and kept on line, and at the next shore towed a land bound at the boat's stern with a loaf of bread and a can of beer and banished the King's ships forever.[24]
>
> If any man within the ship do sleep his watch four times and so proved, this be his punishment, the first time he shall be headed at the main mast with a bucket of water poured on his head. The second time he shall be armed, his hands hauled up by a rope, and two buckets of water poured into his sleeves. The third time he shall be bound to the main mast with certain gun chambers to his arms and as much pain to his body as his captain will. The fourth time and last punishment being taken asleep he shall be hanged on the bowsprit end of the ship in a basket with a can of beer, a

loaf of bread, and a sharp knife, thus to hang there till he starve or cut himself into the sea.[25]

Apart from the attempt to induce pneumonia, the archaic punishments seem mild for the time and certainly did not include the instruction to flog, which was used to cower and impose discipline in later centuries.

Although Audley made no mention of desertion it too was a crime for which a maximum penalty could be inflicted and this included punishing those who left their ships without a licence to depart. In June 1513, Thomas Howard had cause to make his anger and his views on this subject known to the Privy Council. His musters had revealed that many men had departed without licence and he was determined to make an example of two he had recaptured: '...if I can prove that they were departed, I shall not fail to cause to be hanged tomorrow.'[26] – while others, he felt: '...it were well done that the King's grace should command some of them to be put to execution, which shall put others in fear; and if some might be brought hither against my return, to be put to execution here, methink it should be well done.'[27]

Not all wrongdoings reported were major crimes. In June 1513 William Knight informed Wolsey that problems had arisen in the fleet: '...in consequence of the ungoodly manner of the seamen, robbing the King's victuals when the soldiers were sea-sick.'[28] Although it would be difficult to envisage a more understandable action commited by seasoned sailors for the benefit of their landlubber companions, undoubtedly a certain amount of disciplining would have been required to restore harmony.

The willingness of senior aristocrats to go to sea indicates that they recognised advantage in accepting the responsibility: an advantage that compensated sufficiently for their absence from court and not being in the king's presence, which was regarded as essential for any man on the make. Yet, even if the king was not present, he made sure that his sea commanders knew that someone higher than them would take the major decisions and that they needed to keep him fully informed. Thus Lisle wrote to Henry on 21 July 1545:

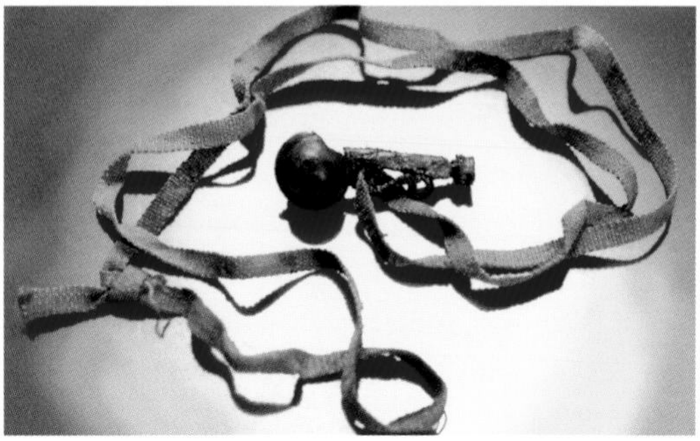

This tiny boatswain's call was used for piping orders to the crew about the ship, although decorative versions were also used as badges of office.

> In no other enterprise being never so feasible, I will not attempt, your Majesty being so near, without first making your Majesty privy there unto; and not without your Grace's consent thereunto...But I have your Grace no doubt of any hasty or unadvised presumptious enterprise that I shall make, having charge of so weighty a matter under your Majesty, without being first well instructed from your Highness; for if I have any knowledge in any kind of thing, I received the same from yourself.[29]

When it is considered how long Lisle and Henry had known each other and how much service the admiral had rendered his king it is a sad reflection on both the power-crazed monarch and the fear in which he was held that a commander as experienced as Lisle felt obliged to write in such a grovelling and self-deprecating manner.

Until naval commanders had the confidence that their well-intentioned actions, whatever the outcome, would be studied sympathetically and knowledgeably by their superiors then the free spirits of a Drake or Nelson would not emerge. Moreover, whatever the restraints placed upon the English admirals it was to be the captains of *Mary Rose* who were responsible for ensuring that their ship could capably and safely execute whatever task they were assigned. And they, in turn, would only be able to do this with if they were well served by experienced masters.

CHAPTER 5

Masters of the Narrow Seas

THE MASTERS APPOINTED TO *Mary Rose* were the best in their profession. They included Thomas Spert, who was to rise to the highest post open to a man of his background. Spert, who sailed in *Mary Rose* for the 1512–14 war against France, was an experienced master. His father had served in the same capacity in *James of Topsham* during Henry VII's reign, so we can assume his was a seagoing family. Thomas was also a shipowner in his own right, having two vessels, *Valentyn of London* and *Mary Sperte*, trading on his behalf. After his time in *Mary Rose* he joined Thomas Wyndham in *Henry Grace à Dieu* as her first master, and then went on to become, in 1524, Clerk Controller of the King's Ships, a position of such significance that, had he discharged it other than to his highly efficient best, the standing navy might have foundered on the shore side shoals of incompetence, indifference and malpractice. He was knighted in 1535 and ended his active life undertaking, between 1538 and 1540, the construction of the new fortifications that were being erected at Gosport. His was a life of professional competence, whether at sea or afloat, but it was as master of *Mary Rose* that his competence would have been most tested and scrutinised.

The first task of the master of *Mary Rose*, once the ship was crewed and victualled, was to get her safely under way and into open waters. John Smith gives a very descriptive account of how such work was done:

> The Master and the company being on board, he commands them to 'Get the sailes to the yards, and about your geare', or, 'Worke on all hands, stretch forward your maine Halliards, hoist your Sailes halfe mat high. Predyl', or, 'Make ready to set saile. Crosse your yards [hoist the yards to the mast head] bring your Cable to the Capsterne. Boatswaine, fetch an Anchor aboard. Breake ground', or, 'Weigh Anchor! Heave a head! Men into the Tops! Men upon the yards! Come, is the anchor a'pike?' That is, to heave the Hawse of the ship right over the Anchor. 'What, is the Anchor away?'
> 'Yea, yea!'
>
> 'Let fall your fore-saile. Tally!' That is, hale off the Sheats. 'Who is at the Helme there? Coile your Cables in small fakes! Hale the Cats! A Bitter,…belay,…loose fast your Anchor with your shank-painter! Stow the Boat!'
>
> Set the land, how it beares by the Compasse, that we may the better know thereby to keep account and direct our course.[1]

The maritime world into which *Mary Rose* was sailing was about to change. In 1509 England was just part of an offshore island with limited overseas trade and ambitions. The one-time French possessions, a need for Breton canvas, and a desire for French wine, meant that a trade existed between the southern ports of England and the French Atlantic coast, but this was often carried out by French merchants. So important was this commerce that it left its mark for all time with the acceptance of the *tunne* as the measure, at first capacity, and then weight itself – the tunne being a barrel of Bordeaux (252 gallons) and a ship's size being related to the number of tunnes she could carry. From the east, ships of the Hanseatic league brought the fish and timber of the Baltic to London, while the spices of the orient were delivered by the Venetians to both London and Southampton. The main export of English merchants was wool or cloth from the east-coast ports to the Low Countries or through Calais where the local guild often caused them problems.

So, the majority of English shipping plied short, well-known and traditional routes. Although John Cabot was the first European to reach the North American mainland (in 1497), and a few of his adopted countrymen sailed as far as Brazil, by and large England was a coastal nation whose sailors were seldom more than a day's journey from shore. *Mary Rose*'s furthest journey north was to Newcastle and her furthest west to Brest. The contrast with southern, Atlantic-seaboard Europe could not have been more marked. For most English mariners, therefore, navigation comprised the art of pilotage and coasting, with some feeling for navigation beyond the sight of land but without the need for astronomical observations, apart from marking the zenith of the sun at midday and knowing the phase and bearing of the moon for tidal information. The fact that charts were scarce or non existent did not matter when young men learned early and well the coast along which they sailed. Fog and the darkness of night were countered by either anchoring or steering away from danger and by keeping a good lookout and a sharp

This modern painting by Bill Bishop of *Mary Rose* gives a good idea of the majesty of the ship when under sail.

Navigational equipment: the ship's pilot in a coastal navy needed few instruments but a long apprenticeship in order to navigate in safety.

ear for the sounds of the shore. The latter was, of course, much easier to sense in the days before machinery played havoc with the fine sensitivity of a well-tuned ear or nose. Historian of Tudor and Elizabethan navigation, D W Waters, sums up the key to safe coastal navigation succinctly: 'Knowing perfectly by sight all the capes, ports and rivers met with, how they rise up and how they appear from the sea.'[2] As long as this simple method was all that was needed then the skills of the ship's master remained static, and there is very little difference between Chaucer's seaman and those at sea during the early Tudor period:

> As for his skill in reckoning his tides,
> Currents and many other risks besides,
> Moons, harbours, pilots, he had such dispatch
> That none from Hull to Carthage was his
> match.
> Hardy he was, prudent in undertaking;
> His beard in many a tempest had its shaking,
> And he knew all the havens as they were
> From Gottland to the cape of Finisterre,
> And every creek in Brittany and Spain.
> The barge he owned was called *The Maudelayne*.[3]

Although written in 1387 Chaucer's description of a sea captain would have been as recognisable 150 years later, but things were changing. Instead of a skipper trading wine from the French Atlantic coast a new generation was emerging, men to whom the broad Atlantic would be home and whose cargo would be slaves and sugar, not wine and wool. Weeks out of sight of land would replace days, and inaccurate sun sights and unpredictable trade winds would take over from the certain knowledge of capes, ports and rivers around the British coast. England's skippers were about to venture beyond familiarity. *Mary Rose* floats where the local tide meets the global current that would sweep the English around the world.

Henry was well aware of the deficiencies of his master mariners in the art of blue-water navigation and he recruited instructors from abroad to compensate for this scarcity and to pass on their skills to his own subjects. In 1540 the French ambassador observed that English ships were 'full' of Ragusans, Venetians, Genoese, Normans and Bretons, many of whom, one could surmise, were pilots. In 1544 a Frenchman was appointed as the nation's first Hydrographer and John Dudley, Lord Lisle was to appoint another as his fleet navigator.

To navigate with safety through these coastal waters required a number of aids, but the most reliable remained the master's eye, experience and knowledge. With navigation and charts so rudimentary and the coasts so unforgiving it is no wonder that ships ran aground. And they did, frequently, for many centuries to come. Sometimes the effect was disastrous, as with the piling up of Sir Cloudseley Shovel's fleet upon the Scillies in 1707. Often the incident could be just embarrassing as with the events recorded by Graham Moore, captain of *Syren*, when part of Sidney Smith's squadron in 1794–96. Making a passage across the Channel could be particularly risky with strong cross currents, little idea of speed made good through the water, and a superfluity of rocks and shoals lying in wait. Moore summed up the feelings of many masters and commanders when he wrote in his diary: '... the fact is that we are all afraid of the dangerous coast which is certainly formidable enough.'[4]

To keep ships off the rocks and shoals professional masters needed to be in charge of the navigation. It was they who, adding to their local knowledge and instincts – and a system to give them an idea of course, speed, time, tide and depth of water – would keep the ship safe. To do this they needed to rely on judgement born of experience and a few simple instruments. Those recovered from *Mary Rose* represent the earliest group of such artefacts existing in Europe, often predating other examples by decades. On board *Mary Rose* local time could only be determined, with any degree of accuracy, once – at midday – and that relied on the sun being visible at its zenith passage. At night, the movement of the Great Bear around Polaris would have given another idea of time and a simple instrument, the 'nocturnal' was carried for the purposes of taking the reading. It worked by lining up a central hole with Polaris and then measuring the angle between that and Kochab, the brightest star of the 'guards'; much extrapolation was needed, and the time worked out was never more than approximate. Another indicator of time could be provided by masters who spent their lives in the English Channel and its approaches, and thus had a reasonable idea of the time of sunrise and sunset throughout the year.

On board, however, life was regulated by the hourglass, on whose accurate and constant flowing sands the smooth running of the ship depended, for the knowledge of time passing had both a navigational and a domestic relevance. The crew needed to know when watches were to be changed and when meals were to be served. To regulate these activities only a reliable, relative measure of the time needed to be kept and this could be satisfied by the use of a sandglass, the turning of which would have been controlled by the officer of the watch. To ensure that the watches ran their allotted time and that no helmsman tried to warm the glass – thus expanding it and enabling the sands to run faster – the system used would have been based upon a boatswain's mate having a half-hour sandglass and the officer of the watch an hour one. Thus, on the hour the sand in both glasses should have run out together. At each half hour the ship's bell would have been sounded to inform the company of the passage of time. From eight bells at eight o'clock

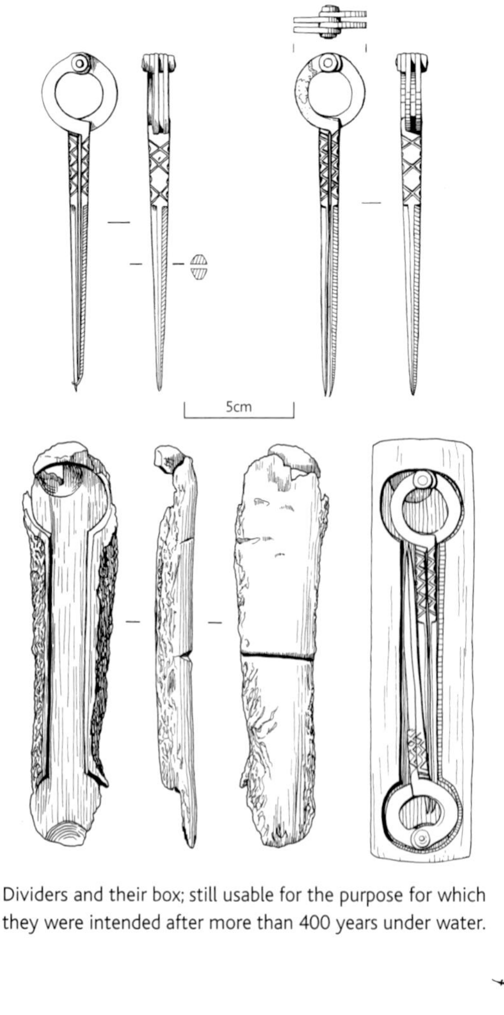

Dividers and their box; still usable for the purpose for which they were intended after more than 400 years under water.

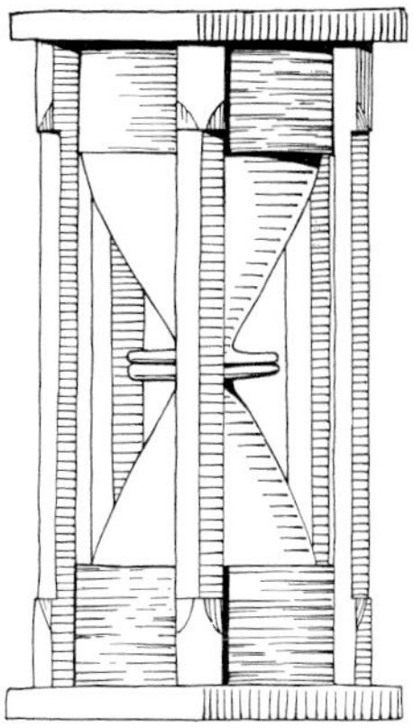

Conjectural reconstruction

Reconstruction of glass

Hourglass. Timekeeping at sea was inaccurate and varied from ship to ship: what was important was that ship's routines were regular and fair.

in the morning watch, one, two, three bells would have been struck, the number increasing every half hour until eight bells at noon started the whole process off again. With a two-watch system it was necessary to divide the day into an uneven number of watches so that sailors did not keep the same watch day after day. Thus the period between 4pm and 8pm would have been divided into two with eight bells being struck at 6pm.

The importance of this regulator of ship-borne life can be gauged by the existence of ships' bells cast from very expensive bronze. The one from *Mary Rose* is a five-kilogram beauty which proudly states in a Flemish inscription around the top, 'I was made in the year 1510' – probably at Malines near Antwerp. The bell had another function at sea, which is still practiced to this day; it was rung loudly and often in foggy weather to warn approaching vessels of the ship's presence. Several of the ship's company had their own system of telling time by means of a pocket sundial. These were beautifully made items fitted with a magnetic needle to line up the dial and a small gnomon, which could be raised to cast its shadow on a scale marked with the hours. The status conferred by possession of such a timepiece probably outweighed its accuracy.

Given a degree of supervision, and periodic checks with the noonday sun this system of local timekeeping ran well, but the glasses had another purpose signified by their being referred to as 'running glasses'. They were a vital part of the pilot's tool kit. Out of sight of land he needed to know how long the ship had been on any particular course. This information, when linked with the estimated speed made good, gave him the vital speed-time-distance equation, which he would mark out on a pegged plotting board so as to gain some idea as to his whereabouts. And if time was uncertain, speed was even more so. The famous 'log' that was to give an idea of speed through the water was first described by William Bourne in the 1574 *Regiment for the Sea*:

> And to know the ship's way, some do use this which is very good: they have a piece of wood, and a line, to veer it out overboard, with a small line of a great length which they make fast at one end, and at the other end and middle they have a piece of line which they make fast with a small thread to stand like unto a crowfoot; for this purpose that it should drive astern as fast as the ship doth go away

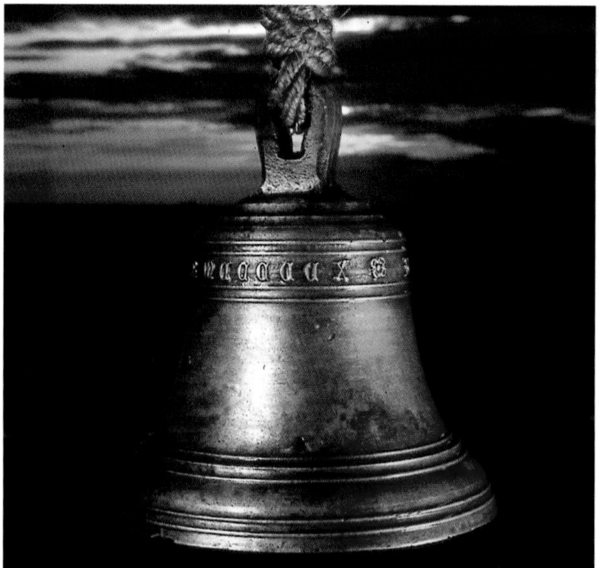

The ship's bell: cast in 1510 this is one of the few objects that would have stayed with the ship throughout her long career.

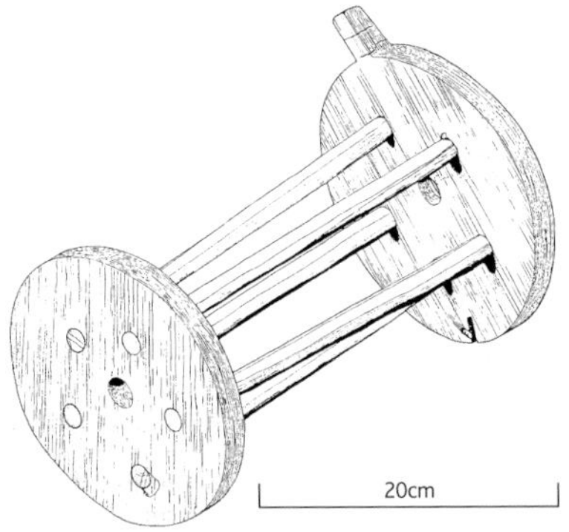

Log reel. Until this was raised from *Mary Rose* it was thought that the log and line was not invented until at least fifty years later.

> from it, always having the line so ready that it goeth out as fast as the ship goeth. In like manner they have either a minute of an hour glass, or else the known part of an hour, by some number of words, or such like, so that the line being veered out and stopped just with that time that the glass is out, or the number of words spoken, which done, they haul in the log or piece of wood again, and look how many fathoms the ship has gone in the time… they multiply the number of fathoms by the portion of time or part of an hour. Whereby, you may know justly how many leagues and parts of a league the ship goes in an hour.[5]

It was thus a revelation when the divers on the *Mary Rose* brought up what was undoubtedly a ship's log. It is a sturdy instrument consisting of two 340mm-diameter wooden discs that were separated by five, probably oak, rods just under half a metre in length, around which the line was coiled. This structure would have been held above his head by a sailor at the stern of the ship so that the line could run out unimpeded until the thirty-second running-glass sand had run through. Then, in the method described by Bourne, the line would have been recovered and the number of fathoms run out measured. A sophistication of this was to tie a number of knots in the line, each one or group corresponding to one nautical mile an hour. The navigator was then able to read directly the ship's speed from the line, a method that has enshrined permanently the word 'knot' as a measure of ship's speed. The most accurate measurement of speed was found by trial and error to be when the distance between the knots in the line was fifty-one feet but, sadly, no knotted line has been recovered from *Mary Rose* to enable us to check her own calibration.

Running glass and log thus gave the navigator an idea of distance run but he also needed to know in what direction he was travelling. Once again, celestial indicators were often present. The bearing of the sun at sunrise, sunset and midday would have been useful, as was the position of Polaris and the rotational movement of the Plough constellation at night. However, there is no indication that northern mariners, spoilt to a certain extent by the existence of Polaris ever developed a sophisticated star-path navigation system such as the one used by the Polynesians. Instead, from very early on the use and development of the magnetic needle into a compass was the key to direction finding in the northern hemisphere.

Three compasses are listed in the 1514 inventory of *Mary Rose* and three were found, but it is probable that others existed for use as spares. One of them was found in the cabin supposedly used by the pilot, while the others were aft on the upper deck, which is where they might have been expected to have been used by the helmsman and the navigator. They are beautifully made and cared-for pieces and, although their precision is unknown, the skill with which they are crafted and their obvious importance, indicates that they were considered to be very important instruments. Their construction is based upon a compass card onto which was drawn the thirty-two points of the compass, while beneath was glued the magnetic needle which was pivoted on a brass pin. All this was sealed in a box with a glass top but in such a way that the card could be easily replaced or removed to remagnetise the needle.

An added feature was that the compasses were mounted on gimbals so that the compass card remained relatively stable whilst the ship pitched and rolled. It probably goes without saying that these are the earliest surviving examples of gimbal-mounted compasses. With log, running glass and compass the master could order a course to be steered and know how long he had been on it and at what speed. He also needed to know, during the course of the day, what the resultant of each course steered was, in other words, after the day's run, where he was in relation to the position from where he started. To achieve this he needed to record every alteration of course and the distance run on each course. To help him work this out he would have had a 'day-worker' – a slate or board on which would have been pegged out each course run and their length. A protractor would have been used to give compass bearings at each way-point. A piece of string linking, on longer passages, the noon position on the previous day to the noon position as computed on the current day would have given the twenty-four-hour course and distance run. Some evidence of this system exists in *Mary Rose*, with the discovery of the remains of a slate disc displaying the points of the compass on one side and work lines on the other, but the lack of further evidence might well be because she was a ship used in coastal passages and journeys across the well-known Channel and thus seldom beyond sight of land.

Slate disc with points of the compass enscribed on it.

English ship masters would not, therefore, have much call upon charts to inform them of the geography of unknown coasts and, when such knowledge was necessary, there is every indication that foreign pilots were employed. There were exceptions. Evidence from a case brought before the High Court of Admiralty in 1533 indicates that the plaintiff, the English master, John à Borough, possessed a chest containing his personal navigational instruments and charts covering as far as the Levant. It would have been strange indeed if such charts had been recovered from *Mary Rose*, since even those drawn on durable vellum would have rotted rapidly underwater. But there is a small indicator that such charts did exist. Among the objects raised were some short sticks with knobs at each end which could have served as rods for holding charts. Their size indicate that only a small chart could have been suspended from them, but that purpose remains a possible use. Then there are the dividers. Four pairs of these classical navigational instruments were raised from the ship. Their main purpose is to mark off distances and courses on charts. They could, however, also be associated with the existence of a 'day-worker', referred to above. Either way they show that the ship's passage was being carefully, but perhaps not accurately, recorded.

Until a ship goes alongside a jetty it is a truism, often forgotten, that the closest point of land to the vessel is that lying directly underneath her keel. Given the range of tides around England, the master of *Mary Rose* when closing the coast needed to know both the direction of the tidal stream and the state of the tide. As tides are influenced by the moon's passage and position relative to the sun, the state of tide at any hour on any day is not fixed, and therefore has to be calculated for each port and each day of the year. This was a three-stage process. Firstly, the master needed to know the time when the full moon was directly south of any port. He then had to know the effect that any local coastal irregularities had on delaying or advancing that time, 'the establishment', and the age of the moon. The establishment he would know from experience or notes, while the latter would be

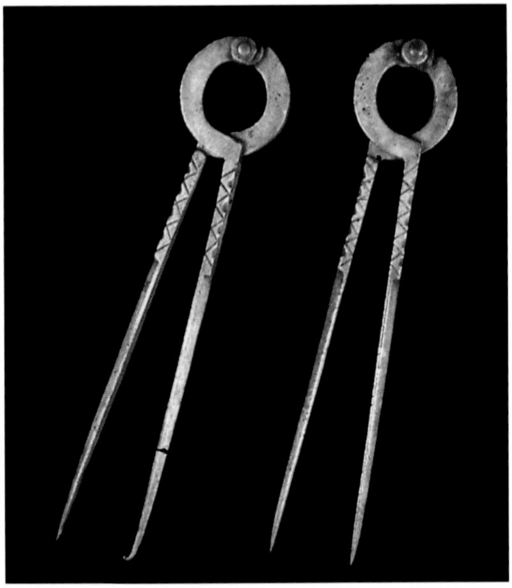

Two dividers, used for the limited chart-work of the time.

written into an almanac; or, he would carefully write into his notes the day on which he observed the full moon. A difficult but constant mathematical sum was involved in calculating the moon's age. It was the same sum that the Church used for working out the dates of Easter, and was based around finding a golden number or prime based on the nineteen years that it took for the moon to complete her orbital cycle in relation to the sun and begin again. Knowing from these linked calculations the moon's age, the master could then use one of those wonderful astronomical coincidences to estimate the time of high water on any day. To do so he used the thirty-two points of the compass as a clock. Taking due south as marking the theoretical time of high water, each compass point represented a forty-five-minute change in 'the establishment'. Then, knowing that on each day after full moon the tide was forty-five minutes later he could use additional compass points to represent the age of the moon, ending up with a time of high water for the day that he needed it. That this – once mastered – simple calculation was used in *Mary Rose* is evidenced by the discovery of a personal wooden compass card that seems designed for this purpose.

The establishment of Portsmouth was recorded in contemporary guides as being, 'Before the Isle of Wight and Portsmouth South and by East Moon.' This meant that at the time of spring tides, when the moon was full or new, high water occurred when the moon's bearing was 167 degrees. On each subsequent day the time of high tide would be forty-five minutes later, or one compass point westward. Robert Hicks gives a detailed explanation of how the calculations of high tide were worked out.[6] The mathematics appears at first to be complicated but as the formula, once grasped, was standard, it could be applied by any master to any location.

However, knowing the time of high water and the presence of tidal streams was only part of the process of making safe entry to port. The master still needed to be aware of what depth of water lay beneath the ship at his present position. To help him discover this he used one of the oldest navigational instruments known, the lead and line, eight of which were recovered from *Mary Rose.* They were simple but multi-purpose instruments. Firstly, of course, they gave a reading of the depth and for this reason the line would have been marked at defined distances with a number and range of easily identifiable materials: from *Mary Rose* these include leather, yellow wool, red silk thread and madder, making this the earliest example of what was to become the standard English lead-line markings. When closing the coast in murky weather the master would want to know not only the depth of water but any other information that might give indication of his whereabouts. To help him in this important calculation the sounding lead had dimpled bases that were 'armed' with tallow. On striking the bottom the tallow would collect a small sample of the seabed, sand or mud or gravel or shell which, by referring to notes, might give a clue as to the ship's location. *Mary Rose,* in common with other ships carried two types of lead. In deeper water, it would have been necessary to ascertain how the land was shelving, but at less frequent intervals. Here a heavy 10–14lb lead was used, its weight helping to 'plum' to the greater depth more rapidly and thus in a straighter line. As the ship sailed close to the coast the depth would have had to be checked both more accurately and more often so a lighter, 7lb-lead-weighted line was used as an aid to the lodesman.

Keeping the ship on his chosen course was something over which the master exercised anything from total to little control, depending on the tides and currents pushing against the hull below the waterline and the play of the wind upon the freeboard and the sails. Tall-sided carracks, such as *Mary Rose*, had a lot of windage that would have pushed the ship bodily sideways and the master would have often had to steer well off course to make the track that he intended. To steer the ship he relied on the rudder and the sails, a task that became easier with the introduction of the lateen sail on the after masts, as they could be set and adjusted swiftly to help the helmsman.

The mechanical means by which the helmsman steered was a short tiller attached to the head of the rudder. In strong seas several sailors would have been needed both to move the tiller and to keep the ship steady on the ordered course. When extra men proved inadequate, tackle had to be rigged and secured to bolts on either side of the ship just to keep some control on the plunging, frisky ship. Later, in order to enable ship design to progress further, better means of steering – such as the whipstaff, and eventually the ship's wheel – were introduced. From his position well aft on the upper deck, although the helmsman could steer and ordered course by means of the compass in front of him, he could often not see where he was heading and he would have been conned by orders shouted to him by the master or officer in charge of the watch.

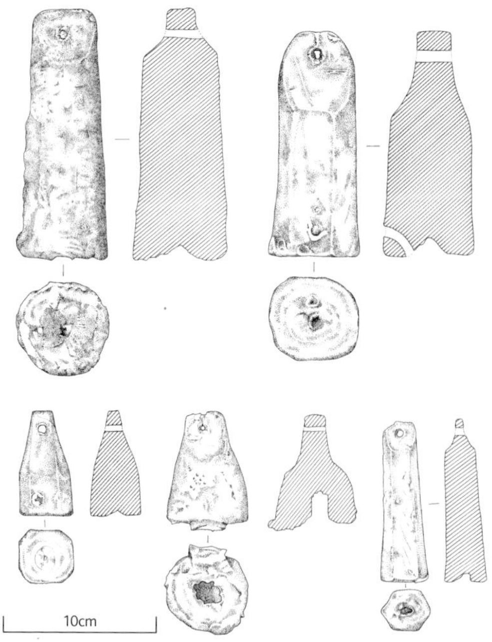

Examples of leads from *Mary Rose*. The lead and line was arguably the most important instrument for safe pilotage.

Although the masters of the navy royal did not have the same imperatives of timekeeping that could worry the merchantman, the time spent by Howard and his fleet in port waiting for a favourable wind added up to months of idleness while, at sea, the speed made good, over the ground, was often far less than the ship's theoretical capability. Even during the exhilarating race around North Foreland the ships were hardly behaving like greyhounds of the ocean. Columbus's carvels are recorded as achieving, on occasion, eleven knots, but the guidance used in London for the time that a voyage might take was based on an average speed of one knot. During their passage ships might have been blown back on their course, becalmed, forced to seek shelter from storms, attacked by pirates, driven ashore or run out of food and water. Marine vegetation created drag on the hull making progress even more sluggish so, although *Mary Rose* could, theoretically, move more swiftly than a coach on the notoriously poor English roads, overall her movement at sea was as slow and often as uncomfortable.

There is good reason to suppose that the fleet might anchor overnight while on coastal passage to avoid the dangers inherent in a night passage. Certainly, being at anchor was the preferred way to spend the night off the French coast. On passage through the Channel against adverse winds ships would often anchor until a favourable tide could carry them towards their destination, only to anchor again when the tide turned. This made for a laborious passage. Given these conditions it is difficult to calculate a typical passage speed for *Mary Rose* and her accompanying vessels. The best opportunity occurs in the record of the attack on Morlaix in 1522.[7] We know that Thomas Howard was in Dartmouth in the late afternoon of 30 June. It is evident that he landed his forces in the Bay of Morlaix on 1 July. Given the dangerous nature of that coast he is unlikely to have entered the bay after sunset. He thus had to cover 145 nautical miles in about thirty hours at the outside, giving a speed of approximately five knots, which would have been impressive progress with a fleet of ships of varying capabilities.

Added to the dangers of the sea that could only be avoided by alert and competent navigation were those imposed by the seaworthiness of the ships themselves. Here again the care taken of the navy royal would indicate that even the parsimonious purse-string holders realised that it was more efficacious to repair and maintain rather than wait for a ship to leak and rot. And rot they could. Carvel-built ships relied on the efficiency of their caulking to keep them reasonably watertight and much was demanded of this method of driving oakum into the seams and then tarring over them. The timbers moved, warped, stretched and shrank and this black mastic had to adjust to this. In time, just as with sealant inserted around a bath today, it decayed and even sprang out as it is recorded doing in an English ship in the 1530s.[8]

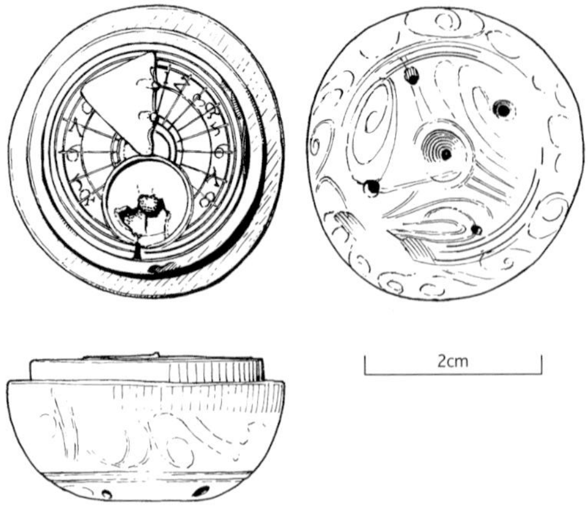

This pocket sundial is a wonderful piece of miniature craftsmanship, but was probably carried more as a status symbol than an accurate time piece.

Good seamanship was a matter of doing a thorough and timely job while at the same time guarding against close encounters with danger, such as rock and tempest, fire and flood. Fire is the mariner's nightmare, bursting upon him suddenly, often on a calm sea and a quiet passage. The need for flame, either for the galley or for candlelight in peace, or for artillery in war, was a well-recognised, dangerous necessity and, in the best ships, it was a well-regulated one as well. Ships did catch fire; spectacularly, like *Regent* and *Cordéliere*, or as a result of accident, carelessness or violent movement as happened to *Mary and John*, which had to be extensively rebuilt. Yet, once again, the navy royal does seem to have had a good record of damage control. Of the ninety ships that at one time or another comprised Henry VIII's navy, Arthur Nelson records the following untimely fates: capsized (1); condemned (16); captured (5); lost at sea (1); wrecked (3), and burnt (4),[9] which is a reasonable record from an age of timber ships, naked flames, gunpowder and primitive navigation.

The handling of a four-masted ship in any sort of weather so as to get the best performance out of her was a masterful art, and one that was only achieved through years of experience at every level of seafaring. A wonderful evocation of what was involved was written in *The Complaynt of Scotland*:

> Then the master cried, 'Top your topinellis.
> Haul on your topsail sheets! Veer your leeches
> and your topsail sheets! Veer your leeches and
> your topsail trusses, and haul the topsail
> higher! Haul out the topsail bowline! Hoist
> the mizzen and change it over to leeward!
> Haul the leeches and the sheets! Haul the
> truss to the yard!'[10]

The thrill of the seaman's life and the reason it appealed to so many can be gleened from those few lines. At its very best it was teamwork and professionalism carried out at a level far in advance of any other calling available at the time.

CHAPTER 6

A Life in the Day of...

FOR MOST MEMBERS OF THE CREW OF *Mary Rose* the day began with the hands being called at around 0700. A dutyman would have descended to the main deck and piped shrilly on his boatswain's call after which he would have stepped on or over the off-watch crew to shake those still asleep. This would give them time to carry out routine ablutions and have something to eat before, at 0800 and eight bells, they relieved the sailors on watch. The off-watch crew would not have had a comfortable night. They had neither bunks nor hammocks, and had to sleep on the decks or on gratings wherever there was space for them to curl up and be wedged against the rolling of their ship. Before hammocks provided a sort of overnight mezzanine deck the main deck of a ship at sea at night would have been a mass of bodies.[1] A permanent or improvised palliasse may have given some comfort, but a hard deck was the most common mattress. In the cabins it would have been easier, for the officers and petty officers had the space and permanency to give themselves some softness for their bony hips.

Primitive, too, were the lavatory arrangements. The designated area for crewmen to relieve themselves was called the 'beakheads' (or heads), an area right forward where two boxes with holes in would have been placed overhanging the sea whose waves took on the role of a flush.[2] This may have been reasonably efficacious at sea but when anchored, in harbour or alongside it would have been both more unpleasant and more exposed to onlookers. Certainly, in harbour, some sort of slopping-out arrangements would have been in place while, at sea, however scouring the waves might have been, there would still have been a need to clean up the area. This was a job for which there would have been few volunteers although, as in modern ships, there could always be found someone who could see advantages in being left alone while carrying out such an odorous task. The next best thing to a volunteer would have been a man under punishment. Thus, in John Smith's *Sea Grammar*, it is stated:

> The Liar is to hold his place but for a week, and he that is first taken with a lie every Monday is so proclaimed at the main mast by a general cry of, 'A liar, a liar, a liar!'; he is under the Swabber and only to clean the beakhead chains.[3]

Urinals were also not present and it would be naive to suppose that our waking sailor would join an orderly queue to use the facilities up forward, especially on a dark, wet, cold morning. There would have been many buckets, the contents of which were poured overboard or else, after a careful check on relative wind direction, the sea would have received the bladder's contents direct. There was, however, a 'daille', a trough-shaped timer used to discharge waste water via a pump from the bilge and this would have had an ablutionary use as well. Officers would have used a 'piss pot' in the privacy of their cabins.[4]

These primitive arrangements do not indicate that the crew were either unhygienic or unkempt. They had their own combs, individually designed, manicure sets and ear scoops,[5] and they would have been regularly shaved. Circumstance rather than slovenliness would have been the cause of poor sanitation. Thus, the crew would have had to sleep in their clothes which, while not being uniform, would have been fairly standard throughout. Over a rough linen shirt they would have worn a woolen under-jerkin over which they would have worn a leather jerkin with long skirt pieces that would have provided some protection from rain, spray and wind. Generally, the jerkins would have been fastened together with laces, the ends of which would have been stopped from fraying by aiglets. Some jerkins would have had button-fastening but, whatever the method, no two recovered examples are the same, confirming the evidence that this was an age of individuality. The design meant that the jerkin could be reversible, although what purpose this might have served is unclear.

Sailors' breeches would have been simple woollen garments held up by being laced in to the shirt. They were probably loose fitting around the upper leg and tied above the knee. Below this the sailor was barefoot when working the rigging and shod in leather while off watch or working below deck. Hardened soles and strong toes would have developed from clambering up the rigging, while well-trained feet and hands would be employed handling the sails and ropes. It would have been when wandering around the ship before going on watch that the seamen wore their shoes or slippers, of which there was also a number of distinct designs. They were, for the most part welted, but a small percentage was of the earlier turn-shoe design. When necessary they would have been repaired on board and one of the crew would, undoubtedly, have earned a few pence for his cobbling skills. Senior officers would have walked the deck in thigh boots.

Besides his clothing the sailor would have come on board with few personal possessions: a bowl for drinking; a wooden plate; a tankard, a spoon, a ballock, or other knife, a comb, and a 'housewife' or sewing set. Some may have had leather bottles to fill with water, for their diet was a very salty one. Apart from that they would have neither needed nor desired much else. Many had chests to hold their bits and pieces but few of these would have held anything of value. Theft would have been both tempting and easy,

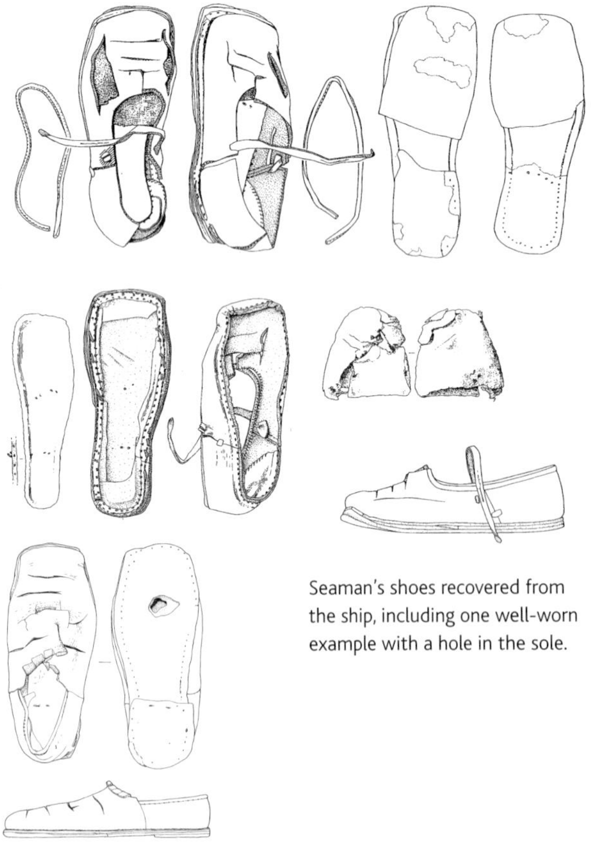

Seaman's shoes recovered from the ship, including one well-worn example with a hole in the sole.

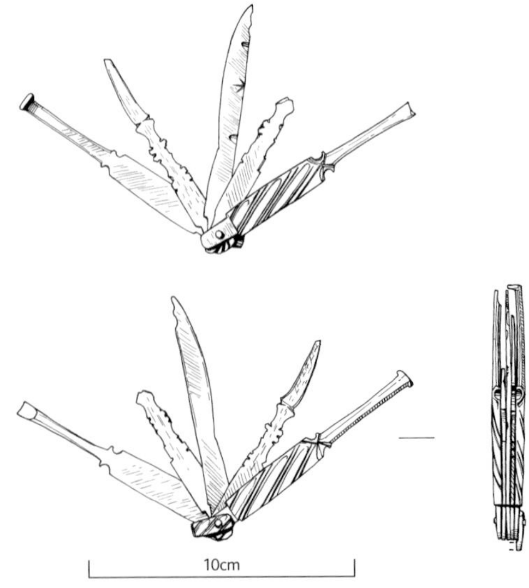

A manicure set. Objects such as this put paid to the idea that the seamen were unkempt and unhygienic.

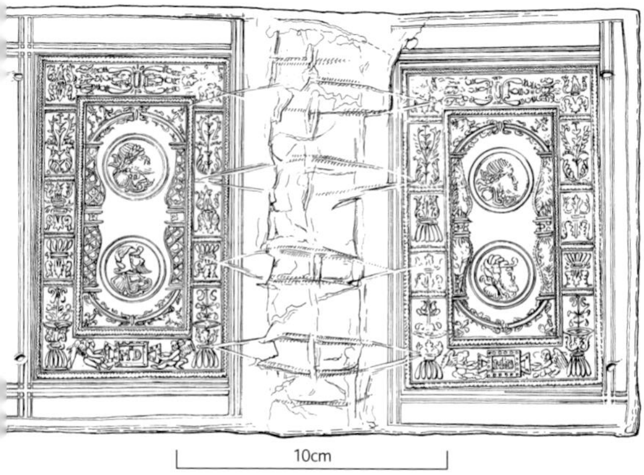

Cover of a Bible, the intricate pattern of the leather work still clearly showing after its long submersion.

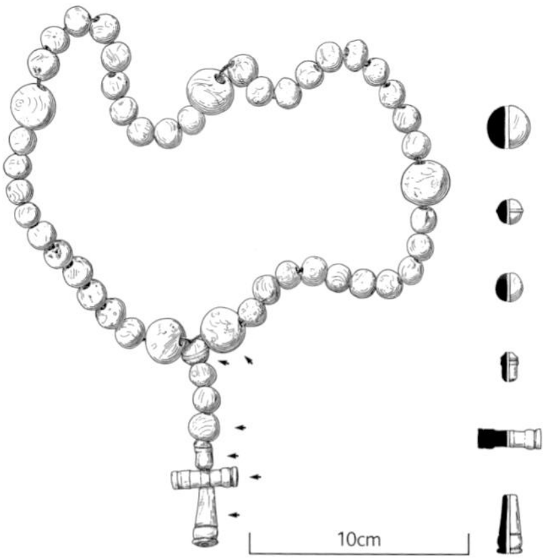

A rosary, another example of piety among the crew.

a fact that has influenced the seriousness with which this crime has always been dealt with on board ship. Pay – and the seaman was in a job that paid regularly, well, and in cash – in contrast to much work available on shore, was often made at the end of the voyage, a system that kept temptation at bay. The manning of *Mary Rose* was, as far as skills were concerned, a simple business; what varied greatly was the number of people on board and this depended very much on the business in hand. When that business was war an influx of soldiers made the normally cramped living conditions disagreeably uncomfortable, and good management would have been needed to ensure that disturbances did not break out on board.

The watch system worked at sea would generally be devised around dividing the crew into port and starboard watches, with each keeping alternate watches of four hours. John Smith details how the watch system was organised at the start of a voyage:

> The Captaine or Master commands the Boatswaine to call up the company. The Master, being chiefe of the Starboard watch, doth call one, and his right hand Mate on the Larboord doth call another, and so forward, till they be divided in two parts. Then each man is to chuse his Mate, Consort, or Comrade, and then devide them into squadrons according to your number and burthen of your ship as you see occasion. These are to take their turnes at the Helme, trim sailes, pumpe, and doe all duties each halfe, or each squadron for eight Glasses or foure houre, which is a watch.... The next is, to mess them foure to a messe, and then give each messe a quarter Can of beere, a basket of bread to stay their stomacks till the Kettle be boiled, that they may first goe to prayer, then to supper; and at six a'clocke sing a Psalme, say a Prayer, and then the Master with his side begins the watch. Then all the rest may doe what they will till midnight; and then his Mate with his Larboord me, with a Psalme and a Prayer, releeve them till foure in the morning. And so from eight to twelve each other, except some flow of winde come – some storme or gust – or some accident that requires the helpe of all hands, which commonly, after such good cheere, in most voyages doth happen.'[6]

While on watch the seamen would have carried out such tasks as working the sails, pumping out, sweeping, washing down, adjusting the standing rigging which, because it was made of hemp, would have constantly become slack or taut with the effect of water and sun, steering the ship and keeping a lookout. On most passages this was work enough to keep most of those on watch gainfully employed.

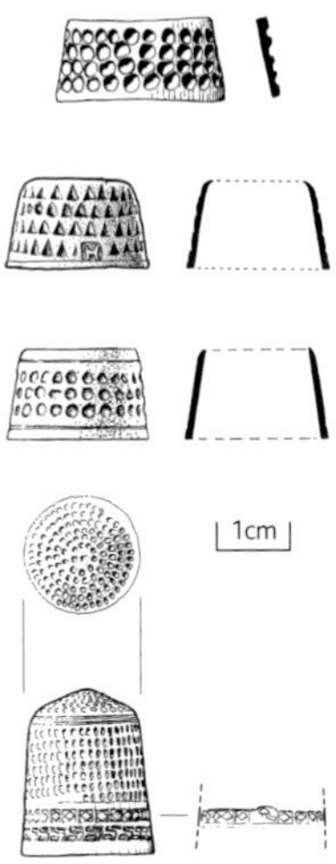

Thimbles found in the ship: apart from their specialist use by sailmakers, it is likely that most of the crew would have mended if not actually made their own clothes.

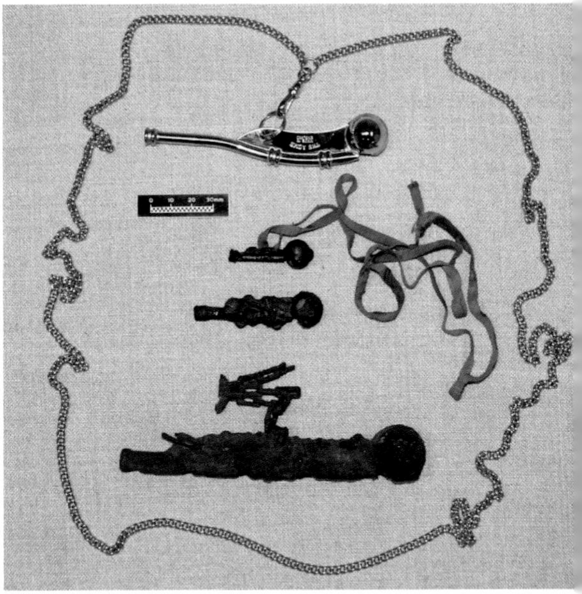

Three boatswain's calls with modern equivalent – yet another example of a continuity of design and tradition.

If the chimes of the bell controlled the watches, the shrill calls of whistles controlled activities around the ship where the sound of wind and sea and the creaking of the vessel may have drowned out human voices. In their place was introduced a system of pipes and trills each one signifying a command. Thus the boatswain could control the setting of sails and the working of rigging, and also inform the crew when dinner was ready or that it was time for quiet between decks: 'pipe down' as a common expression had to await the arrival of tobacco. The use of the whistle became well known even away from the sea. Shakespeare refers to it in *Henry V*:

> ...behold
> Upon the hempen tackle ship-boys climbing,
> Hear the shrill whistle, which doth order give
> To sounds confused.[7]

– a perfect summary of why the whistle was so efficacious. The shipman's whistle, more popularly known as the boatswain's call, served another purpose as well; smaller, decorative silver whistles were worn as badges of office while gold ones, often highly decorated, were reserved for senior admirals and the monarch himself. Henry, who wore his with pride and blew it with vigour, ordered in 1532: 'Masters of the ships or other vessels and mariners to wear whistles of silver, with the chain of silver to hang the same upon.'[8]

Five silver boatswain's calls were found in *Mary Rose*. One of them has such a chain of silver attached while others have silk ribbons. Unlike modern calls, which have a curved stem they are all straight stocked, but, like modern ones, they all have a moulding at the mouthpiece so that they could be clenched between the teeth while the owner's hands were otherwise occupied. Today on board naval ships the duty quartermaster wears a boatswain's call as a mark of his office and is called upon to use it to pipe 'call the hands' in the morning and 'pipe down' in the evening. It is also used to warn of the approach of the Officer of the Day on evening rounds and to 'pipe the side' for the arrival or departure of a commanding or senior officer, or as a mark of respect to a passing warship. It represents, therefore, yet another living link with our Tudor past.

Although the ship's company tend to be listed as either seamen or gunners there were many individual skills, besides those of the master and the boatswains, that were necessary for the ship to work well or even survive. Foremost amongst these, in this wooden world, was that of the carpenter. *Mary Rose*'s material well-being depended on the presence of skilled shipwrights or carpenters to tend her frames, planks, masts, spars and fittings and, very importantly, her pumps. It was on the shipwright and his mates, therefore, that the safety of the ship's company could ultimately depend. Storm, shot or shoal could put the ship in such straights that only the shipwright could keep her afloat or, in the most desperate of circumstances rig a raft or boat by which the crew could endeavour to escape. He would have been a much-respected craftsman and not only in the dire emergency. The shipwright would have been able to make or repair a plate, a bowl, a tankard or a chest, a box in which to keep precious possessions or a shelf on which to stow other items.

The shipwright, or 'chippy' as he became known, has always been a beloved figure on board ship. To call such a man a carpenter is, therefore, to misunderstand and underestimate his training and responsibilities. His wooden world flexed, breathed, swelled, shrank, warped, sprang and bowed, and every time it did so the unforgiving elements of wind and water tried to prize her open or break her apart. He had to understand her language of creaks and leaks, her habits and her limits, her frames and her seams, her frailties and how to minister to them. As he walked her planks he would have kept his eyes, ears and nose attentive to her moods, his feet sensitive to her movements, his hands aware of her breathing flanks. No master of horse had responsibilities for his stable as great as that of the shipwright for his charge.

The carpenter would have been expected to make daily rounds of the ship looking out for leaks or decaying wood work, checking in the bilge to see if standing water was threatening the integrity of plank or mast. In the most extreme conditions he could organise the replacement of a mast or spar and would have been able to construct a boat if ever this was needed. In some instances carpenters managed to bring about the rescue of their shipwrecked companions by building just such a boat from wreckage deemed sufficiently seaworthy for a long voyage to be undertaken to safety or to alert rescuers. As he made his rounds the carpenter would have worn around his waist a belt from which, suspended in a wooden sheath, hung a knife, a spike and a chisel – the tools needed to probe for sprung or spongy wood and to prise out loose caulking.

Shipwrights have always collected their own personal tools with which to carry out their work. As far as working with wood is concerned these have scarcely varied over the centuries and would be as recognisable in a workshop today by any woodwork enthusiast as they were in Henry's time. The standard tools were the same: saws, planes, gauges, brace and bits, rules, augers, gimlets, chisels, axes, mallets and hammers. All are in evidence and their design is instantly recognisable. Most were kept in the carpenter's cabin, which lay beside that of two of the other key professionals on board, the pilot and the barber-surgeon. At some stage, a carpenter on board *Mary Rose* became dissatisfied with his own quarters and decided to allow more light to enter. Disregarding the ship's physical integrity, he cut himself a window. Margaret Rule, the Mary Rose Trust's Research Director, describes it thus:

> He had to survive in a dank, airless cabin on the main gun-deck with no gun-ports to

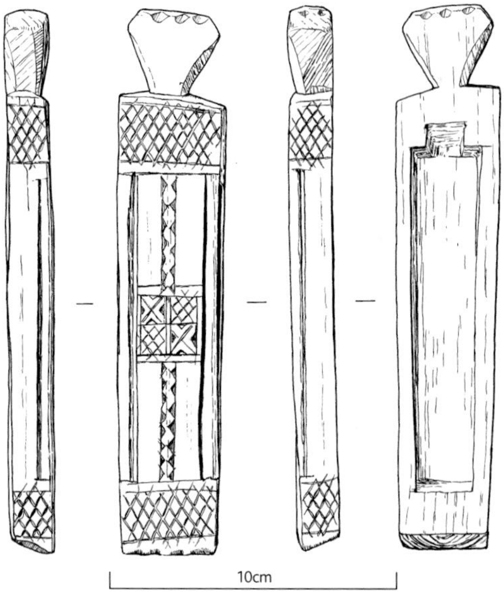

A whetstone holder. Most seamen would have been responsible for ensuring their knives were well honed: their lives could depend on their possessing a sharp knife.

provide fresh air – and so he has cut a hole through the side of the ship straight the way through one of the main load-bearing stringers, one of the most important timbers of the ship, in order to give himself some fresh air. To his surprise he found it went straight through to the chainplate outside (a large wooden ledge) and so he could not open his clandestine little window. So he also cut through the chainplate. The man wanted to live comfortably and if that meant weakening the ship a little, he was not bothered. The man was a rascal.[9]

If the carpenter's duty was to keep the ship afloat a great demand was made on him every time that another professional, the master gunner, required the ship to stand in to danger so that he could perform his duty. The damage resulting from enemy fire could require the carpenter to work both inboard and over the side. For example, during a lull in action John Smith's captain ordered:

> 'Master, let us breathe and refresh a little, sling a man over boord to stop the leakes'. That is, to trusse him up about the middle in a peece of canvas, and a rope to keepe him from sinking, and his arms at liberty; with a malet in one hand, and a plug lapped in Okum and a well-tarred tarpawling clout in the other, which he will quickly beat into the holes the bullets made.[10]

On board *Mary Rose* and the other main ships of the navy royal was another professional whose skills the sailors relied upon for their health, safety and the repair of holes made by bullets – the barber-surgeon. The reputation of the sea doctor has not been an unsullied one. To a certain extent this may be due to the suspicion that the most competent physicians probably stayed ashore leaving the unpleasantness of life at sea to those who could not support themselves on dry land. There is also the widespread belief that surgery was basic and brutal, supported by medicine that was worthless and fake. The sad tale of the failure to recognise the cure for scurvy and the misery that this inefficiency created is probably another major factor that has obscured the pioneering work of William Clowes, chief surgeon in the fleet that opposed the Spanish Armada, and his predecessors. The evidence raised with *Mary Rose* indicates that in the field of surgery the navy royal did its men proud.

Barber-surgeons were just one branch of the medical profession in Tudor times. At the top were the physicians and surgeons, university graduates with many years of honing their skills. Next came the

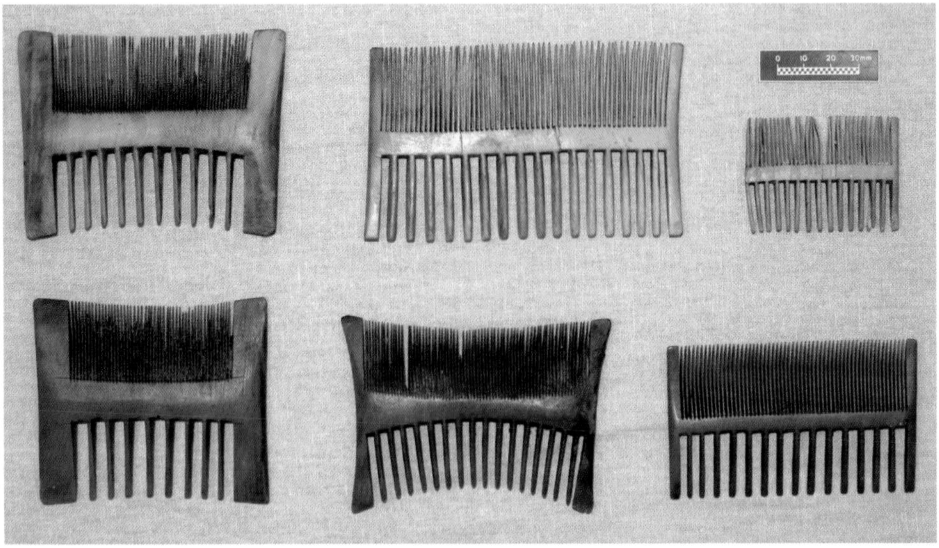

Although cheap, no two combs were made indentically, indicating a great pride in the making of these humble objects.

A re-enactor showing off the work of the apothecary.

barber-surgeons, men who had completed a seven- to nine-year apprenticeship with a master surgeon. They could also cut hair and trim beards but this activity was probably best carried out by the barber members of their profession. Finally, as far as recognised qualifications were concerned, came the apothecaries, the forerunners of the modern chemist.

Regulation followed from the recognition that there were definite skills that could save life and cure illness, and that these needed encouragement at the expense of the popular quacks and charlatans to whom the people entrusted their faith and their fortunes. Henry, a hypochondriac himself, was determined to make quackery a thing of the past. This he did by legislation which, regrettably, he was forced to amend when popular outcry called for the 'quacks' to be restored. However, his recognition of the importance of the barber-surgeons, was clearly demonstrated by the fact that he had his portrait painted with them; the latter wearing felt hats similar to the one recovered from *Mary Rose*.[11]

Special attention appears to have been given to the appointment of these well-qualified men to serve at sea. The Accounts for 1513 list thirty-two naval surgeons serving under four masters and a chief surgeon. On board *Mary Rose* was Robert Sympson with his assistant Henry Yonge. Throughout Henry's reign reform and reorganisation meant that the training of these seagoing surgeons was raised to the highest possible standard, for it was recognised that the task at sea was more onerous than that performed by the equivalent professional in the army. However, it is highly unlikely that these men served for long periods of time on board. Rather, their appointments would have been for the duration of each major campaign. Nevertheless, space was provided on board for them to set up their surgery and operating table.

In *Mary Rose* there are two small cabins that have been linked to the surgeons because of the items found inside. These contents included a chest within which the handles of many an instrument were found, the blades having rusted away. Other finds linked the occupant to both the role of barber and surgeon. There were combs, razors, a shaving bowl, ointment jars, glass bottles, a large, ominous-looking syringe (for irrigating wounds and drainage tracks), ear-wax scoops, and a lot more besides: every indication that the medical department was well prepared for both action and

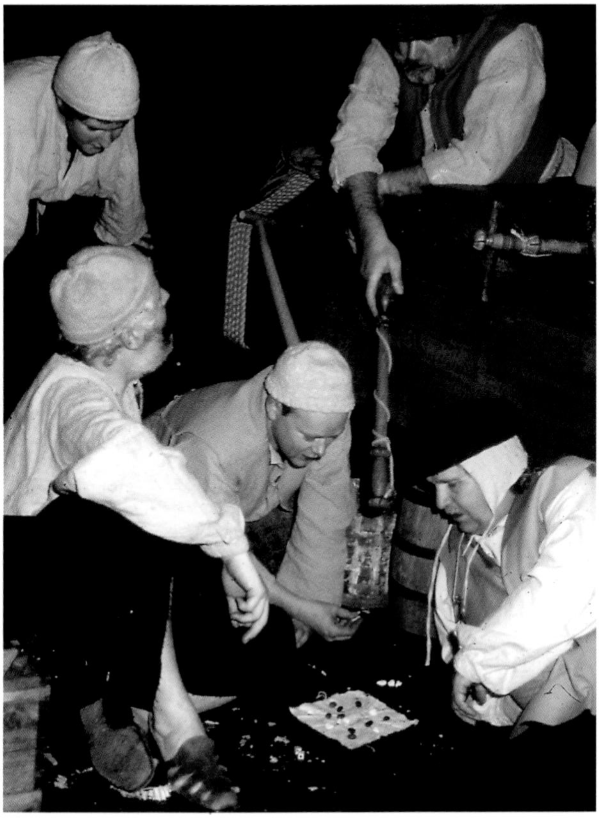

Although officially discouraged, artefacts recovered from the ship prove gaming was common.

every-day care. Generally, the ailments and abrasions that the surgeon dealt with were the commonplace problems linked to life on board. Clambering barefoot around a rolling vessel and lifting and shifting heavy weights would have created a fair number of bone breaks and bruises. Ann Stirland found evidence of a few fractures to hips, legs and feet and a few depressed fractures of the skull and ribs.[12] But the surgeon would have had the usual daily visit from those with cuts and bruises, black eyes and upset stomachs.

James Watt, in a fascinating and thorough article[13] makes much of the fact that the surgeons' cabins appear to have been unoccupied at the time the ship capsized, but that there were many skeletons in the hold, the traditional place for doctors to operate. It can be presumed that none of these skeletons were battle casualties, but could they have needed treatment for another reason? Watt hypothesises that they might have been among the earliest victims of the dysentery that Lisle reported to the king on 2 August had struck the fleet and caused great sickness. If so, Watt goes on, the ship's company might not have been able to react with alacrity to the problems that so fatally struck her on 19 July 1545. Watt also hypothesises on the fact that a shawm, a musical instrument that was the predecessor to the oboe, was found close to the barber-surgeon's cabin. He considers that this might be evidence that music was used to sooth the patient and those awaiting treatment. From this developed 'barbers' music' and, presumably, the much later 'barber-shop' singing.

The presence of a qualified surgeon was just one of the several benefits that the ordinary sailor had better access to on board ship, compared with what would have been available to him at home on land. Two of the most miserable elements of life ashore were totally absent at sea – mud and dust. In an age of unmade road and unplanned housing, mud and mush would have greeted the residence of any small or poor community at their front door and down their street until summer's baking heat dried it out into a dust for the wind to blow in their faces. Neither did the seaman have to work the long hours demanded by a landowner during harvest, nor the backbreaking chores associated with agriculture prior to the introduction of machinery. He could also expect regular 'square meals' – reputedly a naval term brought about by the advent of the square trenchers of which six examples have been found on board *Mary Rose*.

If the carpenter and barber-surgeon kept ship and sailor in good repair it was the cook who was supposed to keep them content. His was a troglodyte existence, a fact that persists to this day, with the ship's cook usually being the most pale-skinned individual on board any vessel. But his was a life others on board might envy. Down in the bowels of the ship he was free from the shouted command or rebuke from officers, and was working in a dry and warm environment albeit, at times, too hot and smoky. From his two-galley range he was expected to provide two hot meals a day from very similar ingredients to which only his own skill could add variety and, hopefully, pallatability. What would have been certain is that he would have had few enemies; cupboard love in a hungry home would have maintained his popularity until any such time that he made a complete mess of the victuals.

Meal times would have been a time for relaxation as would the early evening when the day's work had been done. Sailing at an average of four knots would have made life pleasant and undemanding while the ship was on a steady course. The sailors would have played a variety of games although some forms of gambling, such as cards and dice, had been banned by the king, even though he himself was a devoted gambler. The sailors circumvented this

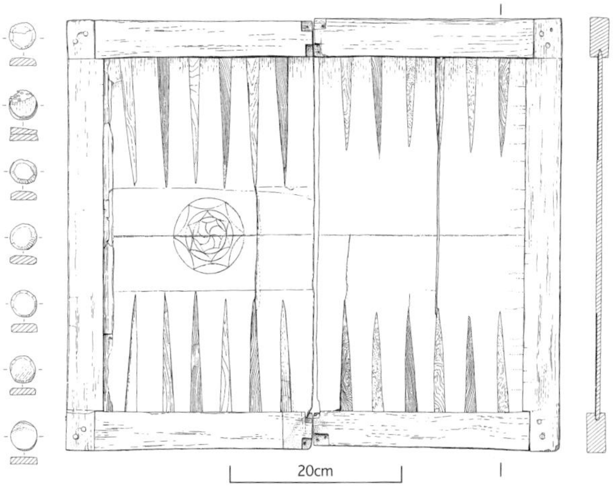

Backgammon board: the earliest example in England and a clear indicator that relaxation was important in the quiet moments on passage.

Re-enactors playing replica sixteenth-century instruments. Extant sea songs from the period show that sailors enjoyed a sing along.

directive by producing dice so small that they could easily be hidden if an officer approached. The officers too had their games, backgammon being one of them, although presumably, in accordance with the king's directive, this was not played for money.

There was no shortage of music to accompany the soughing of the wind and the creaking of the masts. The ship's band, with shawm, pipe and tabor, fiddle and drum, could play tunes for all occasions: sentimental songs for homesick sailors, or rousing shanties to accompany major evolutions. The musicians' main task, apart from lending support to major evolutions, would have been to play courtly music in the evenings to the admiral and his staff to remind them of the brilliance from which they were separated.

The more contemplative and better educated would have read in their spare time, but probably from a choice limited to the Bible and prayer books. When a priest was carried on board he would have said the daily offices and the ship's company would have been summoned to prayers. A small folding table, such as the one recovered from *Mary Rose*, would have made an ideal portable altar.

As the sun set so the sounds on board would have died down of necessity. Below decks, even in daytime, all was gloomy for, with the gun-ports closed, the limited light that penetrated only lit the area beneath the overhead hatches, while some extra light filtered through the small ports fitted above each gun. Lanthorns would have been burnt even in daytime but most of these would have been doused overnight. With nightfall those off watch would have retired and, for the most part, they would have slept uncomfortably but content enough.

For the sailors moving about the ship a life at sea would have been theirs by choice. Stories of press-ganging belong to a later century and even then they are largely exaggerated. Seamen were specialists and hard to come by, they certainly could not be replaced by layabouts hauled away from town stews or country lanes. If, as the 1583 census revealed, there were only about 12,000 seamen in the country, of which the king needed 3,000 for his fleet, scarcity would have encouraged attractive conditions of service. Supply and demand is reflected in the level of wages that the government paid its sailors. At the start of Henry's reign this was five shillings a month for an ordinary seaman, plus a coat, conduct money – a sort of travel expenses – and free board. This was being paid at the time that a labourer was lucky to get four pence a day, from which he had to feed and clothe his family. By 1545 inflation had increased the latter's wage to sixpence a day, but the seaman's wage had risen to 6s 8d to keep the employment competitive. So competitive in fact that men of several nationalities were prepared to serve in Henry's fleet. Paying them on time was, however, as always, a different matter. In April 1513, John Dawtry complained to Wolsey that he lacked money to pay wages a month in advance as agreed and that his money 'goes away very fast' for many reasons.[14]

In 1543 seamen were exempted from service in the army but conditions ashore were improving and many of them did feel the urge to abscond. The king was not prepared to tolerate this desertion and ordered:

> Forasmuch as mariners and soldiers serving in the king's ships have at times past and yet continually do, use not only unlawfully to depart from their ships unto the towns near...His Majesty's pleasure and straight commandment is that no mariner or soldier...depart or go from their ships without testimonial signed with their captain's hands...upon pain of death.[15]

The majority of sailors saw no reason to risk their lives departing for what was a harder and often more lawless, unpredictable life, ashore. Early Tudor England suffered a series of bad harvests and in 1528 there was a famine. Enclosure of common land, rack-renting and the harsh treatment of vagrancy meant that for the agrarian poor who constituted the majority of England's population of four million, scraping a livelihood was hard. Ket's rebellion of July 1549 was just the final frustration of an under-privileged class.[16] The seaman was far better cared for and better fed.

CHAPTER 7

Sailing on their Stomachs

AVARICIOUS, AMBITIOUS, ACQUISITIVE, sensuous, venal and cunning, Thomas Wolsey would not have enjoyed the opportunity to indulge his vices had he not possessed the virtues that earned him his position of power in the first place. Popular history has been unkind to him, concentrating on his baser nature, but few men have shown so great a capacity for loyal, sustained hard work than Wolsey. Fewer still could have held, as a commoner – Wolsey was always derided by his enemies as 'that butcher's son' – such a precarious position for so long while jealous lordly limbs stretched out to trip up his corpulent figure.

It was Dean Wolsey, in his role as Master Almoner, who was able to demonstrate that the idea of a standing navy was a sustainable one. This new creation was twice blessed; firstly, that it came into being at a time of war, thus justifying both its existence and expense and, secondly, that it had a civil servant as able as Wolsey to steer it through administrative shoals no less dangerous than those in which the fleet itself had to operate. No member of the traditional warrior caste had the competence to do what was required or was prepared to ink his fingers with scribblings about the necessary details. Wolsey, however, was. The war with France confirmed his ability and his authority; the former the noble lords could acknowledge, the latter they would abhor and never forgive. No better summary of Wolsey's crucial role exists than that given by his biographer, Francis Hacket:

> The war was in sight. Dean Wolsey, the Master Almoner, stood on no ceremony. He discarded the priest to reveal a rough-shod organiser with a stinging will. Into his hands he gathered the reins of somnolent England – army service, transport, ordnance, budget, sanitation. The war to him was the manipulation of a national economy. He created a national workshop. He raised and spent sixty million dollars [*sic*]. If there was

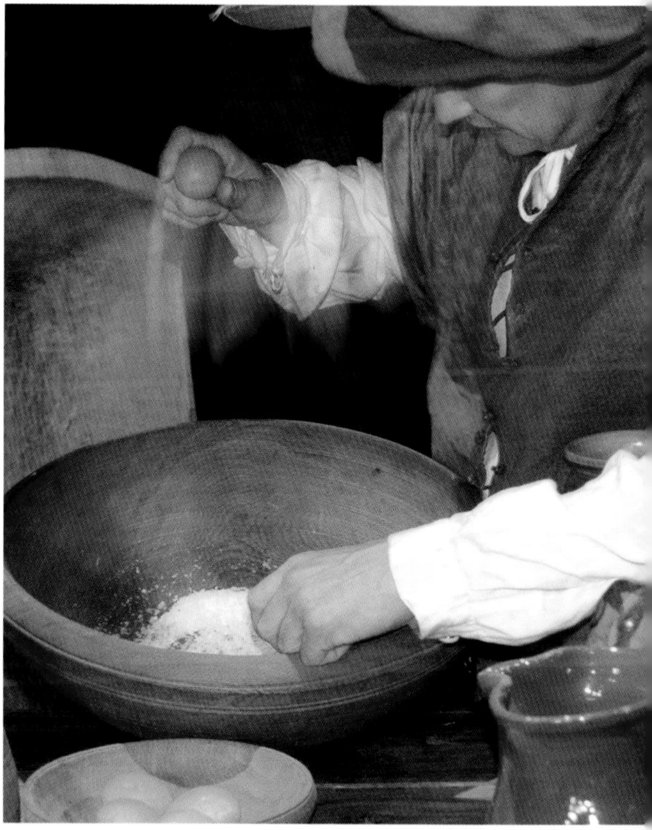

The cook was probably the most important individual as far as maintaining good morale on board. Here a re-enactor uses replicas of culinary equipment found on *Mary Rose*.

> no wind for the windmills, he foresaw water-mills, since biscuit there must be. He controlled bake-houses, breweries, foundries, tanneries, smithies. He planned for pilots and surgeons, hutments and docks. He ordered dry cod, ling, cheese, beef and bacon. Trinity House and the College of Physicians were, in a sense, his war-babies. He personally signed contracts for everything from twenty-five thousand fat oxen for salting to the hire of fourteen mares to haul a culverin.[1]

Richard Fox, the Bishop of Winchester, as Lord Privy Seal, had some idea of the strain under which Wolsey was operating. Writing to him on 12 May 1513, he said:

> I pray God send us with speed, and soon deliver you of your outrageous charges and labour; and else you shall have a cold stomach, little sleep, pale visage and a thin belly, *cum rora degestione,* all of which, and as deaf as a stock, I had when I was in your case.[2]

Wolsey grew fat on the challenge and although those for whom he catered might have gained thin bellies, he provisioned the fleet well enough to keep it in being. Although it mewled for more when it did not arrive as expected, Wolsey, like a stern parent, fed this newborn creation when he judged it needed to be fed, not generously but with a sufficiency to keep it alive. The opportunities for failure in this unprecedented commitment were legion, and many lessons had to be learned, including the need for a great deal of money. Yet Wolsey avoided failure, found the money when it was needed, and kept the fleet, for the most part, as a fit and fighting force.

That the Master Almoner was personally responsible for this provision gives another indication as to the importance that Henry place upon this task. Under Wolsey came special commissioners, who set the rate to be paid for provisions and decided which brewers and bakers were to be used. They were required to deliver provisions to the quayside where each ship's purser had to pay for them and get them moved on board. The deliveries to which they were entitled were the staples: baked biscuit, beef and beer with salted fish, butter and cheese. These were generally delivered in barrels (or foysts), and accounted for by the 'pipe'[3] and, if there was a shortfall, the shore staff could always blame those on board for not returning the empties. Fox, in the letter quoted earlier, informed Wolsey that, 'John Dawtry wants empty pipes for the beer, and I fear that the pursers will deserve hanging for this matter.'[4]

In 1512 a victualling allowance of five shillings a month was made for each of the 411 men on board *Mary Rose.* This, at twelve pence to the shilling, worked out at two pence a day, which may seem extraordinarily little for the provision of two daily meals. The present allowance for seagoing ships in the Royal Navy is about £2.20; in prisons it stands at about £1.20, while recent political debate and a popular television programme has focused on increasing the allowance for one school meal a day to fifty pence per pupil per day.[5] Two pence for very active, fully grown men may seem inadequate but if the accepted multiplier of 300 is applied to equate with today's prices then it would seem that the victualling allowance was equivalent to a healthy £3 per day, a more than adequate amount. It was certainly sufficient to enrich the commissioners, one of whom, John Dawtry, has left evidence of his wealth in the very fine Tudor house that he had built in Southampton.

Yet, if men like Dawtry became rich, there is no evidence to suggest that they did not pass sufficient food on to the fleet; rather it was the failure of the logistics train to deliver that was to cause the greatest problems. The allowance that Dawtry was commanded to deliver meant that the men should have been provided with the following weekly rations: 7lb of biscuits; 8lb of salt beef; ¾lb of stock fish; ⅜lb of butter; ¾lb of cheese and seven gallons of beer. This was based on a twenty-eight-day month with half rations on Fridays. In a letter from William Cecil, Lord Burghley, to the Privy Council more than 60 years later, the issue of rations is further itemised as shown in the following table:

Weekday rations breakdown

Day	Description	Allowance per person
Sunday	Flesh Day	1lb biscuit; 1 gallon beer; 2lbs of salt beef
Monday		1lb of bacon; 2 pints of peas
Tuesday	Flesh Day	1lb biscuit; 1 gallon beer; 2lbs of salt beef
Wednesday	Fish Day	1lb biscuit; 1 gallon beer; 1 qtr stockfish *or* an 8th part of a ling; 1 qtr lb cheese; 1 qtr lb butter
Thursday	Flesh Day	1lb biscuit; 1 gallon beer; 2lbs of salt beef
Friday	Fish Day	Half Rations
Saturday	Fish Day	lb biscuit; 1 gallon beer; 1 qtr stockfish *or* an 8th part of a ling; 1 qtr lb cheese; 1 qtr lb butter

A half-ration day seems an ominous prospect and scarcely the sort of policy to encourage the happiness of the crew, especially when, given the unpredictable exigencies of life at sea, Friday could have been a day of great demand on a ship's company's energy. Logic would suggest that this was in fact the day when the cook was encouraged to use up the left-overs from earlier in the week and to produce a tasty, nutritious stew so that Friday's fare was actually something to look forward to. It would also have given the purser an opportunity to dispose of the produce from less well-preserved barrels.

Nine barrels raised from *Mary Rose* contained a large quantity of cattle bones from immature animals whose carcasses were halved and with joints cut to a standard size. The distribution of similar joints from different animals within separate barrels suggests a consistent butchery technique. It would also appear that produce susceptible to rapid decay, such as marrow bones or offal, were deliberately excluded. There was just one barrel of pig bones but several dozen carcasses were found on the orlop deck just forward of the galley. Elsewhere, there were indications of the storage of both mutton and venison. Fish, mainly cod, was plentiful and appears to have been both dried and salted. Fresh fruit was also present, as indicated by the discovery of numerous plum stones in the wreck, while peppercorns show that the food was also spiced.

It would be wrong to imagine that the official diet (*see* table above) represents the sole intake of the crew. The hinterland of Portsea Island was an area of market gardens and, given the difficulties of transport, it would have been in the local farmers' interest to sell their produce to the navy. The pursers would have been approached regularly by farmers wishing to sell their produce, especially in an age before

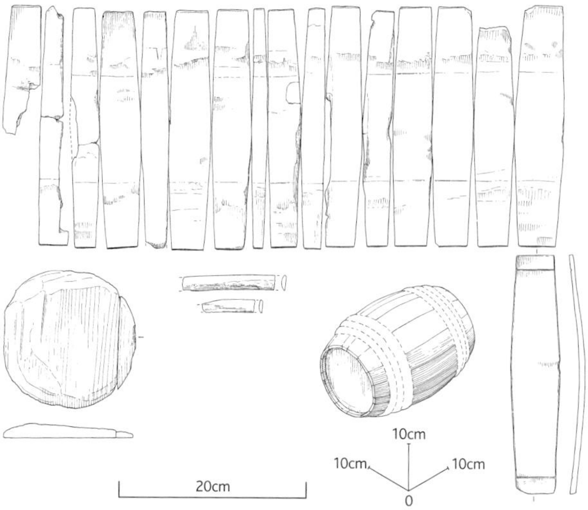

Some of the many barrel parts found on board. Most supplies, dry and wet, were delivered in barrels and the stowage and return of empty ones a major problem.

refrigeration or even cold rooms enabled decent storage to take place. And not on the quayside alone would the sales have taken place, for boats would have been hired, or even owned by those farmers to take their produce around the fleet. An archeological audit of victuals on board *Mary Rose* can only report on what was present and identifiable at one moment on one summer day. Every ship that has ever sailed has been meticulous in 'ditching the gash' – throwing overboard its waste on a regular basis. To fail to do so not only filled extremely cramped conditions with useless garbage but also, as far as un-bagged and stinking foodstuffs were concerned, created an unpleasant health hazard. One can be fairly certain that, by the time she sailed towards the French in July 1545, *Mary Rose* had rid herself of her garbage, which would have included things such as vegetable peelings and bones.

Much of the food available would have been seasonal, for very little could be kept fresh without salting, which would have been inappropriate for fruit and vegetables. In July the ship could have expected to take delivery of plums, but not apples or pears, and some seasonal greens. The main harvest of fruit was still some months away. Thus the absence of evidence of a richer diet does not imply that additional items other than those uncovered did not supplement the sailor's diet. The statutory provisions for the fleet also reflect the prejudice of the governing classes. To them, vegetables, with their proximity to the earth, were not suitable fare for the gentry who thus preferred meat and game. In 1539, Sir Thomas Elyot wrote in his *Castel of Helth* that fruits were: 'noyfulle to man and do ingender ylle humours, and be oftetymes the cause of putrified fevers, if they be moche and continually eaten.'[7] Henry and his court ate much and often but not well. His sailors probably ate more moderately and healthily.

Those seamen would have been brought up on a diet that included a variety of herbs and wild plants – the traditional fare of those excluded from the main markets by virtue of poverty. It made for a wonderfully tasty and healthy cuisine and it was food for free. As an example, two major coastal wild crops that would have enhanced the diet and enriched it with vitamins would have been scurvy grass and samphire. Both would have been available in abundance in the salt marshes of Portsea and the latter would have been a most tasty supplement. The seventeenth-century herbalist, Nicholas Culpepper describes it as, '...a safe herb, very pleasant both to taste and stomach, helps digestion, and in some sort opening obstructions of the liver and spleen'.[8] While the gentry were developing a taste for expensive spices the poorer kept healthier by the use of traditional and free herbs whose uses and properties would have been far better known by them than by those responsible for their victualling at sea.

Shellfish would have been similarly available for free and in large quantities. Hungry sailors within reach of dietary supplements such as cockles and mussels would not have sat idle, bemoaning their fate. Once their ship was anchored close inshore, foraging for whelks, mussels, oysters, shrimps, crabs and other crustaceans would have taken place while, given the opportunity, any wader, water fowl, indeed any bird, would have been snared. This was an age when if it moved it was eaten. Upper-class sensitivities would have meant that these excellent supplements would not have been tasted by the officers. Their own diet might have been more varied, occasionally more exotic, but, on the whole probably not as wholesome. The idea that the officers ate better is a common one but it is probably not true measured by either calorific or vitamin intake. A well-fed sailor is a happy sailor and it is certainly not possible to work a ship with hungry hands.

There was one other source of wholesome seafood available to the Tudor seaman that is far less plentiful today – freshly caught fish. In the sixteenth century the seas around Britain were some of the richest in the world, with vast shoals of mackerel and herring present in both the Channel and the North Sea. Fishing tackle was carried for this purpose and a hook dangled over the side would have soon rewarded the angler. Even when underway, the slow speed of the ship through the water would not have hindered fishing. All that was then needed was for the catch to be taken below to the galley.

On first appearances the galley in *Mary Rose* appears to contain two very basic types of cooking vessels. These consist of a large copper cauldron, with a lead rim, suspended over what could best be described as a cuboid brick barbecue oven. The cauldrons are huge. They are built around a small base widening out from which are eight overlapping panels of copper alloy, attached by copper rivets. They were supported over the brick firebox by wrought-iron bars and at the top affixed to the brickwork by means of a leaden lip. The whole structure was about 2m long, 1.5m wide and 1m high. The ovens were located at the bottom of the ship, which gives rise to the important question of how heat and fire were controlled within a wooden vessel. At the bottom end, over the keel, it is assumed that the ovens were bricked over a base of ballast which would have prevented heat travelling down to the hull timbers. Above the cauldrons there appears to have been no flue to draw away the heat. Instead, the hot air emerging from the arches of the furnaces simply rose through a partitioned shaft on the orlop deck and then through the hatches to the upper deck.

The reconstructed galley at work in Portsmouth Historic Dockyard, showing the 'dangle-spit' in operation.

Heat in a wooden warship can, in wintry seas, be a precious commodity and there is every reason to suppose that the sailors on board *Mary Rose* congregated around the furnaces whenever they were off watch and in need of drying out. Not only does common sense suggest this but the record supports it. A document of 1618 describes reasons for moving the cook rooms away from their traditional position in the hold. These include that the heat caused the oakum (that formed the caulking between the planks to keep the ship watertight) to dry up and spew out, and also that the cook rooms took up a great deal of the area that could be used for storing victuals, requiring his Majesty to hire additional transporters at great expense. But, and perhaps this was the main reason; 'The cook room draws much company to the hold, both out of sight and far from their labour.'[9]

It can be assumed then that the officers were reluctant for the men to congregate down below and out of sight in a place where the soporific warmth of the galley and the gentler motion lower down in the hold could breed mischief and spread rumour and, of course, rock those who might be expected to be alert, to sleep. Even today naval tradition holds fast to the idea that all rumours emanate from the galley. But modern galleys have banned the other major activity that would have taken place down here at the warm core of the ship: the drying out of clothing and soggy leather footwear – it would not have been only gossip that hummed in that atmosphere.

The logs that fuelled the furnaces were mainly of birch and *Mary Rose* carried almost 1000 of these cut into three-foot lengths, ideal not only for throwing to someone while loading the ship, but also for wedging into the furnace so that they would stay put in the fire when the ship rolled. How the galley itself worked once fired up remained a point of conjecture until Christopher Dobbs, the Trust's maritime archaeologist, reconstructed one in 1999 using the evidence from the ship and supported by a detailed inventory for 'Repairs to the Kitchen' of *Sovereign* in 1513. The rebuilt galley was as authentic as it was possible to be, with the right-sized bricks, the same mortar mix and, of course, a cauldron of the same materials and capacity. The latter was found to be 600 litres but with an operational capacity of about 350–400 litres. Whether, given the scarcity of water on board and the difficulties of replenishing it, the liquid within the cauldron was ever used for making

The steaming cauldron on the top of the reconstructed galley.

Some of the galley equipment recovered from the ship.

a broth to be ladled out to the ship's company is debatable. Instead, when the water was heated it was shown to be possible to cook a variety of meals by floating pottery cooking jars within it. Peas or other greens would have been wrapped in muslin or other fabric, and in fact whole meals for individual 'messes' could have been prepared in this way. It was also possible to roast meat by the simple expedient of using a 'dangle-spit' whereby joints were suspended from a bar above the furnace arch. Full use of the differing temperatures would allow for other cooking activities, such as the baking of bread, to take place at the same time, an assumption supported by the discovery of three bread troughs in the wreck. The fact that the ship had two cauldrons might indicate that they were fired up alternately, with the one that was cooling being used for bread making. Today, one of the most popular attractions during major festivals in Portsmouth Historic Dockyard is the operation of the recreated galley from the *Mary Rose* which, once lit, fires up both food and the imagination.

Although victualling the navy has always been regarded by some as a way of making extra money at the expense of the poor sailor, the archaeolgocial evidence would suggest that the crew of *Mary Rose* was well catered for. An analysis of the bones of the crew by Dr Ann Stirland of University College London indicated that, although many showed signs of having suffered from dietary deficiencies in childhood, there was very little evidence of such problems affecting them as adults.[10] Indeed, it would seem that they were healthier than many of their contemporaries ashore where famine was still to be experienced during the sixteenth century. The main reason for this would have been the short duration of any voyage and the ability to return to a home port for victualling. But generally, less crowded conditions and a galley that could serve a whole range of hot food would have made a major contribution to maintaining a healthy crew.

Of course, there were setbacks. It is only to be expected that illnesses were present on board Tudor ships, and in 1545 the fleet in Portsmouth suffered a severe outbreak of dysentery and plague. However, we are, occasionally, guilty of forgetting how quickly an infection can spread on board even a modern vessel. A quick glance through recent news archives will reveal stories of modern cruise liners having to put into port because salmonella or gastric enteritis or some such ailment has stricken the passengers. It is probably also true that instances of disease on board royal ships were far more likely to be recorded, while similar outbreaks among civilians in towns and villages – unless of plague or similar proportion – passed by unheeded. The state of teeth is also a good indicator of the adequacy of diet and those from the skeletal remains of the crew of *Mary Rose* have been examined by a group of dentists from Birmingham University Dental School. They found that her ship's company had better matching teeth and dental arches than their modern-day counterparts. There was, however, more significant wear, which indicates a coarser diet. This implies the consumption of more roughage and thus, in one important respect, a better diet. However, their pattern of tooth decay was surprisingly modern. This suggests that they could have had a significant intake of a sweet substance. The use of sugar was not widespread at the time so this could have been honey or some other substance that has left no archaeological traces. Whatever caused this decay it was sufficiently widespread to indicate that at least ten per cent of the crew could have had toothache at any one time.[11]

The adequacy of the crew's diet did not depend solely on the quality and range of goods supplied but also on the timely replenishment of victuals. This was one area that took many years to master, much to the dismay of Henry's admirals. In March 1513, Edward Howard made it very clear to Wolsey that he had been forced to depart for France before his pursers could victual their ships. To reinforce his need for supplies he then wrote to the king on 22 March:

> Sir, for God's sake, haste your Council to send us down our victual, for if we lie long here, the commonest voice will run that we lie and keep in the Downs and do no good but spend money and victual, and so the noise will run to our shame...[12]

Once at Plymouth, Howard kept up the demand for better victualling, writing to Wolsey:

> ...I assure you was never army so falsely victualed. They that received their proportion for two months' flesh cannot bring about for five weeks, for the barrels be full of salt: and when the pieces keepeth the number, where they should be penny pieces they be scant halfpenny pieces, and where two pieces should make a mess, three will do but serve. Also, many came out of Thames but with a month's beer, trusting that the victualers should bring the rest, and here cometh none.[13]

Howard was even forced to give some of his own beer supply to the *Katherine Fortileza* leaving *Mary Rose* so short that he had to send to Plymouth for more, which he paid for out of his own pocket. At the same time he drummed home to Wolsey that it was useless the latter protesting that half the fleet was well provisioned when the other half was not:

> Sir, if some be well victualled, the most part be not; and you know well, if half should lack, it were as good in a manner that all lacked, in consideration to keep the army together.[14]

That sentiment is a key component in both good management and the maintenance of morale. Servicemen will, together, endure any hardship as a united body if they know that all are suffering equal deprivation. It is the knowledge that some might be better off that causes morale to plummet. Howard was establishing here Drake's idea that all be of one company and was endeavouring to drive the message home to gentlemen in England in far more comfortable and safer conditions. Howard's decision to leave his pursers ashore in London, in the unrealised hope that they could hasten the delivery of victuals, meant that neither he nor his ship's captains knew the true condition of their stores. Eventually he was forced to come up with several suggestions to ease the situation. Firstly, he proposed that providers all along the coast be commissioned to bake and brew so that the fleet could be kept on station. He then suggested that the provisions be brought to Dartmouth for collection and that Spanish ships be ordered to bring further provisions down from Sandwich.

It was not only the inadequacies of the supply chain that worried Howard, parsimony was another fear. In a letter to the king dated 12 April he wrote:

> And if victual serve us, as your men and ships are determined, we shall this year make a bare coast of all the realm of France that boundeth on the sea coast, which shall never recover it in our days. Therefore, for no cost sparing, let the provision be made, for it is a well spent penny that saveth the pound, for...was wont to be spent in 3 or 4 year on the sea with one expense now, we shall do more good than in 4 year by driblet.[15]

A fortnight after the letter quoted above was written Edward Howard was killed in action and his brother, Lord Thomas Howard, was appointed as his successor. He was to find himself in command of a fleet where the lack of victuals was making a significant contribution to very low morale for, as he reported to the king, his captains and noblemen when asked: '...answered with one whole voice and in one tale...they had great default of victual, and had not in their board for 3 days.'[16]

The victuallers that had been sent from London, and those gathered at Dartmouth, seemed to have made no effort to move the supplies onwards to the fleet which was, therefore, obliged to come to them. Wolsey carefully avoided taking responsibility for this lapse, writing to Thomas Howard on 25 May 1513:

> My lord, I assure you it is not possible to furnish your revictualling if Foists [barrels] be not more plenteously brought from the navy to Hampton than they be, which is a great lack and default, for ye cannot be provided elsewhere of any foists for money. And if the foists amongst the navy be not kept and reserved, but wastefully burnt and broken as I hear say they be, ye cannot be sufficiently revictualled to tarry any longer on the sea, for whereas ships have received 10 weeks past 756 pipes, they have redelivered scantly 80 foists of them. What as it appeareth is done by some lewd persons that would not have the King's navy continue any longer on the Sea. And therefore, My lord, for God's sake, look well to this matter so that such substantial order may be taken that the empty foists may be continually rescued...[17]

Wolsey's letter contains just the necessary suggestion of treachery and incompetence that would make a new commander very aware of his precarious position on the rickety career ladder up which the servants of Henry had to climb and jostle. Wolsey's threat worked for, on 8 June, Thomas Howard wrote to the Privy Council about both bows, arrows and foists:

> And as touching the receiving of bows and arrows, I shall see them as little wasted as shall be possible. And where your lordships

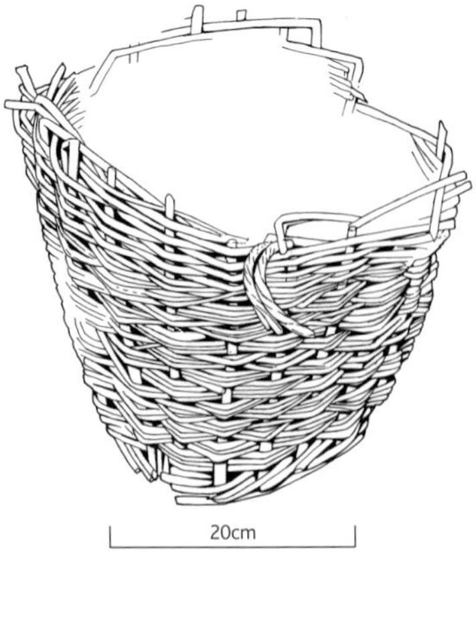

A basket used for delivering items such as fish and bread. The contents would have had to be carefully stored on board to avoid rat and other pest infestation.

write that it is great marvelled where so great a number of bows and arrows be brought to so small a number, I have enquired the causes thereof: and, as far as I can see, the greatest number were witch bows, of whom few would abide the bending. But as for that was done before my time, I cannot call again, but from henceforth, if I do not the best I can to keep everything from waste, I am worthy blame, which I trust I shall not deserve.

> And as touching the safe keeping of foists, assuredly, before my coming was great waste, and since my coming I trust few or never one hath been wasted, nor shall be.[18]

– thereby exonerating Wolsey, blaming his brother and, most importantly, shouldering the blame for future shortfalls: out-manoeuvered before he had scarcely been to sea! Wolsey, of course, was sure of his facts. Some weeks earlier, on 21 May, John Dawtry at Southampton, had written to inform him that the correct number of empty foists were not being returned and that he suspected that many were being burned.[19]

Few lessons appear to have been learned from these episodes. Nine years later Thomas Howard, now the Earl of Surrey, writing to the king from on board *Mary Rose* was still complaining along much the same lines as formerly:

> ...your grace is deceived for the furniture of victuals for your army, where it was promised that by the last day of May we should have had the whole complement for 5,000 men from Portsmouth of beer and from Hampton of all other victual, with much difficulty we be furnished now, which is the 20 day of June, from Hampton of flesh, fish and biscuit for the said two months, and from Portsmouth by no means we can have none than for one month of beer. And where the Vice-admiral was promised before this day to have had his whole complement, none of his ships have full furniture of all victuals passing three weeks, and of those right few, and some but for 8 days, and for the most part not passing 14 days...And where all their doubts hitherto hath been ever for lack of casks for the beer, I cannot perceive but that they be as far or further behind them with flesh, biscuit and fish as with beer, wherein I think there is some negligence. Most humbly beseeching your grace to consider that it shall not be possible for me and the company here to accomplish all that we be determined to attempt unless we be better furnished with victuals.[20]

But Surrey did not simply complain; he suggested improvements or made them himself. He invited the king to send some 'substantial man' to go to London 'for the hasting forth of that is there' and to send another 'wise man to Portsmouth for to see diligence used for the beer there.'[21]

Beer was to become a major business for Portsmouth, but in the early days of the standing navy this was not so. In the orders for setting forth the king's army for the sea the towns ordered to provide both beer and ale[22] are those close to London, which indicates the dominance of the capital and its environs at the time. This dominance, as far as the creation of an effective standing navy and its support was concerned, needed to be reduced so that administration alone remained within the capital. Transporting beer was a costly and damaging process for both beer and barrels. Leakage and spillage had to be compensated for by the existence of a brewer's dozen of anything between thirteen and fifteen barrels. It was much better for the breweries to be established close to their market.

Portsmouth had always taken its production of ale seriously. One of the first officers of the town had been the ale-taster who had to supervise brewing, see that no extra-strength ale was brewed and that none was sold in 'unstamped' measures. This arrangement was sufficient for the needs of the fifteenth-century citizens of a town with just one brew-house, but it was insufficient for the needs of a standing navy so, in 1513, Henry ordered four more breweries to be built. These, the 'Lyon', 'Dragon', 'White Hart', and 'Rose', were built in the area around Penny and Nicholas Streets near where St. Jude's School presently stands. They are shown clearly on a map of Portsmouth dated 1540[23] and in the Cowdray engraving[24] grouped around a pond of fresh water, a precious commodity in low lying and marshy Portsea Island. As well as being used for brewing the

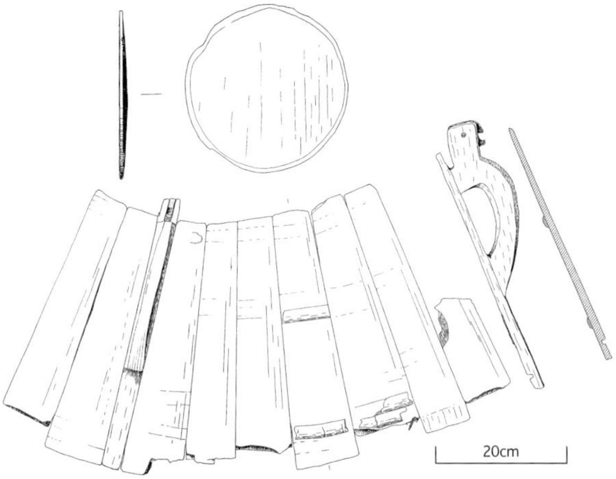

Wooden tankards were built up of staves, like barrels.

pond had many other domestic uses, such as laundering, which would have provided a distinct additional flavour to the brew.

Even so, a gallon of beer would have provided a sailor with about half his daily requirement of calories, many of the essential nutrients to keep him healthy, and a good dose of Vitamin B. Far from being a luxury, it was the stuff of life itself on board. Along with the new breweries, two new bakehouses named 'Ye Anker' and 'Ye Swan' were also established to produce both bread and biscuit for the fleet. Portsmouth's development as a fleet victualling yard was underway. Once the town had commenced brewing on a significant scale it rapidly established a good reputation. Thomas Howard was certainly impressed, writing in June 1513 to the Privy Council:

> Here is the goodliest sort of brewhouses that I ever saw and already do brew 100 tons a day. And the great pity is were it that there should not provision be made shortly to ship the same. Also, the beer is put in the vessels, there is no houses to lay it in, but are fain to lay it abroad in the street, where now, the weather coming on, it shall shortly be destroyed. Wherefore, I have commanded William Pawne to cause great trenches to be digged and to be covered with some boards, turves, sedges and such stuff as may be gotten to keep the heat therefrom. Also the beer that came hither for my Lord Lisle is such as no man may drink for the most part. As much as may be drunk is delivered to the ships, and the rest I shall send again to London. I know not what the King payeth but I assure your lordships much of it is as small as penny ale, and as sour as crab. I doubt not that your lordship will see the brewers punished...[25]

The month in which this letter was written is significant, for summer beer did not keep as well as that brewed in March or October which could last all year. Of course, these good-quality, enduring beers were the more expensive and generally provided to wealthier customers. The sailors' beer had to be wholesome and refreshing and, as in the warm months copious amounts would be needed to slake their thirst, not too strong. Howard's action in digging up the roads seems a novel way of creating storage trenches but one with which many motorists today might be in sympathy. His desire to bring retribution on the brewers of bad ale would be one with which every sailor would be in sympathy but Portsmouth seemed determined not to be found wanting.

Other brewers were not so lucky. In May 1513 the Privy Council received a slightly irate letter from a Nic Kirkehn who had interests in West Country brewing.[26] He complained that Howard had ordered the fleet not to purchase oaten malt brewed in the west as it did not keep as well as barley malt, although the sailors had drunk copious amounts of it without complaint. On other occasions the weather forced the fleet to unexpectedly return to or tarry at anchorages, resulting in considerable pressure on local brewers to increase their output.

Timely provisioning of both food and beer remained the bugbear affecting fleet operations throughout *Mary Rose*'s career. Surrey, always determined to prove that he was desirous of action, even if hampered by incompetent victuallers, demonstrated this in a letter to Wolsey penned from the Bay of Morlaix in July 1522:

> I report me unto your grace, notwithstanding undoubtedly as soon as we shall have wind to depart hence and to draw beyond the Trade we shall not fail to do so, and shall not return as long as we have any beer left, though in our return we should drink water.[27]

Although a few days without beer, especially if it was on the homeward run, might not seem too harsh a condition for even the most drunken sailor, this was, however, a life-threatening proposition. The reason so much beer was taken on voyages and poured out at a gallon a day was that it was far safer to drink than water. The latter came in barrels from unchecked and unpurified sources and soon became contaminated so that, by the time the fleet was ready to make its return voyage, the water would have been dangerous as well as unpleasant to drink. Howard was threatening to take a great risk with his sailors' health. The brewing process kept the bacteria at bay, and beer lasted better than water. Reducing this beneficial effect through watering the beer was a very serious offence, although the full strength of the original was not necessarily that great. If it had been powerful stuff then, on a ration of a gallon a day, the fleet would have been manned by sailors in various degrees of stupor and there is no evidence of that. In fact, drunkenness was always viewed as a serious offence and a threat to good order and naval discipline. Getting the crew drunk and then punishing them for being inebriated would not have been a great example of man management. By way of comparison, the modern naval rating is rationed to three cans, or just over one-and-a-half pints a day.

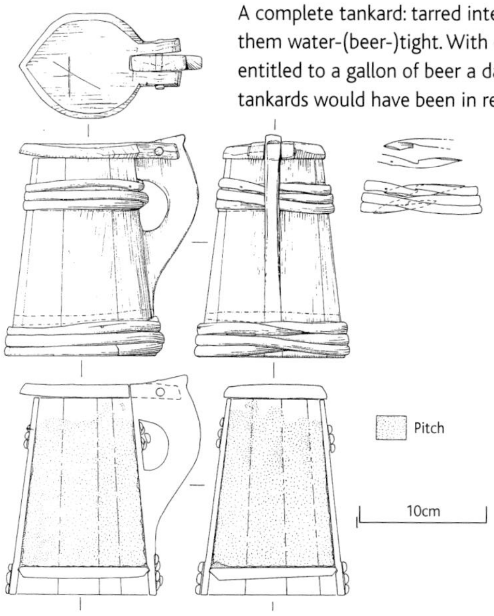

A complete tankard: tarred interiors kept them water-(beer-)tight. With each man entitled to a gallon of beer a day these tankards would have been in regular use.

Having a gallon of beer a day on board in no way curtailed the sailors' desire for drinking when they came ashore. Once on land, and after several rounds of drink, there often followed the boisterous behaviour for which sailors the world over have become renowned. The crew of *Mary Rose* was no exception and in June 1539 several men appeared before the Admiralty Court to account for their conduct. The court record gives a rare insight into the behaviour of the ordinary matelot.[28] The case was brought by a Portuguese pilot, Gonsalianus Cassado and a trader, Petro Falcon, who were on board the 'good ship' *Saynte John de Cangas in Galicia* while she was at anchor at St Katherine's Pool in London. They alleged that at midnight, while all the crew except two boys were asleep below decks, six or seven sailors had boarded her. The boys were driven below by being beaten with the 'flatlong part' of the sailors' swords and everyone else was kept below by the threat of violence. The sailors had then spent an hour looting the ship. Their haul included a valuable mix of northern cloth, kersey, broadcloth and second-hand shirts as well as sundry other items, indicating an opportunistic raid rather than an act of serious theft. The raiders threw these items into their boat and departed, but not before casting off the ship's

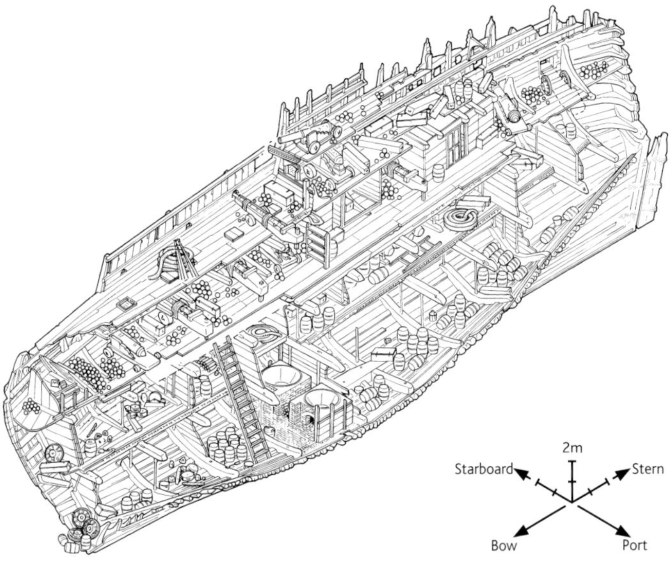

A view of the surviving hull structure showing where the various finds would have been placed. The twin brick cooking ranges are a major feature in the hold.

boat so that they could not be pursued. The morning revealed that it had not been a totally successful sally, however. The thieves, landing in the oozy river mud, had been forced to leave some of the haul behind from where it was recovered on the north shore opposite Greenwich. Nevertheless sufficient had been taken for the merchants to report the incident.

How the deed was traced back to the crew of *Mary Rose* is not stated but, given the farcical nature of the event one could almost believe it was through following a trail of muddy footprints. Be that as it may, several crew members were hauled up to be examined. On the June evening in question *Mary Rose* was lying at anchor off Deptford. After supper on board a sailor named Richard Baker and three of his messmates decided to go ashore and 'make merry at an honest man's house'. Baker was a Londoner and so probably knew where good ale was to be had. Anyway, by 10pm they had had enough and wandered back to the river's edge to hail the ship for a boat. Baker states that when they got no response they used their initiative, well whetted by ale, and decided to 'borrow' a wherry and row themselves back. The craft they selected had no oars but a couple of spars seemed an ideal substitute. Jumping on board they pushed off and managed to bump alongside the *Mary Rose's* boat, which was lying astern of their ship. However, a strong tide swept them away and carried them downstream where they fetched up against the hull of a 'Portingale' merchant ship.

According to Baker, the crew of the merchant ship did not welcome their fellow tars but instead flung stones down upon them breaking open the head of his shipmate, William Oram. This hostile act elicited a response and the English seamen boarded the Portuguese vessel, fell about their assailants with flat swords and drove them between decks. Honour satisfied, they made their way ashore and all, bar one, managed to turn up for work on time the next day. However, the story becomes a bit complicated when the statement of another of the party, Robert Grygges, was heard. According to Grygges, having found themselves the worse for drink and lying against the anchor hawse of the Portuguese ship, one of the company said, 'Vengeance on him, here lyeth a Portingale,' at which call to arms two of their number, Oram and Baker, had boarded the ship and were followed, after cries were heard, by their fellows coming to their rescue. Somehow, and Grygges knew not how, some bits of cloth had been cast into the wherry, but there had been no intention to steal them. This was why they had been thrown on the mud where the men of Greenwich, alerted by the cries from the ship, had found them. The mud-smeared Grygges then fell asleep in a hay barn at St Katherine's, leaving there around 10am the next day. His memory of the night's events was distinctly hazy, but he did remember Oram having been hurt. He could not recall when this had happened and, no, they were not all armed, having just one sword and a short knife, called a 'matchan', with them.

Sadly, we do not know the outcome of the enquiry, nor is the evidence of the other witnesses extant. But the tale is certainly rich enough without these missing details! The contradictory evidence, the protestations of injured innocence, the blaming it on the drink, all are vividly conveyed – as they are today at many a captain's table or Magistrates' Court.

CHAPTER 8

'A Noble Man Ill Lost'

By 1511 Henry had been handed the excuse that he needed to justify going to war with France. The papacy, disgruntled that a joint pillaging expedition against Venice had left its partner, Louis XII of France, with the greater share of the spoils, had decided that such behaviour was an affront to Christianity. Ferdinand of Aragon, the pope's fellow aggrieved ally – he wanted to seize French Navarre for himself – saw advantage in encouraging his son-in-law to join a Holy Alliance against France. Henry had never made a secret of his bellicose aspirations and antipathy toward France. In August 1509 the abbot of Fécamp – described disparagingly as 'a fat man' – came to Henry as the ambassador from France to confirm peace between the two countries only for Henry to respond: 'I, ask peace of the King of France; who daren't look at me, let alone make war![1]

Whatever Henry's intentions towards France, he would need to keep one eye on the Scots. In June

Symbolising the threat from north of the border, James IV of Scotland built a huge carrack called the *Great Michael* of which this is a model. Inspiring the English king to build his *Henri Grace à Dieu*, the Scottish ship proved too expensive to keep, and was sold, after James's death at Flodden in 1514, to the French, having grounded on their coast. It replaced *Cordeliére* and was thereafter known as *Nef d'Ecosse*.

1509 he received information that: 'The King of Scots is having artillery made here, for field and ship, and buying harness...It is rumoured that they intend to attack England.[2]

James IV of Scotland was actively seeking support from the French at Dieppe to assist with his own shipbuilding programme. An arms race was getting underway and Henry was purchasing weaponry both from domestic and foreign suppliers. Artillery was ordered from Flanders while, in England, agents were sent into the shires to procure bows and sheaves of arrows and to place orders for hemp for bowstrings.[3] The political build-up to war also continued apace and was well reported. Rumour and report abounded in this age when every head of state had his spies in the field. Henry's treaty intentions, the number of troops he planned to put into the field and the gains that he hoped to make all appear to have been common knowledge.

In 1511, with the increased harassment of English shipping, Hopton was dispatched to hunt down the pirates whose activities so often presaged war. Edward Howard also volunteered to track down another pirate who was preying on English shipping, the Scottish privateer, Sir Edward Barton, who had been plaguing merchants trading with the Low Countries.

In 1512 the alliances that Henry needed to give him the confidence to challenge France were formed. The king's main partner was to be his father-in-law, Ferdinand of Aragon, who undertook – supported by an English contingent – to invade southern France and take Navarre. In return, Henry was to regain control over Gascony, that low-lying, wine-producing and fertile land that stretched from the Gironde to Bayonne on the Spanish border, and had once been ruled by his forebears. There is no doubt that Henry was considered the junior partner in this alliance, from whom much could be demanded and little returned. Of course, this was not how the optimistic, bellicose and gullible English king saw things, but at this time he was no match for the experienced and wily Ferdinand. The plan was for an English force of some 12,000 men, under the Marquess of Dorset, to sail to Guyenne, link up with the Spanish and march on Bayonne. While this was taking place Henry's new navy was to be mobilised to take control of the Channel and to seek out and destroy the French fleet and its allied merchant shipping.

The navy might have been new to the idea of mobilisation but the reaction was good. On 25 January 1512 parliament agreed that war should be made on the French king: by 29 February orders had been issued for 'setting forth of the King's army of the sea'. These included:

> (i) Indentures and instructions to be devised for the admiral and treasure won (half the prizes were to be reserved for the king).
> (ii) The appointment of a substantial person in every ship to oversee the king's victuals and control their expenditure by a rate delivered to them.
> (iii) The indenture of the captains of every ship with the king.
> (iv) Mariners coming to Greenwich to be assigned what ships they shall go in; bursars to note their day of entry and to provide pay and victuals till their setting forth.
> (v) Number and portage of the ships to be determined and the number of deadshares [a paper increase in crew numbers in order to boost their wages] and their allotment to the crews.
> (vi) Ascertaining the number of guns of every sort and the amount of shot and powder necessary; also the number of bows, arrows, bowstrings, 'man pikes' and bills, and that 'a substantial man may be appointed in every ship to have charge of them'.[4]

The troops were also to be given 'conduct money' of 6d a day to cover their expenses from their homes to the place of shipment. This was based on a day's journey of twelve miles, which gives some idea of the state of the English roads and also why, whenever invasion threatened, it was necessary to gain good intelligence as to either the intended place of landing,

The Anthony Roll illustration of *Peter Pomegranate*, *Mary Rose*'s smaller consort that was part of the fleet mobilised in 1512.

in the case of the French, or the site of the border crossing, in the case of the Scots. Get either of these badly wrong and the defending forces could be rapidly outmanoeuvred.

The arrangements for the ships were supervised by Edward Howard, who authorised payments for ordnance and other necessary equipment, but it was not until 7 April that he was formally appointed as admiral of a fleet of eighteen ships of which:

> The said Admiral shall have under him in the said service 3000 men harnessed and arrayed for the war, himself accounted in the said number, over and above 700 soldiers, mariners, and gunners that shall be in the king's ship called the *Regent*. Of which 3,000, 18 shall be Captains, 1750 shall be soldiers, 1237 shall be mariners and gunners. The said Admiral shall have for the maintenance of himself and his diets, wages, and rewards daily, during the voyage 10s.; and for ever one of the said Captains, for their diets, wages, and rewards, daily, during the said time 18d. except they be of the number of the King's Spears, which shall be contented with ordinary wages.[5]

The mariners, soldiers and gunner were to be paid five shillings a month with the same amount being made available for their victuals. Naval service, and therefore wages, was reckoned to begin on 17 April, and on 16 April the king approved the sending of £6,000 to John Dawtry in Southampton for him to provide victuals. Of Howard's fleet only three vessels, *Regent*, *Mary Rose* and *Peter Pomegranate*, were the king's own, and of these Howard selected the newer but smaller *Mary Rose* to be his flagship in preference over *Regent* which was, in fact, not yet ready for sea. The remainder of the fleet consisted of armed merchantmen. Nevertheless, it is possible to see this deployment as the starting point of the navy royal, the birth of that greatness which was to become the Royal Navy.

The plan for the naval ships was for Edward Howard to keep the Channel clear of French warships so that the Earl of Dorset's expeditionary force, which he was to escort as far as Ushant, could sail unimpeded to Spain. Thereafter, Howard was to cruise between Brest (the Trade) and Calais, seizing all that the war made it legitimate, or excusable, for him to seize.

The French were aware of these preparations but were dismissive of the English force, Margaret of Savoy being informed that:

> Of the English there is no great talk. It is assumed that the King of England still wishes to invade France; but with the French victory at Brescia and their good fortune they are now confident of being able to resist.[6]

Be that as it may the French, Channel-coast seamen were soon living in fearful expectation. Edward Howard began operations by sailing in mid-April on a commercial raiding cruise that was to last a fortnight. He had, at this stage, it seems, no intention of seeking out the French fleet. Instead, he intercepted and plundered every merchant ship that he came across and which he could claim was a legitimate target. As a result, ship movements around Brittany came to a stop and all vessels in Normandy were ordered to Honfleur to be prepared for war. The French were also aware that their limited number of warships in the Seine might encourage the English to invade lower Normandy where, wishful but faulty intelligence reports led the English to believe the countryside would rise in sympathy, as there was great dissatisfaction with the 'reduction of money and the tax of four shillings in the pound'. Henry was, however, cautioned against landing in Upper Normandy, Pays de Calais, Abbeville and Picardy

The main street of Plouarzel, close to Le Conquet, birthplace of the Breton hero and captain of *Cordelière*, Hervé de Portzmoguer.

where Lieutenant General D'Angouleme had prepared the defences, possibly in response to intercepted – and wildly inaccurate – reports by Venetian spies that Henry would cross over to Calais with 100,000 men by the end of June. There were other sources of information available to anyone diligent enough to nose them out. On 19 April, for example, the Bishop of Durham wrote to Lord Darcy apologising for the fact that he had been too busy setting forth the king's army for the sea to write but that the force would be landed at Fuentarrabia.[7]

Howard returned to England to collect this force and sailed again with minimum delay. This second, and equally swift, departure of the English fleet for Brittany reaped the rewards of a surprise attack. On 3 June Howard left the Isle of Wight with Dorset's force and arrived undetected and unmolested off Ushant three days later. Having ensured Dorset's safe onward passage he entered Bertheaume Bay and, unopposed, burnt and seized whatever was available for such treatment. On the following day he burnt

Le Conquet and included in his ravages the retributive pillaging of the ancestral home of Hervé de Portzmoguer, at Plouarzel, some twenty miles from Le Conquet; Portzmoguer, a well-known captain and corsair, had recently seized twenty English vessels. Portzmoguer, the captain of *Cordelière*, was thus very much spoiling for a fight when the English returned in August. Keeping the defenders guessing, Howard then crossed back to Crozon where he was so full of confidence that he offered battle, although the local forces numbered some 10,000 against his own 2,500. The French declined saying that; '...only by compulsion were they defending the French King against the Pope.'[8]

Howard was benefiting from the fact that Brittany had only recently been absorbed into France proper[9], in that he had probably encountered a large band led by local dignitaries resentful of the disappearance of their quasi-independent duchy. The next day they requested a six-day truce and a cessation of the burning. The contemporary comment that they were, '*bien mal dispose; il n'a que la langue et un petit de coeur*'[10] seems very accurate, and is supported by the fact that in August the French naval crews at Brest were reported to be plundering the countryside as they had neither pay nor provisions. Howard sternly informed the Bretons that he had been sent for war not peace, but he still laid on a banquet for their entertainment. He was so delighted by his successes that he used the authority invested in him to knight eight of his accompanying 'Spears'.

The incident at Crozon does reveal, however, a certain diplomatic naivety in Howard. The Breton nobility had every reason to object to the king of France taking over control of their duchy. If the English wished to embarrass Louis they would have had greater chance of success here in Brittany, where local support might have been forthcoming, rather than in more distant Guyenne or in Picardy to which the French army had easy access. Whatever agreement might have been reached unofficially ashore, at sea it did not prevent Howard from seizing twenty-six Flemish hulks and forty smaller Breton ships. Word spread rapidly among the fishing and trading communities and by the end of the month the Channel was all but empty of coastal trading vessels. Howard, satisfied with his achievements, returned to Portsmouth.

This summary of Howard's early operations hides a number of facts that a study of the nautical charts reveals. He was using all the advantages of English superiority at sea to keep enemy land forces guessing as to his intentions, and then forcing them to march great distances to challenge him. Le Conquet to Crozon is forty kilometres by sea (only thirty if one lands at Camaret); it is over eighty by land. Moreover, by making his presence felt on both the north and south shores of the Gulf of Brest the admiral was demonstrating to the French that he had them bottled up in port.

Yet to keep control of these waters safely placed great demands on the English. They were operating in notoriously treacherous waters close to the Ile d'Ouessant or Ushant, as they called it,[11] whose

A Flemish 'hulk': twenty-six of these were seized by Howard during the campaign of 1512.

ship-wrecking coast was to become infamous during the Napoleonic Wars, when the British endeavoured to achieve a close blockade of Brest. Leaving aside the dangers of being embayed on a lee shore, the rocks and islets of this area are fearsome even with accurate charts. The skills of Howard's ship masters, although never stated, must have been superb.

The third phase of the war of 1512 began with Howard sailing once more for Brest with a fleet that had been increased to twenty-five ships. On this occasion he was privileged to have a royal send off for, in July, Henry came down to Portsmouth to review his fleet and to offer his captains a banquet before they departed. It is not recorded which ship he dined upon, but we can assume *Mary Rose* hosted the royal visitor for, although *Regent* was the larger, the former was the flagship and the one which the king himself had commissioned and favoured.

Howard arrived off Brest in the late morning of 10 August and yet again he caught the French unawares. So unprepared in fact that they were partying at anchor in Bertheaume Bay to celebrate the Feast of St Lawrence, although why that particular saint needed a celebratory shindig might be difficult to appreciate. He was a Roman citizen, put to death by being roasted on a grid-iron, thus becoming the patron saint of armourers, brewers, butchers, cooks and vintners; perhaps, the very combination needed for an excellent party. The main celebration was taking place on board *Cordelière*, the Breton flagship which had been built on the personal orders of the Duchess Anne of Brittany, who had also appointed the local hero, Hervé de Portzmoguer, to be her commander. Portzmoguer had taken the opportunity of being anchored off his native land to invite the local Breton nobility and their families on board. The unanticipated arrival of the English brought an unwelcome premature end to the party. Unable either to land his visitors in the time available or to discuss tactics, Portzmoguer was forced to sail towards his foe burdened with frightened passengers. He may have sailed with less support than expected, for the majority of the French fleet seems to have decided to head east towards the safety of Brest.

Although the two fleets were about equal in numbers *Regent* and *Sovereign* far outweighed their French and Breton counterparts, *Grand Louise* and *Cordelière*, while *Mary Rose* was the most modern ship in either fleet. The English also had the advantage of infantry although the French fleet seems to have had more large guns. If the English were to prevail, therefore, they needed to close rapidly and grapple with their foes. Indeed, despite the discrepancy in armament, the English gained first blood when *Mary Rose* shot away the main mast of *Grand Louise*, the French flagship. Even so she was unable to take advantage of what would seem a crippling blow, for the French admiral, René de Clermont, retired to Brest having, according to French sources, had 300 of his men killed. Although there is no reason to doubt this account it does seem strange that *Mary Rose* could have dismasted her opponent and yet been unable to close to close quarters to prevent her escape having, presumably, closed to less than 100 metres to effect the damage to the mast. Perhaps Howard tried and got drawn away from the few French ships that stayed behind to fight, for there is no record of *Mary Rose* being involved in what was to be the major engagement of the day.[12] Although this would indicate the lack of a battle plan, this inconclusive engagement marks a highly significant first in the history of naval warfare, for *Grand Louise*, like *Mary Rose* and *Cordelière*, was fitted with gun-ports, making 10 August 1513 the first occasion on which ships so fitted engaged each other.

Meanwhile, Anthony Ughtred, the captain of *Mary James*, had come alongside *Cordelière* and was endeavouring to board his much larger opponent who was unsupported apart from the *Nef de Dieppe*, whose gallant captain, Rigault de Berquetot, stayed to fight and remained engaged for a staggering seven hours against seven English ships. The main battle, however, raged alongside *Cordelière*, which *Sovereign* also tried to board, only to drift aft. Her place was taken by *Regent*, commanded by Sir Thomas Knyvet. The exchange of fire between the gunners and soldiers of *Regent* and *Cordelière* must have been devastating, frightening,

Grand Louise, the flagship of the French Admiral René de Clermont, engaged by *Mary Rose* on 10 August 1512 in the first combat between ships with gun-ports.

thunderous and vicious. A whole range of man-killing weapons were being discharged at point-blank range at exposed personnel with no place to hide. The ships were grappled together and in such circumstances there was no opportunity for either to break away; the engagement had to be pursued to its climax.

The close-quarters fighting raged on, with some 400 Englishmen, according to the chronicler Raphael Holinshed, storming onboard the French carrack to engage in the butchery of hand-to-hand fighting.[13] It would not have been long before *Cordelière* would have been taken, but before that moment a fire broke out. Some accounts state that this was a deliberate and desperate attempt by Hervé de Portzmoguer to avoid the disgrace of capture, others that a fire in *Regent* spread onto *Cordelière.*[14] Whatever its origins the fire took hold with devastating results. A dramatic French painting shows flames licking up into the rigging and the crews of the two ships leaping for safety.[15] Few reached it. The flames reached the *Cordelière*'s powder magazine and the two ships that had been locked together were blown apart. The carnage was enormous. From the wreckage of *Regent* just 120 of her 700 men were rescued. Of *Cordelière*'s passengers and crew of 900 just twenty lived to tell the tale. And the great explosion also affected those ships lying off in support. *Mary James*, who picked up survivors from both ships, took much of the force of the blast and, on her return to England, had to pension off sixty of her crew as unfit for further service.

While the Bretons lost a hero in Hervé de Portzmoguer, Henry VIII had lost a friend in Thomas Knyvet and a loyal servant in Sir John Carew, *Regent*'s second-in-command, the first of several members of this West Country sailing family to die in the king's service during Henry's reign. Thomas Knyvet, a great jouster, would have been remembered by the court with affection. (In one carousing that got somewhat out of hand, he had been stripped naked by the public and forced to shin up a pillar for his own safety.) His loss indicates the importance that the king placed on having his great ships captained by men whose status ashore reflected their significance as commanders of his most prestigious instruments of war. Knyvet had also been Howard's brother-in-law and his loss affected the admiral greatly. On 26 August Wolsey wrote to the Bishop of Worcester:

> Sir Edward hath made his vow to God that he would never see the King in the face until he had revenged the death of the noble and valiant Knight Sir Thomas Knyvet.[16]

Edward Howard was to have another personal reason to seek revenge. Stunned by her husand's death, Lady Knyvet, Howard's sister Muriel, fell into despondency and forecast that she would die within five months of her husband. She did just that on 12 January 1513.

The combined losses suffered by *Regent* and *Cordelière* make their engagement one of the most bloody in naval history. It also marks, probably, the last major engagement fought under the medieval idea of warfare at sea being the stationing of floating castles of soldiers alongside one another, although two decades later Audley's Fighting Instructions would describe how best to carry out such a tactic.[17] The enormity of the loss can be gauged by a comparison with that much more famous French magazine explosion that led to the loss of *L'Orient* at the Battle of the Nile in 1798 commemorated in the much-parodied poem 'The Boy stood on the Burning Deck'.[18] In that disaster several hundred of the crew were lost, while French deaths during the whole of the battle probably amounted to some 1600, just a few more than died on board *Cordelière* alone. It was a sad sacrifice for Saint Lawrence's Day, whose anniversary in the Catholic Church is recorded with the burningly apt lines:

> ...a glowing bed made ready
> The torment-bearing instrument
> The grid-iron glows suffering
> Roasting his very viscera[19]

The disaster off Brittany was of sufficient magnitude that even Wolsey, who otherwise seems to have been a cold fish, was moved by it. In the letter to the Bishop of Worcester referred to earlier, Wolsey wrote:

> And to ascertain you of the lamentable and sorrowful tidings and chance which hath fortuned by the sea, our fleet, on Tuesday last fortnight, met with 21 great ships of France, the best with sail and furnished with artillery and men ever was seen. And after innumerable shootings of guns and long chasing one another, at the last the *Regent* most valiantly boarded the great carrack of Brest, wherein were 4 lords, 300 gentlemen, 800 soldiers and mariners, 400 crossbowmen, 100 gunners, 200 tunnes of wine, 100 pipes of beef, 60 barrels of gunpowder and 15 great brass cortains with so marvelous number of shot and other guns of every sort. Our men so valiantly occupied themselves that within one overfight they had so utterly vanquished with shot of gun and arrows the said carrack and slain most part of the men with the same. And suddenly as they were yielding themselves, the carrack was once a flaming fire, and like wise the *Regent* with the turning of one hand.[20]

The combat between *Cordelière* and *Regent*. This contemporary French painting showing the fire and explosion that wrecked both ships was painted to illustrate the epic 500-verse poem in Latin written by the French court poet, Germain de Brie.

The almoner and financier in Wolsey's character does, however, show through. The listing of stores, especially wine, seems a singularly inappropriate inclusion in such an account of loss; but Wolsey probably felt it an important ingredient.

Edward Howard, with *Regent* sunk and *Mary James* badly damaged, considered that he still had left a formidable force for the job in hand. Over the next two days he flaunted his naval superiority by burning twenty-seven small ships, capturing a further five and, on 13 August, seizing 300 Breton prisoners. Moving away he harried the coast of Normandy and Picardy, capturing or burning many ships before returning once again to a delighted Henry who appointed him an Admiral of England with the reward of £66 13s 4d.

Curiously, the French king did much the same, rewarding René de Clermont, with 100 francs, but this was based on the latter's false report of the engagenment, which so incensed the gallant captain of the *Nef de Dieppe* that he wrote a letter accusing his admiral of cowardice and challenged him to a duel. The French account states that *Cordelière* was surrounded by twelve vessels and succeeded in putting several out of action while driving others away and dismasting Sir Charles Brandon's ship. Then, at the point of triumph, an English ship threw on board a mass of fireworks that took hold. Portzmogeur, recognising the danger he was in drove his ship, 'like a floating volcano' into *Regent*'s side and:

> ...like a huge incendiary torch...pitilessly grappled her, and wound her in her own floating robe. The powder magazine of *Regent* blew up, and with her the hostile ship, her commander and thousands of burnt and mashed limbs went into the air; while *Cordèliere*, satisfied, and still proud in disaster, blew up also.[21]

A statue of St Lawrence (Laurent in French) in a church near Le Conquet clearly showing the grid iron on which he met his fiery death – a painfully appropriate symbol for the fight between *Cordelière* and *Regent*.

While this successful, but limited, foray against the French fleet was taking place the English land forces in Guyenne were faring far worse. It became very obvious almost from the moment of landing that Ferdinand had no intention of providing any support to his allies from England. Dorset had landed at Fuentarrabia intending to advance on Bayonne, but found not only an absence of allies, but also that there was no provision for tentage or victuals. More importantly, there was no beer, which meant that the English quaffed vast quantities of unpleasant red wine and got diarrhoea. As a contemporary wrote, 'The hot wines of Spain increased the evil. Worst of all, no beer to be had and the English had not yet learnt to fight without it.[22]

In the meantime, using the English presence as a decoy, Ferdinand skirted around the French forces, occupied the part of Navarre he desired, and closed his campaign. Dorset's forces, loathing the heat and the rain, lying sick and unused, mutinied. Their commander was forced to re-embark and sail for home. It was another 302 years before a British army drove across the Bidasso at Fuenterrabia and on into France, but then they were to be a professional army commanded by a military genius, Wellington. However, some things do not change. General William Napier in his account of Wellington's

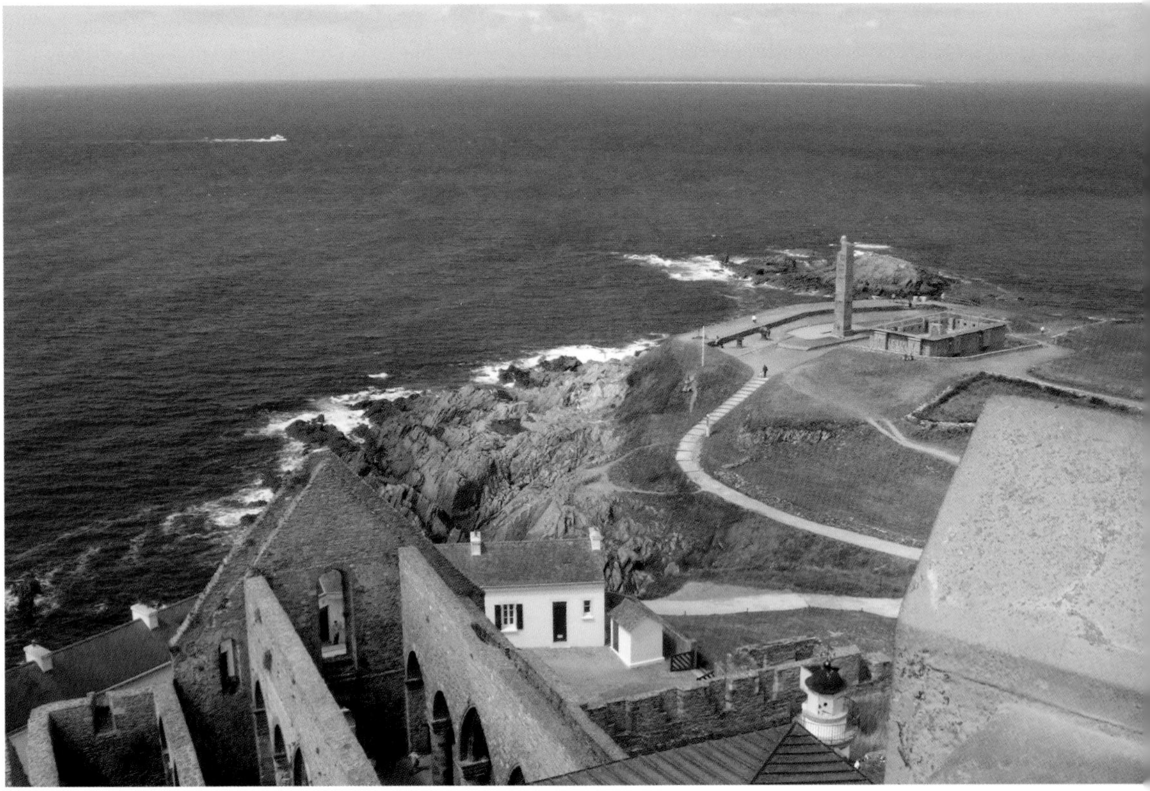

The ruins of the monastery at Point St Mattieu. In 1512 the monks would have had a perfect view of the clash between the English and French fleets below them, and must have watched in horror as *Regent* and *Cordèliere* blew up.

campaign states that the British needed the port facilities at Fuentarrabia because they had, '...to sustain the perverse negligence always, and often the hostility of the Spanish authorities.[23]

Despite the letters he had received keeping him informed of the failures of the deployment, Henry was furious with his commanders and berated them publicly and in front of his council and the Spanish ambassador. What he did not seem to realise was how fortunate his army had been to be able to return unmolested across the sea.

The Earl of Dorset had left Spain on 30 October and arrived in England eleven days later, having successfully sailed past Brest without the French emerging to attack. Given the fact that spies were everywhere and the embarkation of the English would have been both witnessed and reported he was a lucky commander. Even more so in that the king of France had ordered reinforcements, in the form of galleys, to sail from the Mediterranean to Brest to strengthen his fleet for the next season's campaign. The galleys sailed in the late autumn under the command of a skilful and seasoned admiral, Prégent de Bidoux, the very antithesis of the English aristocratic, amateur commander. If he had come across Dorset's fleet things would have gone badly for the English and Portzmoguer would have been more than revenged. Prégent was a Gascon who had been in action at sea more or less continuously for the past fifteen years. He had fought the Turks and was a Knight of Rhodes acting on the frontline of Christendom; he had defended Naples against the Spanish and in 1510 fought a brilliant action against the Venetians. Now he had sailed north to fight a foe ill-versed and badly equipped to deal with even a small flotilla of well-armed galleys.

Galleys had undergone a revolution in their fighting ability, brought about by the introduction of

A street sign in Le Conquet: Portzmoguer is a local hero remembered to this day.

the heavy ship-sinking gun. Until its introduction, galleys had relied on their rams to crash into an opponent splintering his side, snapping his oars and then pouring arrows and small arms onto the decks before boarding for hand-to-hand fighting. Physical contact was necessary to conclude any engagement; then the guns arrived and the game changed. Until 1510, when galleys were first fitted with heavy guns, the advantage in any sea engagement involving galleys and carracks had generally been with the latter, who could run down the lightly sided craft with impunity. The advantage, in calm waters, had now reversed but it is unlikely that the English, given the newness of the galley modifications, were aware of this. Prégent, however, was ready to exploit it. His ships were fitted with three basilisks of which it was reported enviously by one Peter Martyr that: 'One shot of those marvellous guns can sink any man-of-war.'[24]

They would certainly have wrought havoc if unleashed on Dorset's slow and bulky transports. Perhaps the weather had turned too brisk for the galleys to venture out to sea. On their first outing of 1513, sailing to attack Plymouth and Falmouth in mid-March, they indeed were forced back to harbour because of bad weather. Those stormy northern winters meant that it was the accepted doctrine to lay the fleet up for winter, but in 1512 the English decided that it would be necessary to keep some ships at sea to defend against 'skulkers and adventurers'. Howard, with his usual gift for the felicitous phrase, wrote to Wolsey:

> I dare lay my life on it…let the *Lizard*, my bark and the new bark that Sir Stephen Bull is in, with one good ship to lie for and stale in the Camber and another at Wight then…there shall not stir a Frenchman but he shall drink to his oysters.[25]

Mary Rose was not one of the ships selected for the rigours of a winter in the Channel which, given her handling qualities and newness, might be surprising. Perhaps, she was thought too valuable to risk in a stormy winter. She was sent to the Thames with some other ships including *Mary James*, which was considered as being 'unfit for a man to venture in this winter'. Once in the river she unloaded her guns at Blackwall and entered the new dock at Erith to winter. In February this arrangement would be reversed to prepare the ship for the coming season. In the meantime Wolsey assured the king that he would be 'sending out boats and ships daily and nightly to descry enemies' and that he would (not surprisingly) 'not fail to advertise the king of any enemy attempt to land.'[26] However, there was a general feeling that the nation was safe and that, 'there is nothing to be feared from great ships which dare not keep the Narrow Seas these winter nights, without harbours.'[27]

There was one other fleet at sea that winter. In September a group of Spanish vessels, promised by Ferdinand to augment the English forces, arrived in Southampton, too late to be of any use to Howard. They remained alongside for three months before sailing for Spain at the end of December. On land and at sea Ferdinand was proving to be an unreliable and mendacious ally. Henry, who was determined to continue his war with the stated aim of freeing the Church, 'from the savage tyranny of the King of the French, who is the common enemy of all Christian princes'[28] needed a more reliable ally. The only candidate was the Holy Roman Emperor, Maximilian. He was persuaded, on promise of a large sum of money, to join Henry so, with the emperor on side, Henry could revert to the traditional route in to France – an attack across the Channel through Calais. If the four allies could agree to launch a coordinated attack France was doomed. They couldn't. Ferdinand reached his own private settlement with Louis. Nevertheless, Henry decided to lead his troops in person across the fields where his predecessors had won both their spurs and their glory. He would take an army to France.

At sea it was felt sensible to keep to the successful strategy of 1512 and to attack the French at Brest. This was to be done as an entirely independent operation, although its success would guarantee that the army could cross over the Channel and be supported free from seaborne assault. During the winter months the fleet had been refitted, replenished and added to: Cornelius Johnson, the King's gunmaker, had been paid £1366 22d for repairing weapons and making twelve new serpentines for a new galley; a gunsmith John Green was paid for supplying six serpentines for *Barbara*;[29] *Mary Rose* received some new guns;*Anne Gallant, Dragon, Henry Galley* and *Great Bark* had been built; and eight other ships had been purchased.[30] Howard's command was growing into a formidable and expensive fighting force of which much would be expected. Now, instead of just three king's ships as he had had in the previous year, the admiral's fleet of twenty-eight ships included twenty-three royal vessels and just five merchant ships taken up from trade. There is also a record of *Mary Rose* having her own bark to whom a man called Davison was appointed as master.[31] The Anthony Roll shows just such a small vessel secured to *Mary Rose* and one can assume that Davison and his crew only manned it when required for such duties as taking messages around the fleet or laying off during battle to rescue men from the water.

Mary Rose, with Howard embarked, and the rest of the Thames-based ships sailed on 19 March, having been visited by the king the previous day and, it is believed, on several other occasions, for he was sending his navy out on what he saw as a, 'just, holy and somewhat necessary war'. He wanted to show his personal support.

Across the Channel, Louis, determined not to be caught unprepared for a second year running, ordered his new admiral, Guyon le Roy, Signeur du Chillou, to sail from Honfleur at the same time that the English were getting underway in the Thames. In the quiet season Louis had also purchased from his Scottish ally their very impressive, but not overworked, great ship, the 1000-ton *Michael* as a replacement for *Cordelière*. Yet, on paper, the numerical advantage still rested with the English. Du Chillou had only some eleven ships ready for action in Brittany with another sixteen on their way from Normandy to Brest. But he did now have a deadly weapon in the formidable presence of Prégent's galleys. Ever since his arrival in northern waters the influence of this energetic commander had been felt, and his arrival must have lifted the moral of a force much deflated by the loss of *Cordelière* and their fleet's previous poor showing against Howard.

Howard's fleet sailed into choppy seas. The wind, which had been westerly, veered to the east-north-east and would have driven them on to the shallows. They thus anchored on Palm Sunday for the whole day until the wind changed once more and they could sail to round North Foreland. When they got underway Howard ordered a sailing race. With the ships underway in a long line it might not have been easy to recognise the winner except that *Mary Rose*, which started some four miles behind the lead vessels, appears to have sailed past them all. Howard was delighted, and his letter explaining the race to the king in great detail exudes his pleasure with the occasion and the performance of his flagship in particular although, it has to be said, to the modern reader, the letter is somewhat unintelligible. But there is no doubt as to Howard's views on *Mary Rose*: 'Sir, she is the noblest ship of sail [and] great ship at this hour that I trow be in Christendom.[32]

He refers to her also as, '*Mary Rose*, your noble ship' and 'the flower of all ships that ever sailed'.[33] To win these accolades *Mary Rose* had not only to sail well but to execute some clever manoeuvres in treacherous waters where sandbanks abounded, while coping with strong and changeable winds. When these winds blew from astern it gave the ships a chance to attach their bonnets to the sails, thus increasing the area under canvas, and to haul on the bowlines to keep the sails taut so as not to spill any of the wind. For a few glorious miles they must have flown along before coming to anchor at the Foreland, each ship's arrival being recorded by Howard with 'pen and ink'. The evolution not only showed the skills of the English masters, but also Howard's confidence in their ability to carry out his commands in a safe and seamanlike way. This race is the first example we have of an admiral ordering ships under his command to carry out an evolution other than that of engaging the enemy. What is more, it was an exercise designed to test the ability of his subordinate commanders. Howard thus set a pattern that was to be followed for many generations to come.

No sooner had the fleet anchored at the end of the race than a fierce wind blew up from a dangerous quarter:

> Northerboard so strainably that we could ride no longer there without great danger, [so] we weighed to get us to the Downs through the 'Gowles' [Gull Stream]. And when we were in the midst, between the 'Brakkes' and the Goodwin, the wind veered out again to the west-south-west, where we were fain to make with your great ships three or four turns, and God knoweth ...row channel at low water. As we took it, the *Sovereign* and the *Mary* stayed ...a quarter of a mile off the Goodwin Sands, and the *Maria de Loretta* offered her...would none of it, and was fain to go about with a forewind back...where she lyeth...I fetched the Downs with many turns, and thanked be to God I...Downs at anchor in fast.[34]

From exhilaration to desperate straits in a few moments for, whatever the difficulty in an exact deciphering of this description, there is no problem in understanding the dangers that Howard is describing as his ships tacked and turned to keep off the treacherous sands. The fleet survived this crisis and what was to be a stormy spring. On 5 April Howard ends a letter to Wolsey with a postscript:

> Sir, I need not to write unto you what storms we had, for you know it well enough. Sir, I saw never worse; but thanked be to God all is well, saving the loss of one of our galleys; all ill go with her...[35]

Bertheaume Bay: having driven the French from here in both 1512 and 1513 Edward Howard used this sheltered anchorage for the English fleet from where he could watch in safety French shipping movements in Brest harbour.

– and then, in a few words that link Howard with all lovesick and lonely sailors everywhere: 'Sir, I send you in this packet a letter to my wife; I pray you deliver it to her.'[36] We are lucky to have many of Howard's writings to the king and Wolsey; none give us the feeling for the man as do those nineteen words.

Sailing via the Isle of Wight to Plymouth, Howard received news from Brest that the French, whom it was reported had, '100 ships of war besides the galleys' were ready to sail and would not 'fail to come out and fight'. This delighted the seasoned warrior and on 10 April he crossed the Channel, encountering strong winds on the way and surprising, off Brest, a small group of French ships that fled to the safety of the inner harbour as soon as they sighted the English. Howard referred to them as 'cowards'; 'wise' might have been more apt a word. For Brest, where the main French fleet lay, appeared to be impregnable, and the weather was not helping Howard either:

> ...the wind shot out to East-North-East, and the ebb came that with all the turning we could make, we could get no further than the mouth of the entry of Brest water, where we saw riding all the fleet of France to the number of fifty sail, which we should not have missed if the wind and the ebb had not come. And so we weighed anchor in their sight, determining that the next morning if we could have wind to lay on a-board, that we would have them where they lie. For, Sir, this ship cannot get in by the castles but at an high water and a drawing wind.[37]

Howard's main concern was that the French ships would remain secure beneath their defences while the frustrated English chaffed and watched as their victuals shrank and smelled. Howard pleaded to the king for more supplies: 'Sir, we lose no time, I warrant you, for we think upon none other thing but how we may best grieve our enemies. If victual serve us.'[38]

Yet danger for the English still lurked at sea, for Prégent had taken his galleys into St Malo where, equally secure, they posed a flanking threat to the English ships blockading Brest. Not that Howard placed great store in Prégent's force, as he explained to the king:

> Sir, as for the galleys, we make great way with them ... if there come any other by day or by night, the boats and small vessels and rowbarges and row-galleys shall lay them

The Goulet, the confined approach to the harbour of Brest. Contrary winds and then sunken hulks prevented Howard passing through this narrow channel to attack the French fleet safely anchored inside.

> sharply aboard, and rather than they should escape us, I have assigned William Harper, the *Thomas of Hull*, my bark, Sir William Trevynan's bark and two or three small ships...though they should run them aground for to make them sink. And, Sir, if they come amongst us, they shall not escape clean with good.[39]

On 13 April Howard resorted to what was become the traditional tactic of a blockading admiral unable to draw his enemy out of their haven. He landed a contingent of 1,500 men to pillage and burn the countryside. Very soon they found themselves opposed by a force reckoned at 10,000 men and, sensibly, returned on board. At the same time the French sealed off the harbour by drawing hulks across the mouth, increasing Howard's frustration still further. This was only partly relieved by taking his men to land on the opposite side to the French force where he fought two 'battles' and burnt some more houses. But it was small reward compared with what he had intended. Lying off an enemy coast in treacherous waters inevitably creates dangers for the blockading force. On 17 April Howard had to inform the king in a letter carried by the unfortunate, aristocratic captain, Arthur Plantagenet, that the bearer had lost his ship, *Nicholas of Hampton*, which had foundered on a concealed rock:

> Sir, I have taken all Master Arthur's folks and bestowed them in the army where I lacked, by reason of death, by casualty and otherwise; and, Sir, have given him licence to go home, for, Sir, when he was in extreme danger, he called upon Our Lady of Walsingham for help and comfort and made a vow that, and it pleaseth God and Her to deliver him out of peril he would never eat flesh nor fish till he had seen Her. Sir, I assure you he was in marvellous danger, for it was a marvel that the ship, being with all her sails striking full but a rock with her stem, she was broke not on pieces at the first stroke. Sir, we shall have a great want of him out of your noble army, for I know no man...that, considering his power, should better have served you if the fortune had not been.... And, Sir, he would not have departed but for that vow he should do here in a manner your grace but small service, and to himself great discomfort to see every man shipped, and to see his own place and his men divided from him.... I have sent him to your grace, beseeching your grace, to be his good and gracious lord. I assure you he shall do your grace good service wheresoever... both for his good order and hardiness. And, Sir, he is the sorriest man I ever saw, and no man here can comfort him. Therefore, I beseech again your grace to give him comfortable words to be his good lord.[40]

The humanity of Howard has been remarked upon and in this letter it positively runneth over. 'Sirs' and 'graces' tumble into just about every line, whereas in other letters and, indeed, in the remainder of this letter, they are used far less frequently and often simply, formally, just to begin a paragraph. Howard was pleading for clemency for his elderly, although possibly inexperienced, and probably culpable, junior officer (what was he doing under full sail in unchartered and unfamiliar waters?). The admiral realised that the king's wrath might do great harm to Plantagenet and he was, as the king must have realised, humbling himself at a distance, on behalf of the unfortunate captain. He even employs some guile for he would have known that Our Lady of Walsingham was the king's own favourite shrine and he could not but approve of Plantagenet's desire to go there on pilgrimage. Howard's pleas were rewarded; Plantagenet was forgiven and appointed to command the elderly *Trinity Sovereign*, one of Henry VII's surviving carracks.

The rocks of Brittany claimed another victim. In late 1513 Walter Loveday, captain of *Anne Gallant*, was given £6 12s so he could give each of his soldiers 2s:

> ...because they lost all their victuals by the sinking of the said ship in Plymouth Haven

where she was grounded in order to arrest
such hurts as she took upon the rocks
in Brittany.[41]

Even so, the navigation record of the ships' masters in such difficult waters was a commendable one.

On 22 April the threat from Prégent's six galleys materialised and the fight did not go the way that the optimistic Howard had forecast for, in an aggressive attack, Prégent threw the English into disarray. The galleys sank one merchantman, commanded by Ned Compton, and badly damaged Sir Stephen Bull's 240 ton *Lesse Bark*, by holing her in seven places. Prégent claimed even more success. In a letter of 28 April he wrote that on the Eve of St George's Day he met fifty English ships and sank two immediately and that another two sank during the night.[42]

Whatever the truth of this claim – and it does seem to be exaggerated – there is no denying the great success that Prégent would achieve, in quite a different setting, on St Mark's Day three days later. There is no record of the English inflicting any counter-damage on Prégent's swift galleys. The galleys retired into Anse des Blancs-Salons (Whitesand Bay) near Le Conquet, where they added to their protection by placing gun batteries on the cliffs commanding their berth, and to the English problem by posing a threat on their flank. This was classic galley tactic. They were moored stern to the shore with their main armament pointing seaward. Here, safe in this well-protected haven they could take on fresh food and water at leisure; land the sick and take on fresh troops; provide, if needed, reinforcements to Le Conquet; discuss tactics with the shore commanders and, simply by virtue of their presence, cause their enemies a major headache. In contrast, the English were running short of victuals and enduring all the discomforts that went with maintaining a close blockade. From the moment that Prégent arrived on the scene it would be no exaggeration to say that the major preoccupation of English ship design, strategy and tactics was how a sailing warship could best a galley in combat. Howard was in the unfortunate position of being forced to take the matter to conclusion in a situation over which he had no control, short of acknowledging defeat by retiring to Plymouth. He was not that sort of admiral.

His initial response to the threat posed by the galleys was to land 6,000 troops nearby with the intention of marching them over to the bay to take the galleys from the shore. It was a reasonable idea but an aggressive French response forced him to desist and to re-embark. If he was to destroy the galleys he was going to have to do it through a frontal assault. Sitting in his cabin in *Mary Rose* he drew up what was always going to be a very risky plan of assault by boat. In coming to this dangerous decision Holinshed suggests that Howard was feeling pressured by the king himself. In response to criticism of his lack of progress he appears to have invited the king to come and take command in person. Henry, not a great voyager or one to put himself in harm's way apart from at the jousts wrote back, 'commanding him to accomplish that which appertained to his duty'. Goaded by this chastisement and, sure of the likely reception he would receive at court if he returned without success, the admiral drew up his fatal plan. Plausible although this story may be, there is no evidence to support Holinshed's version of events.[43]

Howard had in his fleet not only the barks which acted as tenders to the great ships but a number of rowboats and galley-like vessels which could operate in the shallow waters where Prégent's galleys lay close to the shore. He decided on what was to become known as a cutting-out operation – an attack by ship's boats against an enemy at anchor with the intention of capturing or destroying them. He summoned some of his experienced fighting men to assist him. These included, Lord Ferrers, Thomas Cheyne, Sir Henry Sherborne and Sir William Sidney, courtiers who would wish to seize this opportunity for achieving a glory that would be reported favourably to their king. They were to attack using two galleys, a row-barge and two crayers, with Howard's vessel having 160 men embarked and the rest, presumably, being similarly crammed with men and weaponry. There would have been many a dry mouth and a nervous laugh as they pulled away to their destination, for the French, as Edward Echyngham, one of Wolsey's victuallers, wrote to Wolsey on 5 May were, 'protected on both sides by bulwarks planted so thick with guns and crossbows that the quarrels and the gonstones came together as thick as hailstones.'[44] Howard drove on through this deadly hail, a grappling iron was flung onto Prégent's galley, and the admiral and seventeen of his men jumped onboard. Very quickly, probably with memories of the blowing up of *Regent* in mind, the grappling-iron line was attached to the galley capstan from where it could be veered in case of fire, thus letting Howard's own galley drop back away from danger. However, someone cut the line, the boat drifted away and so, in Echyngham's poignant words, 'they left this [noble Admiral in the] hands of his enemies.'[45] Howard called over the water in desperation, 'Come aboard again! Come aboard again!' For whatever reason they did not. The end was inevitable.

One of the assault party, although badly wounded, managed to jump overboard and swim back to his boat to tell the tale. Howard, pinned to the galley's side, had one final gesture of defiance in him. He ripped from around his neck the chain on which hung the gold boatswain's call that denoted his badge of office and flung it out to sea. Like a Roman legionnaire protecting his standard, Howard was not going to allow this precious token to fall into the hands of his enemies. So fierce was their assault that a moment later he too was flung overboard on the end of their pikes. And so died the man who was England's first professional fighting admiral. The way he commanded, the way he cared for his men, and the way that he led from the front created a tradition that has continued to the credit and glory of the Royal Navy ever since. Echyngham summed him up most effectively:

> There was never noble man so ill lost as he was, that was of so great courage, and had so many virtues, and that he ruled so great an army so well as he did, and kept so great order and true justice.[46]

Distraught, defeated, disconsolate and leaderless, the English withdrew. In the afternoon a delegation led by Thomas Cheyne and Richard Cornwall returned to the shore, under a flag of truce, to enquire after Howard's fate. They were met by Prégent (whom the English referred to as Prester John). He told them that he had:

> No prisoners English within my galley but one, and he is a mariner, but there was one that leapt into my galley with a gilt target on his arm, the which [I saw] cast overboard with morris pikes; and the mariner that I have prisoner told me that the same man was your admiral.[47]

Later, back in Whitesand Bay, Prégent found Edward Howard's body and sent word to the French king and queen to ask how they wished the body to be buried. It would appear that he also recovered the admiral's gold whistle, for this was sent to the queen as a token. One of her ladies, Madame Claude, received Howard's clothes but for what reason it is not possible to ascertain. The body, it is believed, was interred close to the shore nearby.

The result of the battle was reported differently elsewhere. Dr William Knight, Henry's ambassador to Spain, noted that Ferdinand was resolved to keep the truce between Spain and France and that the news received on St Mark's Day of the victory gained over the French at sea by the English fleet had given Spain no satisfaction. Ferdinand, so Knight reported, was actually grieved that any ships of his had contributed to the victory. Some ally, some father-in-law!

Howards' failed assault has been cited as a major example of the disastrous consequences of Henry's policy of appointing his favourites to command. In Steven Gunn's opinion:

> Henry VIII seems at times to have judged distinction in the joust suitable for reward not

Whitesand Bay, and its easily defended headlands: secure in such an anchorage, and with supplies readily available from the shore, here the galleys were invulnerable to an attack from the sea. The present-day fort only dates from the Napoleonic era, but shows how gun batteries could be mounted to command the waters of the bay.

> only with chivalrous honours ... but even with senior naval and military commands. This policy was doubtless misguided, but less for any inherent irrelevance of tournament to warfare then because it encouraged the deployment in real war of the sort of bone-headed tilt-yard rashness that led the magnificent jouster Sir Edward Howard to his death in a vastly outnumbered attack using rowing-boats against the entire becalmed French fleet.[48]

Yet, given the clear and present danger that a protected galley fleet posed to his force there was no alternative available to Howard but to meet the threat head on. He did so. He failed. The failure does not belittle the reasoning, only the excecution. The English might have suffered worse had they not attacked, for at least the galleys did not sally forth to inflict further damage. The opportunity so to do disappeared with the English fleet's reaction to Howard's death. It fled home. It was a dispirited fleet. Not only had the Admiral been lost, but the crews were also short of food. Echyngham had escorted some supplies over but these would soon be used up. But it was morale rather than victuals that was at the lowest ebb and dictated what followed next. The fleet had seen what damage Prégent's galleys could inflict and they did not want to be exposed to further attack. In ones and twos, leaderless, but of one purpose, they sailed away and back to England where Henry had appointed Edward Howard's elder brother, Thomas, as their new commander.

All now depended on whether the new admiral would, as his brother had done when Thomas Knyvet had been blown up in *Regent*, swear revenge, or be true to his character and act with caution. History indicates that he favoured restraint. What is certain is that from 1513 until well beyond Henry's reign the fear of French galleys would be the spectre that haunted English naval operations.

CHAPTER 9

A Fleet in Fear

On 7 May 1513, immediately after writing a letter to the king, Thomas Howard wrote a more detailed account of his brother's fate to Wolsey. In the opening paragraph he gave his assessment of the king's fleet in the aftermath of the events off Brest:

This contemporary engraving of a battle between carracks and galleys demonstrates the greater manoeuvrability of the oared craft that allowed them to approach the sailing ships where their defensive fire-power was weakest, and, conversely, the small target presented by their low profile and tendency to attack head-on.

> Never man saw men in greater fear than all the masters and mariners be of the galleys, in so much that in a manner they had as lief go into Purgatory as to the Trade [Brest].[1]

That fear was to dominate English maritime tactics and strategy for another 60 years.

It would be difficult to put a positive spin on the position in which Howard now found himself, but the need for an enquiry meant that he was able to meet on board *Mary Rose* all his commanders and to form an opinion of their mettle far more immediately than if he had joined them at sea. Many of them he did, of course, already know; for they were drawn from the same small social group from which he himself came. Now he needed their help to enable him to report back to both Wolsey and the king on two issues: the circumstances surrounding his brother's death, and why the fleet had abandoned its station, the latter quite possibly having contributed to the former occurrence. The eye-witness accounts indicated that, in the other galley, Lord Ferrers fired off all his ammunition, that the master of the row-barge was killed, and that Sir Henry Sherborne's crayer drove against the galleys, breaking her oars. Thomas Howard – who had good reason to want to get to the truth, beyond any personal wish to justify his brother's apparent foolhardiness – found little fault with the actions of the attacking force. He told the king that:

> ...there were [with my brother] 175 men, of whom were left of life but 56, and of those [of] my Lord Ferrers' men, 25 slain and 20 hurt; and may...my galley had not fallen on ground, being near the shore, then the [other in like] wise boarded as the other did, and of likelihood few had escaped. [Sir Henry] Sherborne and Sir William Sidney boarded a galley, they being in a small [crayer], and yet by fortune had but three men slain and seven hurt. Cheyne and Wallop, being in a little crayer, boarded in like wise, and yet had no man slain nor hurt. William Tolly and his brother Sir Robert, of all men had 12 men slain and above 20 hurt. Wiseman boarded not but he had all his men slain or hurt. Sir Wystan Browne had three men slain, and divers other boats had many men slain and hurt.[2]

With such a butcher's bill, and with so little to show for it, Howard could only draw one conclusion:

> Please your grace that, as far as I can understand by any man's report [it was] the most dangerous enterprise that ever I heard of, and the most manly handled of the setters on, insomuch that I see no likelihood [nor] possibility to bring the mariners to row the galleys or boats to [shore without] other bargain.[3]

Howard also commended two captains, Thomas Gurney of *Janet Purwyn* and Lewes Southern of *Elizabeth of Newcastle*, who appear to have suffered many casualties and considerable damage in action around the same time. Thomas Howard would have felt an attachment to *Janet Purwyn* – she was one of Andrew Barton's ships that he and his brother had captured in 1511. However, in the letter to Wolsey, Howard departed from the previous blanket exoneration:

> Here is two men that, as I hear say, did their part very ill that day my brother was lost; one was [William] Coke; the Queen's servant, in a rowbarge, and the other Freman, my said brother's household servant. If it be truth, I shall punish that all other shall take example.[4]

The record remains silent as to what action Howard did take or the reasons for his criticism of these men. What is certain is that it was not his brother's actions that would now dominate his thinking, but the ever-present, looming danger of the galleys that had precipitated them. Thomas Howard was not going to be the admiral to overlook that problem.

Howard then turned to the serious matter of why the fleet had abandoned its station. In answering this question there appears to have been some

Henry's personal interest in finding a counter to the galleys eventually led to a class of 13 small vessels called row-barges. This is the Anthony Roll illustration of one of them, *Rose in the Sonne,* built in 1546 supposedly to Henry's own design, but they were launched too late to play an effective part in the war, and in the long run were not judged a success.

collusion ahead of Howard's arrival for, on questioning his captains:

> … they answered with one whole voice and in one tale they did it upon divers and reasonable grounds. One was that they had great default of victual, and had not in their board for three days…One other cause was all your captains and masters generally say that, [if] they had continued there and one day of calm had come, if the galleys being within three mile of them would have done their worst unto them, as it is to suppose they would have done, if they should not a-failed to have sunk such of your ships as they list to have shot their ordnance unto; which ordnance, if it be such as they report, is a thing marvellous.[5]

The captains knew that Henry had been preoccupied by the galley threat and had created a class of ships – his row-barges – that he believed could respond. Howard was told, however, that:

> …one of the galleys in a calm would distress your two galleys and row-barges, and to drown with their oars as many boats as came within reach of them.[6]

Possibly emboldened by the fact that Howard was wiling to listen to them, the delegation of commanders laid it on thick. The inexperienced admiral seems to have reported their words verbatim:

> And also all the masters say that if the wind had blown strainably at South-West or West-South-West, or West and by South, there had been no remedy [and] they must have run into Crozon bay, where they should have lye…near the shores of both sides being already sore

> bulwarked, that without [they] had been able to have beaten the Frenchmen from the land, the said French [with] their ordnance might have destroyed all your fleet lying there.[7]

It is true that being embayed on the Brittany coast was an ever-present risk in the days of sail, but Howard's commanders wanted it all ways for, as he reported:

> The captains...have answered that, considering the great fortification, the great danger of the galleys if calm come, the great danger of winds afore rehearsed, if they fortune to blow strainably, they see no likelihood nor possibility but that there shall rather turn to our great reproach, loss of ships and [men] otherwise. And also they all think it not possible, the premises considered, anything that may rebound to the honour of your grace, your realm and our poor honesties, unless that your grace would so furnish us with [that] we might be able both to keep our ships and also to defend them [against] your enemies for five or six days; which done, all the expert captains and masters think verily your grace shall not cause us to destroy [the ships] of France with the galleys, but also put your enemies to the [word missing]...that ever they had in Brittany.[8]

This position would not have stood up to a closer cross-examination but Howard, possibly by dint of his own limited experience, does not seem to have queried the captains' convenient, and evidently jointly planned defence. Perhaps he felt it might reflect upon his brother's lack of planning. Perhaps, given that he found himself with a totally dispirited command, he felt he needed to show understanding and support of his officers if ever he was to lead the fleet back across the Channel with morale restored. Howard reassured the king that he would, 'demand of them what service shall be possible for us to do', which sounds somewhat less assertive than any response his brother might have given; indeed, there are many indications that the elder sibling had weaker blood coursing through his veins. One is that he finished his letter to the king, 'Written in the *Mary Rose* in Plymouth haven, the 7 day of May, at 11 a'clock at night'. It is followed by the letter to Wolsey, to which reference has also been made, which ended, 'Scribbled in great haste in the *Mary Rose* at Plymouth, half an hour after 11 at night, the 7 day of May.' Three weeks later he ended a letter, 'Scribbled in great haste, the 28th day of May at 6 a'clock in the morning'. One year later it is, 'Written in Dover Road, the 27th May at 7 at night.' Was he trying to impress his masters with his dedication to the job?

Despite the reduction in the fleet's manpower caused by death and desertion, Howard gave the impression that he wanted to sail for Brittany just as soon as he had had time to replenish the fleet. This delay gave him time to get to know *Mary Rose*'s new captain, Edward Bray, who was appointed with effect from 9 May for two months at a rate of 18d a day, which he might have considered little reward for taking an inexperienced admiral off to war in confined waters. Howard had the unusual problem of over-manning in his own vessel. He had been provided with a force of 200 soldiers to join him in *Mary Rose*, but had to write and say that he could not accommodate 111 of them until, 'a great part of the retinue of my brother Sir Edward Howard, were despatched'. In the meantime Thomas issued instructions that the 111 soldiers were to be paid one month's wages of 5s per man. He also gave orders that a pair of gallows be erected at the waterside from which he was prepared to, 'hang a dozen knaves' who had jumped ship as an example to others who might be so tempted for, 'the soldiers be abroad in the country and rob and steal and do much harm'.[9]

Henry's instructions, received on 13 May, by both Howard and Charles Brandon, now Lord Lisle, were for them to return to Brittany with sufficient land forces under Lisle's command to 'distress the navy of France'. The plan was for Lisle to embark at Plymouth but Howard, quite rightly, saw that this could cause problems if, with the army embarked, he was unable to sail. Before Plymouth's breakwater was built many centuries later its anchorages lay open to prevailing wind and seas meaning that it could often be impossible to depart from there in a sailing ship. Howard summed up the location's shortcomings succinctly in his response to the king's command:

> And where your grace willeth me to remain here till my said cousin Sir Charles's coming hither; Sir, under your correction, it is not to be done, for divers causes. One is we lie here in the most dangerous haven of England for so many ships, and lie moored together in strait room, and divers of your ships hath been in great danger, and nightly fall together; howbeit, God be thanked, there is no hurt done. Also, the wind blowing any part off the South, it is unpossible to get hence.'[10]

Plymouth and the surrounding waters as depicted in a contemporary map. The Cattewater, from which Howard had so much difficulty warping, is shown centre right with ships at anchor, while the Sound is the broad area into which the two carracks are sailing.

The problem of leaving Plymouth against an onshore wind was later to confront another English admiral in more dire straits sixty-five years later. Luckily, Sir Francis Drake managed it in one day and sailed on to challenge the might of the Spanish Armada. Howard, having made the very sensible proposal that the fleet embark the ground forces at Southampton, took another fortnight before he could write to Wolsey to say that he was, '...warping with much pain from the Cattewater to the Sound'. It was probably not until 23 May that he reached Southampton.

The time in Plymouth with the ships lying far too close to each other for comfort in those choppy waters would have been unpleasant and exhausting. A full watch of sailors would have been required at all times to fend off ships as they were driven down on to each other, with the danger of spars interlocking, anchors staving in sides and upper works being crushed. Even those off watch would have had an uncomfortable time; probably wet and cold, they would have been rocked erratically as they lay down, while the timbers creaked and the wind howled through the rigging. It is no wonder that some of them felt that desertion was a better option. Howard was a careful recorder of the chaos:

> We be all ready, and have been these six days; and now these two or three days past, the wind blowing at West-South-West, which is the best wind possible to bring us to Hampton, hath and it doth blow so strainable that we have been forced every man to lay out shot, anchors and all, and have broken many new anchors and cables. Assuring your grace that whosoever bought your new cables hath done you shrewd service, for they be made of the worst stuff that ever man saw, as at my coming to Hampton your grace shall well perceive by an example I shall send you of the same.[11]

Although unable to sail himself, Howard stationed watchers off the French coast and gleaned information from incoming vessels. Thus he was able to inform Wolsey that he had heard that twenty Spanish ships with 6,000 men had sailed for England. Howard viewed this intelligence with justifiable skepticism, as it was not long before he was made aware that Henry's father-in-law, Ferdinand of Aragon, had unilaterally agreed peace terms with France, leaving England in the cold. Howard saw advantage in even this betrayal, however. He had been informed that fourteen Spanish ships were sailing from Bordeaux to Flanders with a cargo of wine. These he intended to intercept, asking only for Wolsey's approval that he escort the vessels to London, no doubt with a handsome profit on board for both men. Of potentially greater value to the progress of the war was the news that a rebellion at Brest Castle, led by local Bretons, had been put down by the French king's lieutenants. However, yet again, the English took no advantage from this manifestation of disquiet amongst the Bretons. All this intelligence Howard dutifully reported to Wolsey. Occasionally, sycophant that he was, and despite his dislike for the cardinal, he apologised for the volume of correspondence in his usual ingratiating way:

> And whereas I write unto you often, and peradventure every cause I write of be not of great gravity; yet I require you ascribe not the same to my default, for I assure you I had rather the posts took pain in sparing their horses than I should be found too slow in writing or working when time shall require.[12]

Howard knew that the French were also gathering intelligence and, in a letter to the king dated 18 May, he stated his belief that his move to Southampton could lull the French into thinking that he no longer intended to attack Brittany, and thus weaken their guard. On the other hand, were the French to discover that he was planning to move against Brest, they might withdraw their ships to the safety of La Rochelle and Bordeaux, in which case his assault, which he assured the king had every chance of success, would be frustrated. Two days later, he informed Wolsey that

England seemed to have won what, for his time in command, had been a war of posturing and positioning rather than outright engagement:

> The Bretons...say that they have taken their ordnance out of their ships and had it into the castle, and will no more meddle on the sea this year...but against the next year they will make ships enough to defend the sea....And I have straitly examined him; who saith that the mariners that came from Brest by stealth, having no will no longer to serve in the ships of war, say that the ships of war were come forth from the castle and would return to their countries; and that the hulks that were at Brest said they would go homeward and convey the Admiral to Honfleur, where he intended to lay up his ship for this year....Also he saith that the ships of Brittany that be home be hauled up into creeks and digged in pits, not thinking to come to sea this year.[13]

Howard's purpose in drawing this news to Wolsey's attention was to have his attack on Brest called off for, as he saw it, there would be little to be gained from assaulting an empty port. He did, however, dispatch three ships to Brittany to capture a fisherman from whom the veracity of the rumours might be confirmed or not. Howard was also informed that France was reinforcing and that, '...the French King hath sent Mons. de la Motte into Scotland with money to pay the wages of five Scottish ships and 18 of Denmark.[14]

Henry had indeed changed focus. Now he intended a glorious land campaign against France, which he would lead with his new ally, the Emperor Maximilian. The king's plan was implicit in his directive to Howard in mid-May when the latter was ordered to send three ships to patrol the Straits of Dover. Howard himself was kept in the dark, outside Henry's inner circle at court. And it hurt. The king confirmed that he wished to cancel an assault on Brest when he visited Howard at Southampton on 4 June but, in a letter to Wolsey written the next day it is clear that Howard had indicated quite clearly to Henry that he had no stomach for this fight:

> Which enterprise being debated before his grace, I showed his grace I durst not enterprise the said feats unless that his grace would discharge me if any misfortune fell by the same.[15]

Those few lines, sum up the character of the man, so unlike his derring-do brother, Edward: his concern as to his position so similar to that felt by that far more attractive personality Walter Raleigh when he engraved on glass for his sovereign, Queen Elizabeth, to see, 'Fain would I climb, but fear I to fall'[16]

Having exposed his reticence, Howard blusters on in print:

> And thus most heartily, I beseech you, if my misfortune shall be to do no acceptable service, to be means for me to the King and his Council to consider that never man endured more pain than I shall do to see all other where the may do good service if they will, and I can do none but his enemies will adventure as well as I. And, for God's sake, let his grace and his Council command me to some hard enterprise to see if I will follow the same...[17]

The insincerity drips off the page but it seems his main concern was that others would be given a chance to shine that would be denied him. Reading beyond the hypocrisy in his letters to Wolsey it is evident that Howard was livid at not being kept informed of the king's intentions while Wolsey was. In early June Howard was informed by Lisle and the Bishop of Winchester that he was no longer required to 'enter the water of Brest', but even this personal debrief appears not to have completely clarified the king's intentions for, the next day, Howard informed Wolsey that, '...tomorrow I will take the musters and with as much haste as may be possible I will depart to Brittany-ward.'[18]

The cause of consternation, a mid-sixteenth-century galley. This is a Venetian example, but the French galleys were identical in basic layout. The projecting prow was not used for ramming but could be a useful boarding bridge in action.

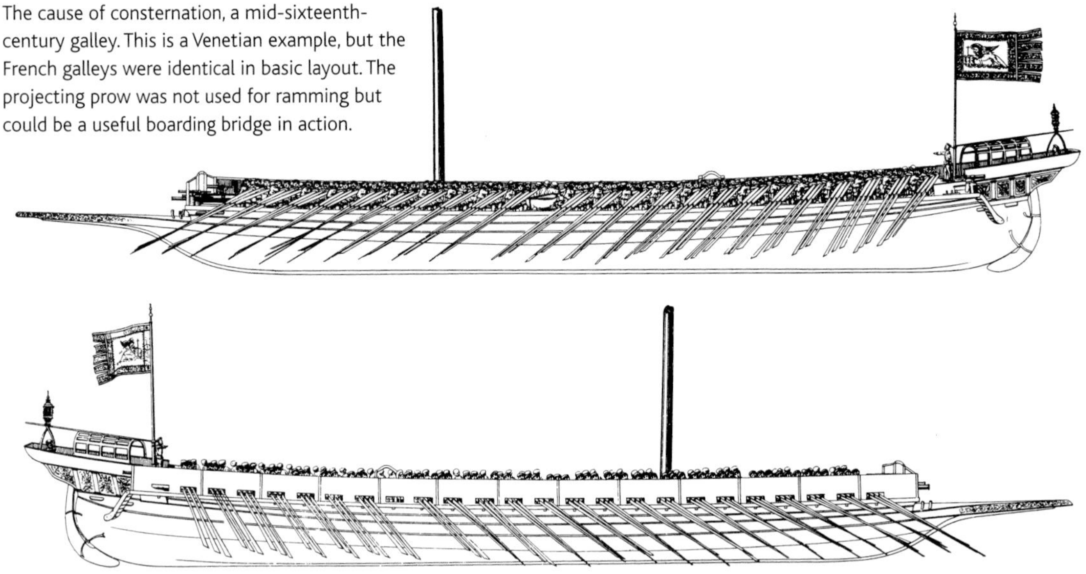

Howard's confusion over his deployment continued for the next few days, with Howard informing the Privy Council, on 8 June, that he could think of nothing that he would rather do than to return to Brest. A study of the correspondence between him and Wolsey during this period does little to clarify his thinking except to confirm that, however cunning, conceited and calculating he might have been, he was far from clever. There was, however, as so often seemed to be the case when Howard was required to take action, a problem. He had to inform the Council that desertions had continued and that, for example, Lord Ferrers was more than 100 men short but had caught two whom he intended to hang if it were proved they had left without licence. Howard also informed the Council that Hereford gaol was full of deserters, although why this particular town should be singled out either for comment or as a centre for deserters was not made clear.

Ships from the fleet continued to be sent towards the Narrow Seas. In mid June, the *Carrack of Savona*, *Katherine Fortileza* and *Mary George* had sailed from Portsmouth and, '...with them many small men, some with the King's mounts of the New Forest.'[19]

Given the size of New Forest ponies it would appear, on a first reading of the above, that short men were being dispatched to form a sort of mini-cavalry, but the 'small' probably refers to the land holdings of the gentlemen concerned, rather than their stature. Howard then sent another three ships after the first group to warn them that a Danish warship was in the area along with some French galleys in Dieppe. The admiral's fear of the latter surfaces once again in this letter: '...if the galleys meet with our ships, little good would be done, and peradventure if a calm came, much danger might ensue.'[20]

At this stage Howard, although aware that the king intended to take the army to Calais, still believed that he himself could be bound for Brittany. As a result *Mary Rose* was being kept in fighting trim, with invoices being raised to cover the costs of such items as iron work, nails and ropes and two gallons of vinegar to make, 'fine powder for hand guns'. To complete this work Howard and his purser had to deal with sixteen named suppliers and many more whose contribution can be deduced; the shore support of the fleet was obviously still very fragmented and conducted on an *ad-hoc* basis. Howard also authorised additional ordnance to be fitted into *Great Carrack* in time for Henry's crossing to Calais, by which time *Mary Rose* had moved to Sandwich to protect the passage of the army.

The English force began its crossing of the Channel on 6 June. Henry himself followed on 30 June, travelling with an entourage more suited to a royal tour than a war campaign. He spent three weeks showing off to the burghers of Calais, then marched forward at the rate of three miles a day towards Thérouanne. The rainy weather drenched the men, allowing Henry the opportunity to emulate Henry V and pass through the camp at night sharing the lot of his bedraggled troops. By 1 August the English had reached Thérouanne, which they beseiged for three weeks. During this time, Henry's elderly ally, the Emperor Maximilian, arrived with a small body of men and, seeing how crestfallen Henry was by the size of his forces, volunteered to fight personally under the English flag. On 16 August the French relieving forces appeared and disappeared in quick succession, the scene of their rout being recorded ignominiously by the title, 'The Battle of the Spurs', referring to the speed with which they urged their steeds away from the English. They left behind much materiel and a few old warriors, such as the much-admired Chevalier Bayard and the Duc de Longueville, captives whom Henry treated with great respect. Thérouanne fell some five days later and, as it had refused to surrender, was put to the flame. Pleased with these limited achievements Henry was determined to advance on Paris, only to be dissuaded by Maximilian who did not wish to see the European balance of power upset. Instead, the emperor persuaded the king to retire to Lille to be regally entertained by his daughter, Margaret of Savoy, a savvy widowed lady, whom Henry only embarrassed by trying to arrange a marriage between her and his favourite – but still a mere courtier – Charles Brandon.

Refreshed by the revelries of Lille, Henry returned to the war to lay siege to the cathedral city of Tournai, which Maximilian saw as an unwelcome

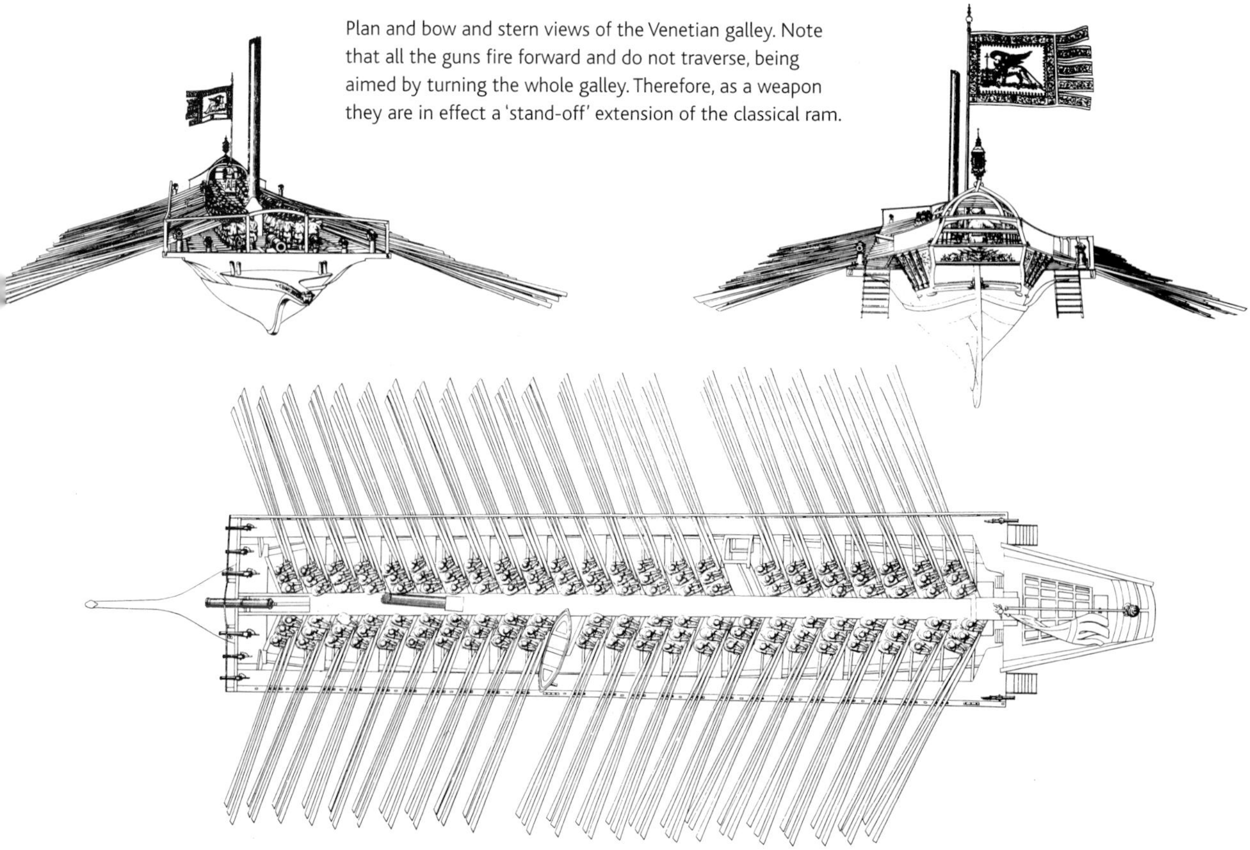

Plan and bow and stern views of the Venetian galley. Note that all the guns fire forward and do not traverse, being aimed by turning the whole galley. Therefore, as a weapon they are in effect a 'stand-off' extension of the classical ram.

isthmus of French territory protruding into his lands. Having heard of the fate of Thérouanne, the citizens of Tournai were more pragmatic; observing the great guns that the English had set up before the city's gates they handed over the keys before the first linstock was lit, making Wolsey, who was promptly enthroned as the city's bishop, a much richer man in the process. Before the walls of Tournai Henry knighted William Compton, Edward Neville and William Fitzwilliam, the latter of whom had been, 'sore hurt with a quarrel' in the fighting with Edward Howard off Brest in 1513, and would go on to serve in *Mary Rose* in the next decade as Thomas Howard's vice admiral. After Tournai, desultory and inconclusive campaigning continued in France until 22 October when the king returned to England, having racked up a debt of hundreds of millions of pounds (in modern values) for little return. In his absence Katherine, who was acting as regent in his absence, had achieved a far greater – and far cheaper – victory in what had been a proper battle.

On 8 September, James IV, having crossed the border from Scotland at the head of his army, reached Flodden Edge in Northumberland. Facing him was an English force that had been heartened by a rousing address from Katherine before it set off north. It was led by the very elderly Earl of Surrey, whose son, Thomas Howard, had sailed in *Mary Rose* to Newcastle to disembark for some land campaigning of his own and the chance to shine by leading the English vanguard. Being the man he was, Howard probably regarded his potential rivals serving with the king in France as a greater threat to his future political security than any Scottish claymore. He was right. The Scots were routed, their king killed on the field of battle. Flodden was a Howard victory. Surrey had commanded; Thomas had led the vanguard and Sir Edmund Howard, who was felled three times, had acted as the Knight Marshal of the army and commanded the right wing. It was the Lord Admiral's repeated assaults on the Scottish centre, under James himself and Bothwell, that secured the victory and it was his seadogs who kept those attacks going. A tradition of naval involvement in land campaigns, that reached its apotheosis with the Naval Division of World War I, had been born.

Flodden turned out well for the Howards. Surrey was restored to the dukedom of Norfolk and Lord Thomas Howard moved up to replace him as Earl of Surrey, by which title he will be referred to from now on. As for Scotland, with Flodden the English placed a throttling thumb on the thin throat of the infant heir to that throne, James V; the other thumb, at Solway Moss in 1542, would squeeze his life out, and with it any future hope that the Scots would have had for remaining an equal partner in a divided island.Thus the Howards achieved the most significant land victories of Henry's reign without the presence of the king who prided himself on his generalship. Katherine, probably unwittingly, rubbed salt in her spouse's wounded pride, by describing Flodden to the king as:

> ...the great victory that our Lord hath sent to your subjects in your absence. To my thinking this battle hath been more than should you win all the crown of France.[21]

She was right. One can only wonder if Henry remembered this in the darker days of their divorce.

During the land campaigns both in France and against Scotland *Mary Rose* and the fleet remained strategically placed in the North Sea so as to be available both to support the king's crossing, and also to intervene against any attempt by the French and Danish fleets to link up with the Scots. When the campaign season ended the existence of a standing fleet meant that Henry was again able to keep ships at sea during the winter. This force, made up of sixteen ships and 1,500 men under the command of Sir Weston Browne, was divided into small patrolling units whose job it was to keep an eye, most especially, on the Narrow Seas.

The winter passed without incident and in March, John Browne relieved Thomas Spert as the master of *Mary Rose* ready for a spring and summer campaign, for reconnaissance operations had indicated that significant preparations were being made by the French at Honfleur, St Malo and Dieppe. Yet Surrey seems to have felt that no immediate threat was apparent. He was wrong. At considerable risk to his galleys from inclement weather, Prégent de Bidoux launched an assault on Brighton in April 1514. The attack was nearly fatal for the French galley ace. While standing by the boats in the surf trying to recall his men from a raid that had been easily repulsed, Prégent was struck by an arrow in one eye, and nearly died. Repulsed as it had been, Prégent's attack irritated Henry who was determined to avenge the insult. But his Holy Alliance had faded away by this time. Ferdinand had already agreed terms with Louis; Maximilian was concluding a secret treaty. Both had assured Henry that they would be part of a triple alliance for the 1514 season; both played false. As much as to show Ferdinand and Maximilian that he could do just as well without their support, Henry ordered his fleet to sea in early April. He also planned to send reinforcements to Calais in preparation for raids into France.

With his fleet at sea Henry could exert pressure on his enemies without the great expense and danger that landing an army on foreign soil would entail. Surrey had all the advantages of mobility with none of the constraints of a land army. The French, however, were not prepared to come out and fight. In May, a force under Sir Henry Sherborne, the new captain of *Mary Rose*, and Sir Stephen Bull (whose *Less Bark* had been so grievously damaged by Prégent de Bidoux and his galleys off Brest in 1513), was dispatched to Boulogne to try to position itself between Prégent's galleys and the harbour, but the French withdrew in time to avoid a clash. As a result, Surrey began to show frustrations similar to those that had been so fatal to his brother; but he was not going to repeat Edward's mistake. Instead, he proposed landing 3,000 soldiers two miles from Boulogne. He believed that, '...without danger [to this landing force] the said galleys would be put in great danger.'[22]

In support of his plans he wrote to the Council:

> I would be assured that nothing should be omitted that may be feasible, with God's grace with the next fair wind that may possibly serve to go and come, I will go over in the King's *Less Bark* with such company with me of small ships as with God's grace shall do that is possible to be done. And if they abide without the bulwark, I doubt not to displease them without great loss; and if they go within the bulwark, as far as I can understand it is...dangerous...which is not to be adventured with none but them that will cast themselves away wilfully. And my lords, if this enterprise will not take effect... methink it were not honourable that all the army should remain here for fear of the said galleys.[23]

Typically, Surrey was promising action but hedging his bets, for it would have been most unlikely that Prégent, having been forewarned by Henry Sherborne's foray, would have left harbour to ride at anchor to await a fresh assault.

Something else was happening that May that was to have implications for the command of the navy of the future. The Council and the admiral started to discuss how the fleet should be deployed in order to deliver the nation's strategic aim of controlling the Channel and the seaways to Scotland. Hitherto ships had very much followed where the admiral led them, with few being dispatched on independent operations. In June the previous year Howard had ordered three ships to the Narrow Seas to cover the crossing of the army to Calais, but generally he had kept his forces together. This disposition was now being questioned. On 17 May the Merchant Venturers were petitioning for 'wafters', or escorts, to protect them against the French galleys on their passage to

---

OVERLEAF A contemporary illustration of a naval attack on Brighton. It is conventionally dated to 1545, but in all probability it shows the raid carried out by Prégent de Bidoux in 1514. Note the galleys drawn up on the beach, in effect acting as landing craft for the raiding party ashore.

1545
Julye 37
Hen viij
the wynde milles
hove Churche
hove village
Shippes may ride all somer
within di a myle the towne in
v fathome water

the frie comme Cage

Grynell commyng from howne towne to briethampton

The East pte of briethampton reysing onelam clere home

here landed the Galeys

whese shippes rydeng hard a bode shore,
into the hille and also the way to see of parte of the
the Countrey dare not aduenture to

Calais. Two days later, Fox, the Bishop of Winchester wrote to Wolsey expressing his hope that ships would be sent at once to scour the Narrow Seas and 'waft the hoys to Calais'. Fox was concerned that some ships had already been lost and tried to impress upon Wolsey the need to keep ships in harbour until escorts were available.[24]

Coupled with this pressure Wolsey was also being informed by Lord Dacre, Henry's ambassador to Scotland, that the Scots were going to try to link up with the French, a task they believed would be made all the easier, 'because the English fleet keep together'. This idea supported one put forward a year earlier by Lord Darcy that, 'If ships lay at Dover and some upon the North Sea' they would gain honour through engagement with the enemy.[25] The pressure for deployed flotillas and independent commands was mounting.

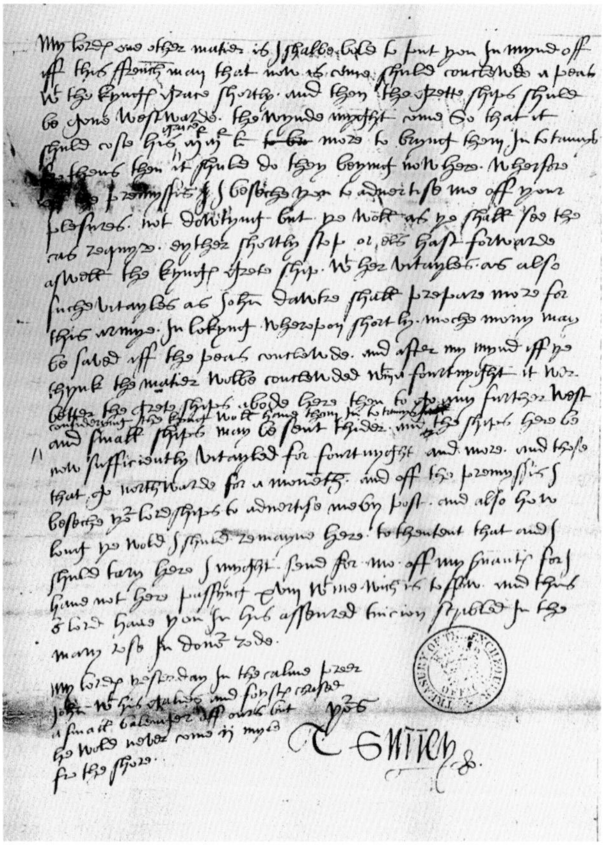

The letter from Surrey in which the Lord Admiral refers to the 'fear of the galleys'. This is the (secret) reverse of the public letter, 'scribbled in the *Mary Rose* in Dover road'.

By the end of the month, Surrey was writing of sending ships east to convoy merchantmen from Zeeland, and north to watch for any Frenchmen sailing for Scotland. He himself was uncomfortable at anchor in the Downs or off Dover. He wished to reduce the number of ships on patrol in the Narrows to a number just sufficient to deal with the galleys should they venture out, and wanted to leave one of his commanders, Weston Browne, in command in the east while he took the remainder of the fleet west to annoy the French.[26] He was creating a truly Channel-long command.

Surrey showed the letter described above to his captains. In a secret addition, written on the other side(!), he opened discussions about the future deployment of the fleet should peace be concluded within the following weeks. Very sensibly he proposed that it would be cheaper to leave the fleet in the Downs than to sail it west where it could cost a great deal to bring it back to the Thames to lay up once a peace treaty was signed, especially if the winds were contrary.[27] A few weeks later, Howard was able to report to the king and Council about a successful raid on the land around Cherbourg, although he did not attack the 'marvellous strong town and castle' itself. He had also dispatched another party of some 700 men thirty miles along the coast and, although at the time of writing he was waiting for their return, he was satisfied that the great plumes of smoke he could see signalled their success. As he said to the king, 'I trust your grace be not in the French men's debt for burning late of Brighton.'[28] In an act that replicated that of his brother two years earlier, Surrey also claimed to have burnt Prégent de Bidoux's own house.[29] He understood the king's mentality well and that ending the war with a successful act of retaliation would be just the sort of thing to keep him in Henry's favour. With that raid in June 1514 the war ended and peace with France was concluded in early August.

On the same day as the raid on Cherbourg, Henry had been enjoying himself at another naval occasion. He had taken boat from Greenwich to Erith and launched his mighty new flagship, *Henry Grace à Dieu*. At 1500 tons with, reputedly, five decks and more than 200 bronze and iron guns, the *Great Harry* was a formidable expression of royal might and a valuable propaganda weapon. Henry ensured that all the ambassadors were invited down river for the occasion and that it was marked by an appropriately extravagant degree of carousing. He was delighted with his new creation and dressed for the occasion in a long tunic of gold brocade under which he wore breeches also of gold cloth and scarlet hose. Around his neck he hung a large golden bosun's call encrusted with jewels and this he blew frequently, 'near as loud as in a trumpet or clarinet' rejoicing in his role as an armchair commander. *Great Harry* was launched too late to serve in the war for which she had been built and in which the rest of the navy had acquitted itself well. It would be a test of Henry's nerve and Wolsey's skill and commitment to see if she and the other great ships such as *Mary Rose* could survive the peace until they were next required.

One element of that peace was Henry's agreement to wed his young sister Mary to the prematurely elderly Louis of France, whose own wife, Anne, Duchess of Brittany, had just died. Thus political expediency led to Mary, a vivacious eighteen year old who had already expressed her own desire to wed the king's favourite Charles Brandon, being sacrificed to Louis, an elderly fifty-eight year old. A strange way to treat a supposedly favourite sister. After a mildly erotic 'proxy wedding' ceremony in Greenwich between Mary and the French king's representative, the Duc de Longueville, the princess sailed for France. Louis, who rode out to meet her was enraptured and, '...kissed her as kindly as if he had been five and twenty and came in this dress and on horseback the more to prove his vigour...[30]

Mary was showered with gifts, diamonds and a huge ruby, so much in fact that, when it all went wrong (see below) the requirement to return some of these gifts became most contentious. Her entry into Paris was a great success and she was likened to the *rose vermeille*, the fabled shrub that adorned Jericho, so her link to the Tudor emblem was very evident even in France.

The morning after the wedding night the French king informed the Venetian ambassador that he had, '...crossed the river three times that night and would have done more had he chosen'. However, although Mary might have enchanted the king she had not won over the French court. Despite her tearful pleadings, she was ordered to send most of her retinue back to England. Even her letters to Henry and Wolsey, written in her distress, received little sympathy, suggesting that there was not the closeness between sovereign and sister that has been believed, or, at the very least, that it was not sufficient to overturn the needs of international diplomacy. On 28 December Louis wrote to Henry to tell him how satisfied he was with his bride. Then, on New Year's Day, he died, exhausted, by all accounts, by his young wife, but having thoroughly enjoyed his many 'crossings of the river' in the matrimonial frolic that ended with his death. Thus Henry achieved through *amour* what he had failed to achieve through armour.

Wolsey and the king immediately planned to marry the widowed Mary to the Archduke Charles, the Emperor Maximilian's grandson and the king of Spain's nephew. So, before the period of court mourning was completed Henry sent his much-loved courtier Charles Brandon, Earl of Suffolk, to recover Mary, his childhood sweetheart, from her widowed isolation and the unwelcome pesterings of the new French king, Francis I. Understandably at this point, Mary's love for Suffolk now outweighed her sense of duty to her brother, and their (briefly) secret marriage placed them in danger of being charged with treason. For once, however, love triumphed over politics and the chastened, but heavily fined lovers, were allowed to live together in peace. Sadly, Mary died in 1533 at the age of thirty-eight, her life span just exceeding that of the ship which popular tradition claims bore her name.

CHAPTER 10

Biting Back

THE ADVENT OF PEACE meant that the king now owned a large number of vessels for which he was still responsible. He could not, as had his predecessors, return ships to their merchant owners or lay a few vessels up in the Hamble. He thus faced a large programme of maintenance to keep his vessels both seaworthy and available for bringing back into service at short notice, a contingency that the uncertainty of continental politics demanded. The English did not have a good record in keeping laid-up ships in a seaworthy condition and had often employed foreign experts to manage this task, for the nation as yet still lacked the maritime traditions and dock-side skills to be up to the job. Techniques such as careening – turning a ship on to one side for cleaning, caulking or repair – were unknown in England and were first introduced by these foreign workers. Of significance was the recognition that, because of their carvel construction, after four to five years in the water a great deal of re-caulking and re-timbering was needed before vessels built this way could go to sea again.

If Henry was to preserve his new navy then a system of planned maintenance needed to be introduced for his reserve fleet. The fleet was now too large and represented too great an investment to be disposed of privately, besides which the creation of purpose-built warships meant that the hulls could not be readily adapted for trade. So, once again, the fate of *Mary Rose* and her sister ships was to lie in the hands of civil servants. Foremost of these was John Hopton, who had been appointed Comptroller of the King's Ships in 1512. He was responsible for the new storehouses that had been built at Erith and Deptford in 1512–13 during the height of the war to support Howard's fleet. The importance of the creation of Hopton's post, and the existence of these storehouses cannot be underestimated for they represent the administrative keel on which a permanent navy could be kept afloat. N A M Rodger goes so far as to say that:

> The reason why Henry VIII's navy did not go the way of Henry V's on his death is partly because of the mortal danger to England which Henry VIII left as his legacy, but also because an administrative and logistical structure had been created which was capable of maintaining a permanent navy. Nothing like it had existed in England before, and nothing like it then existed in any other country outside the Mediterranean (except perhaps Portugal).[1]

Hopton's position made him *de facto* senior to Brygandyne, who was to retire in 1523, although the two men do seem to have exercised separate areas of authority. The Thames, where *Mary Rose* was to spend the five years from the autumn of 1514 to 1520 was definitely within Hopton's patch. On 27 July *Mary Rose* arrived, in company with *Peter Pomegranate* and *Great Elizabeth*, at Blackwall to be secured to moorings in the river. Over the next few weeks her fittings were landed and a careful inventory made.[2] It was a lengthy, and one can presume, definitive list. It included the masts and yards, the standing and running rigging, the sails and parrals, brass sheaves, compasses, hourglasses, the ship's boat and its oars, even down to the last kitchen utensil. Minor armament, such as bows and muskets were delivered, along with barrels of gunpowder and shot into the safe keeping of one John Miller and one Thomas Elderton, but there is no record of the guns themselves being landed at this time. Instead they were placed under the care of the master of the ship, John Browne and the purser, John Bryarley. The care with which all these items were recorded, and presumably stowed, meant that the ships could be brought back into commission very efficiently and at short notice. For the time being, as empty hulks, the ships were referred to as being 'in ordinary' – meaning that they were charged to the routine budget, not from money raised for contingencies such as war.

Empty of fittings *Mary Rose* might have been, but she had five ship keepers on board to carry out routine maintenance and, most importantly, to check for any leakages that could spring and spread with remarkable rapidity in any untended wooden ship. Such leaks were not just caused by general wear and tear. Moored in the tideway the ships could be rammed by passing vessels or even, in the severe winters of the time, struck by heavy floes of ice. Wind, wave and tide would also have made it difficult to carry out regular inspections from outboard.

In the summer of 1517, therefore, Hopton was instructed to 'make and cast a pond' in a meadow at Deptford large enough to float *Mary Rose, Great Galley, Peter Pomegranate, Great Barke* and *Lesser Barke.* The specifications required it to have:

> ...a good, able, and sufficient head for the same pond, and also certain able sluices through which the water may have entry and course into the said pond, as well as spring tides as at neap tides.[3]

If Portsmouth was the home of the nation's first permanent dry dock, Deptford was to have one of the earliest naval basins. And it did not come cheaply: Hopton was to be paid 600 marks for the work but a careful clause in the contract specified that, should the five ships not ride comfortably in the pond, the money was to be returned. Obviously, investing money now to save on long-term expenditure was a sensible decision, but it still took foresight and commitment.

This foresight meant that *Mary Rose* could be re-commissioned for Henry's attempt at diplomacy by extravagance that was 'The Field of the Cloth of Gold' in June 1520. For his crossing from Dover to Calais, Henry summoned his ships to escort him. He even had a new ship built, his royal yacht, which was named *Katherine Bark* but also, and more touchingly, referred to as *Katherine Pleasaunce.* Some years later a picture, considered by many to depict the king embarking at Dover, was painted (artist unknown). Like many paintings of the time it has its inaccuracies. The king is shown on board *Henry Grace à Dieu,* which had too deep a draught to enter Dover, but the artist was probably more concerned with the impression than the historical accuracy of what he depicted. There are fifteen ships shown in the painting, fifteen being the number of vessels over 180 tons in the navy royal at that time, so what is being depicted is a fleet review by the monarch. The five largest and most conspicuous ships in the foreground appear to be, from left to right, *Katherine Fortileza, Gabriel, Royal Sovereign, Henry Grace à Dieu* and *Mary Rose.* If these are indeed they, then the painting has to be showing a scene from 1520, for that was the last time these ships could have served together. The unfortunate *Katherine Fortileza* was condemned after a storm in 1521, by which time Henry VII's *Sovereign* had also to be removed from the establishment as, after thirty-two years of service, she did not warrant repairing. However, subject to artistic interpretation the painting might be, it still represents a formidable fighting fleet. The ability to rendezvous at Dover with this number of seaworthy vessels was a credit to the much improved system of upkeep.

The empty extravagance of the Field of the Cloth of Gold is best reflected by the fact that the eternal amicable brotherhood that Henry and Francis swore to each other lasted just two years. This was not helped by Henry's friendly meetings with his wife's nephew, the new Holy Roman Emperor,

Charles V – Francis' greatest European rival – both immediately before and after the Field of the Cloth of Gold. The amity established between Francis and Henry – two green young monarchs desperate to prove themselves – was, in fact, a confirmed cordiality of hatred.

Following Henry's triumphant return from France *Mary Rose* sailed back to Deptford where she was kept in a state of readiness so that when hostilities between England and France were renewed in 1522 she was ready to sail, having been pumped out and re-caulked in October 1520. Before he could go to war with France Henry needed reassurance that the Emperor Charles was firmly committed to their new alliance. Charles was returning from the Low Countries to Spain, presenting an ideal opportunity for the two heads of state to meet at Dover, and Charles arrived there in late May 1522. He was to

be entertained on board *Mary Rose* before being escorted to London via Gravesend where the royal party would embark by barge for Greenwich. Orders were therefore given that all ships along the route be 'adorned with streamers and with ordnance ready to fire as the Emperor passes'. Later, while the two rulers were still together, they declared war on France and, as a sign of their alliance Surrey was appointed by Charles as an admiral in the Imperial Navy. The document conferring the appointment also refers to Surrey as an admiral of Normandy and Aquitaine, and to Henry as king of France; the continental aspirations of the English died hard.

Henry's navy at Dover prior to 'The Field of the Cloth of Gold'. The king is shown on board *Henry Grace á Dieu*, the ship setting sail on the right.

Mobilisation of the fleet had begun at the end of 1521 and followed a familiar pattern, with Surrey ordering the fleet to muster at Southampton for victualling and the embarkation of troops. In May Howard issued his directions to his captains, which formed part of the growing body of fighting instructions for use at sea. He clearly directed what he expected of his subordinates, often reinforcing his desires with the ominous phrase, 'on pain of death'.[4] That aside, they form an early example of standing orders to enable the admiral to keep command of his force, and they were clearly spelt out. Among the nine commandments:

> No ship, except those appointed, to give chase…on pain of death.
> Every master to keep his lead and sound out of any danger, according to the old customs.
> No one to enter port without authority.
> Before sunset every ship to come under the lee of the Admiral to know what course to keep.
> Every ship had to have a quartermaster and boatswain.
> When they land soldiers, the crew and gunners to defend the boat must not leave it on pain of death.[5]

Conversely, it was during the period of stand off with the French that Surrey and his advisors developed further the concept of the independent command that had come into being towards the end of the previous war. Hitherto, although the admiral had dispatched units of his fleet to carry out tasks away from the main group these had generally been supporting operations, such as reconnaissance or convoy escorting. Now the fleet was to be divided into separate commands, each with its own geographic area of operations, and authority delegated to the local commander to act as he saw fit. One flotilla, consisting of four ships, with John Cary in the 60-ton *Katherine Galley* in command was placed on Channel patrol to cover the area between Winchelsea and the Channel Islands. A second, under the experienced William Gonson in the 300-ton *Christ* was to be stationed off the southern entrance to the Irish Sea, while the third, composed of four ships, with Captain John Maryner commanding from on board the 80-ton *Sweepstake*, were to guard the Narrow Seas – precursors of the famous Dover Patrol. The larger vessels, including *Mary Rose*, *Peter Pomegranate* and the *Great Harry* seem to have formed a strategic reserve ready both to sail where most needed and, more especially, to act as the offensive arm of the fleet taking the fight and the forces over to France.

The thinking behind these deployments would remain appropriate until the union of England and Scotland for, if successful, it would have sealed off the Channel and provided a reasonable challenge to any enemy convoys heading towards Scotland. However, although he had issued his orders, Surrey himself was to play a less prominent role. Much of the operational work was delegated to William Fitzwilliam the vice admiral in *Henry Grace à Dieu*. It was Fitzwilliam who, despairing at the state of Portsmouth's defences, ordered an expensive rectification programme that included the provision of a chain to be drawn across the harbour mouth to the appropriately named Fort Blockhouse. The Portsea end of the chain, from where it was raised and lowered is remembered today in the delightful little 'Capstan Square'.

As always in the days of sail the ability not only to remain on station but also to get there in the first place was weather dependent. Fitzwilliam who, with Surrey absent with the king and emperor, was himself on board *Mary Rose* had a difficult time trying to head down Channel from Dover in early June. Adverse weather conditions had forced him from Dover on the day of the king's departure eastward to seek shelter in The Downs for several days, after which a temporary improvement in wind direction and strength allowed him to sail again only for a southwesterly to blow so 'exceeding strainably' that they had to return to The Downs. It was during this period of difficult sailing conditions that Fitzwilliam was able to compare the sailing qualities of *Mary Rose* with that of the *Great Harry*. The latter impressed him and he wrote to the king to say that she:

> sailed as well as any ship that was in the fleet, and rather better, and weathered them all save the *Mary Rose*. And if she go by the wind, I assure your grace, there will be a hard choice between the *Mary Rose* and her.[6]

Having entertained the two sovereigns Surrey then took passage to Southampton and the Solent where he was to suffer the common frustrations of lack of wind and absence of victuals. His letters, which had previously been sent in almost equal number to Wolsey and the king, were now addressed mainly to the latter and he did not make light of his problems. He summarised his position by stating that unless the victualling was sorted out satisfactorily then Henry would expend much, 'without some great displeasures might be done to the enemies'.[7] In a side swipe at Wolsey he also suggests that of the two factors influencing his activities he was, 'doubting much more of the victual than wind'.[8] This latter remark, quite subtle for Howard, would indicate that he now felt much surer of his own position vis à vis Wolsey. The reference to high expenditure would have touched a raw nerve with the king, especially as Howard also informed him of the wretched state of defences and preparations at Portsmouth.

This was not a surprising state of affairs. Henry had bankrupted the Exchequer to pay for the first French war. He had spent a fortune to disport himself at The Field of the Cloth of Gold, and was now having to dig deep in his commodious breeches to find even loose-change to support the latest war. Surrey must have been aware of the state of the economy but he stuck to his task, moaning all the while. Two days later, on 23 June, Surrey wrote a very terse letter to Wolsey requesting action over the victuals.[9] Although still addressing the cardinal as 'your grace', there is none of the sycophancy of the correspondence some nine years earlier. This letter, and the one that followed,[10] clearly reflected Howard's

The Bay of Morlaix showing the numerous islets and rocks threatening any fleet entering without local knowledge.

growing confidence. When the time came he was ready to play his part in the overthrow of the upstart butcher's son.

On 24 June the under-victualled Surrey was back at sea battling against a wind so contrary that the ships had to anchor during the flood tide and only move westerly when the ebb carried them that way. It was a slow passage; three days to Portland and a further two to come to anchor off Dartmouth, a port that impressed Surrey greatly. Surrey had himself and his advisors rowed into the haven about which he waxed lyrical in a letter to the king, telling him that: 'In my life I never saw a goodlier haven nor more sure lying, after all our opinions, for your said ships, than here.'[11]

Surrey thought Dartmouth itself very defensible but recommended that castles be built to protect against an attack launched from Torbay. He even suggested that it would cost the king less to establish Dartmouth than it would to repair Portsmouth and, in a final effort to sway the argument, he had his letter countersigned by some of those who had accompanied him into Dartmouth. He then dispatched the letter for personal delivery by Nicholas Semer, the Mayor of Dartmouth who would, undoubtedly, have reported most favourably on the virtues of his town. Although Henry did not follow up his admiral's suggestion to station ships at Dartmouth a fort was built at Brixham and another south of Dartmouth at Bayard's Castle. Anyone who has tried to enter or leave Dartmouth with a strong wind blowing will be thankful that Surrey's enthusiasm did not persuade the king to respond in like manner.

The fleet's main purpose in sailing had been to attack the French fleet gathering at Francis's new port of Le Havre and then to continue down the coast to assault Brest. There was very good reason for this. Surrey was charged with the safe delivery of the Emperor Charles from Southampton to Spain. Charles had, in fact, written to his own secretary on 7 June to inform him that ahead of his passage the English would have, 'dispersed the French navy on these coasts'.[12] Surrey, however, was not exactly rigorous in attending to this task. On 13 June he wrote to Wolsey explaining why he had not attacked Le Havre,[13] and to the king – somewhat ambiguously with regard to his own presence – that Venetian galleys would, '...accompany the Emperor under my command, till he be past the French coast, and defend him if attacked.'[14]

But Howard assaulted neither Le Havre nor Brest, preferring to sail due south to ravage the Breton port of Morlaix in what could have been a disastrous operation. The approaches to Morlaix resemble the mouth of a monkfish or, as the French call it more expressively *loup de mer*. The wide, open mouth is guarded by lines of sharp black, rocky teeth after which it narrows into the throat of the river of Morlaix up which the town lies some fourteen kilometres from the open sea (about the same distance as Caen from the D-Day beaches). Even those with local knowledge would be advised to enter the bay from the sea in daylight, near high water and with a favourable wind. The Admiralty Pilot states, very understandably, that pilotage is compulsory for vessels over forty-five metres in length and goes on to state that:

> The bay is obstructed with islets, rocks and shoals and access is difficult; local knowledge is recommended before attempting any of the approach channels.[15]

Surrey would certainly not have risked entering the bay without making certain that he had access to that local knowledge which, with English merchants resided in Morlaix, may have been available to him. However, with the navy royal increasingly manned by its own professionals and the fact that Howard seems to have acted on impulse the greater likelihood would be the presence of a Breton pilot in English pay. The discontent caused by the union with France might have led disaffected Bretons to seek just such employment.

Once past the offshore hazards, the bay itself is capacious enough for a fleet to anchor in sheltered waters with a good holding ground of sand, mud and shell beyond the range of most shore artillery. But in order to penetrate further upstream to Morlaix itself, Howard would have needed information beyond that which could be provided by local pilots. For, as well as the state of the tides, he needed to know about the presence or absence of batteries, troops and garrisons both on the banks and in the town and its nearby chateau. For this Surrey needed a traitor; he had no time to conduct his own reconnaissance.

Morlaix is a delightful town. Its present charm is firmly rooted in its affluent past of which the apogee was probably the fifteenth and sixteenth centuries when the merchant classes grew wealthy on the export of cloth and salt and the trade in wine. The booming town also attracted the sons of the Breton gentry who were in need of cash to maintain the pleasant lifestyle encouraged by a thriving semi-independent Brittany. Several of their houses still remain adding much charm to the town, which sits snugly in its deep valley at the confluence of the rivers Jarlot and Queffleuth. From the town quays the tidal river Morlaix flows between steep wooded hills until the estuary opens out into the Bay of Morlaix with the open sea beyond. Like the more famous river Rance nearby, the tidal length of the river is subject to an enormous tidal range creating huge mud banks and a limited and winding channel at low water. Any ships, however successful their passage upstream, could be subject to devastating and unavoidable point-blank fire from ordnance brought up to the river banks. Enemy shipping, if alerted in time, could also seal the bay allowing no vessel to escape. And yet, aware of the potential for failure, the usually cautious Surrey launched a raid that stood as small a chance of success as the far better-planned Dieppe raid of 1942. He met with success.

It was not just the town that Surrey wished to attack. Morlaix's naturally protected position had encouraged its townspeople to indulge in another form of enterprise whenever trade was slack. The place was notorious as a lair of pirates, a reputation that is exploited today in many a local pantomime, children's playground or show. The most notorious of these corsairs was Jean Coatanlem who, in 1490, sacked Bristol and whose cousin, Nicolas, built the *Cordelière* at Dourduff on the east bank of the river Morlaix. It has been suggested that Surrey's attack was to avenge this Bristol raid, but there is every indication that the filibusters of Morlaix had never ceased to take advantage of the strained relationship between England and France to seize English vessels or ships bound for England on an opportunistic basis. If they were doing so it could only have been with the encouragement of the governor of Morlaix, Mériadeck de Guicaznou, who had been a chamberlain to Duchess Anne of Brittany and was an equerry to the king of France.

De Guizcaznou's residence, the chateau of Lezireur, lay some miles from the town on a plateau to the west of the Bay of Morlaix close to the little village of Henvig. The chateau lay well hidden from the sea but Surrey knew both where it was and how to approach it; another indication that he had access

The river below Morlaix at high water.

The same scene at low water.

Henvig church tower showing look-out platform.

to some first-class local intelligence. In an act identical to that of his younger brother when the latter burnt Hervé de Portzmoguer's home in 1512, Surrey divided his forces, with one group directed against Morlaix and another tasked with assaulting Lezireur. The path to the chateau from the bay runs up the side of the fast flowing stream, the Frout. Unusual among all the saline, brackish waters of the rivers that empty into the Bay of Morlaix, the Frout is a source of fresh pure water that even at low water runs clear into the bay. It was, therefore, an ideal spot at which to land to replenish the ships' casks, regardless of what lay upstream. There was also, in all probability, a small jetty here for, in the days before fields of artichokes and tobacco replaced the trees, this was a heavily wooded areas with dense stands of oak, sweet chestnut and beech growing right to the water's edge. The quickest and easiest way for the governor to move between his chateau and the town would have been by water.

Lezireur was torched. Even although it was rebuilt Surrey's attack sounded the town's death knell. All that remains today is a crater, which was the mill pond, a wall of doubtful origin and, in the grounds of the small country house that stands on the site, a large granite basin, some 7.6m in circumference. The rest has disappeared. Of all Surrey's actions during the raid on Morlaix, it is the destruction of Lezireur that indicates most clearly his determination that piracy against the English would be revenged.

While Lezireur was being destroyed Howard's main force was moving up stream, under cover of darkness, for the main assault on Morlaix. The approach had to be made by boat for on both sides of the main estuary not only thick forest but also muddy tributaries, such as those of the Pennelé and Dourduff, would have impeded progress by land. Although the Admiralty Pilot states that, '...the river is navigable by vessels up to 63m in length with draughts of 4m in springs and 3m at neaps.'[16] – it goes on to say that, '...the channel is tortuous and contains

Basin at Lezireur – all that remains today of the chateau destroyed by Thomas Howard.

some bends which, for vessels exceeding 50m in length, can present some difficulty in negotiation.'[17]

The Pilot is referring to vessels with, at least, auxiliary power. To sail a single large vessel, let alone a fleet, up to the town would be a remarkable feat of seamanship and would mean that the ship would have to spend several hours on the mud for, with a tidal range that can be as much as 7.7m the town is cut off from the sea for many hours each day. Contrary to the impression given by some writers,[18] Howard would not have risked his larger ships beyond the throat of the bay. Yet any force sailing up river in small boats could easily have been destroyed by a small group of archers hidden amongst the trees. Howard seemed to be taking an enormous gamble. Or was he?

At the time of the attack the military based in Morlaix were absent, having been summoned to manoeuvres at Guingamp, some fifty kilometres away. The senior merchants, who might have provided alternative leadership, were also absent at a fair in Noyal-Pontivy, away to the south. The town appears to have been left defenceless and blissfully unaware of its impending doom. The English were able to move upstream unreported and unimpeded until they were spotted by some foresters working in the woods on the river bank opposite the great church of St Françoise Cuburier. With great presence of mind the woodmen rolled great trunks into the water thus blocking any further progress by the boats and forcing the soldiers to disembark a few kilometres from the town. Thus the alarm was raised some time before the first English troops arrived outside the town.

Today only a small section of the stout walls and the strong castle on the nearby hill remain, but in 1522 these defences should have been able to fend off an English assault that lacked heavy weapons. Yet the town fell almost instantly. Here is another clue that Surrey had insider information, and also active assistance, for a lieutenant of the garrison, named Latricle, who appears to have remained behind when the rest of the garrison went on manoeuvres, was later accused of lowering a drawbridge to let the troops in.

Once inside, the marauders ran wild. Houses and churches were torched and the inhabitants that did not flee were beaten up, raped or slaughtered. Everything of value that could be removed was hauled down to the river bank. Even English merchant houses were pillaged. Resistance appears to have been minimal. The names of only two defenders are recorded. One, Jehan Pinou, chaplain of the town's College de Mur, raised the drawbridge and then, using his musket to good effect dispatched a number

The monastery of Saint Françoise Cuburier on whose opposite bank the English were forced to land.

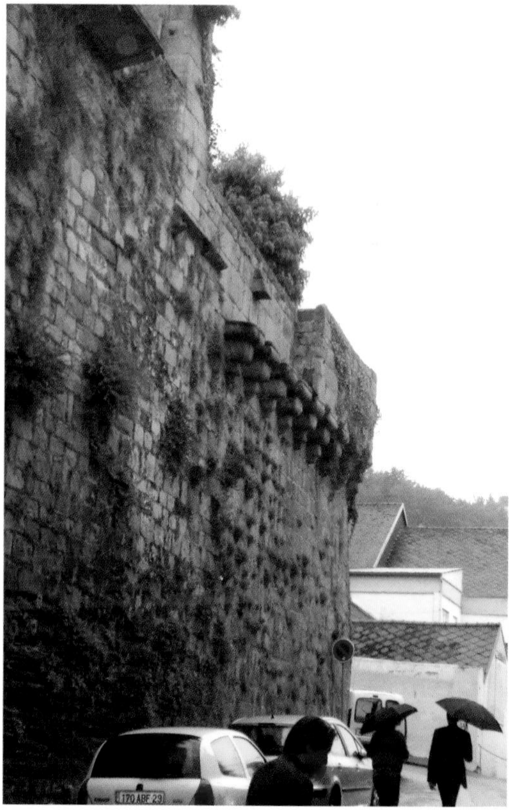

Remains of the ancient walls of Morlaix.

of the attackers before being shot himself. The other to win renown was a chambermaid, Suzanne Le Borgne, who worked in one of the great houses on the Grande Rue. She enticed over eighty of the soldiers to enter her cellar, which led to the river, barricaded them in, then opened the sluice gate and drowned them. Chased upstairs by their vengeful colleagues she was defenestrated and then, for good measure, trampled to death on the street below. Apart

No 18 Grande Rue, Morlaix, where Suzanne Le Borgne was thrown out of the top window.

from these isolated examples of resistance the English had a free hand. Overnight the plundering became more degenerate as the soldiers found a rich red-liquid booty stored in the cellar of most of the houses. By dawn, and their recall, many were too inebriated to make it back to the boats.

Tired and thirsty many congregated by two fountains that sprang from the rocks a short distance from the town. Here they were found by the Count

Les Fontaines des Anglais, where the drunken and soporific English were slaughtered by the French.

of Laval's men who had returned in haste from Guingamp once the alarm had been raised. They slaughtered, or so it is claimed, some 600 to 700 drunken English in such a dense gathering that the waters of the fountains ran red. Today they are still referred to as *Les Fontaines des Anglais* and one, dramatically is called the Red Fountain.

The survivors struggled back with their booty and rejoined their ships. Others came back on board vessels seized at the town quays. After a day's delay caused by contrary winds Surrey sailed back into the Channel probably more than satisfied with his three days' work. In practical terms Surrey razed the town, destroyed seventeen ships and captured three prizes: *Mary of Homflete* (90 tons) re-named *Mary Grace*, *Bark of Boulogne* (80 tons), re-named *Bark of Bullen*, and, *Bark of Morlaix* (60 tons) re-named *Bark of Murless*. Although these vessels were taken into the king's service they were last heard of in 1525 thus, presumably, proving to be of limited value. For all this

Surrey had risked a large part of his fleet and his own neck! There was, however, the booty, reported by some to be in the order of 800,000 ducats. If this amount is correct, then the attack was a very notable success as was the planning and execution of the raid itself.

Certainly, there had been some hot action, for Surrey knighted Francis Bryan, one of the king's friends, and John Russell, who was to hold the post of Lord High Admiral from 1540 to 1542. Even the slaughter at the *Fontaines des Anglais,* although avoidable, was small for such a daring raid. The disaster at Dieppe, a similar operation in 1942 resulted in a fifty-per-cent loss with thousands killed or captured. Its failure was put down to insufficient information, bad planning and lack of surprise. Surrey had avoided all of these pitfalls. Yet he seemed strangely reticent about his achievements. He told Wolsey little,[19] stating that the latter would learn about the episode from the king to whom Surrey had written. However, that letter no longer exists and there is nothing in the Norfolk family archive at Arundel Castle to show how much personal gain Surrey may have derived from the venture. Thus, his major operation as the Lord Admiral has mainly been left unrecorded, except in Brittany.

Morlaix took ten years to recover from the destruction. Alarmed by the ease with which the English had managed to attack the town the merchants petitioned the French king to provide them with further defences. The result was an inspection of the seaward defence by the Duc d'Etampes, which resulted in the fortress of Taureau being built on an island in the throat of the Bay of Morlaix to guard the mouth of the river estuary. Today this picturesque fort is a major visitor attraction. One other visible local record allegedly commemorates the incident. The coat of

Wealthy merchants' houses at Morlaix.

arms of Morlaix depicts both a French leopard and an English lion and carries the legend, '*S'ils te mordent, mords les*' ('If they bite you, bite back!') referring, some say, to the incident at the *Fontaines des Anglais*.

Something very strange seemed to have affected Surrey for those few days in July. On sailing from Morlaix, his habitual caution returned and he abandoned plans to attack Brest on the grounds that it was too well defended. Not that he was prepared to explain this to Wolsey, for in his letter to the cardinal from Morlaix Surrey attributed the fleet's limited activities to a lack of victuals:

> Great pity it were to see this well-willed company, for lack of victual, to leave undone that we here be in mind to essay, and what danger it shall be, with so little victual, to put ourselves so far from the coast of England upon the coasts of enemies I report me unto your grace, notwithstanding undoubtedly as soon as we shall have wind to depart hence and to draw beyond the Trade we shall not fail so to do, and we shall not return as long as we have any beer left, though in our return we should drink water.[20]

The drinking of water instead of beer may seem a mere detail. But the impurity of the drinking water of this period means that Surrey was saying he was prepared to risk inflicting dysentery and other water-borne diseases on his crews in order to accomplish his task. The fact that he seems to have had no intention of doing so does not detract from the force of the argument. However, an account of the fortunes of Sir Francis Bryan does indicate that Surrey also attacked Saint-Pol-de-Leon in the Bay of Morlaix some days later, and followed it up with an assault on Brest. There is also a sufficient gap in the coverage of Surrey's activities to have allowed him to have escorted the emperor beyond Ushant so, perhaps he did play a more active role as the imperial admiral. What is certain is that Surrey and Bryan were summoned to join Henry's land campaign out of Calais leaving Fitzwilliam in sole command at sea.

Morlaix coat of arms. The motto, which translates as 'If they bite you – bite back', is said to refer to the slaughter at the Fontaines des Anglais.

The younger admiral also seemed to have got the measure of Wolsey. In early August Wolsey sent him a list of captains and the ships and men that they should command. Rather than complying, which is certainly what would have happened years earlier, Fitzwilliam explained to Wolsey that he had no intention of carrying out the order:

> ...yesterday my lord Admiral departed towards Calais...Afore whose departure he appointed as well the ships as the captains and number of men to keep the sea, whose names shall appear unto your grace by a book which I send unto you herewith, which is not possible now to change.[21]

The newly formed navy was showing its unwillingness to accept interference from gentlemen ashore in matters pertaining to fleet operations. In the same letter Fitzwilliam told Wolsey that *Gabriel of Topsham* and *Trinity George*, for which the cardinal had certain plans, would do better to be sent west both to convoy the returning Newfoundland fishing fleet and to watch for the French sailing to Scotland. Fitzwilliam also questioned Wolsey's plans for the laying up of *Mary Rose* as well as the proposal to send him to Calais:

> And as touching my going to Calais, the King's highness can command me to go into no place in the world that I shall refuse. And in case his pleasure be that I shall go thither;

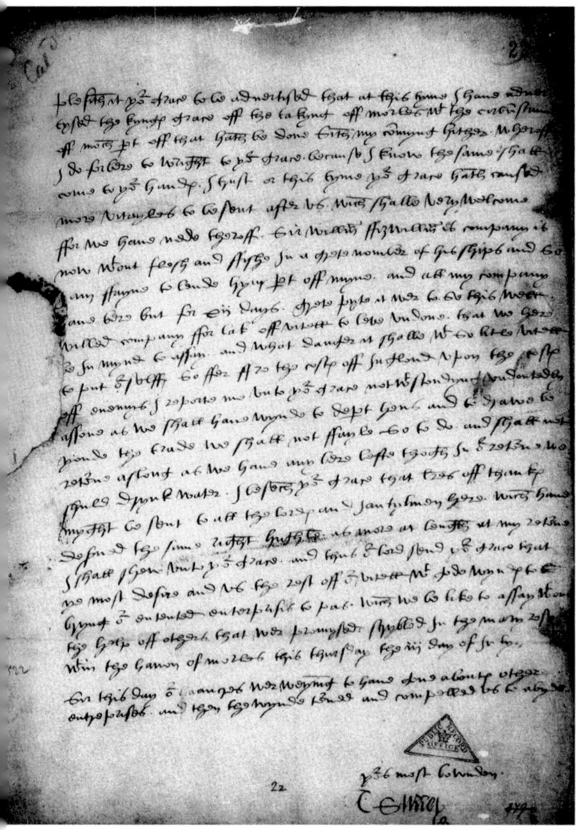

Surrey's letter of 3 July 1522: he refers to the raid on Morlaix in just four words.

> then I beseech your grace I may not only be advertised thereof with diligence to the intent that I may send my folks thither and provide myself of such things as I have need of...And, if the King's pleasure shall be that I shall go to Calais, that then I may know his grace's pleasure whether Gonson shall be Admiral.[22]

This was a major challenge to Wolsey's authority. Fitzwilliam was stating that he would obey no operational order without a clear indication that it was the king's command. At the same time, his query as to the appointment of Gonson as admiral went to the heart of the appointment system; Gonson, although a very efficient seaman, was a commoner and his appointment to command the king's navy was certainly not one that Wolsey could make on his own authority.

Operationally all was quiet along the Channel coast but the Scots were rumoured to be planning something. To soften them up William Sabyn, a successful member of that new breed of seagoers, equally at ease either trading or fighting, was dispatched to the Firth of Forth to create mischief. He achieved some success but failed to prevent a flotilla of four French ships entering Leith with reinforcements. Otherwise the season drew to a close without further major incident and *Mary Rose* was laid up in Portsmouth that winter.

The next year the Scots seized the initiative by carrying out a short blockade of the Humber and then planned to seize the fishing fleet returning from Icelandic waters. Howard was, therefore, compelled to send ten ships to the far north to escort the boats home, which they did without incident. Later, a sea battle off Leith between a French ship and a ship commanded by one of Henry's 'Spears' and past captain of *Mary Rose*, Sir Henry Sherborne, ended with Sir Henry being killed and his son being deafened. The North Sea command was assumed by Christopher Coe, another shipowner who had fought well in the war of 1513 and who enjoyed a bit of privateering on the side.

The desire for personal profit did sometimes mean that commanders were found wanting in their main role. Even Fitzwilliam succumbed to the temptation when, in 1523, he abandoned his Channel patrol. One of the main objects of this patrol, and the flotillas in the North and Irish Sea, was to prevent the Scottish regent, the Duke of Albany, from returning to Scotland with reinforcements as he was being encouraged to do by Henry's sister Margaret – the dowager queen of Scotland and Albany's one-time enemy – to renew the fight against the English. Albany had been reconciled with Margaret when he returned briefly to Scotland in 1521. Perhaps too much so, as the pair was accused of being 'over tender' and Henry, on being informed, railed against the duke for 'damnable abusing of our sister'. Henry now took one step too far. He demanded that the Scottish Estates expel Albany on threat of breaking the truce between the two nations, and thus gave the Scots the reason they needed to do just that themselves.[23] Albany's 1522 incursion into England had been a fiasco but, with reinforcements, he believed he could make a greater impression. He had, therefore, returned to France in October 1522 to raise an army with which he could return to Scotland. It was this army whose departure Fitzwilliam was deployed to prevent.

And prevent it he did, at first, forcing Albany and his 3,000 troops aboard some dozen vessels to seek shelter in both Dieppe and Boulogne where Fitzwilliam planned to cut them out in a night raid. This was prevented by an offshore wind, so the frustrated Fitzwilliam landed at nearby and much-assaulted Le Tréport, burnt the village and loaded his ships up, presumably with fish so perishable that he had to return to England to unload his booty. By the time he was back on station Albany and his ships had slipped out from Dieppe and Boulogne, sailed west past Sir Anthony Poyntz's flotilla in the Irish Sea and landed at Kirkudbright. Once again, his incursion into England, late in the season and with a reluctant Scottish host, was unsuccessful, and Albany retired well ahead of the repulsing force commanded by Fitzwilliam's ever-vigilant boss, Surrey. In the spring of 1524 Albany left Scotland for what was to be the last time – thus sparing Fitzwilliam from having to explain why his desire for fish from a French village had led to battles in the north of England.

The year 1524 proved very similar to 1514, which had seen the end of the previous war: little happened on land or at sea while the diplomats worked out a way to end hostilities. *Mary Rose*, if she was brought out of her winter quarters would have seen little action. Peace was eventually made at the Treaty of More in August 1525 and *Mary Rose* was placed in ordinary at Portsmouth where she remained until around January 1530. Once again the maintenance of a standing navy in good repair proved its worth. Without the necessary arrangements ships would have been hauled up on mud banks and abandoned. Five years later they would have been in no condition to put to sea. The existence of a Clerk of Ships meant that a system was in place to appoint and supervise ship keepers to keep those vessels in reserve in a reasonable state of repair. From 1523 the clerk was Thomas Jermyn, who succeeded John Brygandyne. He kept between six and twenty-one ship keepers on board *Mary Rose* and introduced an annual overhaul as part of her maintenance package.

When hostilities ended a survey was made to ascertain the state of the king's ships. *Mary Rose* was found to be in need of caulking 'from the keel upward, both within and without'. This work was undertaken in June and July 1527 and, as usual, a detailed record was kept by Thomas Jermyn. This indicates that a thorough job was done. The ship's side were 'burnt' to soften all the old caulking so that it could be scraped out easily and completely, for seams can leak if new caulking is forced in between planks where the old material is still present. Several other ships needed similar treatment, so the shipbuilders had a lot of work on their hands and needed the appropriate facilities to carry them out. To this end a second dock was opened at Portsmouth in 1528 specifically to carry out such repairs. The dockyard itself was increased in size and provided with improved facilities.

Following her overhaul in 1527 *Mary Rose* disappears from recorded history for nine years during which time concerns over the seaworthiness of the king's ships were raised in several quarters. In 1536, Chapuys, the long-standing imperial ambassador to the English court, reported that Henry's major warships were in such a poor state of repair that it would require eighteen months' work to make them seaworthy. This view seems to have been reached also by Thomas Cromwell who, in the same year, wrote a justification of the work that he had had done to the king's ships since he became chief minister. This included the statement that he, 'new made the *Mary Rose*, the *Peter Pomegranate*, the *Lyon*, the *Katheryn Galley*, the *Bark*, the *Minion*, the *Sweepstake*'. If this were so then it would represent a major expenditure on the navy royal at a time when funding for other ventures was very tight. But England's growing international isolation meant that Henry needed to look to his defences at this time.

In the absence of a documentary record, the research carried out by Christopher Dobbs of the Mary Rose Trust on the ship herself after she was raised provides the best evidence as to what work was carried out on *Mary Rose* during this period.[24] Dobbs undertook a detailed visual inspection of the hull and extracted core samples for analysis by dendrochronology. The amount of material available for analysis was limited. Ideally, samples would be taken using the sapwood of timbers, which would indicate the last growth ring of the tree felled. However, shipwrights would have been reluctant to use this soft timber, preferring to build only with the harder heartwood. Nevertheless, sufficient wood was available for Dobbs to draw some very positive conclusions from his study. Firstly, he was able to confirm that the riders in the hold and the diagonal and vertical braces that are so noticeable a feature of the ship were secondary timbers dating to the time of a refit. The difficult task of fitting the braces would not have been undertaken lightly and in all probability they were positioned to strengthen the vessel prior to the addition of more guns. They represent, yet again, a first for *Mary Rose* for, until she was raised, it was not believed that such braces were introduced

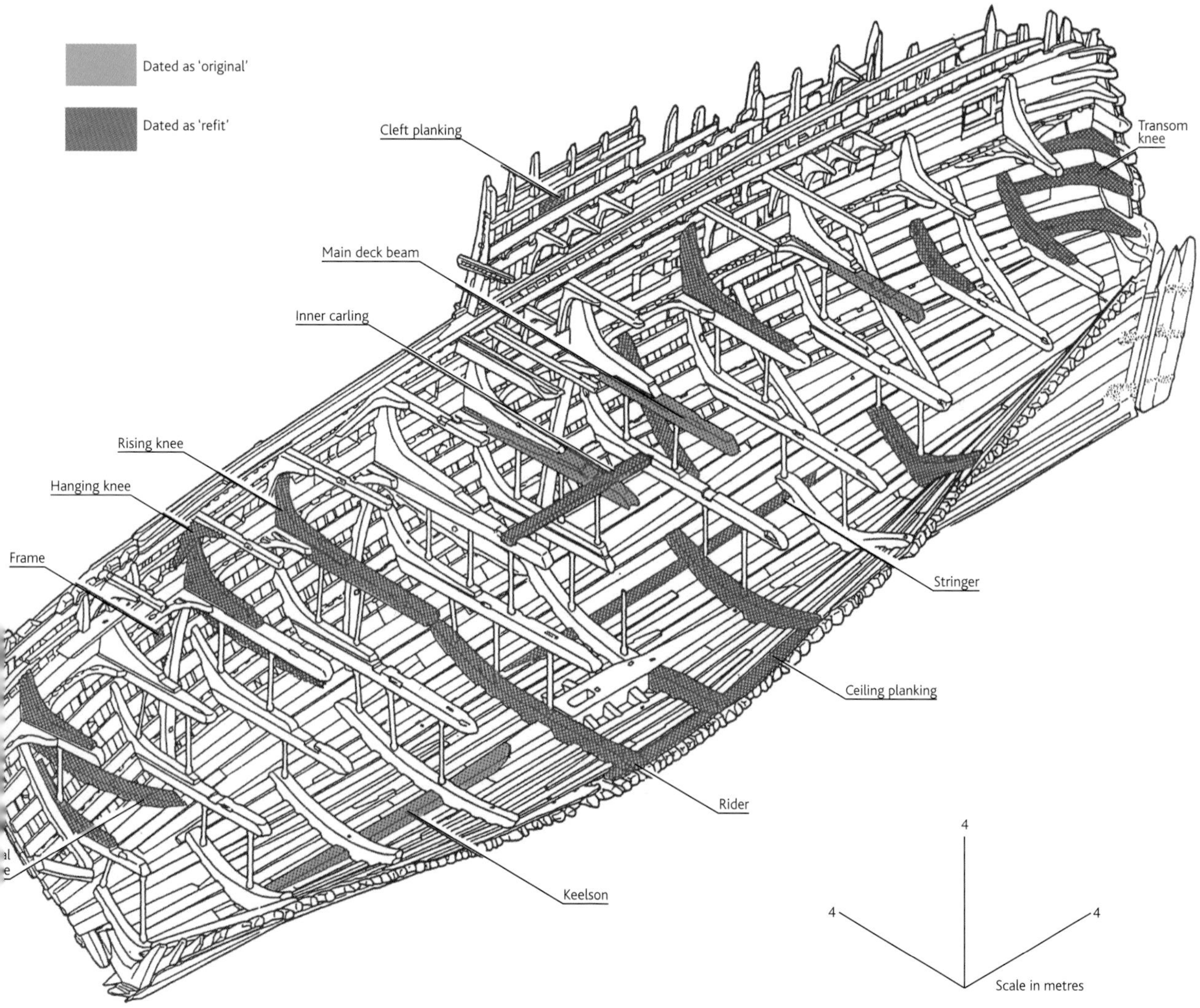

until the late eighteenth century.

Dobbs was also able to show that the main-deck knees and one of the main-deck beams were also retrofitted, probably in the Thames, for although the original timbers seem to have been re-sourced from woodland in Hampshire and neighbouring counties, possible refit timber derived from Kent, Essex and Suffolk. But was she refitted or rebuilt? The addition of the braces would suggest that major modifications at the very least had been planned for the ship. Of these, the most speculative but not entirely discountable, would be that a complete extra deck was built. This supposes that the ship was originally built without the present upper deck and that, during a refit, the weather-deck was covered over. This would have created more room for heavy guns but would also have meant that her freeboard would have been reduced, bringing the gun-ports closer to the waterline with the resulting serious consequences.

The record of the ship's tonnage might also indicate that major changes had taken place since her original design was agreed. The document of 1510 that gives the first indication that *Mary Rose* and *Peter Pomegranate* were to be built refers to vessels of 400- and 300-tons burden respectively, tonnages that remain constant up to the end of their building in 1511. However, by 1525, *Mary Rose* was being referred to as, 'being of portage 600 ton' – too early for the effects of additional refit weight. In June 1545 the English Order of Battle drawn up by Lord Lisle lists *Mary Rose* as being of 800 tons, while the Anthony Roll inventory of 1546 lists her as being of 'Tonnage – 700'. This evidence would suggest that she had doubled her tonnage from that originally conceived. Extreme caution has to be exercised in relying on any of the aforementioned documentary evidence, however. Even the observable fact that the construction of the weather-deck differs from that of other parts of the ship cannot lead to the positive conclusion either that *Mary Rose* underwent a major refit in the 1530s, or prove definitively which parts of the vessel were altered and in what way. Nevertheless, the difference in tonnage between that of 1510 and that of 1545 indicates some major alterations which, combined with more and heavier armament, would have had a detrimental effect on both *Mary Rose*'s sailing qualities and stability. After many a summer, the flower of all the ships that ever sailed was settling lower in the water.

CHAPTER 11

A Nation in Need of a Moat

THE PERIOD FOLLOWING HENRY'S divorce from Katherine of Aragon in 1533 saw both the Act of Supremacy – confirming Henry's position as Head of the Church in England and rejecting papal authority – and the dissolution of the monasteries. Internal disturbances, such as 'The Pilgrimage of Grace',[1] indicated to all that the king's reforms were not universally popular. Moreover, in 1538, Pope Paul III called for a holy war against England, a call that saw a brief alliance between the Holy Roman Emperor and the king of France. This was the era of Reformation in Europe: Emperor Charles was a Catholic – just like his discarded aunt Katherine. His earlier friendship with the English king was now defunct. Henry no longer had powerful allies who would help him ride across the northern plains of France; now England, not France, was the nation most likely to be isolated on the European political scene. So, in 1536, when the Emperor Charles clashed once again with the king of France, Henry saw no merit in becoming involved. Instead he issued a proclamation of 'upright and indifferent' neutrality, directing his subjects, 'on pain of the King's high displeasure and indignation and forfeiture of all their goods and also imprisonment of their bodies' not to take advantage of the belligerents by seizing their goods.[2]

However, Henry's proclamation of neutrality was a unilateral statement; it did not give his seafaring subjects any reciprocal guarantee of safe passage from the predators of other nations. Low-level piratical activities continued to irritate the English merchant fleet. Pirates were reported off the Isle of Wight in 1537 and the king duly dispatched four ships to deal with them. Pirates were also operating off the coast of Kent coast in response to which more vessels were sent to sea. The navy seems to have had little success against these adversaries, for the complaints by merchantmen continued.[3]

Of far greater concern than the privations of pirates was the threat of a papal-inspired alliance against England. By this time Henry had married, then executed Anne Boleyn in 1536, marrying Jane Seymour later the same year. She died in giving the king his longed-for son, Edward, in 1537. Henry still needed international allies and, in endeavouring to provide one, Thomas Cromwell now overstepped the mark, by arranging Henry's marriage to Anne of Cleves. The lady's charms quite escaped the king, and he married and divorced her within seven months in 1540. For the first time Henry found himself – because of the break with Rome – with more potential enemies than friends. In these circumstances he realised that a declaration of neutrality alone would not secure his borders. Abandoning the long-held – but fanciful – dreams of further English expansion on the continent at the expense of France, Henry's thoughts now turned to consolidation: the creation of a defensive moat to keep Europe out.

In both Europe and England new ideas about the building of forts and castles were emerging, influenced by the growing menace of heavy artillery. Interestingly, as with the reduction in height of the 'castles' in the carracks at sea, these new ideas leaned towards the construction of more robust, but lower castle walls able to mount more and heavier guns with a greater field of fire. Henry was very aware of these developments, and laid down ideas for the improvements of his enclave at Calais. However, in 1538, it

An aerial photograph of Southsea Castle, completed in 1545 as part of the great programme of coastal defences undertaken by Henry in the early 1540s.

A map of the fortifications erected or improved by Henry VIII in the south of England.

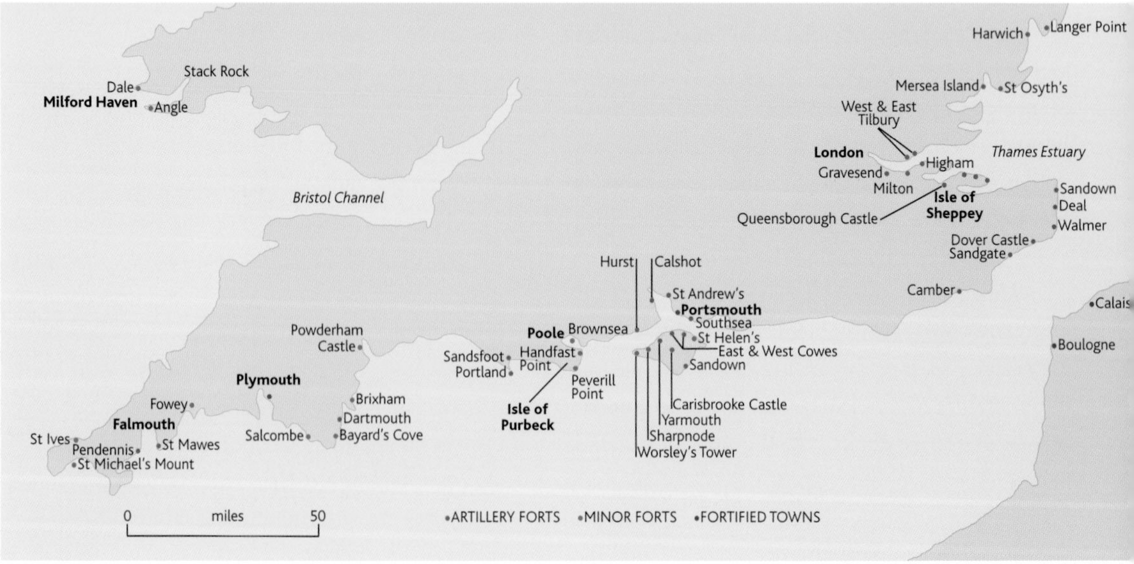

was the papal bull of excommunication and the growing amity between Franics I and Charles V that stirred him into action – not in Calais, but in the improvement of English coastal defences. From 1539 to 1546 numerous military coastal fortifications were begun that could serve as a wall on the edge of the Channel 'moat'. In 1539 Richard Morison wrote:

> What a realm will England be, when his grace hath set walls according to the ditches, that run round about us. England will then be much like a castle, than a realm.[4]

Twenty-four new fortresses manned and armed by the end of 1542 included the major castles of Deal, Walmer, Sandown, Sandgate and Camber, Calshot, Hurst, Portland and St Mawes in Cornwall. Southsea Castle completed the fortification of the Solent in 1545. Between each of these major castles lay lesser forts and gun batteries so that between Portland and Portsmouth there were ten artillery forts and six minor forts, as well as the defended city of Portsmouth itself.[5] Across the Channel the capture of Boulogne was to mean further building work had to be added to that already underway in Calais. The cost was extraordinary, and the bankrupting of the kingdom continued.[6]

At Portsmouth, the rebuilding of the town's fortifications was well advanced by 1539. Two years later, however, the walls were reported to be in such an unsatisfactory state that the king himself descended on the town to supervise the repairs. Neither were there men enough to man them. Sir Anthony Knyvet, in command of Portsmouth, had to plead for more men in 1544 when, instead of a hundred gunners he had only fifty. He had also been forced to impress bakers, butchers and brewers to help with the rebuilding of the walls.

That Henry was, for the first time in his reign, seriously worried about an invasion of England by a foe other than the Scots, can be seen in a proclamation that he issued in 1544, authorising:

> ...some number of his subjects skilled and exercised in the feat of shooting in handgun and hagbusshes as well for the defence of the realm against enemies as annoying of the same in time of war ... give licence and liberty to all and singular his majesty's subjects born within his grace's dominions being of age sixteen and upward that they and every of them from henceforth may lawfully shoot in handgun and hagbusshes without incurring forfeiture loss or damage for the same.

Although this freedom was withdrawn two years later it is perhaps not too fanciful to see within it the birth of a citizen's right to carry arms, which became enshrined in the American constitution nearly 250 years later. If Henry was building walls and arming those needed to man them, he and others were also making efforts to secure the moat and counter the threat of the French galleys. In 1541, Chapuys, the Spanish ambassador wrote to the emperor that:

> The King has likewise sent to Italy for three shipwrights experienced in the art of constructing galleys but I fancy that he will not make much use of their sciences as for some time back he has been building ships with oars according to a model of which he himself was the inventor.[7]

If the model was the galleasses or the row-barges then it cannot be claimed that Henry's involvement in naval architecture was a proven success. However, with war approaching, it was manpower not ship design that was the critical factor. In 1542 the Lord Admiral Lord John Russell passed an order enabling seamen to be pressed for the 'voyage de conserve' – the passage of the wine fleet to Bordeaux[8] under escort, a state of convoy that had been in existence since 1338. The order allowed the agents in both Poole and Southampton, where the wine fleet lay idle for want of crews to, 'take up so many mariners as they shall need, to be taken at Lyme and from there to the westward.'

By 1543 the idea of neutrality had disappeared. The king now issued a proclamation to equip ships

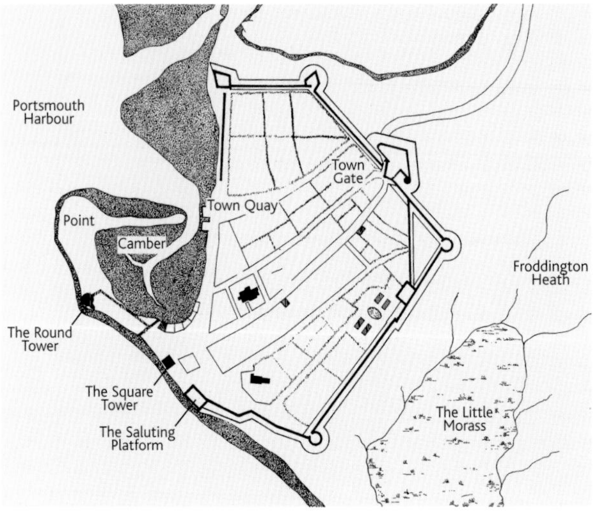

A map of Portsmouth's defences in the 1540s.

against the Scots and French. Antagonism was encouraged by all who wished to benefit from a little plunder, for the king:

> Giveth full power and licence to all and singular, his subjects of all sorts, degrees and conditions, that they and every of them, and, at their liberty, without incurring any loss, danger, forfeiture, or penalty,...prepare and equip to the sea such and so many ships and vessels furnished for the war.[9]

And in return they:

> Shall enjoy to his and their own proper use, profit and commodity, all and singular such ships, vessels, munitions, merchandise, wares, victuals and goods of what nature and quality soever it be.[10]

This declaration of open season was a wonderful opportunity for those whose trade would be adversely affected by the conflict and, at a time when the addition of a few guns could transform any ship into a vessel of war, the opportunity for plunder must have been hard to resist. However, simply letting loose everyone who would wish it upon the enemy had its disadvantages, and the king was going against the sober advice of an earlier age when Sir John Fastolf stressed that allowing a free-for-all could mean that some would not be too particular as to whether or no they robbed the king's enemies or his friends and allies. Mistaken identity is an easy defence in a maritime environment.

The war of 1512–13 had seen the English fleet sail without an embarked army and act in an independent role. As a result of the experience of those campaigns and the lessons learned, both then and subsequently, the time had come for the navy to be regarded as a separate arm of state and, as such, it needed to develop its own fighting instructions. Thomas Howard, when the country was at war in 1522, made the first tentative steps towards written instructions, but his ideas were mostly limited to points of etiquette, as one might expect from such a blue-blooded admiral. The first attempt to codify command and conduct at sea was written by Thomas Audley[11] in 1530, a Norfolk lawyer, at the behest of the king. Although influenced by the galleys that had hitherto been the main naval weapon of war, Audley made a very clear attempt to lay down sensible procedures for the mixed fleet of vessels that the king owned. Inexperienced in matters of the sea, Audley was able to turn – as the English frequently had to do in maritime affairs – to the continent for advice.

Alonso de Chaves who served at the court of Charles V wrote, but did not publish in about 1530, the first treatise on maritime strategy. His views were, however, well known (the English geographer Richard Hakluyt later wanted Chaves to receive a lectureship in navigation in the school he was trying to establish in London). Chaves produced basic and well-argued principles:

> Some may say that at sea it is not possible to order ships and tactics in this way, nor to arrange before hand so nicely for coming to the attack or bringing succour just when needed and that thus there is no need to develop an order of battle since order cannot be kept. To such I answer that the same objective binds the enemy, and that with

> equal arms he who has taken up the best formation and order will be victor, because it is not possible to break up an order with wind and sea as that he who is more without order shall not be worse broken and the sooner defeated. For ships at sea are as war-horses on land, since admitting they are not very nimble at turning at any pace, nevertheless a regular formation increases their force.[12]

Although spelling out the logic he was forced to use land based examples to support his argument. Until maritime fighting instructions could stand without this comparison they would not develop into a science of their own. Although Hakluyt might dream of a navigation school, Chaves's audience was the military grandee who, with more experience of a siege than the sea, might be put in command of a flotilla of warships. The Spanish, up to and including their great enterprise against England in 1588, relied on such men. The English, for their salvation, developed the new profession of naval officer.

Chaves's instructions began with establishing the role and duties of the sea commander and went on to show him how, by seizing the weather gage, he could gain the upper hand of his enemy until he came alongside. As the fleets approached the flagship was called upon to sound a trumpet, after which, as they came into maximum effective range, the ships:

> ...shall commence to play their most powerful artillery, taking care that the first shots hit, insamuch as they are the largest, they strike dread and terror into the enemy; for seeing how great hurt they suffer, they think how much greater, it will be at close range...[13]

And so the idea of 'shock and awe' was developed to demoralise an enemy at sea. Chaves showed, with his idea of the trumpet being heard throughout the fleet, that he was more a theorist than a practical and experienced lecturer. This inexperience was borne out by his suggestion that, having fired the guns from one side of the ship the ones from the disengaged side could be wheeled over for firing while their companions were being reloaded. The 'loose cannon' could be said to have been created officially in this document! This desire was, however, only part of Chaves's wish that everything possible be thrown at the enemy as the range decreased: missiles, harpoons, stones, hand-guns, cross-bows, fire-balls, calthorps

Modern painting of *Mary Rose* at anchor off Southsea, safely under the town's guns. The main seaward fortifications, the Round Tower and the Square Tower, can be seen, respectively, forward and aft of the ship. Despite his investment in fixed fortification, ultimately Henry's kingdom would depend on the floating assets of his navy.

[spikes], stinkbombs and grenades were all to be hurled over, ahead of the first attempt at boarding. The obvious desire was to create so much mayhem, noise, smoke, fire and stench that the enemy would be too dispirited to offer much resistance.

Audley's *Orders for the King's Majesty's Navy by the Sea* drew upon Chaves, but his own land-based and sedentary background was evident in some of his suggestions. As with Chaves, it is the idea of command and control at sea that Audley was trying to convey, rather than telling his commanders precisely how they should employ their weaponry:

> If they meet with the enemy the admiral must apply to get the wind of the enemy by all means he can, for that is the advantage. And if they chase the enemy let them that chase shot no ordnance till he be ready to board, for that will hinder his ship's way.[14]

As the melee developed Audley still recognised the necessity to maintain discipline:

> Let every ship match equally as near as they can, and leave some pinnaces at liberty to help the overmatched.[15]

He then described the boarding technique in some of the most quoted words of early English naval tactics:

> In case you board your enemy enter not till you see the smoke gone and then shoot off all your pieces, your port-pieces, the pieces of hail-shot, crossbow shot, to beat his cage deck, and if you see his deck well ridden then enter with your best men, but first win his tops in any wise possible. In case you see rescue, scuttle the enemy ship but first take the captain with certain of the best with him, the rest be committed to the sea, for else they will turn upon you to your confusion.[16]

Audley's imagination had to take the place of actual experience in his proposal for the use of a smoke screen to mask a Parthian manoeuvere at sea, fleeing and luring the enemy into a disorganised chase, before turning to destroy them in their confusion – hardly an easy or well-disguised evolution.

From the fanciful, Audley returned to the practical: how should a fleet control an impetuous commander who might risk all on a whimsical notion? Audley's answer was to make him aware of his limitations and the need for consultations:

> The admiral shall not take in hand any exploit to land or enter into any enemy harbour with the King's ships unless he call a council and makes the captains privy to his device and the best masters in the fleet or pilots, known to be skilful men on that coast or place where he intendeth to do his exploits, and by good advice. Otherwise the fault ought to be laid on the admiral if anything should happen but well.[17]

– and, even if despite the risk the matter works well, lawyer Audley had his answer:

> And if he did an exploit without assent of the captains and it proved well, the king ought to put him out of his room for purposing a matter of such chance out of his brain, whereby the whole fleet might fall into the hands of the enemy to the destruction of the king's people.[18]

That Audley's writings were not just theoretical is evidenced by the fact that the most famous admiral cited for not holding a council of war was none other than Sir Francis Drake, whose court martial for entering Cadiz without discussion with his commanders in 1587 was demanded by his vice admiral, William Borough. It was to be several years before the opportunity arose to put Audley's ideas into practice.

The Channel and North Sea remained restless but not stormy. In 1533 the navy had been mobilised but attempted little. In 1535 Sir William Fitzwilliam was again at sea investigating reports of 'rovers' in the Channel but found nothing of significance to report. Preventive action was also taken in case the

The Anthony Roll illustration of *Galley Subtile*. Built in 1543 prior to the war, she was Henry's only true Mediterranean-style galley and he needed to employ a Spanish captain and a Venetian master to command her, so limited was the English experience of galley tactics. However, when employed as part of a sailing fleet, as in the raid on Scotland in 1544, her captain was the Englishman, Richard Broke.

leaders of the Pilgrimage of Grace decided to challenge the king at sea as well as at land but nothing came of this either. Throughout the 1530s the story is much the same, with complaints being made about piracy and a few of the king's ships being deployed in response and, if opportunity arose, indulging in a little piracy themselves.

The year 1539 saw a greatly increased level of naval activity but this still did not involve *Mary Rose.* As usual preparations were reported to the European powers both enemy and ally alike by the well-placed ambassadors and spies. Thus, in January 1539, Castillon wrote to Montmorency, the Constable of France in Paris that the English were seeking permission to purchase up to 3,000 pieces of sailcloth from France which, as most ships only required 20 to 25 pieces, Castillon saw as clear indication of preparations for war. He advised not only that not a single piece be exported without licence, but also that extra vigilance be exercised, as he knew that French merchants would trade anyway, with or without such authority.[19]

The usual English fleet deployment from the Thames in April was also reported with the numbers of ships manned, according to French reports, ranging from eighty to 150: certainly enough to descend with purpose upon the coast of France. The real figure seems to have been somewhat fewer, with possibly a maximum of thirty-seven ships rendezvousing in Portsmouth and 'five or six' being deployed around the coast.[20]

Having ships at sea did keep a peace of sorts and policing did achieve results. In 1540 six Portuguese pirates were caught and executed but numerous others must have evaded capture. The fleet was not involved solely in anti-piracy operations. The joyful escorting of Anne of Cleves to her miserable and short-lived marriage to Henry involved the navy mounting its usual display of ceremonial and pageantry for the short sea crossing from Calais to Dover. Gonson estimated this cost his budget £2,000, a sum he probably resented considering the more pressing needs for military preparedness at the time.

In October 1542 the navy royal suffered a sad loss. The army, marching to Scotland under the command of one Lord Admiral, Thomas Howard, Duke of Norfolk, ably supported by another, William Fitzwilliam, by now Earl of Southampton, both of whom had flown their flag in *Mary Rose*, stopped at Newcastle where Fitzwilliam fell ill and died. His elder brother had been one of the few casualties on the English side at Flodden, illustrating once again the casualties that a few noble families suffered in the insignificant campaigns waged by their king. The Scottish campaign did achieve one notable success at sea, the capture of the galley master Prégent de Bidoux's nephew, Pierre, Sieur de l'Artigue, and his ship *La Ferronière*, off Dartmouth in November 1542. After several months in jail l'Artigue indicated that he was willing to trade his freedom for information that might be of use to King Henry. The traitor evidently proved his worth for Henry granted him an annual bounty of £50. The timing of l'Artigue's release makes it possible that he was able to give the king advice on the fitting out of *Galley Subtile* ahead of the renewed war against France.

As with so many of Henry's military initiatives the build up to that war took longer than the event itself. So the year 1543 saw another annual mobilisation of naval forces greater than normal but with little to show for it by the onset of winter. Lisle took up his appointment in January with Sir William Woodhouse specifically charged to be the Admiral for the North Sea in February, with four vessels taken up to patrol between the Humber and the Tweed. Gonson was given convoy duties and a second squadron, under Andrew Flammock, was based at The Downs. General instructions commanded that French and Scottish vessels were to be seized but that Flemings, Spaniards and Portuguese should be left unmolested. The fleet maintained a pressure on its potential foes so that it came as no surprise to them when Henry issued an ultimatum on 21 June 1544. By August, England was again at war with France.

At sea it was already open season. A skirmish in the Straits of Dover between Vice Admiral Sir Rice Mansell with six ships, and eleven French opponents resulted in one small enemy vessel being taken, and signified that the war at sea had begun. In the north Henry's land campaigns and diplomatic strategies had achieved little so he resorted to the use of an amphibious expedition against the Scottish capital. In a very short time the Earl of Hertford had raised a force to be conveyed in 200 transports from Newcastle to the Firth of Forth. The Lord Admiral commanded the escorting vessels.

This limited operation was a huge success. A large Scottish force was routed at Leith and Edinburgh was sacked. When the English sailed away the Lord Admiral was able to add to his fleet *Salamander* and *Unicorn*, their capture from the Scots made all the more pleasant by virtue of the fact that they had originally been French warships. Hertford himself, with his army, was unable to re-embark because his transports were laden with booty. He therefore marched down to Berwick destroying all in his path.

Across the Channel Henry was commanding an army of 40,000 in person, from the litter in which his gouty condition forced him to travel. In a surprisingly rapid advance the English had seized Boulogne, which Henry refused to return. Francis had already agreed a peace with the Emperor, thus leaving him free to concentrate on England. With an English force for the time being safe within Boulogne, and another, under Thomas Howard's command, retreating rapidly from Montreuil, the war in France petered out. But it continued at sea.

Boulogne had been battered during the siege and was initially vulnerable to counter attack. The town needed support from the sea and this task was given to Sir Thomas Seymour, a man whose standing in the king's household probably endured more because he was the brother of Jane Seymour, the king's beloved late third wife, than through any personal merits so, despite his ambitious, hot-headed, and somewhat spiteful nature, he remained on call for middle-ranking duties. In 1537 these had included

The Anthony Roll illustration of *Unicorn*, a galleass taken from the Scots in 1544. This ship, and the similar *Salamander* captured at the same time, were ex-French and are the only ships in the Anthony Roll with clearly identifiable figureheads.

sailing under Dudley in a four-ship squadron to intercept and deter pirate activity along the coast. The pair reported much and achieved little, and it was not until after Seymour had been replaced by Sir Gawen Carew that pirate vessels were attacked and seized.

Seymour managed to deliver supplies to Boulogne in early November 1544. He was then required to harass the ports and shipping of Normandy but found himself gale bound at Dover, where he learned of the presence of a French fleet at Etaples. Deterred by this opposition he proposed attacking Brittany instead, only to be lured towards the Seine on news of some more French ships anchored in the bay. Bad weather again intervened and Seymour retired to the shelter of the Solent without leaving any ships on patrol in the Channel as he should. An angry Henry forgave him for what had been a costly deployment in both ships and men. A hired Bremen vessel had been driven ashore on the Isle of Wight, losing all but forty-one of her 300-man crew; another ship had been lost on the rocks at Dartmouth, but most of her crew had been rescued. At least the human losses were not English sailors. Henry, flush with ships was very short of suitable manpower and could ill afford to lose the latter.

Seymour, unsuccessful as an admiral, eventually went on to marry the king's widow, only for his excessive ambition to lead to his execution for treason in 1549. Unpleasant though he may have been, his high rank and connections at court illustrated yet again the importance that Henry placed in his emerging navy by appointing such people to its high command.

English sailors were, however, making their presence felt in the Channel. Chapuys, the Spanish ambassador, reported that Henry told him that:

> English privateers, not in his service, had captured twenty-three French vessels and shortly before as many more had been sunk, burnt or captured. He calculated that his people had taken no less than 300 ships since the beginning of the war.[21]

Until this time the navy's main problem in getting the fleet to sea was the lack of victuals and the inadequacies of the supply chain. The Howards had concentrated on little else. By the 1540s the victualling problems of the king's ships seem to have been resolved. Now it was manpower that was causing frustration. The nation was running short of trained, available and willing seamen. London and the ports were scoured for recalcitrant crews who had received their conduct money but not reported for duty. Those who were discovered were in for a shock if the letter of the proclamation of 24 January was enforced for, after the preamble:

> ...contrary to the most just laws of his Grace's realm the said mariners and soldiers do run and steal away from the said ships, taking the King' wages, prests and conduct money to their most extreme perils; by which means, contrary to the King's majesty's expectation and trust, his said ships are constrained for want of men to lie still in the harbours and docks, neither being able to do any enterprising themselves nor yet to defend the King's majesty's travelling in the seas...[22]

– it went on to sentence death for such desertion. Of equal significance, however, it was also announced that a seaman's wages were to be raised from the long-standing five shillings a month to six shillings and eight pence, making the occupation attractive once more. It is not possible to estimate when this shortage of seamen first made itself felt, but it could have been one reason why the great ships did not see much activity in the 1530s. It also made far more sense – if convoy duty and anti-piracy patrols were the main call upon the navy – for these to be carried out by a number of smaller vessels with smaller crews and shallower draughts for entering ports and pirates lairs, than by the great ships with their deep-draughted hulls and hundreds of men on board. Better to keep the larger vessels in reserve until they were really needed for such occasions as a French invasion of England.

For, if Francis was not to recover Boulogne by negotiation then he was determined both to take it back by force and to raze the English equivalent. To achieve the former he needed to cut the town off as much by sea as by land. Content that he had the forces to seal the land approaches Francis knew he needed to destroy Henry's navy if reinforcements were not constantly to arrive and frustrate his purpose. The first serious invasion of England since 1066 was prepared and allies sought by France to support her enterprise. At the beginning of January 1545, Francis had written to Denmark stating that he planned:

> ...to invade England when the season arrives, as the best way to constrain the enemy, to make restitution and satisfaction and, perhaps, with God's grace, deliver the people of England from his tyranny.

Francis believed that Henry was, 'hated by his nobility and subjects for well-known reasons and exhausted by two years of great expense,' so that he would be 'deserted by his own subjects.' Yet, for all his talk of deliverance, Francis had neither the forces, either at land or sea, to mount a full-scale invasion nor, from the evidence of the landings on the Isle of Wight, the military commanders competent to secure a beachhead and march inland.

A great fleet of some 324 vessels – far larger than the more famous Spanish Armada – was gathered in the Le Havre and Baie of Seine area. They included twenty-five galleys, brought round from the Mediterranean and placed under the experienced

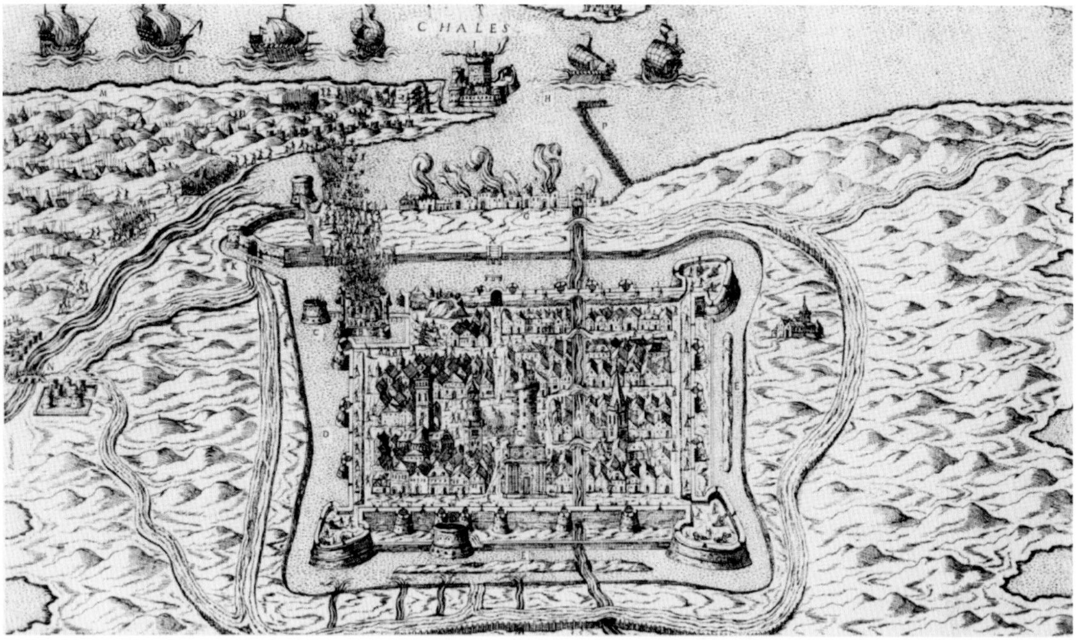

Henry's continental campaigns were facilitated by the possession of a heavily fortified toehold on the European mainland in the form of the town of Calais. Although it was expensive, Henry held it with little difficulty, and – as shown in this contemporary engraving – it did not fall until the reign of his daughter Mary, when the fleet was unable to come to its relief.

command of Antoine Escalin and Leo Strozzi. When it is recalled how much damage and consternation Prégent's six galleys had caused in 1512, the threat of Francis's new flotilla, to which could be added six new vessels being built in Rouen and a further six stationed in Scotland, would have been viewed with some trepidation by the English. Francis obviously considered that they would prove effective weapons both offensively and defensively in the calm waters of the Solent during a northern summer. Their usefulness was to be proved even before then.

Francis also had a number of large carracks, barges for transporting horses and an army of some 30,000 men to assault Portsmouth or other Channel ports. As ever, Henry was fully aware of these developments and he did not wish them to proceed undisturbed. He ordered his navy to descend on the French, which they did twice but not with significant success. The first attack, led by the High Admiral, was foiled by the galleys when the winds were light, then had to be aborted altogether when stronger, but onshore winds drove the galleys away but threatened to ground the deeper-draughted English ships.

The second attack relied upon the weapon that Drake was to deploy so devastatingly against the Spanish Fleet up the coast at Calais in 1588: fire-ships. A fleet of thirty fire-ships designated for this purpose was brought across the Channel by Lisle, but they were captured merchant ships with an understandably reluctant crew on board. Taking advantage of a strong wind the would-be fire-ships made off with the English navy in pursuit. A warning shot from *Less Galley* failed to dissuade them but the saker that was fired exploded and its iron fragments severely injured her captain Sir John Berkeley in the chest and shoulder.[23] Sir John was to die of his wounds some three weeks later but the Cowdray engraving shows a figure standing in the stern of *Less Galley* with what appears to be an arm in a sling! Away from Le Havre thing were different. On 6 July, the Lord Admiral, Viscount Lisle, met twenty-one French galleys off Alderney in calm conditions that boded ill for the English. However, much to the latter's surprise, the galleys fled.[24]

Southsea Castle from landward. This was where Henry chose to pitch his headquarters to resist the expected French assault.

When it came time for the French to sail, true to their reputation for being *bon viveurs*, they held a dinner party onboard the flagship *Carraquon*. On 6 July, Francis was entertained by Admiral d'Annebault, who would have been proud to show off this 800-ton vessel with its 100 bronze guns; it was considered the finest warship in Europe. Dinner may well have been judged a success, but the aftermath was not. Shortly after the king had gone ashore and climbed the heights of Caux Head to watch his fleet put to sea fire broke out on board the flagship. It spread rapidly and, as magazines and weapons exploded, a terrifying firework display hurled lighted debris around the fleet destroying nearby craft and rescue boats. However, there was time for many of the crew, and the treasury, to be transferred or picked up before the ship burnt out. A shaken d'Annebault then raised his flag on the almost as impressive *La Maitresse*.

If the French had a plan for their amphibious assault on Portsmouth it was both ill conceived and ill concealed. From the gathering of the fleet in the Bay of Seine the English seem to have been aware of both their enemy's movements and intentions. With the whole south coast of England open to the French it was with unerring accuracy that Henry gathered his forces at Southsea, a dead-end from which a withdrawal to another beach-head, should the French land elsewhere, would have been a lengthy and untimely process. Either the king made a very successful gamble, or his intelligence services were proving most competent. From the French point of view there is a hint of Gallipoli about their preparations – a landing about which the enemy were well aware but which, nevertheless, went ahead resulting in inevitable failure. They were also throwing down a gauntlet that they hoped Henry would not be able to resist. The French commentator, Du Bellay, who was present, wrote:

> Our admiral had news that the King of England had come to Portsmouth and he thought that if we made a landing on the Isle of Wight and fired the countryside in the sight of the King and killed his people only a handsbreadth from him, the indignation he would feel at such an insult, the pity he would have for the wounding and death of his subjects, and the spectacle of the wasting and burning of his realm, would make him send his ships to the rescue, especially as they were barely two cannon shot away. But if he did not act, then the displeasure of his subjects, who would see themselves abandoned by their Prince, although he was present, might produce sedition and mutiny.[25]

This shows a complete misunderstanding of Henry and his relationship with his subjects. It also indicated that the French had failed to grasp the strategic position in which they found themselves, for all Henry had to do was keep them in the moat and wait for the tides of time to run out. The result was inevitable.

CHAPTER 12

The Last Battle

THERE IS SOME CONFUSION about timings during the Battle of the Solent. Neither Corbett,[1] McKee,[2] Loades,[3] or Rodger[4] agree as to either the French movements following their departure from Le Havre or the date on which they entered the Solent. There is even some doubt as to whether or not they carried out a preliminary raid on Brighton. So, although there is total agreement as to the fact that *Mary Rose* sank on 19 July 1545, the times of events leading up to her loss are still open to speculation. The account that follows is based on the proposition that the French vanguard were sighted rounding Bembridge Foreland on 18 July, with the main action taking place the following day.

When Henry and his Council arrived at Portsmouth on 15 July they knew that England was facing the greatest foreign threat of the reign. They knew that the French army was a competent fighting force while their own troops were more of a militia. Henry would, therefore, not have committed his person and his best troops to the cul-de-sac of Portsea Island until he was absolutely certain that this was the French objective. If he had misjudged the location, the French could have landed unopposed and reached London before the king's forces could have reached Guildford. The results, for the English, could have been catastrophic. A negotiated peace might have been brokered, but that would have entailed the return of Boulogne, the surrender of Calais and payment of a heavy fine. There is ample evidence to show that the state plans and secrets of all the main European nations leaked out in a fairly constant trickle, and this would have been the case with the French plans for 1545. In Hall's *Chronicles*, compiled in 1548, it is written that, following his raid on the French at Le Havre, Lisle retired to Portsmouth where:

> The king then lay, for he had knowledge by his spies, that the French army intended to land in the Isle of Wight, wherefore he repaired to that coast, to see his realm defended.[5]

Given the strategic stupidity of the French landing an army on the Isle of Wight, Henry must have wondered how accurate these reports were, and would have hedged his bets until the last moment. Whatever the details of French strategy, Henry already knew it was going to be his sea commanders who would have to scotch their plans.

By lunch-time on 18 July Henry was on board *Great Harry* for a meeting with Lisle and his subordinates, including three Carews: Sir George, the vice admiral flying his flag in *Mary Rose*, his uncle, Sir Gawen, in command of *Matthew Gonson*, and Peter Carew, George's younger brother, commanding the 700-ton *Great Venetian*.

These men would have been fully aware of the predicament they faced. Their fleet – despite the presence of the enemy galleys, impregnable at Spithead and within Portsmouth harbour – would probably face rapidly shortening odds in an open mêlée, for the French had the advantage of numbers. Yet, whereas a defeated French fleet could retreat homeward with no threat to their homeland, heavy losses among the English could lead to the seizure of Portsmouth, the destruction of the navy, the opening up of the Channel coast to raids and the harassment and seizure of English merchant vessels.

Lisle was drawing up fighting instructions for a general battle but whether these were appropriate to the situation in which the English now found themselves is still open to debate. To stand any chance of success, Lisle needed to use his different classes of warships – both sailing and oared vessels – as one unit, working to mutual advantage and in support of each other. He therefore issued orders that a vanguard was to be formed from the most powerful vessels at his disposal, which happened to be Hanseatic merchantmen, which he would use to drive a wedge through the enemy to create passage for the king's great ships. This action would be supported by a rearguard of his weaker vessels and two wings of oared vessels.

At some stage during the lunch-time meeting on board *Great Harry* an alarm must have been raised, for the king called for someone to climb the mast and report on the enemy. The young Peter Carew, according to his biographer, leapt forward and, once in the top, called down that he could see three or four sail that he thought might be merchantmen – a curious description given the circumstances, and one which Carew quickly and rightly corrected to a large fleet of men-of-war.

While Henry may have wanted to ensure that his commanders did precisely what he required of them in the hours and days ahead he had no desire to be on board with them during the ensuing engagements. It was as supreme commander of the army that he best filled his regal position so, once the enemy had been sighted, he called for a boat to put him ashore. But before he left he had two other tasks to perform. Firstly, he formally appointed Sir George Carew as his vice admiral, taking off a gold bosun's call and chain from around his own neck and placing it over the head of Carew. Next he gave a short, pithy interview to the Emperor's ambassador, Francis Van der Delft, who had recently replaced the long-serving and exhausted Chapuys. Van der Delft was left with no illusions as to Henry's feelings at being left to face his French enemy alone, following the peace treaty

ABOVE: Sir George Carew, last commander of the *Mary Rose;* oil painting by Holbein.

BELOW: The well-known Cowdray engraving after a near-contemporary but now lost original painting of the Battle of the Solent. The masts of the sunken *Mary Rose* can be seen just above Southsea Castle in the centre.

between Charles and Francis. Having vented his ire the king went ashore to join his troops drawn up on Southsea Common.

The first French ships to test the English mettle were four galleys. Their role was one of reconnaissance and they would have had no wish to engage the English unsupported by their main fleet. They were, however, met by the English, who sailed out with great alacrity and drove them back toward the main body of the French fleet. Neither fleet wanted to engage at close-quarters at this stage, and the exchange of fire that took place, lengthy though it was, seems to have been the ordnance equivalent of hurling verbal abuse. Certainly, by sunset, when the engagement had ceased no damage appears to have been done to either side. Lisle was keeping to his understanding of the strategic requirement. Du Bellay noted:

> After a long fight with gun-shot, the enemy began to slip to the left to the shelter of the land. This was a place where their ships were

> defended by a few forts that stood on the cliff behind them and on the other side by hidden shoals and rocks, with only a narrow and oblique entrance for a few ships at a time. This withdrawal, and the approaching night, put an end to the first day's fighting, without our having suffered notable loss from their cannon shot.[6]

This short passage shows both the high level of French cartographic intelligence and the very significant achievement of Lisle. At this stage of the engagement it was far more important for him to preserve his fleet in being than it was to inflict damage on the enemy. Having sailed on 6 July, the French would by now be running short of water and victuals at the very least.

The feeling on board the ships on both sides was probably one of relief. We tend to stride through history with seven-league boots, moving from one interesting stepping stone to the next, with scarcely a glance at the space in between that becomes artificially contracted. But, between the fierce fighting of the 1512–13 war and this Battle of the Solent, thirty-two years had passed – longer than the period between the end of the First World War and the beginning of the second. Ann Stirland, in her examination of the skeletons raised from Mary Rose, found only one belonging to a man over forty years of age.[7] From this evidence it is highly unlikely that any of the crew had experienced anything other than a little skirmish in their entire lives. Now they were looking at a forest of ships bristling with armament. Although they had not yet felt the effects directly, they would have heard gun fire and seen the smoke and flame; their imaginations, aided by tales of *Regent* and *Cordelière*, would have done the rest. They would probably not have eaten a hearty supper and the grim humour that precedes any engagement would have been strained. Given the period in which they lived the ship's priest may well have been busy that evening, while Carew and Grenville walked the decks discussing the way that they would play out the next day.

Operations that day began with the French deploying in a way designed to draw the English away from their shallow anchorage under the protection of the land batteries. D'Annibault positioned his ships in line abreast in three divisions of thirty-six, while the galleys were placed well ahead to tease and tempt the English to sail after them and toward the main fleet. Weather conditions seemed to favour the French, with the English becalmed at Spithead. The advancing galleys must have been a stirring and scary sight. They were commanded by the Baron de la Garde, Antoine Escalin (known to the English as Paulin), on board the flag-galley, *Reale*, a modern vessel with five rowers to every oar. With him came a wealth of experienced galley commanders, such as Leo Strozzi, a Knight of Malta, who was to advise La Valette[8] on how to defend that island against the Turks, and Pierre de Blacas, another Knight of Malta and a French Chevalier. The conditions were ideal. It was calm, and with their shallow draft the galleys could not only approach across the ship-repelling shoals but could also be safe there from attack by the deeper-draughted English warships. On they came and, for a while, everything went in their favour. Du Bellay wrote:

> ... the weather favoured our attempt, beyond our wishes; for it proving, in the morning, a perfect calm, our galleys had all the advantages of working which they could desire, to the great damage of the English, who, for want of wind, not being able to stir, lay exposed to our cannon. And being so much higher and bulkier than our galleys, hardly a shot missed them; while they, with the help of their oars, shifted at pleasure, and thereby avoided the danger of the enemy' artillery.[9]

If Henry observed this initial skirmish from the shore he would have done so with trepidation. The old arguments about the advantages of sail versus oar in close-quarter situations would have been at the forefront of his mind, especially if what du Bellay recollected had actually happened:

> ...among other damages which the English received, the *Mary Rose*...was sunk by our cannon...Their admiral-ship, the *Great Harry*, was so distressed, that if she had not been supported by the ships which were nearest her, she would have suffered the same fate.[10]

Henry and his entourage on Southsea Common, a detail from the Cowdray engraving. The man riding behind Henry is Sir Anthony Browne, the Captain of the King's Horse and the man who commissioned the picture, whose main purpose was to show how close he was to the king on such an important occasion. © 2007 www.artistsharbour.com www.artistsharbour.com from whom prints are available.

We know from the recovered *Mary Rose* that cannon fire from the galleys was not the cause of her sinking. Nor does the site of her loss tally with the scene of this first galley engagement. However, if things had waxed hot for the English at Spithead why did Lisle not deploy his own rowboats either to drive off the dangerous French galleys or to form a protective screen to keep the galleys outside range? The implication is that the galley threat was not as great as painted by du Bellay, and that Lisle was content to ride it out until a favourable and anticipated breeze got up. Certainly it is strange that a galley force of such size and strength was unable to inflict severe or notable damage upon a group of vessels lying at anchor in conditions that favoured the attackers. The state of the tide would have determined how the English fleet lay and what guns they could bring to bear. Perhaps they had boats out astern towing them round or laying kedge anchors so that they could fire at the approaching galleys. Perhaps Paulin had been told to harbour his resources and tasked to draw the English out, rather than sink them where they lay. This latter option hardly seems probable, and we are left with the impression that the attack was not pressed home when all advantage lay with the French.

The English did have a more mobile form of defence that they should have considered deploying at this stage of the battle. These were Henry's own galley, *Galley Subtile*, galleasses and row barges – oared vessels that could have rowed out to meet the enemy galleys. They did not, which seems strange, as they were designed for these conditions although, for the galleasses – a hybrid that would later develop into the galleon – oars were a secondary means of propulsion. Perhaps the reason why they did not venture out is contained in a note of 21 July written to Lisle from the Privy Council, gathered with the king at Portsmouth, that states:

> That in sending forth row vessels he should take heed lest the galleys cut between them and home, and if the Frenchmen continue landing men in the Isle and to disfurbish their galleys, he might essay and attempt against them.[11]

In other words, the vessels designed to counter the galleys could not be deployed until the threat from the galleys had diminished, because the latter were being used as landing craft!

There is further significance in this failure of the English to deploy their oared vessels. The row barges available to Lisle were not the vessels the king would have liked to use. A new class of thirteen of these long, narrow vessels with sixteen oars on either side, was taking shape in the king's mind, but they had yet to be built. These 20-ton craft, delightfully named after royal heraldic devices, were not commissioned until 1546 when the main threat from invasion had passed. One can conclude that either Henry ordered them too late, or that the contribution of the French galleys to the loss of *Mary Rose* (*see* chapter 13) made him more determined to have such vessels available to him.

The customary afternoon breeze at last allowed the main English battle fleet to get underway from Spithead and head towards the pestilential galleys with alarming speed. Du Bellay reports:

> They bore down full sail upon our galleys. The change was so sudden, that our galleys had hardly any time and room to manage their oars, to tack about; for during the calm, and in the height of battle, they were got so near to the enemy, that they must inevitably have perished by the bearing down of their ships upon them, if they had not shifted their prows, and by this management, with the help of their sails, got, in a few hours, to the distance of a cannon-shot.[12]

Bearing in mind the amount of time it took to turn galleys and their vulnerability astern Paulin would have been cautious, and would have welcomed the arrival of some of the ships from his fleet to give support. Had Lisle closed down on him his best option was to retreat. The English would have been ready as soon as the breeze first shivered their sails. The ships would have hauled in the anchor ropes so that the cables lay up and down to the single anchor that was still out so that it was ready to weigh the instant the order was given. This would have conferred the added advantage of releasing more sailors to man the rigging so that headway could be achieved and increased as soon as possible. The optimum speed could then be reached in the limited distance that lay between the French and English, thus giving the English captains the best chance to overhaul the infuriating galleys. Gunfire would not have been necessary to inflict mortal damage on these light craft. Any sort of collision would have overturned them; a close pass would have sheered away their oars while, from their high stations, the archers could have picked off the crew with ease. It is no wonder the galleys retired towards the protection of the guns of their fleet.

The English guns would have already been loaded and their gun-ports opened; now the soldiers and archers would be taking up their positions and, hopefully, keeping out of the way of the sailors. Led by *Great Harry* the English weighed anchor and sailed after the enemy galleys to where the French awaited

The sea battle as depicted in the Cowdray engraving. A group of four galleys in 'wheel-spoke' formation is just above and to the left of the masts of the sunken *Mary Rose*, which is being fired on by a big ship that is probably intended to represent the *Henri Grace à Dieu*. © 2007 www.artistsharbour.com www.artistsharbour.com from whom prints are available.

them off St. Helen's. The galleys were in a hurry to reach shelter so it is surprising that du Bellay indicates it was a slow passage:

> Through the professionalism of the captains and the skill and experience of the seamen and slaves, the galleys could reverse course quite quickly. Then by rowing fast and the use of sails they returned to the protection of our own guns after a few hours. Then they reduced their strokes and slowed down so as to tempt the enemy to follow as they had been instructed to do.[13]

So, about one hour after the French attack began, their galleys retreated in accordance with their plan to draw the English after them onto the guns of the French fleet. Rather than getting underway in their intended battle formation the French fleet may have remained at its anchorage from where soldiers were being landed on the Isle of Wight. The distance between Spitsand and St Helen's is only six miles; fast-moving galleys being pursued by the enemy should have been able to cover the distance in less than half the time du Bellay indicates above. If his timings are correct, however, it would suggest that the breeze blowing the English towards the French may have been only just sufficient to keep the fleet underway and that the galleys, far from racing for cover, were dawdling just ahead of their pursuers. *Mary Rose* covered less than half the distance. Two miles from where she had been at anchor she foundered. To the south of the sunken vessel the battle continued, although it is hoped that the small boats were diverted to pick up survivors.

The sinking of *Mary Rose*, although devastating, did not represent such a significant loss in the overall strength of the English fleet, for Lisle was perfectly capable of carrying out his attack on the French without his vice admiral. But the battle seems to have fizzled out. The reason why a major fleet engagement did not take place might be attributable to the presence of the galleys and their English hybrids. Du Bellay wrote:

> Our enemies had special ships, which they call ramberges [row-barges]. They are long in shape for their breadth and much narrower than the galleys so they can be steered better in the currents experienced at sea. Their crews are skilled so that they can rival the speed of the galleys. A number followed rapidly astern of our galleys and badly harassed them with their ordnance against which our galleys, with no stern firing weapons, had any defence. Nor could they turn as to do so would have allowed them to be run down and capsized by the enemy fleet. However, Peter Strozzi, unable to endure this ignominy, and having faith in the agility of his galley, began to turn to face the leading English ship which had got ahead of the others and was almost touching the stern of one of his own galleys. However, the English ship, being shorter, turned quicker and steered back to the main fleet. And so the chase ended.[14]

It would seem that both sides held a healthy respect for their enemy's galleys and rowboats and that, without a significant wind, neither side wished to attempt a major fleet engagement. The stand off continued. Yet, without realising it, in their desire to entice the English out, the French had overplayed their hand. They were, in fact, guilty of a fundamental error, which dooms any amphibious operation to failure. They had failed to secure their water boundary before establishing their land one. This error was compounded by the fact that, if the French troops were to be landed in sufficient force and concentration to seize and hold a beachhead, they had to be ferried ashore in galleys – the one vessel that could both win the sea battle for the French and, more importantly at this stage, protect their fleet from an assault by the English.

Once any amphibious landing has been made then the role of the delivering fleet becomes one of support. It needs to focus on ferrying troops and supplies ashore, carrying the wounded back, sending for and receiving reinforcements, and moving to additional beaches as opportunity arises. It is a full-time commitment and cannot be undertaken if the sea commander has still to defend himself against enemy attack. Lisle recognised the mistake his opponent had made in carrying out the landings on the Isle of Wight before neutralising the English fleet. The evidence suggests he knew how best to respond.

The French fleet off St Helen's was not in a defensible anchorage. It was open to the elements and the proximity of the eastward-lying shoals of the Owers off Selsea Bill. Lisle fully realised his advantage and, on 21 July he wrote to the Council. He related that, although the French had survived a gale that had just blown through the Solent, 'even if it blew too a corse and a bonnet off', were the English to sail down on them in such conditions the French would have to:

> ...loose anchor and abide us under small sails; and once loosed they could not with that strainable wind fetch the Wight again and would have much ado to escape a danger called the Owers.[15]

However logical the tactics, the Lord Admiral still felt unable to decide on their introduction without reference to the king. He does not tell the Council that he 'intends' to carry them out but that with:

> ...the King being so near, he will enterprise nothing without his Highness's privity from whom he has learned all he knows [as] being near the fountain it were little joy to die of thirst.[16]

This undue hesitation in deference to the king indicates that, until admirals could take action based on their professional judgement rather than fear of the crown, a professional cadre of senior naval officers would not come into being.

The French troops ashore on the Isle of Wight, however, did not need their ship-borne commander to make any additional errors for them to be placed in a 'strainable' position. Their problems had begun with the decision for them to be landed in several places so as to keep the English forces divided. The landing beaches selected were Seaview, Sandown, Bonchurch and later one at Bembridge.[17] At Seaview the objective was a small fort that had been irritating the French fleet with its fire. It was soon taken, but the attacking troops did not venture further inland other than to set fire to some village houses, nor did they attempt to join up with their colleagues further south. At Sandown the disembarking troops endeavoured to assault the more substantial fort that was nearing completion as one of Henry's new coastal defences. They were met by fire and repulsed with the loss of their commanders.

The main French landing was at Bonchurch[18] and this choice of location again shows a degree of ineptitude. This landing was taking place at the same time that the French fleet was awaiting the English onslaught – yet Bonchurch was more than fifteen kilometres from where d'Annebault and his supporting fleet lay. Not only could the French admiral not witness events ashore, he could not respond to them in a timely fashion, nor could he provide protection for any galleys he might need to dispatch with reinforcements. The landing itself, led by the Seigneur de Tais, General of Foot, went in unopposed but the troops met stiff resistance as they moved away from the shore. Casualties were suffered on both sides and the English were forced to make a hasty retreat. One Captain Fischer, a portly gentleman, found his escape much hampered by its uphill gradient and cried out, 'a £100 for a horse'. Commenting on his loss, Sir John Oglander goes on to say, '...in that confusion no horse could be had, not for a kingdom', a phrase that would later be transformed into one of the most famous in the English language by William Shakespeare.

The French pressed on and up to reach Saint Boniface Down where they stopped for no apparent reason. Witherby suggests that at about this time news of the chaotic landings at Bembridge had reached de Tais, who went off to take charge of that area, giving limited instructions for the commander that he left behind.[19] What de Tais found at Bembridge would have been disheartening. It appears that a disorganised assault had been made and that an ambush by superior English forces had created panic and confusion. The Cowdray engraving shows the French retreating in some disorder from a burning village, while their way across the Yar bridge is blocked by a barricade and advancing English troops.

At a crisis meeting between de Tais and d'Annebault it was decided to withdraw the troops the next day, 22 July. The commanders estimated that if they were to secure the anchorage at St Helen's they would require the equipment and manpower to build three large forts in an operation that could take more than three months to complete. There was no way that such a project could be undertaken given the present dispositions, nor could the fleet be expected to remain safely at anchor in the exposed roadstead of St Helen's.

As the French assault on the Isle of Wight took place Henry increased his troops there until they numbered 8,000. He also sent to London to have 2,000 extra troops dispatched along with additional armament, but he did not cross over to take charge of operations himself – thus avoiding the one trap that the French had set for him.

The Bonchurch landing had, however, one final episode to play out. Close to the landing site there was a spring from which the fleet could be re-watered. A galley captain, the Chevalier d'Aux, was placed in charge of this task and, while it was underway, he climbed to the hill-top to reconnoitre and check the perimeter defences. He was ambushed, wounded by an arrow and then beheaded, thereby wasting a goodly ransom. A counter-attack led by de Tais in person managed to hold the perimeter until the watering was completed but, once this was finished, the French withdrew, never to return. In the course of those few days the French had landed some 1,500 men on the

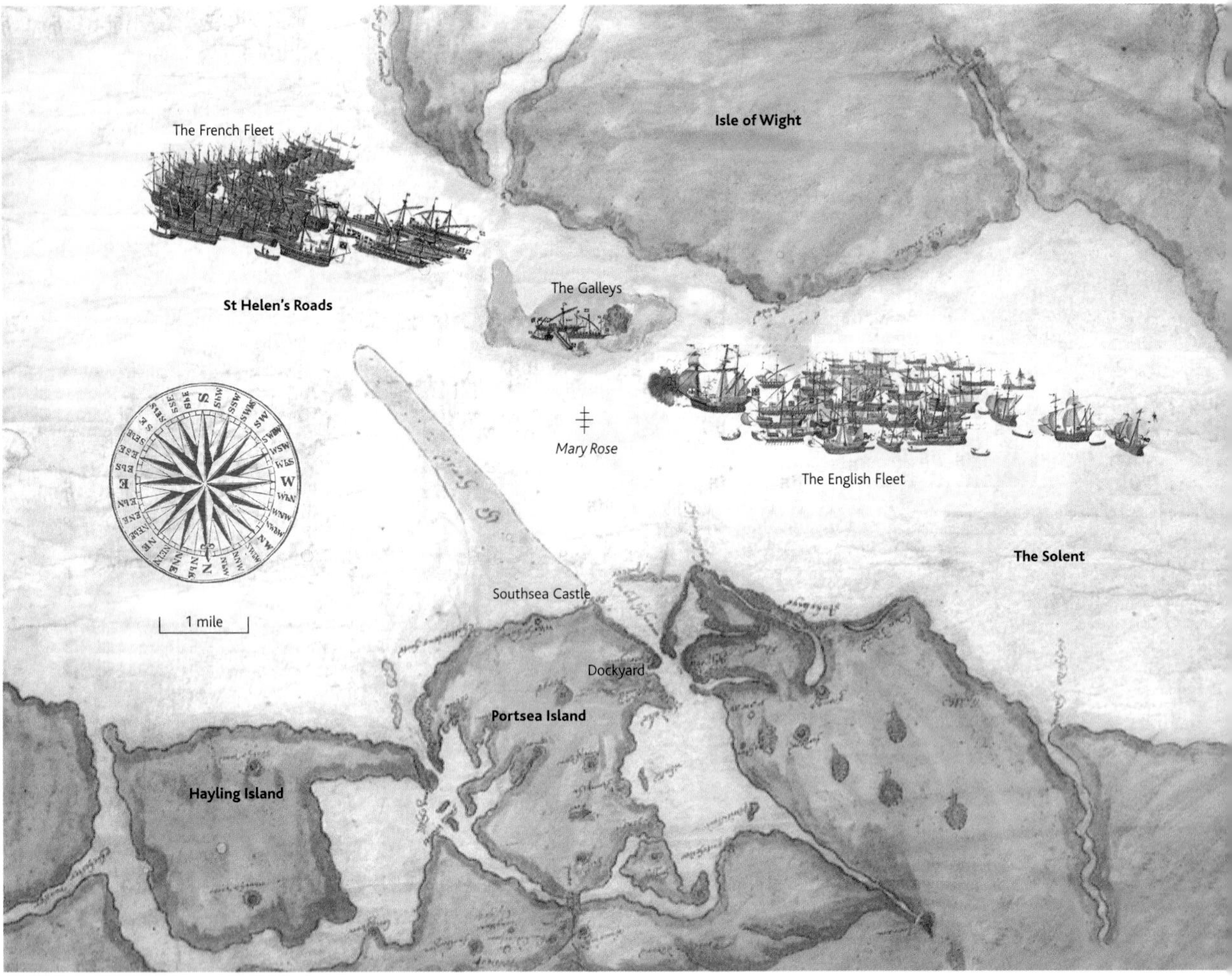

A plan of the final action based on a contemporary chart of the Solent with the ships taken in from the Cowdray engraving.

Isle of Wight out of a total of some 30,000 soldiers in their fleet. This limited effort begs the question as to why only such a feeble assault was made.

There is no doubt that d'Annebault was in an uncomfortable position. Having changed flagships at the beginning of the expedition he now found that his present vessel, *La Maistresse*, was still taking in water from her grounding as he left Le Havre. Lack of victuals and illness were also taking their toll. No longer confident that any good would be achieved by his remaining at St Helen's he weighed anchor and sailed on 22 July. The English could not, of course, be sure that the French had departed for good. On 23 July the Privy Council wrote to the commanders on the Isle of Wight to warn them about an enemy attack on Sandown Castle with a 'camisado'. This pointed to a night landing: a 'camisado' was a shirt worn over armour to identify one's own side at night.

But no such assault materialised on the Island; instead the French landed at Seaford on the English mainland, some forty miles east of the Solent, with a force similar in size to the one that had failed in the Isle of Wight. Here again they made little progress inland. Disorganised, their minds on pillage and destruction rather than military advantage, the French troops charged ashore to the nearest village, which they put to the flame. As they rampaged the local militia closed to within bow range. The onslaught was rapid and effective; the village was abandoned and the fleeing French surviviors were hard pressed all the way back to their boats where reinforcements had to be landed to defend their re-embarkation. Chastened, d'Annebault sailed back to France to land, for the last time, his troops at Boulogne where they joined the besieging army – where they should have been all the previous month.

With the French gone Lisle could concentrate on reorganising his forces and recovering *Mary Rose*. Even now, with the king also departing from Portsmouth, he was not left alone to get on with the task in hand. Sir William Paget, the king's principal secretary, who really seems to have enjoyed his role as the intermediary between the king and his lieutenants, wrote to Lisle that, on crossing Portsdown Hill the king, 'found fault with the lying of the ships and wished that they should repair to the strait on this side of Saint Helen's Point.' Lisle was directed to signify that the ships would lie as the king had commanded. In a terse response Lisle informed Paget that the ships were precisely where the king had commanded except for *Great Venetian*, which was taking on ballast and the two hulks *Sampson* and *Jesus*, which were about to raise *Mary Rose*.[20]

This interference with the commanders in the field continued even when the king and Council were over the hill and far away. Suffolk and Lisle were required to write to Paget to tell him that, by 10 August, Portsmouth would be fully fortified to defend itself in the absence of the fleet. Suffolk remarked wryly that the job would be achieved more quickly if, instead of just shovels, mattocks were sent down by the Council from Winchester to help break up the hard earth.[21] However, on 3 August, a bolder Lisle reported to Paget that the royal idea of sending some ships to lie between the galleys and the fleet off Seaford was not expeditious. It would divide the king's fleet, a disposition of which the galleys would take advantage as they had daily intelligence on the English fleet, and this vanguard would be in danger if becalmed. The prevailing wind, the admiral continued, also meant that the ships would be unable to return and then:

> ...if the galleys essay a number that they cannot resist they would dally with them, keeping out of danger, and meanwhile our ships may be trapped by the French fleet.[22]

The words 'danger' and 'galleys' appear yet again in the same sentence and they continue to do so in reports all through the summer of 1545 and the following year. In the above letter Lisle has at least gained sufficient confidence to contradict the king. He did so again the next day, writing to Paget that:

> The King's pleasure to have certain of his ship's made to row, to attend upon the French galleys, should be done as far as stuff and time permit; but all the shipwrights have been so occupied with making engines to bring up the *Mary Rose* that they have had no leisure for other things.[23]

Simultaneously with this exchange of correspondence, Lisle was also having to deal with a sickening fleet. His men were dying grotesquely, with 'swelling in their heads and faces and in their legs and diverse of them with the bloody flux'.[24] Yet the Lord Admiral stuck to the task in hand, and showed no signs of wanting to reduce his commitment while a French vessel remained at sea. While he was rebutting unhelpful suggestions from the king, managing a sick fleet and supervising the attempt to raise *Mary Rose* the French navy had taken a strategic position off Boulogne to molest traffic through the Channel. In these calmer summer months the galleys roved freely, forcing two English vessels ashore off Boulogne and even revisiting the Solent in early August. Their arrival drew a response from Lisle. He sent four English galleasses, *Grand Mistress*, *Anne Gallant*, *Greyhound* and *Falcon*. Heavily armed and very manoeuvrable, especially in light winds, they would have been more than a match for the galleys which, wisely, retreated.

Lisle was also further developing the fighting instructions that he had debated with the king in July.[25] His aim was to create an order of battle consisting of a vanguard of twenty-four ships, a main body of forty vessels and two wings made up of his forty galleasses that could act as two separate units as each both now had their own admiral. The instructions included practical guidance as to how ships could avoid impeding each other and how, once the enemy line was broken, those that had driven through were to turn and fall back on the enemy. Each ship was required to fly the flag of St George, a concept which was to be kept alive with the flying of the white ensign by all royal naval ships in commission. Lisle may also have made a further contribution to tradition. The watchword he gave his fleet was, 'God save King Henry', and the reply, 'And long to reign over us', perhaps the first hint of a sentiment that would emerge in Georgian times to become the national anthem.

When the winds turned westerly Lisle was able to sail with the largest English naval force so far deployed. He wanted to discover whether his newly issued instructions would help him destroy d'Annebault's fleet, which he presumed was still lying off Boulogne. In fact, drawn out by the same breeze, the French were cruising off the English coast. The two sides met off Shoreham. Once again d'Annebault positioned his galleys so that they formed a fierce gauntlet through which the English would have to pass if they were to reach the French fleet lying at anchor downwind. D'Annebault seems to have been an admiral who liked to battle with his ships stationary at anchor.

Just when it seemed as if the two sides would engage the fickle wind dropped. Lisle was left fuming. Once again the oared vessels on both sides could act where their wind-dependent colleagues could not. It seems that the French galleys, under Baron de la Garde, took the most aggressive position, loosening some 200–300 cannon balls at their opposite numbers, but did little damage save breaking three oars in Vice Admiral William Tyrrell's galleass, *Grand Mistress*. For the most part, if du Bellay is to be believed, the English shot flew over the top of the low-lying French galleys. This point could be most informative when we re-examine (in chapter 13) what might have happened just before *Mary Rose* went down.

At dusk the English also anchored about a mile from the French upon whom Lisle ordered a dawn attack. However, when it became light, early that August morning, the French had slipped away. By 17 August they were back in Le Havre having accomplished nothing of substance at great expense, a fact that did not escape the notice of Francis's tax-payers. Lisle and Henry could, however, be well satisfied. They had kept their fleet in being and prevented a major invasion. Lisle, in his report to Henry of this engagement of 15 August stated that:

> The *Mistress*, the *Ann Gallant* and the *Greyhound* with all your Highness's shallops and rowing pieces did their parts well, but especially the *Mistress* and the *Ann Gallant* did so handle the galleys as well with their sides as with their prows, that your great-ships in a manner had little to do.[26]

Some authorities have used this statement by Lisle to suggest that the naval broadside was born off Shoreham on 15 August 1545. But great care needs to be taken before drawing such a conclusion. Firstly, the vessels referred to were all galleasses or rowed boats so that no direct comparison could be made with their sailing counterparts. Secondly, as Rodger makes clear, there were probably not enough gunners on board to allow a broadside to be fired and, thirdly, such a devastating discharge would have sorely damaged the firing ship. As it was, according to Corbett, the English units involved in the action:

> ...had been so shaken by the weather and the shock of their guns that they were pronounced no longer serviceable without extensive repairs.[27]

But Corbett goes on to say that:

> Of all others the year 1545 best marks the birth of the English naval power; it is the year that most clearly displays the transition from oars to sails...[28]

It was a birth at which *Mary Rose* was a prominent midwife. Yet it was not so much the firing of a broadside that marks the Shoreham engagement as significant for the youthful sailing navy. In a letter to the king on 18 August Lisle wrote: 'The galleys were repulsed before the rest of the fleet came up, at whose approach we anchored to show that we were not afraid.'[29]

Lisle had met with the vessels that his fleet had dreaded since 1513 and contemptuously anchored in their presence. Not that the fear of galleys disappeared on that day. The English were still unsure as how best to handle this dangerous opponent. And if this was true of the great ships it was, of course, far truer for merchant vessels, even those with escorts. While the Channel winds allowed the French to deny the Narrow Seas to English shipping, England could be effectively cut off from her French possessions through fear of the galley patrols. Five thousand soldiers that should have been sent by sea from East Anglia as reinforcements for Calais were not dispatched for this very reason.[30] When the winds were unfavourable the English could do little to dislodge their opponents from their upwind advantage. That August, Lisle was forced to anchor with the ebb and hope that three tides would sweep his ships upstream beyond Beachy Head: a laborious process.

This problem of the galleys continued to enrage the English king, especially when they appeared to be operating with hostile intent while a truce was being negotiated. On 19 May 1546 the Privy Council informed Lisle that:

> The King is this day advertised that notwithstanding the French admiral's[31] promise, their galleys remain at Neyse Point, between Rye and Hastings, watching to intercept victuallers. Thinking it is both dangerous and dishonourable to permit this… His Majesty will have you order some of the galleasses, row barges and greater vessels, with the next tide to meet the said galleys and give them 'the setting on in the name of God.[32]

Success came a few days later when, after a two-day engagement with at least ten French galleys, the English captured one, which they referred to as *Galley Blanchard*, after her commander, the Baron St Blancharde. The galley was brought round to London and, as van der Delft reported to Charles V, 'This has greatly rejoiced the people here'. Among those captured was the galley's Portuguese pilot, Fernando Oliviera, who was to become, as he himself reported, 'Henry's servant, [who had] eaten his bread'. Oliviera had been present at the loss of *Mary Rose*, and was regarded by Henry as something of an expert on galleys and their deployment. Later in life he was to write a erudite work, *Arte da Guerr do Mar*, in which he stated that:

> In the war of Boulogne, the English King ordered some galleys to be built in his kingdom, to remove the fear [of French Galleys] from his men, solely so that his men should see what the thing was, and not be astonished by those of France; which galleys would serve him there for no other thing, and he knew well that they would be able to serve him, and therefore did not make more than a few for show. With which strategy he so emboldened his men that they had no esteem for the galleys of France.[33]

Five vessels in the navy royal of the 1540s are referred to as galleys: *Red Galley*, probably *Galley Subtile*, *Black Galley*, *Mermaid Galley* and the captured *Galley Blanchard*. Of these Henry's only planned true galley was *Galley Subtile*. The earlier *Great* and *Less Galleys* were too heavy at 400–500 tons to be true galleys dependent on oared propulsion. However, in November 1540, Francis I was advised that Henry intended to construct six galleys, while in 1544 the English king offered to buy ten fully equipped galleys from Charles V, only to be told that the emperor required them for his campaign against the Turks.

Two overriding factors conspired against the creation of an English galley squadron; the elements and manpower. As far as the first is concerned, a Venetian report of 1551 provides good evidence:

> They [the English] do not use galleys, by reason of the great strength of the tides in the ocean, so that… the navigation of these seas differs from all others, as unless the tide be favourable the wind is of very little use.[34]

Nor did the English, lacking a tradition of sending convicts to the galleys, have a system in place to 'recruit' the manpower a fleet of such vessels would need. There is evidence that Henry considered using captured Scotsmen to man his future galleys. In May 1544 he issued a proclamation commanding all French nationals to leave the country within twenty days and that:

> Every one of them doing contrary to this proclamation shall be forthwith apprehended, and either sent to his grace's galleys, there to be ordered as shall appertain or to be otherwise used as the case shall require.[35]

A year later it was the turn of, 'all wrongdoers, at the bank [Bankside] or such like naughty places where they much haunt and in manner lie nightly'. All such:

> …ruffians, vagabonds, masterless men, common players, and evil-disposed persons [were to serve] in certain galleys and other like vessels which His Majesty's Highness intendeth to arm forth against his enemies before the first of June next coming.[36]

It never happened, and it was not until the advent of Elizabeth's reign and another naval patriarch, John Hawkins, that a solution was found that would finally end the years of concern about enemy galleys and tip the balance back in favour of the English sailing navy. It required a revolution in ship design that saw the demise of the carrack and the creation of the galleon. The development of an ocean-going navy by both the Portuguese and the Spanish had shown that bulky vessels with high fore- and after castles were not well suited to the wider seas. What was needed for ocean passages were vessels that could hold to a course,

operate with fewer men and provide ample room for stores. For this the English needed a new class of ship. Henry's galleasses had shown the way, but they were only the first step in the right direction.

In 1570 John Hawkins, seaman, shipbuilder and entrepreneur, persuaded his father-in-law, Benjamin Gonson, the Treasurer to the Navy Board, to support his idea of building galleons from new or rebuilt naval ships. The first to be launched, *Foresight*, was so seaworthy, fast and manoeuvrable that her virtues

A later painting by Abraham Storck showing galleys in close combat with a Dutch galleon. The artist needed to cram the whole scene onto his canvas, so he has been forced to show the galleys far closer to their powerful enemy than they would have wished to be. Nevertheless, by 1600 a well-armed galleon, with sea-room and enough wind for steerage way, could generally expect to drive off all but the most concerted attack by galleys.

were immediately apparent. The new design allowed for heavy guns to be carried low in the hull, thus improving both stability and ship-killing ability.[37] Additional gun-ports could also be cut without diminishing the ship's strength. A lower gunroom aft was able to carry six large guns, while additional armament was also fitted on the upper deck. Most importantly, forward-firing guns with a greater range and power than had hitherto been possible could be fitted to these new vessels that have come to represent the apotheosis of Tudor ship design. They marked the final move from the medieval to the modern wooden warship, a journey that had begun with *Mary Rose*. They were ocean-going vessels that could, however, be handled confidently against galleys in confined waters. It is of great significance that the second of the class was named *Dreadnought*, the first to be so called and the first English ship that could honestly be expected to live up to such a name.[38] After sixty years the fear of the galleys was laid to rest.

CHAPTER 13

Drowned like Ratten

THE SOLENT IS DESERVEDLY famed as a mecca for sailing, and Cowes is renowned the world over as the centre for serious yachting and racing. These sheltered but expansive waters are perfect for testing the skills of yachtsmen and the conditions generally promise the opportunity for fine competition, especially in June and July, the period in which Cowes Week is held. Although the summer Solent is generally a pleasant place, Atlantic depressions can still wander up the Channel or, conversely, hot days can set off mighty thunderstorms. What the Solent lacks is a surround of tall mountains down whose gullies sudden squalls might rush to fall upon the loose sail boat and overwhelm it – the Solent is, in fact, a relatively safe stretch of water.

Afternoon breezes are generated by hot air rising from the heated land but, in general, mighty winds do not arrive unheralded. Bright sunny days can be enjoyed by those afloat without too much concern. Yet the windbreak of the Isle of Wight does create an aeolian phenomenon that gives the Solent the equivalent of double tides. A south-westerly wind can divide near the Needles with the main wind continuing up the Solent, while the diverted arm passes around St Catherine's Point and turns back to enter the waterway past St Helen's as a south-easterly. The result is that in the area where *Mary Rose* sank a patch of calm can form that can then be replaced by winds from either direction that then contend which is the mightier. A vessel with its sails set for one can be embarrassed when she is struck by a wind from entirely the opposite direction. The heading on which *Mary Rose* was set when she foundered would have maximised the effect of such a blow.[1]

The summer of 1545 seems to have been a good one. Certainly 19 July would appear to have been a day to enjoy a sail on the Solent, were it not for the fact that the waters were host to opposing fleets. So why, in this balmy weather, did the *Mary Rose* capsize? Was it solely a result of water rushing in through open gun-ports, or was it a combination of this with other factors such as faulty seamanship, poor ship handling and defects introduced from refitting, over-gunning and over-manning?

Later naval disasters resulted in the convening of Boards of Enquiry to establish the facts behind the tragedy, to make recommendations and, where it was felt necessary, apportion blame. This did not happen with the *Mary Rose*. Had it done so the board would have had many factors to consider, including the stability of the ship, manning and tactics. A ship stays afloat because the forces of gravity and the opposing forces of buoyancy acting upon it are kept in equilibrium with a margin of safety; this is called the reserve of buoyancy. If there is an increase in the forces of gravity caused, for example, by additional weight or an inflow of water, the reserve of buoyancy decreases until the ship can no longer float unless drastic remedial action is taken.

The other essential requirement for keeping a vessel both seaworthy and habitable is stability. After all, a tree trunk is buoyant, but there is no telling from one moment to the next which way up it is going to float. Although some vessels, principally lifeboats, need to have some tree-like characteristics so that they will bob upright even when rolled over, a normal

Modern painting of the moment of capsize.

vessel needs to retain a degree of horizontality for its decks. It would be impossible to live on board a ship with buoyancy but no stability. Various factors influence the stability of a vessel. First and foremost is her design: the shape of the hull, especially below the water-line; the ratio of length to breadth – all single-hull ship design is based on the relative advantages/disadvantages of a narrow tree trunk or a very wide raft – and the weight and distribution of the fittings and fixtures above the water-line compared with that below.

Some of these factors are present from the design-and-build stage, but a perfectly seaworthy vessel can still be made unstable by the way in which she is fitted out. Much depends on where weights are introduced, either permanently or temporarily. A heavy object exerts a turning moment, especially if it is placed off the centre-line; the further off and the higher up it is the greater the force it will exert once the ship begins to roll. To counter the effects of the turning moment, a ship has ballast stowed in her hold and, of course, in modern ships the engines are low down to enhance this stabilising effect. Cargo ships load the lower compartments first, and gravity dictates the way in which tankers are able to use their cargo to aid stability.

In a warship, until the advent of the centrally placed turret gun, the major contribution to retaining stability while fitting out was to ensure that the cannon were distributed sensibly and evenly, with the heavier guns being located lower down. As the demand for more guns per vessel increased, so more decks had to be fitted to hold the weaponry; these decks needed to be low down to protect the vessel's buoyancy. This resulted in less headroom for the crew, as evident in the 100-gun *Victory* compared with the equivalent space on board the twenty-nine-gun *Mary Rose*. Thus, as the weight of armour increased, so the comfort of the sailors decreased for, not only was headroom lowered, but more guns required more gunners to man them, placing further demands on already limited sleeping, messing, and storage space.

There is evidence to suggest that stability was not all it should have been on board *Mary Rose* before she sailed towards the French and her doom. As the sails were hoisted and the fleet moved seaward, Sir Gawen Carew, commanding the 600-ton *Matthew Gonson* noticed that *Mary Rose* was wallowing badly. *Matthew Gonson*'s master then made the gloomy forecast that, were *Mary Rose* to heel over, she would capsize.[2] This makes sense when we examine the available evidence.

When she was launched *Mary Rose* was referred to as being of some 500 tons. By the time she sank her tonnage is being recorded as 700 tons, indicating that some major new work had taken place without altering her below-water lines. This could have increased her instability, especially if she had more decks than is at present recognised. From the evidence of the wreck several artist's impressions have been made of the ship. Each contradicts the contemporary drawing featured in the Anthony Roll, and each gives the ship lines closer to that of a galleon than an older carrack with its high fore- and after castles. Yet we know that *Mary Rose* was built on carrack lines. Doug McElvogue, who has been responsible for the most detailed drawing of the salvaged timbers of the ship considers it a very real possibility that she had extra decks added both fore and aft.[3] These would certainly have decreased her stability and helped raise the water-line closer to those fatal gun ports.

The increased weight of her guns would have resulted in many extra tons being placed high up and on the ship's side where they would have exercised the greatest turning moment whenever the ship heeled. Contemporary captains knew of the effect that too heavy an armament might have on a ship's stability. Edward Howard described *Katherine Fortileza*, at the time of the ships' race in 1513, as being 'overladen with ordnance'. Many captains therefore had much of their weaponry stowed well down in the ship, only bringing it on deck when battle seemed imminent, a precautionary measure which could, on occasion, cause the embarrassment of unpreparedness.

The Elizabethan admiral, Sir WilliamMonson, was very critical of the desire to place more armament on a ship than its design made practical. In his *Naval Abuses* he drew attention to the:

...disability of ships...occasioned by the great weight of ordnance which makes them laboursome and causes their weakness. And, considering how few gunners are allowed to every ship, it were better to leave some of these pieces at home than to pester the ship with them.[4]

An increase in the ship's complement by the addition of nearly 200 soldiers would also have had an adverse effect on both her stability and handling while under way, unless they were kept in one position. An indication as to how sensitive contemporary ships could be to the movement of men around the decks can be found in *The Complaynt of Scotland* which states that in a chase:

The master bid all his mariners and men of war hold themselves quietly at rest, by reason that the moving of the people within a ship stops her on her course.[5]

If this were indeed the case, then the presence of these extra men could also have had an adverse effect on accuracy when firing at any great range, with gun's running out and recoiling, thus further adding to the instability. So, if *Mary Rose* had had a large body of troops moving in a disorganised way from side to side in the ship this would have had a considerable effect on her stability, not to mention getting in the way of the sailors who would have been trying to remedy any dangerous list.

The concerned Sir Gawen Carew had hailed his nephew to enquire if all was well. Sir George Carew, it is alleged, told him that he had a ship's company of knaves whom he could not rule. Ruling the ship's company was, of course, not Sir George's role but that of the ship's captain, Roger Grenville. Hooker, states that on board *Mary Rose* there were:

...a hundred mariners, the worst of them being able to be master in the best ship within the realm; and these so maligned and disdained one the other, that refusing to do that which they should do, were careless to do that which was most needful and necessary, and so contending in envy, perished in frowardness.[6]

There is, however, an explanation as to why the men might have been both unruly and capable of being their own masters. *Mary Rose* had not seen sea service for many years as both she and *Henry Grace à Dieu* had spent a great deal of time in ordinary, leaving smaller vessels to carry out the king's business at sea. There is no evidence that either ship had any operational duties between 1526 and June 1545 when *Mary Rose* sailed from the Thames to join Lisle. If this was indeed the case, then a whole generation of seamen who knew how to handle these large vessels had passed on. To man the great ships Henry would have had to bring together men whose experience was limited to that gained on much smaller vessels with fewer masts and sails and ones that were, in all probability, able to answer to the helm more readily. Many of these sailors would have held positions of responsibility in these smaller ships and might well have resented taking on a subordinate role in *Mary Rose*.

From the descriptions above it would seem evident that George Carew was sailing into a fight for which his ship's company was ill prepared. Few of the ship's gunners or mariners had seen action,

Possible first stage of the capsize: the flooding of the lower-deck gunports caused by a sudden heeling of the ship.

and the majority of the soldiers on board, even if they had fought in land battles, would not have fought at sea. Nor is there any record, among the whole of the navy royal, of the officers carrying out gun drills or boarding training. We have the account of Edward Howard ordering a sailing race back in 1513 but not one report of him, or any other commander, ever arranging gunnery shoots. Indeed the parsimonious Wolsey might well have frowned on such unnecessary waste of expensive gunpowder and shot. Nor did

Possible second stage of the capsize of *Mary Rose*: heavy objects on the windward (higher) side cascade to the lower, increasing the heel.

Mary Rose carry a great deal of ammunition for each gun. The average number of shot per gun was sixteen, hardly enough for a prolonged engagement, let alone regular practice. What practice that was carried out would have been non-firing drills that would not have prepared the sailors for the realities of battle.

So the omens were not good. But why not? Although *Mary Rose* had been in service thirty-four years, continuous maintenance ensured that her timbers had not decayed. Stability was a problem but every contemporary accounts emphasise the fact that the weather at that time was fair with very little wind and a flat sea, conditions that should not have tested *Mary Rose.* The Cowdray engraving – which Dominic Fontana of the University of Portsmouth has shown to be very accurate in most verifiable details – gives no hint of a squall in the way that the English fleet had set its sails. Nevertheless, several accounts record that *Mary Rose* fired her guns on one side and that, in turning in order to fire from the other side, she was caught by a gust of wind that heeled her over so much that the water flooded in through her open gun ports and capsized her. Down with her went Sir George Carew, Roger Grenville and some 500 men unable to abandon their ship because anti-boarding nets and chain-mail jerkins prevented them from scrambling away. If this is the full story it is likely that *Mary Rose* was in a state of 'loll' caused by the combination of a greatly increased weight unevenly distributed above the water line with water swilling around in the bilges. When she made a hard alteration of course this water would have rushed over to the lower side, taking the ballast with it, causing an enormous weight to transfer to that side and continue the heel over until it passed the point of no return.

A clue as to why *Mary Rose* carried out such a violent manoeuvre can be seen in the Cowdray engraving. Most historians have been content to accept the explanation that she had fired the guns on one side, probably the starboard, and in altering course to bring her other guns to bear had capsized. But this is too simplistic and probably incorrect. Firstly, such an alteration of course would have steered her away from the enemy and by the time she had come back onto her required heading she would have fallen well astern of the more junior ships in the fleet; hardly the station for the Vice Admiral. Secondly, there is no evidence that she had fired any of her guns; all those on the port side were found loaded and only one on the starboard side was not. Thirdly, at whom would she have been firing?

One of the few statistics that contemporary writers omit from their descriptions of Tudor warship guns is their range but we know this was limited. In the case of the ordnance on board *Mary Rose* we can assume a maximum effective range of some 200 yards. This was dictated not only by the calibre and bore of the weapon, the size of shot, the strength of the gunpowder and the windage around the shot, but also by the accuracy with which the weapon could be aimed. At sea, ship movement drastically reduced the effective range from that obtainable from an identical weapon fired ashore. Even competent naval commanders such as Sir Richard Hawkins and Sir William Monson were cynical about the efficacy of naval weapons at range. 'How much nearer, so much the better' was Sir Richard's motto, which Monson echoed by stating, 'he that shooteth far off at sea had as good not shoot at all.' Add to this the evidence from the *Complaynt of Scotland*, quoted above, that indicates that even men moving around the ship's decks could upset the gunners' aim. While the object of warfare at sea was to grapple, blast and then board, a good maximum effective range was not as important as it would become when ships stood off and tried to sink each other, in which situation the advantage obviously lay with the ship that had the greater range.

A study of the Cowdray engraving clearly shows that there were no French warships remotely within range of *Mary Rose*'s guns at the place where she capsized. If her starboard guns had been fired, then the fact that they were recovered loaded would indicate that an untrained crew had managed to reload them in record time. This simple explanation does not stand up to scrutiny. However, there was a group of ships close by and, what is more, they were the bogey-men of the English fleet – the French galleys. We know that they had already been in action earlier in the day, attacking the English ships becalmed at anchor. Now, in the afternoon, the galleys were drawing the English out towards the French warships, but Lisle knew that once he was grappled ship to ship the sides of his own vessels would have been an exposed and easy target for the galleys. He needed to deal with them first. They, in their turn, were stationed where the English would have to risk sailing past them to reach the main enemy battle fleet.

The devastating capability of the galleys was well known. Their achievements off Brest in 1513 had created a fear among the English that endured for some 60 years. The weight of their armament justified such anxiety. Guilmartin states that:

Possible third stage of the capsize: with water rising on the lower deck, the crew make a desperate attempt to escape up restricted companionways.

> In 1536, the *Capitana* of Don ÁÁlvaro de Bazáán the Elder, Captain General of the Galleys of Spain, carried a large cannon, two half-culverins, three stone-throwers and an array of swivel guns…[7]

– and that some five per cent of the galley's displacement was ordnance, most of which was offensive. It is likely that the French galleys were similarly equipped: these formidable fighting machines lay between the English and their main objective.

A trained squadron of galleys had several well-developed tactics to deploy against opposing warships. One was for four galleys to come stern to stern at right angles so that all their guns pointed out. They would then rotate about their position by pulling on the oars on one side and backing with the others. Thus they could retain a constant rate of fire, forming the equivalent of an infantry square at sea. If one looks at the group of galleys just ahead of *Henry Grace à Dieu* in the Cowdray engraving this is precisely the formation they have taken up. The *Great Harry* is responding to them with her bow chasers, but seems to be on course to try and pass to the south of them.

What of *Mary Rose*? Her original course could have been to the north, but on this tack she might have been passing too close to engage these low-lying vessels with her major armament, which she would then have had to have fired one at a time, altering slowly to port to enable her so to do as her guns were canted at different angles.[8] Had she done this then she would have exposed her bulky beam to the galleys at a range that was ideal for them because her own guns lacked the accuracy and power to wreak similar destruction from a safer range. Further more if, as in du Bellay's account, the galleys under Strozzi had turned suddenly to confront their pursuers then the need for drastic, rapid evasive action would have been all the more necessary. *Mary Rose*'s tiller may have had to have been thrown violently from one side to the other, thereby increasing not only her angle of list but also the moment given to any loose materiel to contribute to her latent instability.

Faced with this problem the best guns for *Mary Rose* to have brought to bear would have been her stern-chasers. The introduction of the flat-planked, transom stern had enabled shipbuilders to place heavy guns in the stern, one of the strongest parts of the vessel. As the planking was flat it would have been easy to build gun ports and this might have been where these essential items were first introduced. The space where these guns were placed became known as the 'gunroom', a place that later became renowned as the area in which midshipmen were accommodated. The Anthony Roll shows eight guns facing aft through *Mary Rose*'s stern.

The advantage of turning stern-on to galleys was well reported in the engagement in 1628 between *Mary Sampson* and the Knights of Malta:

> Captain William Rainsborrow (who behaved himself with brave courage and temper) finding a breath of wind to give the ship motion; considering that he was a great mark on the broad-side, and the galleys very narrow, keeping their prows sharp toward him, and that he could bear little upon them, trimmed his sails before the wind, and brought them to a stern fight…the *Sampson* could then bear upon them two whole culverin in her stern-chase, and two transom culverins in the gunroom and two sakers in the great cabin.[9]

If one were to re-draw the Cowdray engraving to show the moment before *Mary Rose* capsized then a picture very similar to that described in the *Sampson* engagement would be seen. In the morning the English fleet had been becalmed and by early afternoon there was just sufficient wind for them to get underway. Then, as they approached the waiting galleys, a brisker breath of wind was found sufficient for *Mary Rose* to turn away to bring her stern-chasers to bear. Her manoeuvering would have been complicated, possibly involving an initial turn to port and then a hard turn back to starboard. Alternatively, she could have shipped water through her open port-side gun-ports and, in an effort to correct, turned too hard to starboard, resulting in the water rushing over to that side where she was held by the stiff westerly gust that might have been blowing at that time. Either way, the only logical explanation for her foundering where she did and on the heading she was on is that she was either engaging the galleys or endeavouring to get past them outside their gun range.

Her loss was not thus a simple accident but the result of her close-quarters encounter with the enemy. The galleys had, yet again, proved deadly opponents. They were to remain so for many years. Indeed, great store was to be set on the English defeat of galleys at Cadiz in 1587 and 1596, about which Monson waxed lyrical, stating that they set a precedent, 'which has seldom been seen or heard of, for ships to be the destroyers of galleys'.[10] So, if the ship was seaworthy and the weather fair; if she had not been damaged in action or sabotaged, and if her logical – albeit violent – manoeuvre was necessary to evade the galleys, why did she sink? Like the open bow doors of the *Herald of Free Enterprise* in March 1987, were the open gun ports of *Mary Rose* merely the immediate cause of a disaster waiting to happen for a variety of other, underlying reasons? For, faced with the inrush of water the master could have let fly the sails and caused the ship to turn head into wind and thus right herself. He did not, and down she went. In which case it would seem that the reasons for her sinking could have been as much to do with command and control as with ship construction or fitting out. In other words, discipline and drill on board was such as to exacerbate the precarious position that the open gunports had created. Thirty-three years later, Sir Francis Drake, during his circumnavigation on board the *Golden Hind*, called his jealous and grumbling crew together and stated what was to be a vital requirement of leadership on board ship:

> I must...have the gentlemen to haul and draw with the mariner and the mariner with the gentlemen...Let us show ourselves all to be of a company and let us not give occasion to the enemy to rejoice at our decay and overthrow.[11]

On 19 July 1545 did the French rejoice because the rule stated so clearly by Sir Francis Drake on board the *Golden Hind* had not been enforced on board the *Mary Rose*?

The loss of *Mary Rose* was witnessed not only by the king sitting on horseback on Southsea Common, but also by Lady Carew who was in attendance. The king was stunned, but did his best to comfort the distressed lady. The tragedy is best summed up – as was the loss of the *Royal George*, in a similar accident near the same spot centuries later – by a poet:

> Sunk by her own guns
> cannoning to leeward,
> gun ports open to the sea
> The King he screeched
> like any maid:
> 'Oh my gallant gentlemen
> Oh my gallant gentlemen'
> All over. The cry of mun,
> the screech of mun, Oh sir,
> up to the very heavens.
> The very last souls I seen
> was that man's father,
> and that man's.
> Drowned like rattens,
> drowned like ratten.[12]

The point of no return: the final capsize.

Except, perhaps, the ratten swam away. One did not, however; the bones of an individual rat were recovered from the wreck of *Mary Rose* in 1982.

The loss of life was great. Yet, even with the ship healing over so rapidly, she was not in a rough sea, nor was she on her own. On the contrary, she was surrounded by ships, boats and galleys of both England and France. Long-established maritime traditions would have meant that sailors in the water would be dragged out by whoever was able to do so, irrespective of whether they had been mortal enemies a few moments earlier. It was the reported breaching of this time-honoured custom that added to the horror of stories of seamen being machine-gunned in the water by enemy submariners in both world wars.

But only about thirty members of the *Mary Rose* crew were rescued. Why so few? The most obvious answer is that across the upper deck was stretched an anti-boarding net through which no-one could crawl. Those beneath had no chance of scrambling free in the brief moments they still had oxygen in their lungs. Anti-boarding nets were fairly common although, apart from the evidence from *Mary Rose* we have little information about them. In the abortive attempt on the Manilla Galleon in 1709, Woodes Rogers states that the attackers had the, 'disadvantage of a netting-deck to enter upon',[13] so it would seem that they had a long and international history.

Many of the crew, however, would have been above the netting. Certainly, there would have been no place for the soldiery below the nets. They were needed higher up, both to pour fire onto the enemies' upper decks and to board when called upon so to do. A key aim of these early naval engagements was to drive the enemy below so that their upper decks could be taken by a boarding party. In case of the enemy boarding ones own vessel then pikemen, probably seamen, below the netting, and archers and musket men in the castles would have attacked them from both above and below. Another group who would have been above the netting were the gunners of both fore- and after castles. Although the men above the netting faced no obstruction preventing them from jumping into the sea, many of them would not have been able to swim, and it would appear from the Cowdray engraving that there were precious few pieces of flotsam on which to cling. Many of the soldiers would have been wearing protective jerkins

A detail enlarged from a contemporary map showing anti-boarding netting rigged amidships on this warship.

of chain mail. The weight of one of these would have dragged the wearer down in much the same way as those soldiers who, landing at Normandy in 1944, were dropped too far out to sea and drowned through the weight of their equipment. The fact is that a capsizing ship is never easy to escape from, regardless of the circumstances.

When *Royal George* went down in the Solent in 1782 with Rear Admiral Kempenfeldt and, 'twice four hundred men'[14] on board not far from where *Mary Rose* sank, it had been a peaceful day and the ship was being careened when, similarly to *Mary Rose*, a land breeze shook the shrouds and she was overset. The circumstances that overset *Mary Rose* were more complex and the record of events incomplete. The known facts and the theories that historians have created to fill the gaps in between are still open to debate.

In capsizing where and how she did, however, *Mary Rose* preserved for future generations a unique time-capsule of Tudor life and maritime activity. Many of the Royal Navy's greatest disasters have occurred in peace time: groundings, storms, fires, collisions and capsizes have all taken their toll. Of all such tragedies, whether caused by accident or enemy action, the loss of life in *Mary Rose* and *Regent* is both the earliest and among the largest on record. *Mary Rose*, a ship that represents the birth of British naval greatness also represents the start of the recorded tragedy that has always accompanied that greatness.

Few of these lost ships have left anything of themselves to go alongside memorials to their dead. It is different with *Mary Rose*. As the enormity of the loss dissipates through the passing of the centuries, the lives of those who died are remembered daily by all who visit the Mary Rose Museum. Without perhaps realising it, each visitor has undertaken a pilgrimage to a shrine dedicated to all who served in *Mary Rose*. For those who seek a quieter memorial, on 19 July 1984, the bones of one of her sailors were laid to rest beneath the floor of Portsmouth Cathedral in a part of that church that existed in 1545. The body of this unknown sailor was interred during a service specially written for the occasion in such a style that its words and ritual would have been ones with which he himself would have been familiar. Every year, on the Sunday nearest to 19 July, a wreath of the beautiful, fragrant pink David Austin roses - named 'Mary Rose' – is laid on the tomb.

King Henry was not to outlive his favourite ship by many years. Ill and obese by the time of the loss of *Mary Rose* he staggered on for another two years until, on 28 January 1547, he died. His biographer, William Thomas, stated that he was, 'Undoubtedly the rarest man that lived in his time' and that he, 'Wot

Every year a bouquet of 'Mary Rose' roses is laid on the tomb of the unknown sailor in Portsmouth Cathedral.

not where in all histories I have read to find one king equal to him'.[15] Other contemporaries might have felt that both Süleyman the Magnificent and the Holy Roman Emperor Charles had surpassed him. For Henry had not been a great king. Too many of his closest circle had said their final farewells with their heads upon a wooden pillow. Too many of firm belief had entered the fiery furnace like Daniel and lit forgotten candles. Too many of those in error saw their entrails exposed before they expired in agony. Too many great buildings and treasure houses were vandalised and looted; what Cortes and Pizzaro were to do to the New World Henry did to his own kingdom. Too many flaws, too many conceits, too little understanding, too few great rather than grand gestures: a gross rather than a great king.

But then there was the navy. Henry's wooden walls were to be as significant as those on which

Athens pinned her hopes in the Persian Wars; more significant, in fact, for, whereas Athens herself was despoiled, after Henry's creation of a standing navy, the shores of England were never again trampled by a seaborne invader. Yet Henry remained a man of the land. His sea passages were limited to the shortest crossing to Calais and the occasional meal on board ship. In contrast, his Scottish contemporary, James V, was to circumnavigate his kingdom in 1540. But Henry was a king of the home counties, who did not seem to consider such a progress to the outposts of his nation either a necessity or an obligation.

There can be little doubt that on his death bed Henry would not have considered the founding of a standing navy among his great achievements. His vision of empire stretched not much further than the land that can be seen from the white cliffs of Dover on a fine day. His daughter Mary lost even that, but Elizabeth looked beyond Europe and her sailors encompassed the world. Not that they did it with her financial support. The parsimonious queen did not invest in her fleet in the same way that her father had. Rather, with greater

subtlety she invested in men's hearts and minds; they took the risks and she kept faith – and a great deal of the loot. Henry's fleet seized foreign hulls according to the legitimacy of war. Elizabeth's privateers steered a less honest and more prosperous course.

Henry's greatest legacy, a first-class fighting navy. This Vroom painting of the attack on Cadiz in 1596 shows how the race-built galleons of the next generation could – even in the close confines of Cadiz harbour – come up against galleys and defeat them.

Elizabeth had inherited an infrastructure, both administrative and physical, on which she could build. This included a few warships, the great legacy of Trinity House, a defended naval port at Portsmouth and a Navy Board. Operationally, the idea that serving the monarch at sea was just as important – and rewarding – as rendering similar service ashore had taken hold. Unlike Henry, Elizabeth did not have to send young and inexperienced courtiers to sea. With ships such as *Mary Rose* sea warfare had come of age, and men like Drake and Hawkins knew how to exploit its specialist opportunities.

CHAPTER 14

Rediscovery and Recovery

HEINRICH SCHLIEMANN FIRST visited the Troad in 1868 and began his excavations of Troy in 1870, completing them in May 1873. Arthur Evans, having visited the site of Knossos in 1894 began excavations on 23 March 1900, and had completed his main work on the Minoan Palace by 1906. The work of these two archaeologists is ranked among the greatest excavations ever undertaken in the field of archaeology. But, alongside them must surely stand the search for and recovery of *Mary Rose*, for this latter was a far more difficult project. After all, both Schliemann and Evans had significant, identifiable features standing proud of the landscape to help them, with shards and artefacts scattered around as clues. *Mary Rose* lay beneath a blue, featureless liquid and unstable plain, upon whose surface even the most perceptive eye could not pick out the spot where the ship might lie. Her discovery and recovery were a test of faith and determination, against both odds and criticism, which puts the team that achieved this remarkable feat on the same pedestal as that occupied by Schliemann and Evans.

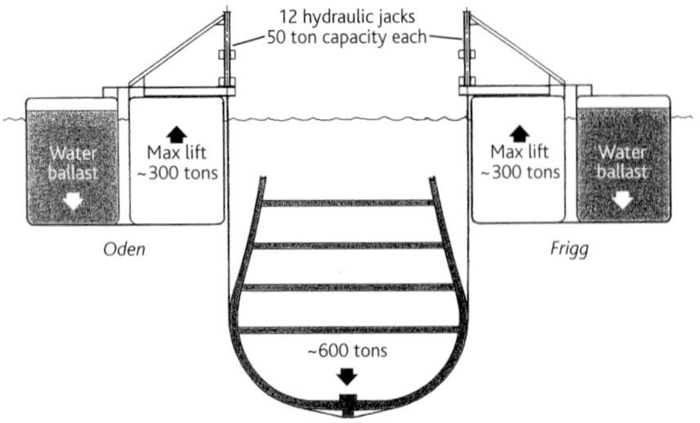

The salvage system as used on *Vasa* in 1965. It is much the same method that was tried and failed on *Mary Rose* in 1545.

Mary Rose did not disappear the day that she sank. She went down to a sea bed that was only six fathoms below the surface at low tide so that the tops of her masts remained visible. Although Lisle was well able to continue his campaign without *Mary Rose*, the fact that she had sunk in shallow waters suggested that her salvage might be a simple and swift task that would not compromise his fighting strength. The admiral therefore immediately ordered her to be raised. Lisle was to be supported in the work by his military counterpart the Duke of Suffolk who, if *Mary Rose* had been named after Henry's sister (see chapter 1) would, as her husband, have had a special and poignant interest in raising the vessel; Mary had died in 1530. No such personal interest is evident but, by 31 July 1545, Suffolk was writing to Paget that, '...for the *Mary Rose*, we intend with all speed to set men in hand for that purpose as shall appertain.'[1]

The salvage work itself was entrusted to two Venetians whose vessel had been detained at Southampton. How experienced Petre de Andreas and Symonde de Maryne were is not known, but the fact that they did not succeed in raising the ship might indicate that they had tendered for the task for reasons other than their own competence in such work. For the job need not have been difficult, and the necessary salvage method was both simple and well known. Indeed, it varied little from how such a task might be achieved today; it was the same principle employed for the recovery of *Vasa* off Stockholm in 1965. The salvors required two large vessels strong enough to bear the underwater weight of *Mary Rose*. These vessels would need to be placed either side of the wreck so that stout cables could be passed between them and underneath the wreck itself. The rise and fall of the tides would then produce the motive power needed to lift the hull. At low water, the slack on the cables would be taken up by the crews of the two salvage ships. High tide would then lift all three vessels the same distance until, after several tides, the wreck cleared the bottom, enabling the salvors to move their charge to shallower water where she would be grounded. There the process would be repeated and the ships moved into shallower and shallower waters where divers could lighten the vessel by helping to remove the heavy weaponry and stores. When the decks broke surface, pumps would have been placed on board to assist with the salvage until, after many weeks the vessel was fully pumped out and afloat once more. Although the French threat meant Lisle was reluctant further to diminish his forces by diverting two large vessels to the salvage work, by 1 August two naval vessels, *Sampson* and *Jesus of Lubeck*,[2] 700-ton carracks, had been emptied of their guns and stores and moved above *Mary Rose* to begin work. The Venetians had provided a list of the equipment that they would need in addition to the two hulks. They required, '...five of the greatest cables that may be had; ten great hawsers; ten new capstans; fifty pulleys; and a great quantity of cordage of all sorts.'[3] As for manpower, they required thirty of their own mariners and one carpenter plus sixty English mariners.

The date of 3 August was set for the attempt, which Suffolk believed would be, 'speedily done as may be for the serving of the tides'. It was not. Certainly some progress was made for, on 5 August, Lisle and Suffolk were able to report that the ships' sails and yards were ashore and that three cables had been secured to her masts. The optimism continued for, on 7 August, Suffolk was informing Paget that Lisle considered, '...that he had good hope of weighing upright of the *Mary Rose* this afternoon or tomorrow.'[4]

Two days later everything had changed. Suffolk had to report the cessation of the operation because the 'Italians' had broken off the ship's masts. They were now preparing to try and drag the ship bodily into the shallows, which they estimated would take six days. In fact considerably more time was needed – some 437 years in all.

The unsuccessful Venetians did not depart empty handed, however, and were given forty marks sterling (£27) for their efforts. The attempt to salvage *Mary Rose* herself might have been abandoned, but the work to raise her equipment continued for a number of years for, in modern values, some £1.7 million of ordnance had sunk with her. In 1547 the Treasurer for Marine Causes paid out £37 11s 5d for the removal of anchors and weapons and, later, an Italian diver was paid a further £20 for similar work. In 1549

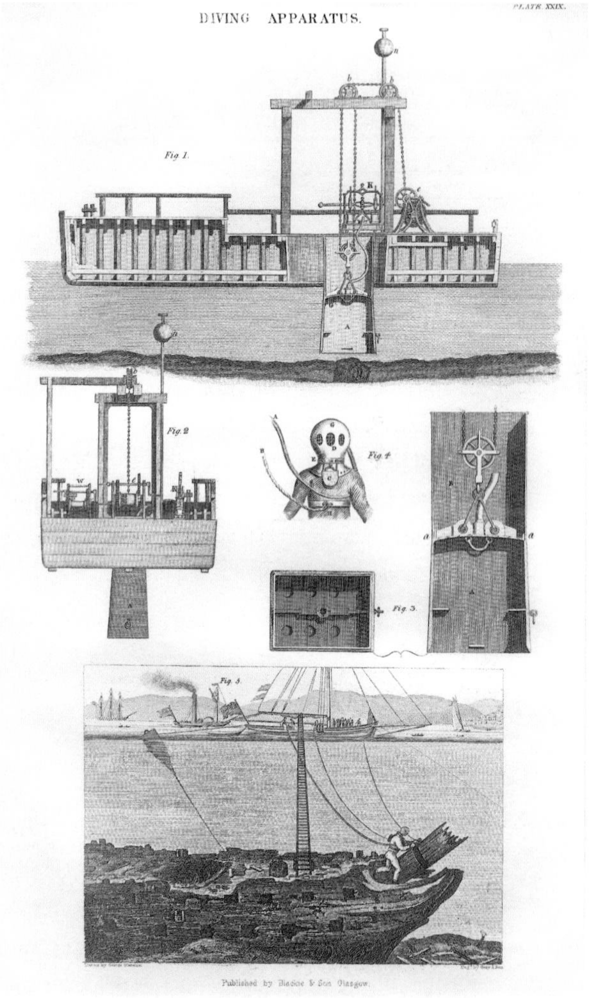

The equipment used by the Deane brothers for working on the wreck of the *Royal George*.

another Italian, Piero Paola Corsi, was paid £50 for the recovery of ordnance. Later he was to be charged with attempting to make off with objects from another Solent wreck. The record of his trial is another example of archival evidence linked to *Mary Rose* throwing light on history in an entirely unexpected direction: Corsi's chief diver was a Guinean black slave and as such was the first black person to give evidence in an English lawsuit.[5] By 1552 salvage work was over. It had cost the crown £559 8s 7d (£168,000 in modern terms) to recover what little they had managed to retrieve. By way of comparison, the three-week diving operation carried out at the wreck site by the Mary Rose Trust in 2004 cost £100,000.

Below the water *Mary Rose* had been undergoing a sea change. She had settled on her starboard side nestling into the soft silts of the old River Solent. Twice daily tides would have scoured out a pit into which she would slowly subside while, like dust in an attic, the same silts settled in her interior. Slowly worm and rot would have worked on her exposed timbers until, eventually, little remained above the sea bed to indicate that here lay a noble ship. The next time she was disturbed was when another Solent disaster, the loss of *Royal George* in 1782 brought salvage divers back to the Solent. Their optimism was just as buoyant as that of those who had sought to salvage *Mary Rose* more that 200 years earlier. Cowper, in his famous poem, included the lines:

> Her timbers yet are sound,
> And she may float again;
> Full charged with England's thunder,
> And plough the distant main.[6]

But success was as illusive as it had been in 1545. Attempts had been made to salvage equipment from *Royal George* within two years of her sinking but with very limited success. Nothing, in fact, could be achieved until the invention of the very first practical individual diving apparatus by the Deane brothers.

In 1818 a barn fire in Kent threatened to destroy a number of horses tethered inside the burning building. Some rapid thinking resulted in a friend of the farmer, John Deane, sticking the helmet from a suit of armour on his head, thrusting the hose from the fire pump underneath it and entering the building while being supplied with fresh air down its length by the working of the fire pump. Amazingly, the idea worked and the horses were saved.

By 1823 John Deane and his brother Charles had secured a patent for 'An Apparatus to be Worn by Persons Entering Rooms filled with Smoke'. The Deanes had maritime connections and it was not long before they were experimenting with using the apparatus underwater: there was money to be made in working wrecks and recovering items of value. Having commenced such endeavours off Kent, in 1832 this brand new business moved to the Solent where so many wrecks lay reasonably close to the surface. Their 'target' was *Royal George*, but while working on her they were asked to unsnag the nets of a local fisherman and in doing so they stumbled across the site of *Mary Rose*. Their discoveries and recoveries here amazed the antiquarian world; they recovered four of the fifteen bronze guns known to have been fitted in the ship and twenty of the seventy-six iron guns plus numerous other artefacts.

In 1840, they placed charges to clear away the sands in an attempt to discover and retrieve more objects. Thankfully(!) this did not prove a success. Soon after this the Deanes' pioneering talents ceased to be called upon, for the brothers sold their patent to a man called Augusts Siebe, who came to be known as the inventor and father of underwater breathing apparatus. One major achievement of the rediscovery of *Mary Rose* in the twentieth century was to restore the Deanes to their rightful place in the history of underwater exploration. Hitherto, the waters of oblivion had washed away their work and its location, just as the Solent had hidden away the site of *Mary Rose*. It was to take a determined effort by a visionary man, Alexander McKee, and the team that he inspired to find her again.

Following the loss of *Mary Rose*, the Solent witnessed several other major disasters. In 1711 *Edgar* blew up and in 1795 *Boyne* did the same. The most famous sinking was *Royal George,* which capsized in 1782 when 'a land breeze shook the shrouds, and she was overset' taking to the bottom brave Kempenfelt 'with twice four hundred men'. Locating these ships was McKee's original aim and to this end he formed an organisation called Solent Ships to look for *Boyne, Royal George, Mary Rose* and ten other historic ships although, from the start, he believed that *Mary Rose* was the 'one really important wreck'.

Once he had located these ships McKee wanted to record and write a book about these ships and note whether any of them might be worth excavation or salvage. McKee's work in the Solent began on 24 April 1965. Like so many enthusiastic 'amateurs' he had very limited equipment with which to begin such a major undertaking. His greatest resource was his own enthusiasm and the loyalty and dedication that he inspired in the small team which he uncannily and unerringly picked to work with him. It was a small and dedicated group of local divers and researchers and they had to endure many a discomfort and disappointment before their eventual triumph.

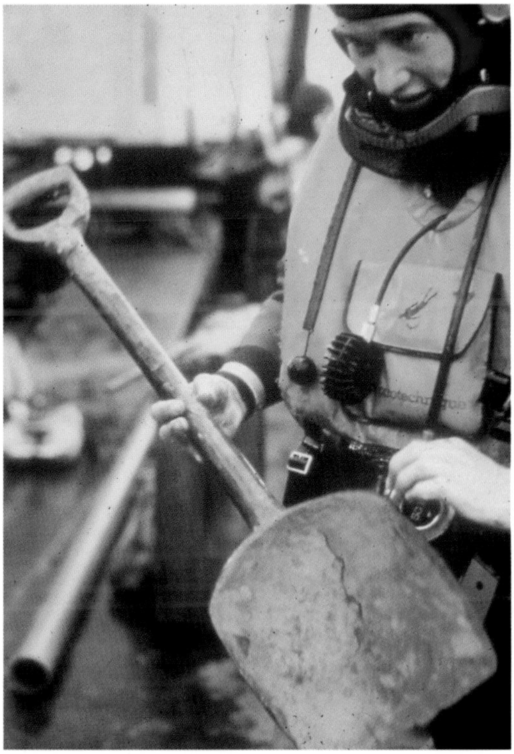

Following the rediscovery of the site by Alexander McKee's diving team in 1971, the slow process of investigating the wreck and recovering its contents began.

On many occasions the elements and the limitations of equipment conspired to frustrate the divers bobbing about in their little boat. Lesser men, under less inspirational leadership, would have called it a day – McKee's team pressed on, like polar explorers defying the elements because of their conviction and dedication. Morrie Young, one of the original team, recalls that McKee would get quite cross when people used such phrases as, 'if we find the ship'. 'Not 'if',' he would say, 'WHEN!' As with any demanding, obsessive task, sacrifices had to be made. McKee was quoted in *The Sun* at the time of the ship's recovery, saying that, 'The *Mary Rose* was a rival to the wives and girlfriends of all of us'. Many a domestic squabble and marital strain must surely be politely hidden away in that statement!

The search for *Mary Rose* by 'Mad Mac's Marauders' – as they called themselves – involved both diving in the likely position of the wreck, and academic research to try to pinpoint the site of the ship with as great a degree of accuracy as possible. It was quickly accepted that very little, if any, of the wreck would be visible above the seabed, so this research was vital. At first the team had a copy of the contemporary Cowdray engraving and some very contradictory statements that gave far too great a search area. The search radius needed to be narrowed down. The breakthrough came in the most logical place – the Royal Navy's Hydrographic Office. On a visit to their records in 1966 McKee was shown a chart drawn up as a result of a survey of Spithead carried out in 1841. Red crosses showed the location of *Royal George, Edgar* and *Mary Rose.* At last, the team had an idea of where to look. Even so, this still only reduced the size of the haystack in which they sought their historic needle.

The next breakthrough was a technical one. In 1967, McKee was given the opportunity to trial a new bottom-searching sonar with a side-scanner. This would give the observer a profile of the shape of the seabed – the seabed-penetrating sonar would reveal any anomalies lying beneath the surface. As so often on such quests, the searchers enjoyed miserable weather conditions to begin the trial; however, they were rewarded with a promising anomaly in the sea bed in what they believed to be approximately the right area. This became known as the 'W' feature and it is worth recording McKee's view of its potential. He wrote to Professor Edgerton of the Massachusetts Institute of Technology, the equipment's champion:

> Looking at the plotted results what we have is:
> (a) an oval-shaped feature about 200-feet long headed towards No Mans Land area:
> (b) the interfaces give the impression of a flattened letter 'W', i.e. they are exceedingly angular and nothing like the rounded shapes of the clay interfaces. They are smaller at the ends than in the middle. Oh, ho!
> (c) the feature appears to form some sort of discontinuity or 'break' in the geological strata, and as this cannot be the result of an earthquake the hypothesis that it results from the insertion into the seabed of 700 tons of battleship seems likely, particularly when we consider that the findings at (a) are consistent with the wreck of the *Mary Rose*.
> If the suspect feature proves to be the *Mary Rose*, then I expect we shall be able to claim the carrying out of the first electronic trenching survey of a sub-mud historic wreck.[7]

What McKee's research had also clearly demonstrated was how a wreck coming to rest on the soft silts of the old River Solent might get covered up and form a hollow, scoured-out feature, caused by the effects of tidal movements around the obstruction. The 'W' feature was consistent with this. Work on the 'W' site began in 1969 with great support provided by both the Fire Brigade and the Royal Engineers. The Fire Brigade was able to bring hoses out to the site to blast away a trench on the site; this signalled the commencement of serious excavation on the site. Nothing of import was found that year but the team could be assured that they were, at last, on track.

At last, in August 1970, came the breakthrough the team's perseverance deserved. At around midday in the last days of the diving programme the divers came across a large concreted object. It turned out to be an iron gun of the sort known to have been carried in *Mary Rose*. Eureka! On 5 May 1971, Percy Ackland, a wonderfully instinctive diver, surfaced to report the discovery of a number of frames. The long search was over. Amazingly, just the ends of three small timbers were protruding above the surface of the seabed. They could so easily have been missed or dismissed. That they were not is credit to the professionalism and determination of the full diving team. The joy upon their discovery is best conveyed in Percy Ackland's own words:

> Mac [McKee] said he would like the end of the excavation dug last season buoyed, as we

Some of the recovered objects were instantly identifiable.

> aimed for today. I attached a length of line to a buoy and coiled it up so it would be released without snags. By this time we were on site and Tony [Glover] had anchored up. I finished knitting up and Mrs Rule, who was doubling up as a log-keeper, acknowledged my departure.... Visibility was a gloomy three to four feet.... I headed south-west for about eighty feet when I noticed a change in the bottom. I swam back and found a ledge. I swam along the ledge and found a fragment of timber. I felt around it. It was not attached to anything. I moved ahead and saw an indistinct dark object. I moved towards it. It looked like a frame. IT WAS A FRAME! Eroded at the top like a pyramid about two inches by ten inches. Six inches away was another one and beyond that yet another. I moved along, noticing they ran north to south; I found more frames – only this time with some planking attached. I touched it, half to reassure myself it was real and half to check the width of the planking which was about four inches. I swam along all the frames visible above the seabed. This must be the *Mary Rose*.[8]

The anticipation of just how much of the wreck might be conserved below the sands was most keenly felt by Morrie Young, a shipwright by profession, who was the first to identify the sternpost and the angle at which it lay. Morrie was, and is, a remarkable man. Having been in at the start he remained with the Mary Rose Trust, which had been created in 1978, as a charming and informative volunteer guide. It was Morrie who put into words what the whole team felt when they knew that they had indeed rediscovered the *Mary Rose*: an overwhelming sense of relief. So great had been the criticism and scepticism that the realisation that they had been right all along was a greater sensation than the thrill of discovery.[9]

Morrie's enduring dedication to the cause was not unique. There was a bug present in the water that affected many of the early diving team so that, once caught, they were unable to withdraw. Thus did Alexandra Hildred became a leading expert on Tudor armament and the author of Volume 3 of the archaeological record of the excavation while, at the same time, taking charge of the 2003, 2004 and 2005 dives. Christopher Dobbs, after a short absence, returned to the Mary Rose Trust where, in addition to filling numerous jobs, he became the lucid, humorous and idiosyncratic voice of the trust in all major TV documentaries. Morrie Young and Eric Sivyer became enthusiastic and modest volunteer guides; Wendell Lewis, the Director of Salvage, became President of the Mary Rose Society to be succeeded, after many years of service, by Adrian Barak, another diver. Professor Seán McGrail, whose involvement had begun when he was at the National Maritime Museum, and a member of the original Steering Committee advised on the five volume *Archaeology of the Mary Rose*. Many, many others remained active or in touch, a tribute both to the magic of the ship and the team leadership and camaraderie that the excavation had created.

With the discovery of what was obviously a find of major archaeological and historical significance the Mary Rose 1967 Committee had to decide whether to (i) leave the vessel undisturbed; (ii) raise a representative sample of objects or (iii) carry out a complete excavation and recovery. Their boldness in going for the third option should not be underestimated. No such major underwater excavation had ever been undertaken and there were numerous unknown quantities including the cost, the commitment to conservation and the storage and eventual display of the ship and her thousands of objects. It was with a very deep breath indeed that the great plunge was taken.

The decision, once taken, involved a change of direction from exploration to excavation. Different skills were needed and this meant a change of leadership. Margaret Rule, a professional archaeologist, had been involved with the search for *Mary Rose* from the beginning. She had been working on the Roman Palace at Fishbourne when she was first asked to

Margaret Rule became the professional Archaeological Director of the project, having learned to dive to get a better understanding of the site. Here she is examining one of the most spectacular objects recovered, a bronze gun.

spend a few days advising the McKee team. This she had done willingly, caught the bug, and had learned to dive herself. Her instructors had been Morrie Young and Percy Ackland, and she qualified in time to make her first dive on the site on 15 May 1971 just ten days after Percy had, at last, discovered the ship. From now on she would have a much clearer idea as to what was going on down on the seabed.

Year after year, despite the occasional setback, more and more timbers became visible and the realisation dawned that as much as half the ship's hull might have been preserved in the silt. This was a major discovery. At first the team had thought that the ship was resting nearly upright in the seabed but this interpretation was gradually seen to be wrong as mote timbers were exposed and Morrie had a chance to consider the evidence with his experienced and professional shipwright's eye. It was not until 1975 that Morrie finally realised the truth about the angle of inclination at which the ship had come to rest and the direction in which she was pointing. With a hunch to prove he dived on the stern and located what he knew to be the sternpost of *Mary Rose*. This confirmed beyond doubt what he had suspected for some time, that the ship was lying at an angle of sixty degrees. When asked by a reporter how he felt at the time Morrie stated that he could only 'truthfully answer "Jubilant but highly embarrassed!"'

It was time for the future of *Mary Rose* to be decided. In 1978 Margaret Rule was a part of the team that made that bold decision to salvage and recover the ship. Put simply the trust was committing itself to:

- (i) remove all the material above and around the hull
- (ii) remove all the silt from within the remaining structure
- (iii) remove all the contents from between the decks and in the scour-pit around the ship
- (iv) reinforce the hull
- (v) lift the hull in one piece and transport it ashore
- (vi) find a suitable site to conserve and display the hull and its artefacts.

It is probably true to say that, had the trust members realised at the time the extent and duration of the work involved, they might well have decided to record the hull *in situ* and just raised the artefacts. Had they been that cautious they would have deprived the nation not only of a wonderful and unique treasure but of watching, on 11 October 1982, one of the most memorable events ever shown live on television.

To get to that great day a highly professional excavation needed to be carried out. Margaret Rule was, therefore, appointed the Archaeological Director to plan and supervise the future programme. The decision to raise the hull meant a change in organisation. The original work had been carried out by part-time, but experienced volunteers; the new working practice required a core of full-time professionals supported by volunteers who could give many weeks at a time to the project. This was not a commitment that many of Mac's team were able to undertake and, with great sadness, many of them had to call an end to their active involvement. To say that the shift represented a change from amateur to professional personnel would be to disparage unjustly the 'Marauders', who had by this time been formed by McKee into the most experienced archaeological diving team in the country, probably the world.

Volunteers remained the core of the work force. In January 1981 *The News*, the local Portsmouth paper, estimated that the Mary Rose Trust had 250 volunteer divers working in shifts on the seabed, supported by a total paid workforce of just twenty-three. Not all the volunteers were divers; many others raised the project's profile or funds in numerous ways. Roger Trise, for example, spent 200 hours making a model cross-section of the hull for display at the London International Boat Show.

From 1979, for the first time, a proper diving vessel, *Sleipner*, which had been used during the recovery of the *Vasa* was made available to the trust when Portsmouth City Council, in one of many acts of support purchased her, thus allowing the Trust time to raise money to repurchase her themselves. The change in diving frequency was manifest. During the 229 days of the 1979 season 6,858 dives, involving 180 volunteers in addition to the permanent team, were made from *Sleipner* and some 600 cubic metres of silt removed. A matrix of scaffolding poles[10] and a meticulous recording system ensured that every object's discovered position and details were meticulously recorded, labelled, numbered, described, drawn and listed. Professional archaeology, in the most difficult environment was ensuring a text-book style project. Nic Rule, Margaret's son, devised a system of reference points to guarantee pin-point accuracy in recording locations. The system, along with many innovations first tested on this site, remains in use today wherever similar excavations take place.

In 1981 it was discovered that corrosion of the nails in internal planks meant that all the internal structure would have to be dismantled before any salvage began. A large subsidiary pile of timbers on the seabed was the result, and again nothing was removed without accurate recording so that it could be restored to its rightful position. By June 1982 all was removed and the hull lay ready for lifting.

The objects that had come from within the structure had amazed all those that saw them. From beautifully cast bronze guns, and bows and arrows, to a gimbal-mounted compass and several pairs of dividers, the finds all showed what an active warship *Mary Rose* had been and the lifestyle of those who lived on board her. Along with the objects were the bones of some 179 of the sailors and soldiers who had drowned with the ship. They were treated with respect and only limited access was given for thorough and proper research.[11] One volunteer, Tom McShee had taken responsibility for cleaning and cataloguing the bones and dedicated two days a week for seven months to this task.

The decision to lift the ship and the debate about how this would be achieved meant, sadly, that old hurts resurfaced. These were all reported in *The News* whose coverage of the whole *Mary Rose* saga was a most thorough, unbiased but supportive, piece of sustained journalism. By 8 May 1981 McKee had made it clear that in his view, '...unless there is a drastic change of direction in plans to raise [the ship] the entire project could founder and Portsmouth could become a laughing stock.'[12] On 15 May 1981 *The News* headline read, 'Mutiny on the Mary Rose' under which an article entitled 'Salvage Row Rocks Project' made clear the differences of opinion between Margaret Rule and Alexander McKee. McKee, who had encouraged Margaret Rule to learn to dive when she joined his project felt that she was too inexperienced in salvage to be entrusted with the incredibly delicate task of raising a Tudor ship from the seabed. Instead he wished to see 'a top salvage man' appointed. His main concern was that, 'At the moment the seabed is holding the ship together. This adhesive will have to be broken at some time and that is when expert advice will be needed.'[13] Dr Rule's view was just as robust and she was quoted as saying, 'The original divers are no longer working on the project and those who have criticised the methods of working are out of touch.'[14]

From such a statement Alexander McKee might very understandably have felt a sense of exclusion from a project that had long been his own. *The News* called for harmony stating that:

> If the Trust's salvage scheme needs to be reappraised in the light of McKee's convictions and if more money has to be raised to guarantee success, then so be it. Raising the ship in haste to meet next year's deadline would be disastrous if it risked repentance at leisure.[15]

McKee and his experts had a valid concern, for the plan at this time involved lifting the ship from the seabed above the water so that she could be transferred to a cradle resting on a barge. Even the level-headed Morrie Young saw dangers in this approach and he was quoted by *The News* as believing that:

> ...the ship can be raised but I would be amazed if they did it without some damage being caused. The finest salvage company in the world could not get it up without it showing some damage.[16]

The Marauders' concern was based on the physical fact that, underwater, *Mary Rose*, was almost weightless; above the surface she would weigh several hundred tons, making the chances of an accident much more likely. While this difference of opinion was aired the Trust continued with preparations to raise the ship. Early September 1981 brought, in the opinion of *The News*, 'Decision Day for Mary Rose' for now it was necessary for the Trust to answer four questions: Could the Trust's recovery plan work? Could the Eastney Museum be built in time and within the trust's budget? Was the ship ready to be lifted? And could the Trust raise enough money to fund the whole project?

The first good news from the brainstorming that took place was the decision to lift the ship on to her cradle while she was still underwater. This delighted McKee and, much relieved, he was reported as saying that he was, 'a lot happier now and I think the chances for success are reasonably good'. It was also decided to reject the use of nylon strops for lifting in favour of securing metal bolts to the hull itself, which would be safer and avoid the hull 'playing' as the strops tensed.

The new plan was ingenious. It called for holes to be drilled through the main frame of the ship into which steel bolts would be passed, linking them by wire attachments to an Underwater Lifting Frame (ULF) that would be placed over the vessel. Once secured, the frame would be lifted up and the ship transferred, underwater, to a cradle situated nearby on the seabed. The cradle was another skilfully designed object. Not only was it capable of receiving the hull at precisely the same sixty-degree angle at which she had lain on the seabed but, at some stage during the conservation period ashore, it was going to be possible to move the cradle and thus bring the ship upright for the first time in more than 450 years. The cradle also had hollow legs into which the legs of the ULF would fit and be locked so that both objects could be raised together to the surface.

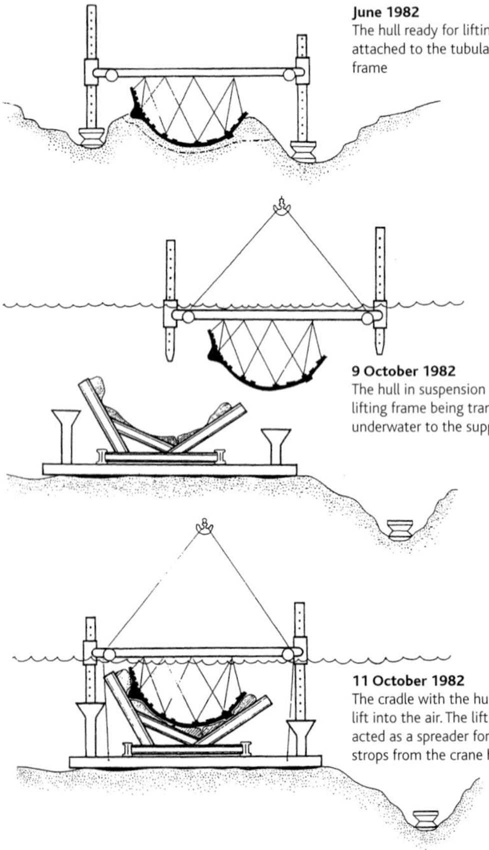

June 1982
The hull ready for lifting with wires attached to the tubular steel lifting frame
9 October 1982
The hull in suspension from the lifting frame being transferred underwater to the support cradle
11 October 1982
The cradle with the hull ready for the lift into the air. The lifting frame now acted as a spreader for the wire strops from the crane hook

The recovery system worked out for the1982 lift was a most sophisticated design in which nothing was left to chance.

In choosing a final resting place for *Mary Rose* on land a site on the easternmost end of Portsea Island at Eastney had emerged as the clear favourite with the City Council. Others were less impressed by this choice, citing problems with parking as well as the distance from the dockyard where the story had begun almost 500 years earlier. Most vociferous in their disagreement was a pressure group called the Maritime Preservation Society who initially preferred a site close to Southsea Castle. In July 1981, a correspondent in *The News*, J J Rattley, was the first to suggest that the most appropriate site would be in the dockyard next to HMS *Victory*. A day later he and his followers were informed in *The News* that the Eastney site had reached the point of no return, a view endorsed by the Chairman of the Trust, Sir Eric Drake, on 22 July when he ruled out any alternative to Eastney.

'Decision Day' was followed rapidly by second thoughts on the Eastney site, however, which would not be ready to receive the ship following its recovery. To address this eventuality the Ministry of Defence offered as a temporary home a dry dock in the naval base. The offer was treated with suspicion by the Eastney faction and the City Council expressed fears that the ship might end up 'in Portsmouth Dockyard for good'.[17]

Few would now argue that this location, which did become the final resting place of *Mary Rose*, was not the most appropriate, but in 1981 the debate was a fiery one, with local county councillor Michael Hancock even suggesting that the Council's pledge of substantial and vital funding should be withdrawn should the dockyard site become permanent. By March 1982 the Eastney plan had been shelved 'for a time', but few believed that it would be resurrected. Nevertheless, Sir Eric Drake had to say that it was still too premature to decide on the final resting place of the ship.[18] *The News*, however, urged the trust to decide on the dockyard.

The final Decision-Day topic was funding, a doubly vexed issue. Firstly, there was the obvious problem of raising enough money to carry on with the work, especially as costs were soaring and, secondly, there was the question of whether such a large sum could not be better spent elsewhere. Portsmouth has many areas of deprivation whose inhabitants might well have preferred their Council to invest in their well-being rather than into the lifting of half a hull of ancient soggy wood. Once again this debate was carried out in both Council chamber and the pages of *The News*, but there was little doubt as to its outcome. The Council could see the benefits that this unique piece of their own maritime heritage would bring to the city once she was on display, and many local people took a pride in the fact that their city's proud tradition of skilled maritime construction was being brought to the attention of the world. The Council's support continued.

Matching that support with private donations – for the ship was being raised many years before the introduction of the Lottery – was the task of the Chairman of Whitbread, Charles (later Sir Charles) Tidbury, a man with a zest for life, a persuasive charm and an indestructible optimism. As Chairman of the Court of the Mary Rose, the trust's fundraising arm, Charles Tidbury worked with the trust's equally tireless Development Director, Ian Dahl, to encourage both corporate and personal donations. Their great coup was to be a challenge by the American billionaire, Armand Hammer, that he would give $100,000 to the Trust if nine similar donors could be found to give the same amount: in other words, raise one million dollars. Armand Hammer duly paid his cheque. Gifts in kind were also most valuable contributions. The most significant of these came when Mr A J Grenville, the head of the Scottish company Howard Davis, pledged to the Trust the use of his massive crane *Tog Mor* to carry out the lift with a charge of just £1 for its hire. This generous gesture was worth over £400,000 to the Trust so, without it, *Mary Rose* would not have been lifted in October 1982, however ingenious the technical plans for that operation had by then become. And they were ingenious.

The recovery programme was approached as a six-phase evolution:

The listing frame containing the ship's remains being brought into No 3 Dock. Her future 'home' was to be under 100m from the site of her construction in 1509/10.

PHASE 1: once excavation was complete the steel frame was towed to the site (in June 1982) and lowered so that its four legs were supported firmly by the seabed.

PHASE 2: involved the drilling of the holes in the ship and the fixing of bolts linked by cable to the frame.

PHASE 3: a steel cradle was placed on the seabed close to the lifting frame.

PHASE 4: the hull of *Mary Rose* was lifted from the seabed and moved to the support cradle.

PHASE 5: the lifting frame was lowered and locked into the cradle.

PHASE 6: *Mary Rose*, secure between the cradle and the frame was slowly lifted to the surface and lowered onto a barge for transportation back to Portsmouth.[19]

To achieve all this required a precision in engineering, design and construction that would have cost a fortune to purchase, but corporate generosity made the dream a reality. Along with Howard Davis, Babcocks were manufacturing the cradle on very favourable terms and BP, Sir Eric Drake's old company, who had been one of the first to give practical support continued to do so well beyond the actual raising of the hull. In addition the Trust was blessed by a very professional hull-salvage recovery team, led by one of the most professional and nicest men to be associated with the Trust, Colonel Wendell Lewis, an ex-Royal Artillery officer with a great deal of experience as a project manager.

The on-site work began with the lowering of the ULF in June and was not completed until October. The onset of autumnal gales had Alexander McKee again voicing his anxieties as to the wisdom of conducting the operation so late in the year,[20] but there was no going back. Originally 10 October, a Sunday, had been set for the lift, but the final move had to be delayed twenty-four hours because of adverse weather conditions. There were many places of work missing employees that Monday morning as millions from all over the world gathered around television sets to witness this unique event – the result of so many years of effort by so many people.

At 0903 the ULF broke the surface and shortly afterwards the hull of *Mary Rose* was seen above water for the first time in more than four centuries. As the lift continued there occurred one of those heart-stopping moments of suspense that was evidently not planned but which remained forever in the viewers mind. A sling slipped. Margaret Rule, who together with Alexander McKee was watching the culmination of their years of work being handled by others, described it thus:

> An unforgettable crunch was heard at the south-east corner of the ULF as a tubular pin used to restrain the leg had given way, and the sheath or collar which connected the ULF to the leg had slipped by more than a metre. All hearts stopped but no damage had been done to the ship. The lift continued and by teatime the whole package was safely on the barge.[21]

As for Alexander McKee, he described the day as 'The most wonderful day of my life', the realisation of a boyhood dream.

Mary Rose may have been placed safely on the barge, but no-one was prepared to relax until the precious cargo was safely secured within Portsmouth Harbour. As the fleet made its slow way towards the harbour Wendell Lewis sent the following signal to the local Flag Officer: 'Request permission for *Mary Rose* to re-enter Portsmouth Harbour after a rather long commission of 437 years.'

Permission granted, *Mary Rose* was home at last. The next phase in her long career – conservation – could begin.

Alexander Mckee standing proudly in front of his find – the triumph of determination over adversity and frequent disappointment.

The ship and its cradle safely in dry dock.

CHAPTER 15

Conservation and Display

In the history of the restoration of *Mary Rose* the names of Alexander McKee and Margaret Rule loom large, but there is another name that should be mentioned in the same breath. For, if McKee found her and Rule raised her, then Dr Mark Jones preserved her, and without this third member of the triumvirate the ship would have rotted and her artefacts would have been left to corrupt and crumble. Dr Mark Jones joined the Mary Rose Trust as its Monitoring Scientist in April 1983. He had just completed his doctoral thesis on marine anti-fouling at the University of Portsmouth and was accepted by the Trust following what, for a young scientist must have been a formidable interview with Margaret Rule and Professors John Levy and Sean McGrail. The task ahead of him was enormous. The marvellous state of conservation of the ship and her artefacts today masks the delicate state in which the majority of these items were found when they were first recovered. Nearly 450 years spent in Solent silt and saline had put material under intense destructive pressures, which affected each material differently. There could be no such thing as a 'one treatment suits all' option. Each item needed its own therapy.

Dr Mark Jones, the head of the Mary Rose Trust's conservation team.

With the ship placed in a covered dry dock next to HMS *Victory* and subject to spraying with cold water to stabilise her timbers, the first requirement of the conservators was to find suitable facilities where conservation of the thousands of other finds could be undertaken. A practical beginning was made through agreeing a contract with Portsmouth City Museums so that their staff would undertake some of the work, as their laboratory was ideal for conserving large metal objects and freeze-drying organic material. The National Maritime Museum at Greenwich also agreed to provide specialist advice on the implications of such a major work of conservation, while a grant from the Leverhulme Trust provided the all-important facilitator – money. With these agreements in place the task of conserving a wide variety of items, both organic and inorganic, could begin. The facilities available to Mark Jones and his team in Portsmouth, although willingly given and gratefully received were not purpose-built for the work that needed to be undertaken; nor was there much data available on exactly how to undertake the work. Much had to be attempted through trial and (reversible) error. Questions led to answers that

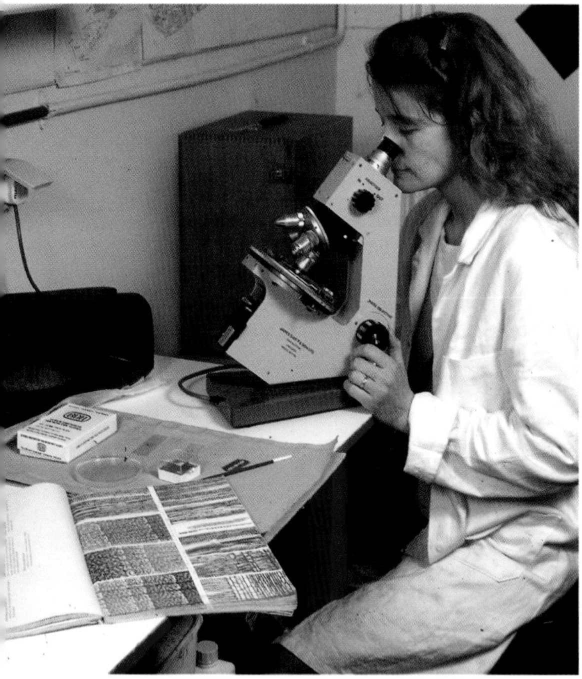

Sue Bickerton, the Trust's conservator, still with much to do after twenty-five years of work.

inevitably posed more questions; the team were going where nobody, not even those involved with *Vasa*[1] – with whom a strong and helpful relationship was swiftly built – had gone before.

Added to the scientific task was the problem of how to protect the hull from the elements while simultaneously allowing the public to see the ship. Mark Jones had to manage the scientific laboratory that the hull of Mary Rose had become, while the public gazed on as the team worked; his was a very exposed job. It was also to be a lengthy one. The conservation process would take more than a quarter of a century. Yet, despite the long hours, seven-day weeks, financial frustrations, lack of proper equipment and paucity of staff, many of Mark Jones's team stayed with the project till the end, including some, such as the conservation specialist Sue Bickerton and the archivist Andy Elkerton, who had began work before the hull was raised.

The predominant material in need of recording, research and treatment was, of course, wood. Ships' timbers, while in water and exposed to oxygen, form a very good diet for organisms such as the infamous *Limnoria* and the ship-worm *Teredinidae* of which the best known is the *Teredo*, whose activities led to the introduction in the seventeenth century of copper sheathing on ships venturing into warmer waters. These crustaceans and molluscs bore long narrow tunnels through the wood, which can form a network of tubes that never link up, the creatures seeming to possess some sixth sense of where their colleagues are active. Left unprotected even the largest block of wood can be eaten up in a remarkably short period. Once recovered the timber, while outwardly appearing in good condition, will be weak and ready to disintegrate. Added to the biological attack, waterlogged wood also decays physically and chemically. Wood cells are subject to fungal and bacterial activity and weakened by cellulose degradation. The result is inevitable. Recovered waterlogged timber left to dry out would distort, shrink and eventually crumble away.

The hull of *Mary Rose* was enormous and before any active conservation could be undertaken it needed to be cleaned. Sediments trapped between the frames were removed by hand and water hoses used to wash out compacted deposits. Ideally the hull should then have been placed in a large tank where her timbers could have been totally immersed in water. Such tanks are very expensive to build and, if one had been

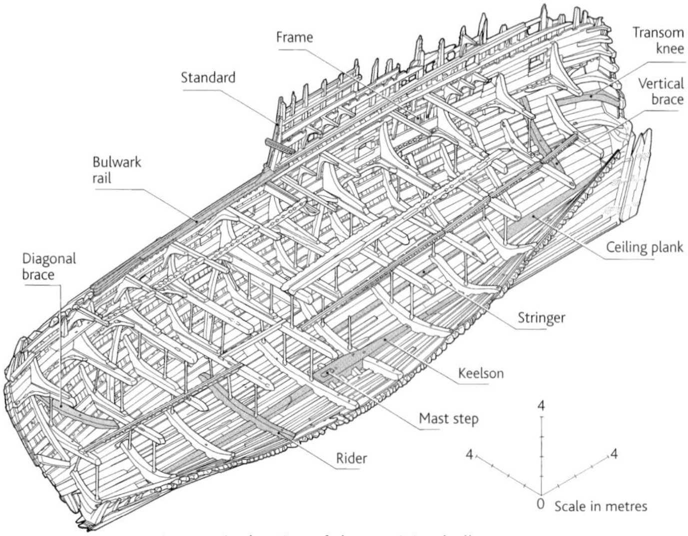

Isometric drawing of the surviving hull structure.

Spraying the hull with PEG (polyethylene glycol).

constructed, the hull would have been hidden from the public for many years. Spraying was the obvious answer.

A low-temperature water-spraying regime was introduced, and it provided several advantages for the conservators. Firstly, it kept the timbers constantly saturated and thus prevented the distortion that drying out would cause; secondly, the low temperature of between two and five degrees Centigrade mitigated against fungal and bacterial growth; thirdly, it was safe and non-toxic and, fourthly, it was compatible with future treatment processes. It also had the major advantage in that visitors could come in their thousands and see the famous ship and watch her conservation taking place. The passive spraying period lasted twelve years and during this time Dr Jones and his colleagues researched the best ways open to them to continue the conservation through chemical treatment. The problem, in lay terms, was that the timbers were no longer solid wood but had assumed the consistency of sponge. If they were allowed to dry out they would collapse on themselves, shrink, distort and crumble. The saturating water, at levels of over 600% of the solid volume in some samples, was what was keeping them in shape. Remove the water and the timber could be lost.

The solution adopted was to fill the spaces within the wood with an inert chemical that would provide structural support and prevent further cellular collapse. The chemical selected for this task was polyethylene glycol (PEG) which, fortunately, was manufactured by a local company, Ineos Oxide, who were more than willing to support the Trust by supplying large amounts of PEG at a very reasonable price. Nevertheless, the conservation remained a very expensive task and it could not have been achieved had the Trust not been fortunate enough to have received a large grant in 2002 (some £4.8 million) from the Heritage Lottery Fund (HLF) and matching funding from, among others the ever-supportive Portsmouth City Council and Hampshire County Council. Several major donations from trustees and their friends further contributed to the funding, while local companies such as Pall Europe, Wightlink, Davis Langdon, Gifford, Lewmar and Sony became regular contributors. The new occupants of the naval dockyard, Vosper Thorneycroft and Fleet Support Limited, gave of their expertise for free.

Before PEG spraying began, the ship was enclosed in a temporary structure that included two galleries from which the public was still able to view her. The spraying and conservation they were witnessing comprised three stages. The first phase used low-grade PEG to enter the timbers and penetrate the cell walls replacing the water as it did so. Phase Two (from 2006–2011) involves the use of a higher-grade PEG to give better rigidity to the badly worn outer timber while, at the same time, sealing in the low-grade PEG. Once sufficient PEG has been absorbed, a five-year programme of controlled air drying will take place during which careful monitoring of the timbers will be necessary to detect any shrinkage or distortion. Over 150 tons of water will dissipate from the hull during this phase. Only after this has been done will the timbers be in a condition to allow the ship to be displayed to the public in a stable state of conservation, without barriers. If this process is completed by 2016 the timbers of *Mary Rose* will have spent as long being conserved as they did in their original service at sea.

In an age where wood was a major material in the manufacture of a whole range of articles it is not surprising that the majority of the finds from *Mary Rose* are wooden. The range is enormous; from the hull itself and its bulky timbers down to ornamental beads and hair combs, bows, arrows and linstocks. As the items were recovered so the range of woods revealed illustrated how carefully the right timber had been chosen for its job. Thus the keel of the ship is formed from tough, rot-resistant elm, while the ship's timbers are of durable oak. Hard boxwood that can take a fine cut was used for the combs while imported yew was used for bows. The parrels that formed a ball race[2] to assist with hoisting the spars were shaped from walnut, which produces its own oils that acts as a self-lubricant.

As they worked, and reported on their progress, so the growing expertise of the conservation team became known throughout the world of maritime archaeology. Originally advice and guidance had been sought from the Swedes who had raised *Vasa* many years earlier, and the two teams had established a close working relationship. However, as Mark Jones's team grew in experience and knowledge so they were in turn able to help the Stockholm team with information based on their experiences with *Mary Rose*. As word got around, the conservators were asked to advise and even restore other finds so that, by 2005, the Mary Rose Trust's own laboratories were handling and advising on, *inter alia*: a fifteenth-century merchant ship found at Newport; an Iron-Age log boat from Fiskerton in Lincolnshire; a Bronze-Age boat from Dover; an ancient wooden circle found off the Norfolk coast (Seahenge); a Bronze-Age ship from Gela in Sicily, and a large carving from the stern of HMS *Colossus* found in the seas off the Scilly Isles.

The research even went so far as to provide indicators on such future concerns as global warming. During the summer dive of 2004 some of the timbers recovered from the site were found to have been colonised by shipworm larvae. Analysis indicated that these were *Lyrodus pedicellatus*, a type of shipworm more normally associated with warmer waters. To find out whether or not these creatures had recently colonised the site a number of modern sacrificial timbers were lowered to the seabed and then sampled for infestation. *Lyrodus pedicellatus* was indeed found in these sample timbers, indicating that this destructive creature from further south had moved into the Solent, whose waters had previously been considered too cool to support its colonisation.

After the hull and its associated timbers the next largest objects recovered from the wreck site were the ship's guns. For conservation purposes these came in two main types; iron guns and bronze guns. The bronze guns recovered were in a wonderful state of preservation due mainly to the fact that their tin content formed a protective layer over the surface. The fine lettering on them was still legible, although they did have areas of bronze disease that formed green rust over the surface. This was easily treated, however, and the conserved gun barrels are a wonder to behold. Among other bronze objects was the ship's bell, cast in 1510, and barely affected by lying in the seabed for so long.

Many of the iron guns were distorted with huge lumps of chalky concretions adhering to their surfaces. Although unsightly, these concretions – because they prevented oxygen reaching the surface of the guns – contributed to their conservation for, without oxygen, the chemical process leading to corrosion could not take place. It followed, therefore, that removal of the concretion could restart corrosion, so preservation had to be swift. There was also a need to get objects on public display as quickly as possible for publicity purposes. The method chosen for the conservation of the larger guns was, therefore, hydrogen reduction in a furnace. This heat treatment drives off dangerous chlorides and converts the oxides of rust back to metal. As this process took only fourteen days to complete it had many advantages over the alternative soaking techniques.

The best way to record archaeological finds is still by their meticulous scale drawing: the task of the illustrator is highly skilled.

Other metal objects, such as pewter plates, on which both the Carew and Lisle crests were stamped, and silver whistles offered corroboration of what was known from the archival record. As these objects were recovered and displayed so knowledge of the ship – until then available only in two-dimensional letters and papers – became three dimensional, real and tangible. The conservationists were bringing history alive.

One wonderful object kept itself hidden. Although gold coins were found in *Mary Rose* the most sought-after gold object was the gold chain and call that King Henry had placed around Sir George Carew's neck as a badge of office before the Vice Admiral sailed to his death. The romance of its recovery awaits a future generation.

Smaller objects could be freeze-dried. This entails freezing the object under great pressure, then removing the water by sublimation by which process the water is expelled as a gas without reverting to its liquid form. Larger objects, which could not fit into the Trust's freeze drier – donated by Pall Europe – had to undergo the lengthy process of drying in air. Of the materials used for clothing the crew, leather was the one that survived the lengthy soaking process the best. So much so that the *Mary Rose* collection includes the best and most extensive range of Tudor leather objects in the world. The leather used came from the skins of cattle, calf, sheep, goat, deer and pig, and was used for making shoes, jerkins, book-covers, flasks, purses, scabbards and many other items, illustrating, once again, the great versatility of the Tudors.

The problem that saturated leather presents to the conservator is how to avoid shrinkage, cracking and distortion as the waterlogged items dry out. While awaiting conservation the leather items recovered from the *Mary Rose* had to be sealed and refrigerated before being washed gently by hand to remove sediments and salts. A series of trials were needed to identify the best method of conservation and then two processes, both involving freeze-drying, were utilised with excellent results, as a study of any of the recovered book-covers, with their fine hand-crafting illustrates.

Although some 260 pieces of cloth were recovered from the ship many were very small and they represent a tiny sample of the textiles that would have been on board. The largest woven item would have been the ship's sails, and sufficiently large fragments of these were recovered to show how their hemp was woven.

Next to the sails the most numerous natural-fibre item used on board was rope. Much of this, in a number of diameters, has been recovered. It is all made of hemp, for they came from an age before the sources of superior fibres such as African sisal or Far-Eastern manilla had been exploited by Europeans. The rope survives in good condition largely because it was impregnated with tar to help its preservation while in use at sea. The efficacy of tar as a preservative can have no better illustration, and the smell, with all its maritime associations still lingers to amaze many of the visitors to the museum, who gingerly sniff the examples on display. Animal fibres, wool and silk were used for clothing, and examples of caps, jerkins, capes, stocking hose and a wonderfully named 'scogger' – or detachable sleeve – have been brought ashore. The finest silk item is probably the barber-surgeon's hat of red velvet, which is identical to those being worn in the 1540 Holbein painting of Henry VIII greeting his surgeons.[3]

The need to handle this huge variety of materials in all their shapes and sizes, with their individual conservation requirements meant that Mark Jones and his team were operating, albeit in a specialist area, on the very frontiers of science. At the same time, much of their work involved elementary processes and methods being taught in science classes in schools up and down the country. The *Mary Rose* team was putting into practice what many children were learning in theory. Opening up the trust's laboratories could bring science alive to these youngsters. The HLF funding for the conservation work enabled this opportunity to be realised.

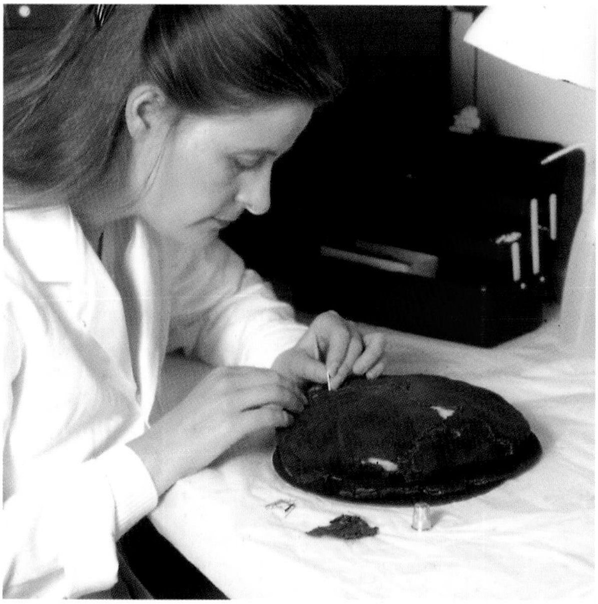

The required conservation expertise covered a huge range of materials, including leather and fabrics.

From 2005 onwards, the number of academic science visits to the trust also grew. At the most specialist end the Trust – in partnership with the University of Southampton, whose marine-archaeology department was headed by Jon Adams, one of the original *Mary Rose* divers – developed an MSc in maritime archaeological conservation. At the juvenile end of the learning scale, primary-school children were instructed in basic science. Looking at the faces of any of these students, either in the laboratories or in the ship hall, one can see the joy of science coming to life. Education at the *Mary Rose* received a further boost when BP Shipping, recognising the value of introducing children to science in a marine environment, provided the trust with a sizeable donation to support such educational work.

After the hull of *Mary Rose* was raised in 1982 it must have seemed that the exploration of the underwater site had come to an end. There was a general belief that the majority of salvable material had already been recovered and that – although further dives to search for such items as the bowcastle would be welcomed – mounting such dives would just be too expensive. Besides which, Mark Jones and his team already had more than enough conservation work to keep them fully employed well into the next century. And so it proved until 2002, when the Ministry of Defence announced its plans to build two new aircraft carriers.

It was always recognised that the wreck site was worthy of further exploration, but at the time of the raising of *Mary Rose* the idea of a return visit was not seriously contemplated. However, in 2001, the Royal Navy's newest warships, not yet built, came to the support of its oldest surviving colleague, the *Mary Rose.* The Ministry of Defence announced that it was to build two large, new aircraft carriers. The biggest ships ever built for the Royal Navy, their deployment would require a re-examination of the entrance into Portsmouth Harbour. There was a perceived operational requirement that these new ships should be ale to sail whatever the state of the tide. In order to achieve this – and guarantee them a safe passage into the port – a new deep-water channel might have to be created, leading in a straight line from the eastern corner of the Isle of Wight to the harbour entrance. The tortuous channel that had defensively served Henry's fleet so well was now an impediment to progress.

Once drawn on the chart it was obvious that the best route for such a new channel ran directly alongside the *Mary Rose* wreck site. Although dredging would not directly disturb the remains, its effects had the potential to cause significant seabed changes to the area where remains of *Mary Rose* still lay. The ministry undertook a survey to evaluate the archaeological impact along the proposed route. The aim of the first year of diving was to take away the arisings and metallic detritus that still lay on the bottom, abandoned when diving ended in 1982. The removal of this rubbish would mean sonar and magnetic anomaly sweeps would only indicate areas of potential archaeological interest rather than a pile of twentieth-century scaffolding. Ironically, the electronic exploration failed to reveal the presence of the five-metre-long iron anchor that was later recovered in 2005. During this skirmishing dive a new trench, forward of the area where the bow timbers had lain, uncovered a large, solid and curved timber. It was immediately thought that this could well be *Mary Rose*'s stem, the curved piece of timber forming the foremost part of the bow. If this were the case, it was an extremely important find.

When *Mary Rose* was raised, in order to ensure that the structure was capable of taking the strains of the lift, the soggy ends that stretched raggedly forward were cut off, leaving the hull with a blunt forward section rather like a roll-on ferry. If the stem was lifted, conserved and placed in its original position the effect, especially for the visitor, would be an enormous improvement. For the first time in centuries, the glorious profile of a sixteenth-century warship would be on display.

Diving in 2004 exposed this timber to its full ten-metre length and it was confirmed that this was indeed the stem. It had to be raised. Meanwhile, plans within the Ministry of Defence had moved on. Not only had the projected carriers reduced in size, but their operational requirement had been amended so that it would be possible for them to use the confines of the existing channel. The final recovery dive planned for 2005 was thus in jeopardy. At this critical moment the Mary Rose Trust was in luck. The new Chief Executive of the Mary Rose Trust, John Lippiett, was a retired rear admiral and he knew the ways of the Ministry of Defence. Applying all his wisdom and experience he was able to persuade the ministry to complete the work that had already been underway for the previous two years. Indeed, not to have done so would have been to have left these historic timbers and artefacts exposed, an unethical position which the ministry wished to avoid.

ABOVE The large anchor recovered in 2005. Ships of the sailing era needed massive ground-tackle like this to secure them from the effects of strong winds, seas and tides.
RIGHT The stem timber. Once restored to its original position the outline of the hull of a sixteenth-century warship will be seen for the first time in centuries.
BELOW *Terschelling*, the diving vessel used in the 2003 to 2005 dives.

A group of her original divers gather around Margaret Rule at the completion of the 2005 dive.

With a beautiful irony the delays meant that the climax of the 2005 dive took place on 11 October, the anniversary of the original lift. Margaret Rule, Morrie Young, Christopher Dobbs and many other members of the original team were among those present to witness the raising of the stem, a large anchor and the ship's crest. Of these, the anchor was the most spectacular, the stem the most significant, and the crest the most romantic. With the ship now at rest in her dry dock under a temporary cover, a home needed to be found in which to display her treasures that had been preserved. The only site available anywhere near the hull, was a 150-year-old wooden boathouse, more than 300 metres from the ship near the entrance to the historic dockyard. This was duly repaired, restored and converted in time to mount a temporary exhibition in 1984. Although temporary, the exhibition, with some modifications and additions, has been on display ever since. Unfortunately, it could only display some ten per cent of the conserved items and there was no opportunity to mount other temporary exhibitions in the limited space available. By 1995 the search was on for a solution that would reunite the ship with its objects in such a way as to display to the public both a 'living' Tudor ship and a far greater quantity of the objects raised. In 2005, with the end of active conservation of the hull in sight, a proposal was put to the HLF for a grant towards creating a purpose-built museum so that *Mary Rose* could complete her 'final voyage' and justify both her potential and the time and faith that so many had invested.

Since she was first displayed in Portsmouth Historic Dockyard more than seven million visitors have flocked to see this remarkable vessel and to wonder at the human endeavour that not only found her but raised her as well. The ship has proved to be enormously popular with schools. With Henry VIII losing none of his appeal and Tudor history still on the school curriculum the ship is a logical venue for school trips. However, she has proved to be more than this, for every school child seems 'wowed' by the sight and many return with their parents in tow to show them what they have found so inspiring.

The potential of displaying the ship and her objects to best advantage, however, had yet to be fulfilled. While conservation was underway the ship, in her dry dock, remained beneath a temporary structure designed merely to provide shelter beneath which, in the correct environment, conservation could take place. The public had to view her through thick glass along two corridors neither of which showed the stunning view of the vessel from outboard. The few items from the ship for which display space had been found were located several hundred metres distant from the ship. Many visitors did not have the time to go to both sites and a significant number of those who did found it difficult to relate the finds, within their glass cases, to the ship from which they came. Nor was it possible to vary the items on display; room did not allow for temporary exhibitions to be staged. Some very important items, such as the guns, had to be placed upright against walls, while there was not space for more bulky, and important items such as gun carriages or anchors.

Over the years from 1982, The trustees of the Mary Rose Trust were presented with several ideas to display the ship once she was conserved and stabilised. The more fanciful involved moving her from the dry dock to another location either in Portsmouth Historic Dockyard, or even as far away as London. One plan called for a huge structure that would dwarf HMS *Victory* which is located in the next dry dock – neither the Trust nor the Royal Navy thought much of that idea!

In the end it was realised that the most cost-effective way to display the ship would be for the hull to remain in the dry dock and for the objects to be returned to their mother ship. This was the nub of the idea that went out to design competition in 2005. Those interested were clearly told that the project required a solution that was designed from the inside out. In other words the most important element was the *Mary Rose* herself, and her artefacts; the building that would house them needed to grow from that function, rather than its own architectural concepts. The competition encouraged forty-five consortia from around the world to submit proposals. After a lengthy elimination process the task was given to a group led by Wilkinson Eyre, a firm rapidly gaining a global reputation for fine design.

Wilkinson Eyre proposal for the new museum building, as it would appear from the south-west.

The Wilkinson Eyre proposal, following the design brief, was to create a virtual hull where, approximately, the missing port side would have been. Onto this structure could be placed the ship's cannon and other objects sited in accordance with their original positioning. Many more items than it was currently possible to display could then be presented to the public in a contextually appropriate way. When it was ready the conserved stem could be returned to the ship to show off the lines of a Tudor warship. Galleries at either end of the ship would tell in-depth stories about the ship's history, its manning and sailing, storing and victualling, weapons of war, and its loss, recovery and conservation. Once completed there would never again be an excuse for anyone to claim that they thought *Mary Rose* had sunk on her maiden voyage.

APPENDIX 1

The Building Specifications for *Mary Rose*

AS IMAGINED BY Dr. Doug McElvogue, maritime archaeologist of the Mary Rose Trust, based on his knowledge of Tudor ship architecture.

Brygandyne and the Master Shipwright would have discussed the ideas laid out below before they could translate the king's wish for a warship into and actual vessel.

1. The ship shall be 105ft long keel, 38ft 9in maximum breadth and 13ft deep under the beam of the main orlop to the top of the keel.

2. From the keel at 8ft height to have twelve beams well bound to lay a false orlop of 1in elm board so far as need shall require, under which twelve beams must be twelve riders well bolted, and where the riders besides the footwales must have sufficient sleepers on every side fore and aft, and the pillars to be bolted sufficiently, the ground timbers and futtocks to be 14in deep and the 'posse' answerable in bigness of white sound and perfect oak.

3. The main orlop to have twelve beams well bound with side knees and standards, every knee having at least two bolts, and this orlop to be laid with 3in planks of sound and seasoned oak and caulked.

4. The second overlop to be well bound and laid with sound and seasoned 2in oak plank, and to be well bound with side knees and standards, every knee having at least two bolts.

5. The half-deck to the mast to be well bound and laid with 2in oak plank, to be well bound with side knees and hanging and every knee to have at least two bolts.

6. To have a forecastle and a barbican to the mast and other buildings above to fit the ship with comeliness.

7. The main capstan to allow the cat to be fair upon that orlop forward with a pair of carrack bitts.

8. The jeer capstan to be made aloft in the waist, and the cobridge heads to be made musket free with elm board.

9. The outside of the ship from the keel to the second wale to be wrought with 4in plank, and so much thereof as shall be above water to be dry stuff and seasoned from the upper wale to the quick side or waist to be dry 3in plank.

10. Above the waist to be 1¼in plank, cleft and fastened direct to the frames, and the rails to be inboard to go to the ship's side; the ship to be painted from 2ft above the chainwales, upward with colours in oil; to be carved likewise and garnished with gold, with galleries about the stern and casement as is fit for such a ship.

11. The making of two ovens and paving the kitchen likewise to be set up and the cook room to be done effectually below the false overlop in the hold of the said ship. The steward rooms, rope room and powder room to be fully furnished with such cabins before every of them as hath been usual, and the bread room to be sealed on the false overlop of the said ship.

12. Cabins to be made upon the lower orlop for the boatswain, the purser, the surgeon and the carpenter, and the quartermaster's cabin where it may be best placed by the bitts; the gunner's room likewise, and cabins therein where places may be had, and elsewhere upon that orlop where it may be thought convenient.

13. Cabins likewise to be made upon the second orlop for the company as place will suffer, and as shall be thought convenient by the lord admiral or the officers of the navy, together with a cabin abaft by the mizzen for the boatswain's mates.

14. The captain's cabin and the master's to be so wrought as they may be sealed to the plank with spruce deals or wainscot for avoiding of mice and rats, and that such windows be therein made as shall be thought fit by the lord admiral or the officers. The steerage likewise to be wrought and sealed with spruce deals, and a dining room for the

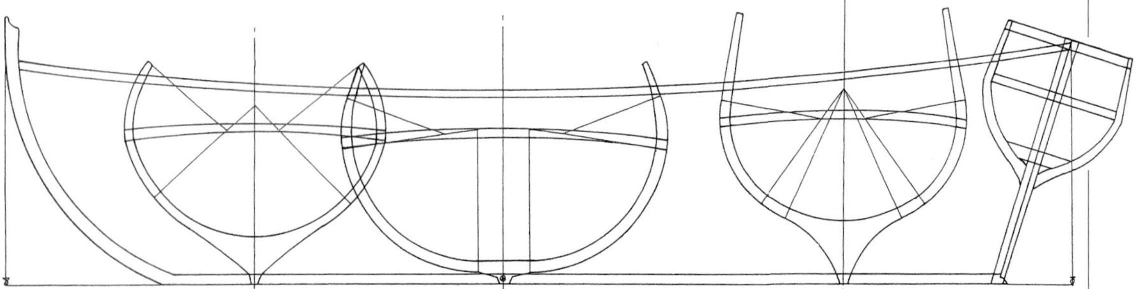

Doug McElvogue's reconstruction of the kind of plan that might have been the shipwright's starting point. It shows the shape of the keel, stem and sternpost, and the principal sections, from which the shape of the rest of the hull could be extrapolated.

captain, garnished and to be furnished with locks, bolts, hinges etc., and such cabins to be made before the steerage and the master's cabin as shall be thought fit by the lord admiral or the officers.

15. The ship to be sufficiently bound with knees, both standards and side knees, where it shall be thought meet, and that the beams be of a sufficient scantling, and the clamps to be 8in thick, the chainwales, wales and rails to be of a sufficient scantling, and with an edge above the flat for the better caulking. The hull is to be fortified and bound under the orlop and below, with timber to brace it and make it strong.

16. All the bolts and spikes, rudder irons and hinges for ports to be of Spanish iron, and the bolts under the chainwale to be of 1¼in through, and above that inch ¼ through, and more or less, as shall be thought meet by the lord admiral or officers of the navy.

17. The ship to be caulked with a thread of oakum and a thread of hair throughout and perfect 'puppett' oakum of hemp under the wales, in the rabbet of the stems, stern post, keel and transoms, as shall be thought meet by the lord admiral or the officers, and about the wales sufficiently as the place shall require.

18. A new boat, cock and jolly boat to be made sufficient and answerable in service for such a ship.

19. That all the masts and yards be made, fitted, set and closed up; and if there be not masts great enough, then to have the spills at her majesty's charge, and to make them up with oak.

20. All the ports to be furnished with ring bolts, and all such as be upon the lower orlop or elsewhere that hath a demi-culverin, port piece, cannon or above to have four ring bolts to a port, the rest two ring bolts to a port, with shackles and rings accordingly.

21. One main pump besides the main mast step in the belly of the ship.

APPENDIX 2
The Eight Other *Mary Roses*

EIGHT ROYAL NAVY VESSELS have borne the name *Mary Rose* and have served with distinction and, sadly, with great loss in battle. Few other ships' names have proved as popular in the history of the Royal Navy.

Battle Honours
Armada 1588; Cadiz 1596; Lowestoft 1665; Four Days' Battle 1666; Orfordness 1666; The Seven Algerines 1669; Sole Bay 1672; Schooneveld 1673; Texel 1673; Jutland 1916; Scandinavian Convoy 1917.

The Second *Mary Rose*
39-gun galleon, 500 tons, built 1556, rebuilt 1589 as 596 tons. In 1590, flagship of Sir John Hawkins. Took part in Cadiz expedition of 1596 and the Azores voyage of 1597 as well as 1599 expedition against Spain. In the latter expedition her commander was George Carew. In 1616, condemned, used to construct part of the wharf at Chatham.

The Third *Mary Rose*
26-gun ship, 300 tons, built Deptford 1623, wrecked 1650 off coast of Flanders.

The Fourth *Mary Rose*
A hired 32-gun ship that saw service between 1650 and 1654

The Fifth *Mary Rose*
Ex-*Maidstone*. 40-gun ship, 555 tons, built in Woodbridge 1654, renamed 1660, captured by French in Atlantic 12 July 1691. On 29 December 1669, Captain John Kempthorne saved a convoy from attack by seven ships of Algerine pirates whom he fought off single handed for four hours. He was knighted for this action. On 12 July 1691 she was captured by the French in the West Indies and fought against the English in 1696.

The Sixth *Mary Rose*
Ex-*Maria Rose*. A 4-gun brig that was captured from the French 18 March 1799 off Acre. Sold 1800s.

The Seventh *Mary Rose*
'M'-class destroyer, launched at Swan Hunter's, 8 October 1915. Took part in Battle of Jutland. On 17 October 1917, while escorting vessels to Norway, she was attacked by the German cruisers, *Bremse* and *Brummer*, seventy miles off the Shetland and sunk along with the destroyer *Strongbow* and nine of the convoy. Only ten of her complement of ninety-eight survived.

The Eighth *Mary Rose*
Fleet tender, purchased 1918, sold 1922.

The Ninth *Mary Rose*
Ex-*Toronto*. 'Algerine'-class minesweeper, launched at Redfern in Canada on 5 August 1943 for the Royal Canadian Navy but transferred immediately to the Royal Navy, and renamed. Broken up Gateshead 1957. She saw service mainly in the Mediterranean and Far East. The Sea Cadet Unit of Basingstoke and Deane bears the title *TS Mary Rose*.

ABOVE: The official crest of the later *Mary Roses*, ships that served in the twentieth-century Royal Navy and Royal Canadian Navy. The ships' badge reflects the Tudor origins of the name. On a white field within a laurel-green wreath a blue fleur-de-lis is surmounted by a rose per pale white and red.

RIGHT: Cadet at the Sea Cadet Unit TS *Mary Rose* in Basingstoke, piping the side.

Bibliography

THE PRINCIPAL SOURCE for anyone wishing to study the events of Henry VIII's reign are the *Letters and Papers, Foreign and Domestic, of the Reign of Henry VIII, 1509–47,* which were painstakingly edited by J S Brewer and his colleagues. They added very readable prefaces that are a mine of great wisdom and interpretation. C S Knighton and Professor Loades collated those letters that had been written from on board *Mary Rose,* and their *Letters from the Mary Rose* provide an excellent short cut to those documents relevant to the ship herself. Where I have considered it appropriate so to do I have referred to their book rather than the voluminous *Letters and Papers.* The recently published five volumes, *Archaeology of the Mary Rose,* is an encyclopaedic and very readable description of all that was found on board the ship and the hull in which they lay, and is essential reading for any student wishing to research the vessel itself in any detail.

Abbreviations

AMR *Archaeology of the Mary Rose*
EHR *English Historical Review*
HT *History Today*
LMR *Letters from the Mary Rose*
LP *Letters and Papers, Foreign and Domestic, of the Reign of Henry VIII*
MM *The Mariner's Mirror*
NRS *Navy Records Society*

Books

(Unless otherwise specified, all books were published in the United Kingdom)

Bellay, M du, *Memoires de Martin et Guillaume du Bellay,* (eds V-L Bourrilly and F Vindry), Paris, 1908–19.
Bindoff, S T, *Tudor England,* Penguin, 1950.
Bradford, E, *The Great Ship,* Hamish Hamilton, 1986.
Brewer, J S, Gardiner, J, and Brodie, R H (eds), *Letters and Papers, Foreign and Domestic of the Reign of Henry VIII, 1509–47,* London, 1862–1932.
Brenon, G and Statham, E P, *The House of Howard,* Hutchinson, 1907.
Byrne, M St C (ed), *The Lisle Letters,* Secker & Warburg, 1983.
Campbell, J, *History and Lives of the British Admirals,* London, 1813.
Clowes, W L, *The Royal Navy, A History from the Earliest Times to the Present Day,* Vol 1, London, 1897.
Corbett, J S, *Drake and the Tudor Navy,* Longmans, 1917.
——, (ed), *Fighting Instructions 1530–1816,* NRS Vol 29, 1905.
Cornou, J, *L'Héroique Combat de la Cordelière 1512,* Sked, Brest, 1998.
Cruickshank, C, *Henry VIII and the Invasion of France,* Alan Sutton, 1990.
Davies, J, *The King's Ships,* Partizan, 2005.
Elton, G R, *England under the Tudors,* Methuen, 1955.
Friel, Ian, *The Good Ship,* British Museum Press, 1995.
Gardiner, J, (ed), *Before the Mast: Life and Death aboard the Mary Rose,* AMR Vol 4, Mary Rose Trust, 2005.
Guilmartin, John, *Galleons and Galleys,* Cassell, 2002.
——, *Gunpowder and Galleys,* Conway Maritime Press, 2003.
Hacket, J, *Henry the Eighth,* Jonathan Cape, 1929.
Hall, E, *The Union of the Two Noble and Illustrious Families of York and Lancaster,* London, 1542.
——, *The Triumphant Reign of King Henry the Eighth,* London, 1547.
Hardy, R, *Longbow,* Patrick Stephens, 1976.
Hildred, A (ed), *Weapons of Warre: the Armaments of the Mary Rose,* AMR Vol 3, Mary Rose Trust, 2006.
Horsley, John, *Tools of the Maritime Trade,* David & Charles, 1978.
Hutchinson, R, *The Last Days of Henry VIII,* Weidenfeld & Nicolson, 2005.
Jones, M, *For Future Generations,* AMR Vol 5, Mary Rose Trust, 2003.
Knighton, C S and Loades, D M (eds), *The Anthony Roll,* NRS, 2000.
——, *Letters from the Mary Rose,* Sutton, 2002.
Leland, J, *Leland's Itinerary of England and Wales in about 1535–1543,* London 1710–12, London 1906–10, reprinted 1964.
Lister, T and Renshaw, J, *Conservation Chemistry – An Introduction,* Royal Society of Chemistry, 2004.
Loades, D, *England's Maritime Empire,* Longmans, 2000.
——, *The Tudor Navy,* Scolar, 1992.
Marsden, P (ed), *Sealed by Time,* AMR Vol 1, Mary Rose Trust, 2003.
—— (ed), *Your Noble Shippe: anatomy of a Tudor Warship,* Mary Rose Trust, 2006.
Mattingley, G, *Renaissance Diplomacy,* Cape, 1955.
McKee, A, *King Henry VIII's Mary Rose,* Souvenir, 1973.
——, *How We Found the Mary Rose,* Souvenir 1982.
Mudie, C, *Sailing Ships,* Adlard Coles Nautical Press, 2000.
Nelson, A, *The Tudor Navy 1485–1603,* Conway Maritime Press, 2001.
Oppenheim, M, *A History of the Administration of the Royal Navy,* 1896.
—— (ed), *Naval Accounts and Inventories of the Reign of Henry VII,* NRS, Vol 8, 1896.
—— (ed), *The Naval Tracts of Sir William Monson Vols I–V,* NRS, Vols 22, and 23, 1902; Vol 43, 1912; and Vols 45 and 47, 1915.
Parry, J H, *The Age of Reconnaissance,* Weidenfield & Nicolson, 1973.
Patterson, B, *A Military Heritage,* Fort Cumberland & Portsmouth Military Society, 1984.
Perrin, W G (ed), *Boteler's Dialogues,* NRS Vol 65, 1929.
Perry, M, *Sisters to the King,* Andre Deutsch, 1998.
Platt, C, *Medieval Southampton,* RKP, 1973.
Plowden, A, *Lady Jane Grey,* Sutton, 2003.
Ridley, J, *Henry VIII,* Constable, 1984.
Robinson, J M, *The Dukes of Norfolk,* Oxford University Press, 1982.
Rodger, N A M, *The Safeguard of the Sea,* Harper Collins, 1997.
Rule, M, *The Mary Rose: The Excavation and Raising of Henry VIII's Flagship,* Conway and Windward, 1982.

Sim, A, *Food and Feast in Tudor England*, Sutton, 1997.
Smith, John, *A Sea Grammar*, 1627; Goell K (ed), Michael Joseph, 1970.
Spont, A (ed), *Letters and Papers Relating to the War with France 1512–1513*, NRS Vol 10, 1897.
Stirland, A, *Raising the Dead*, Wiley, 2000.
Taylor, E G R, *The Haven Finding Art*, Hollis & Carter, 1971.
Unwin, R, *The Defeat of John Hawkins*, Allen & Unwin, 1960.
Waters, D W, *The Art of Navigation in England in Elizabethan and Early Stuart Times*, Hollis & Carter, 1958.
Weir, A, *Henry VIII, King and Court*, Cape, 2001.
Witherby, C T, *The Battle of Bonchurch*, published privately, 1962.
Wood, R, *The Wooden Bowl*, Stobart Davies, 2005.

Books for Youngsters

Norris, S, *Run Away to Danger*, National Maritime Museum, 2005.

Articles

Adair, E R, 'English Galleys in the Sixteenth Century', *EHR*, Vol 35, 1920.
Anderson, R C, 'Henry VIII's Great Galley', *MM*, Vol 6, 1920.
Barker R A, 'Fernando Oliviera: The English Episode', Academy de Marinha, Lisbon, 1992.
Bennell J E G, 'English Oared Vessels of the Sixteenth Century' (in two parts), *MM*, Vol 60, 1974.
Childs, D J, 'Shock and Oar – The *Mary Rose* and the Fear of the Galleys', *HT*, Vol 57 (4), 2007.
DeVries, K, 'The Effectiveness of Fifteenth-Century Shipboard Artillery', *MM*, Vol 84 (4), 1998.
Dobbs, C T C and Bridge, M, 'Preliminary Results from Dendrochronological Studies on the *Mary Rose*', *Proceedings of the Eighth International Symposium on Boat and Ship Archaeology*, Poland, 2000.
Eley, P, 'Portsmouth Breweries 1492–1847', *Portsmouth Papers*, Vol 51, 1988.
Fox, R and Barton, K, 'The Fourteenth-Century Dock in Oyster Street', *Post-Medieval Archaeology*, Vol 20, 1986.
Gunn, S, 'The Duke of Suffolk's March on Paris, 1523', *EHR*, Vol 101, 1986.
——, 'Tournaments and early Tudor Chivalry', *HT*, Vol 41 (6), 1991.
Howard, G F, 'Gun Port Lids', *MM*, Vol 67, 1981.
Jones M, et al, 'Sulphur accumulations in the timbers of Henry VIII's warship *Mary Rose*', *Proceedings of National Academy of Sciences of the United States*, Vol 102, 2005.
Kybett S M, 'Henry VIII – A Malnourished King?', *HT*, Vol 39, 1989.
Laughton L G, (ed), 'Early Tudor Ship-Guns', *MM*, Vol 46, 1960.
Lawson, W, 'The Boatswain's Call: its role in the European Maritime Tradition', Royal Swedish Academy of Music, No 53 (I), Stockholm 1986.
Merriman M, 'Realm and Castle: Henry VIII as European Castle Builder', *HT*, Vol 41, 1991.
McKee A, 'Henry VIII as Military Commander', *HT*, Vol 41, 1991.
Parker, G, 'The Dreadnought Revolution of Tudor England', *MM*, Vol 82 (3), 1996.
Richardson, G, 'Good Friends and Brothers? Francis I and Henry VIII', *HT*, Vol 44, 1994.
Rodger, N A M, 'The Development of Broadside Gunnery 1450–1650', *MM*, Vol 82 (3), 1996.
Scammell, G V, 'European Seamanship in the Great Age of Discovery', *MM*, Vol. 68, November 1982.
Strachan, M, 'Sampson's Fight with the Maltese Galleys, 1628', *MM*, Vol 55, 1969.
Vaughan, H S, 'Figure-Heads and Beak-Heads of the ships of Henry VIII', *MM*, Vol 42, 1914.
Watt, J, 'Surgeons of the *Mary Rose*', *MM*, Vol 69, 1983.
Wood, A B, 'The Laws of Oleron', *MM*, Vol 4, 1914.

Charts and Pilots

NP 27 Channel Pilot, The Hydrography Office.
Charts: 1545 Roscoff and Morlaix.

Notes and References

Abbreviations
AMR *Archaeology of the Mary Rose*
HT *History Today*
LMR *Letters from the Mary Rose*
LP *Letters and Papers, Foreign and Domestic, of the Reign of Henry VIII*
MM *Mariner's Mirror*
NRS *Navy Records Society*

Introduction

1 McKee, Alexander, *King Henry VIII's Mary Rose*, Souvenir, 1973.
2 Rule, Margaret, *The Mary Rose*, Windward, 1982.
3 Bradford, Ernle, *The Story of the Mary Rose*, Hamish Hamilton, 1982.
4 *The Archaeology of the Mary Rose* (AMR), five volumes, Mary Rose Trust, 2003–07.
5 *Letters from the Mary Rose*, (LMR), Sutton, 2002.

Chapter 1

1 LP Vol 1, Pt 1, 5.
2 Ibid, 19.
3 Indeed, without Henry's building and demolition the core estate of English Heritage would be missing.
4 LP Vol 1, Pt 1, 17. Henry VII is referred to as, 'most miserly but of great genius, who has accumulated more gold than that possessed by all other Christian Kings.' His son was to spend it all and more.
5 NRS 1993.
6 Strangely, it was only after the loss of Calais in Mary I's reign that the English looked beyond Europe for their overseas expansion as if, freed from European possessions, they could seek new lands afar.
7 LP Vol 1, Pt 1, 119.
8 Davies, C S, *MM*, Vol 56, 1970.
9 Knighton, C S and Loades, D M (eds), *The Anthony Roll*, NRS 2000 and Pepys Library.
10 Rodger, N A M, *The Safeguard of the Sea*, Harper Collins, 1997.

Chapter 2

1 See *Rudyard Kipling's Verse*, Hodder and Stoughton, 1940.
2 Ibid.
3 The Cowdray engraving is a copy of a painting showing comprehensive depiction of events at Portsmouth on 19 July 1545, and the loss of *Mary Rose*. It was painted for the vain Sir Anthony Browne, Captain of the King's Horse, to adorn his dining room at Cowdray House and to show his guests how close to the king's person he was on that day. The painting was lost in a fire in 1793 but, luckily, a detailed copy had been commissioned by the Society of Antiquaries in 1778, and this version survives.
4 Leland, John, *Itinerary*..., iii, m 81, 82, *c*.1540.
5 The exact location of this dry dock is unknown, but it probably lies close to Number 1 Basin in Portsmouth Dockyard, and within fifty metres of where *Mary Rose* is on display today.
6 Fox R and Barton K, 'The Fourteenth Century Dock in Oyster Street', *Post-Medieaval Archaeology*, 20, 1986.
7 In the cellar of Dawtry's house are two vast roof beams that look far too large for the task. They are, however, of the size of a main beam for a warship: 'the measure of all that's made', perhaps?
8 LMR 1.
9 Ibid.
10 Ibid.
11 Sutherland, William, *The Shipbuilder's Assistant and Maritime Architecture*, London, 1711.
12 Pepys Collection, Magdalen College, Cambridge, MS PL 2820.
13 Now in the Royal Collection at Hampton Court.
14 However, for the smaller *Sweepstake*, built at Portsmouth in 1497, clenching nails and roves were purchased. See, Oppenheim, M (ed), *Naval Accounts and Inventories of Henry VII*, NRS Vol 8, 1896.
15 Ibid.
16 Ibid.
17 Ibid.
18 Horsley, J, *Tools of the Maritime Trade*, David & Charles, 1978.
19 LMR 14.
20 Ibid.
21 Callender, Sir G, *The Naval Side of English History*, London, 1920.
22 Ibid.
23 Such a stump, believed to be from *Sovereign*, was found in the Thames at Woolwich in 1912.
24 Knighton, C S and Loades, D M (eds), *The Anthony Roll*, NRS 2000 and Pepys Library.
25 The grapnel from *Mary Rose* was raised by the Deane brothers in 1840, but has since been lost. Research by Doug McElvogue of the Mary Rose Trust indicates that it had four barbs and was 1.4m long.
26 In May 2006, AmSafe, a Bridport ropemaker, won a £16 million contract with Airbus to make specialist, state-of-the-art cargo restraint nets.
27 Oppenheim, op cit (note 14 above).
28 Ibid.
29 Today, Locronan's houses still reflect the affluence that grew from such trade so that, with cloth production long ceased, it is much visited as one of the prettiest of all Breton villages.
30 Oppenheim, op cit.
31 Ibid.
32 Ibid.
33 Firstbrook, P, *The Voyage of the Matthew*, BBC, 1997.
34 Ibid.
35 Ibid.

Chapter 3

1 The full complement of flags was a banner of St Katherine in metal; five banners of the arms of Boulogne in metal; four banners of the arms of England and Castile in metal; four banners of the Rose and Pomegranate in metal; one of St. Peter in metal; two of the Castile in metal; one streamer of St George in colour; one streamer of the red lion in colour; one streamer of the Castile in colour. In addition she carried eighteen banner staves. See Hobbs, D, 'Royal ships and their flags in the late fifteenth and early sixteenth century', *MM*, Vol 80

(4), 1994.
2 The idea that muzzle loaders were sponged out, recharged and reloaded by sailors working outboard in full view and easy range of the enemy is based on a landsman's eye for the possible, not a seaman's eye for the practical.
3 Quoted in Rodger, N A M, 'The Development of Broadside Gunnery, 1450–1650', *MM*, Vol 82, No 3, 1996.
4 Ibid.
5 Ibid.
6 See Bourne W, *The Art of Shooting in Great Ordnance*, London, 1587; Tartaglia, N, *Three Books of Colloquies*, London, 1588; Collado, L, *Practica Manuale di Artiglieria*, Venice, 1641; and Eldred, W, *The Gunner Glasse*, London, 1646.
7 Cyprian Lucar 1588 English edition of the Venetian Tartaglia's *Colloquies*. See note 6 above.
8 See chapter 5.
9 See chapter 11.
10 Quoted in *The Royal Navy: A History from the Earliest Times to the Present*, London, 1897–1903.
11 Strachan, M, 'Sampson's fight with Maltese Galleys, 1628', *MM*, Vol 55, No 3.
12 A boarding 'beak' up forward had replaced the classic ram. For a detailed discussion of the impact of sixteenth-century galleys, see Guilmartin, J F, *Gunpowder and Galleys*, Conway Maritime Press, 2003.
13 Document in Portsmouth City Museum.
14 From his poem '*Agincourt*' aka '*Fair Stood the Wind for France*'.
15 See Hardy, R, *Longbow*, Patrick Stephens, 1976.
16 AMR Vol 3.

Chapter 4

1 Gunn, S J, 'The Duke of Suffolk's March on Paris in 1523', *EHR* Vol 101, 1986.
2 An indication of the importance that Henry placed on having the right men in command at sea can be gauged from the fact that, of the organisers of the joust to celebrate his coronation (Lord Thomas Howard, Sir Edward Howard, Lord Richard Grey, Sir Edmund Howard, Sir Thomas Knyvet and Charles Brandon), four would serve at sea, two as Lord Admiral.
3 Brenon, G and Statham, E P, *The House of Howard*, Hutchinson, 1907.
4 *The Ballad of Andrew Barton*, author unknown, was written shortly after Barton's death. It can be found in *The Child Ballads*, a collection of 305 ballads from England and Scotland, and their American variants, collected by Francis James Child in the late 19th century. The collection was published as *The English and Scottish Popular Ballads* between 1882 and 1898.
5 *The Ballad of Andrew Barton*, see above.
6 Quoted in 'Lloyd's State Worthies'.
7 Campbell, J, *History and Lives of the British Admirals*, London, 1813.
8 Glanville, P, 'The Howard Grace Cup', *HT*, Vol 44 (10), 1994.
9 See LMR and LP.
10 Brenon, G and Statham, E P, op cit.
11 Weir, A, *Henry VIII, King and Court*, Jonathan Cape, 2001.
12 Ibid.
13 LMR 28.
14 Ibid.
15 Ibid.
16 Froude, James Anthony, *History of England from the Fall of Wolsey to the Defeat of the Spanish Armada*, 1856–70.
17 Sandford, Francis, *Genealogical History of the Kings of England*, London, 1707.
18 The affair of the Maid of Kent was an uprising against the Act of Succession formed around the visions of a poor servant-girl, Elizabeth Barton, who was executed in 1534.
19 The Boltof Conspiracy was a supposed Catholic plot to seize Calais.
20 LMR 7.
21 Ibid.
22 Audley, Thomas, *Book of Orders for the War both by Sea and Land*, 1530.
23 Ibid.
24 Ibid.
25 Ibid.
26 LMR 10.
27 Ibid.
28 Ibid.
29 LP 20, Pt 1, 1237.

Chapter 5

1 Smith, John, *A Sea Grammar*, 1627; Goell K (ed), Michael Joseph, 1970.
2 Waters, D W, *The Art of Navigation in England in Elizabethan and Early Stuart Times*, Hollis & Carter, London, 1958.
3 Chaucer, Geoffrey, *The Canterbury Tales*, Coghill (trans), Penguin, 1963.
4 Cited in Wareham, T (ed), *Frigate Commander*, Pen & Sword, 2004.
5 Bourne, W, *A Regiment for the Sea*, 1574, reprinted, Cambridge, 1963.
6 See AMR Vol 4.
7 LMR 52, 53.
8 Scammell, G V, 'European Seamanship in the Great Age of Discovery', *MM*, Vol 68 (4), 1982.
9 Nelson, A, *The Tudor Navy*, Conway Maritime Press, 2001.
10 Wedderburn, R, *The Complaynt of Scotland, 1550*, Stewart, A M (ed), Scottish Text Society, 1979.

Chapter 6

1 Paul Burgess, of quantity surveyors Davis Langdon, has estimated the space available on the main deck for sleeping to be some 240 sq m. Allowing 1 sq m per person this means that half the ship's company could lie down here at any one time. This, however, makes no allowance for passageways. Some would have slept in both the fore- and after castles.
2 The user could wipe himself clean by hauling a rope whose frayed end dangled from the heads into the sea.
3 When the remains of *Batavia*, a Dutch merchantman that sank off Australia in 1628, were investigated in the 1970s a large black mass in the bilges proved to be human excreta.
4 Smith, John, *A Sea Grammar*, 1627; Goell K (ed), Michael Joseph, 1970.
5 Ear wax was a useful organic product for waxing twine when stitching leather.
6 Smith, John, op cit.
7 Shakespeare, William, *Henry V*, Act III, Prologue.
8 1532 Act of Excess in Apparel.
9 Rule, Margaret, *The Mary Rose*, Windward, 1982.

10 Smith, John, op cit.
11 This portrait can be seen today at The Barber Surgeons' Hall, London.
12 Stirland, A, *Raising the Dead*, John Wiley & Sons, 2000.
13 Watt, J, 'Surgeons of the Mary Rose', *MM*, Vol 69 (1), 1983.
14 LP Vol 1, Pt 2, 1913.
15 Royal proclamation, 24 January 1545.
16 Ket's rebellion was a rising of the poor in Norfolk against abuses by the gentry in July 1549.

Chapter 7

1 Hacket, J, *Henry the Eighth,* Jonathan Cape, 1929.
2 LP Vol 1, Pt 2, 1912.
3 A pipe was the equivalent of 126 gallons and, in solids, represented enough meat to last 100 men for one week of four 'flesh' days.
4 LP Vol 1, Pt 2, 1912.
5 'Jamie Oliver's School Dinners', Channel 4, 2005.
6 William Cecil, Lord Burghley, to the Privy Council, 13 March 1588.
7 Elyot, Thomas, *Castel of Helth* 1539. This was a popular medical book at the time.
8 Culpeper, Nicholas, *Culpeper's Complete Herbal*, 1653.
9 *A Discourse Concerning His Majesty's Ships in the Year 1618*. Author unknown.
10 Stirland, A, *Raising the Dead*, John Wiley & Sons, 2000.
11 Ibid.
12 LMR 13.
13 LMR 14.
14 Ibid.
15 LMR 15.
16 LMR 17.
17 LP Vol 1, Pt 1, 1944.
18 LMR 30.
19 LP Vol 1, Pt 1, 1913.
20 LMR 48.
21 Ibid.
22 The essential difference between ale and beer is that the latter includes hops which, as well as adding flavour, help preserve the brew. Thus ale production was seen as a domestic activity for family consumption, whereas beer was brewed in commercial establishments on an industrial level.
23 Held in Portsmouth City Museum.
24 See Chapter 3, note 2.
25 LMR 30.
26 LP Vol 1, Pt 1, 1864.
27 LMR 53.
28 LMR 57.

Chapter 8

1 Quoted in Starkey, D, *Six Wives*, Chatto & Windus, 2003.
2 LP Vol 1, Pt 1, 83.
3 Ibid. Transportation costs for these and similar items were carefully laid down, for example, ¼d a sheaf of arrows for fifty miles and 2d a mile for every 500 bill heads transported from Birmingham.
4 LP Vol 1, Pt 1, 1661.
5 Spont, A, *Letters and papers relating to the war with France 1512–13*, NRS Vol 10, 1897.
6 Jean de Veau to Margaret of Anjou, LP Vol I, Pt 1, 1075. The slaughter of the civilian population of Brescia is a vivid illustration of the cruelty of sixteenth-century warfare: see, LP Vol I, Pt 1, 1071.
7 LP Vol I, Pt 2, 1147.
8 Ibid, 1268.
9 Duchess Anne of Brittany had married both Charles VIII then Louis XII of France. The agreement had been that Brittany would be enfoeffed to a younger son or an elder daughter. There were no surviving sons from either marriage, but her daughter Claudia then married Francis I who, after her death, simply annexed the duchy to the royal domain.
10 Hector de Vicquernon to Margaret of Savoy, LP Vol I, Pt 2, 1265.
11 Ushant is known to the Bretons as Enez-Heussa (Isle of Terror).
12 The disjointed fighting that took place indicates that tactical thinking had not yet evolved to deploying warships in line astern, *ie* led by their admiral, a tactic on which later broadside gunnery engagements would be based. The first occasion when such a formation was used probably did not occur until 1558, in a fight between the Portuguese, English and French freebooters off Guinea.
13 Holinshed, Raphael, *The Chronicles of England, Scotland and Ireland…*, London, 1577.
14 Ibid.
15 Spont op cit.
16 Brenon, G and Statham, E P, *The House of Howard*, Hutchinson, 1907.
17 Audley, Thomas, *Book of Orders for the War both by Sea and Land*, 1530.
18 The poem 'Casabianca' is far better known by the words of its first line, 'The boy stood on the burning deck'. Written by Mrs Felicia Dorothea Hemans, it was first published in *The Monthly Magazine*, August 1826.
19 See the Mass of Saint Laurence, Old Sarum Rite Missal, Saint Hilarion Press, 1998.
20 Spont op cit.
21 Ibid.
22 Ibid.
23 Napier, William, *English Battles and Sieges in the Peninsula*, London, 1866.
24 Quoted in Spont op cit.
25 LP Vol 1, Pt 1, 1480.
26 Ibid, 1532.
27 Spont op cit.
28 Colburn, H, *Letters of the Kings of England*, Harvard, 1846.
29 LP Vol I, Pt 1, 1704, 1705.
30 The eight ships were: *Katherine Fortileza*, *Gabriel Royal*, *John Baptist*, *Mary George*, *Lizard*, *Great Nicholas*, *Christ* and *Mary James*.
31 LP Vol 1, Pt 2, 1661.
32 LMR 13.
33 Ibid.
34 Ibid.
35 LMR 14.
36 Ibid.
37 LMR 15.
38 Ibid.
39 LMR 16.
40 Ibid.
41 Recorded in the Naval Payments for late 1513.
42 Spont op cit.
43 Holinshed op cit.
44 Spont op cit.
45 Ibid.
46 LP Vol I. Pt 2, 1844.
47 Ibid.
48 Gunn, Steven, 'Tournaments and Early Tudor Chivalry', *HT*, Vol 41 (6), 1991.

Chapter 9

1 LMR 18.

2 LMR 17.
3 Ibid.
4 LMR 18.
5 LMR 17.
6 Ibid.
7 Ibid.
8 Ibid.
9 LMR 23.
10 LMR 21.
11 LMR 25.
12 LMR 23.
13 LMR 26.
14 Ibid.
15 LMR 28.
16 Underneath which line Elizabeth wrote, 'If the heart fail thee, then climb not at all'. See Fuller, Thomas, *Worthies of England*, London, 1840.
17 LMR 28.
18 LMR 29.
19 LMR 31.
20 Ibid.
21 LP Vol 1, Pt 2, 2422.
22 LMR 39.
23 LMR 40. For a discussion of how the fear of the galleys affected English naval policy see, Childs, D J, 'Shock and Oar – *Mary Rose* and the Fear of the Galleys', *HT*, Vol 57 (4), 2007.
24 Spont, A, *Letters and papers relating to the war with France 1512–13*, NRS Vol 10, 1897.
25 Ibid.
26 LMR 40.
27 Ibid.
28 Carried out by Prégent de Bidoux in April 1514.
29 LMR 41.
30 Quote in Plowden, A, *Lady Jane Grey*, Sutton, 2003.

Chapter 10

1 Rodger, N A M, *The Safeguard of the Sea*, Harper Collins, 1997, p.221.
2 LMR 43.
3 Ibid.
4 LP, Vol 3, Pt 2, 2296.
5 Ibid.
6 LMR 47.
7 LMR 48.
8 Ibid.
9 LMR 49.
10 LMR 53.
11 LMR 52.
12 LP Vol 3, Pt 2, 2306.
13 Ibid, 2308.
14 Ibid, 2315.
15 NP 27, *The Channel Pilot*, Hydrography Office and Admiralty Chart 2745.
16 Ibid.
17 Ibid. *Mary Rose* had a length of 38.5m, and a draught of 4.6m.
18 Moorhouse, G, *Great Harry's Navy*, Weidenfeld & Nicholson, 2005.
19 LMR 53.
20 Ibid.
21 LMR 54.
22 Ibid.
23 Bingham, C, *James V*, Collins, 1971.
24 Dobbs, C and Bridge, M, 'Preliminary Results from Dendrochronological Studies on the *Mary Rose*', *Proceedings of Eighth International Symposium on Boat and Ship Archaeology*, 1997.

Chapter 11

1 The 'Pilgrimage of Grace' was a popular and potentially serious uprising in the north of England in 1536, led by the traditional religious idealist, Robert Aske, in protest against the dissolution of the monasteries and other religious reforms. It was defeated through a combination of the rebels' gullibility with the guile of Thomas Howard, by now Duke of Norfolk.
2 Marsden, R G (ed), *Documents relating to Law and Custom of the Sea*, NRS Vol 49, 1915.
3 See Loades, D, *The Tudor Navy*, Scolar, 1992.
4 These words were later famously echoed by John of Gaunt in William Shakepseare's *Richard II*, Act II, scene 1. See also, Morison, R, *Exhortation to styre all Englishe men to the defence of ther countreye, London 1539*.
5 See Merriman, M, 'Realm and Castle', *HT*, Vol 41 (6), 1991.
6 Ibid.
7 Quoted in Oppenheim, M, *A History of the Administration of the Royal Navy 1509–1660*, London, 1896.
8 Admiralty Court Exemplification 1, No 23.
9 Marsden, R G, op cit.
10 Ibid.
11 Audley, Speaker of Parliament from 1529 to 1535, and later Lord Chancellor, is another example of the small coterie upon whom the Tudors relied. His great house, Audley End, built from the dissolved abbey of Walden, descended to Thomas Howard (son of the fourth Duke of Norfolk) who fought against the Spanish Armada.
12 See Corbett, J (ed), *Fighting Instructions, 1530–1816*, NRS Vol 29, 1905.
13 Ibid.
14 Ibid.
15 Ibid.
16 Ibid.
17 Ibid.
18 Ibid.
19 LP Vol 14, Pt 1, 144.
20 Loades, op cit.
21 LP Spanish, Vol 7, 107.
22 Hughes, P F and Larkin, J L, *Tudor Royal Proclamations*, Cambridge, Mass., 1964.
23 LP Vol 20, Pt 1, 7.
24 Ibid, 1023.
25 Du Bellay, M, *Memoires...de plusiers choses adveniies au Royaume de France* .... Paris 1569, reprinted in *Memoires de Martin et Guillaume du Bellay*, Bourrilly, V-L, and Vindry, F, (eds) Paris 1908–19.

Chapter 12

1 Corbett, J, *Drake and the Tudor Navy*, London, 1917.
2 McKee, A, *King Henry VIII's Mary Rose*, Souvenir, 1973.
3 Loades, D, *The Tudor Navy*, Scholar, 1992.
4 Rodger, N A M, *The Safeguard of the Sea*, Harper Collins, 1997.
5 Hall, E, *The Union of the Two Noble and Illustrious Families of York and Lancaster*, London, 1542. Commonly known as 'Hall's Chronicle'.
6 Du Bellay, M, *Memoires...de plusiers choses adveniies au Royaume de France* .... Paris 1569, reprinted in *Memoires de Martin et Guillaume du Bellay*, Bourrilly, V-L, and Vindry, F, (eds) Paris 1908–19.
7 Stirland, A, *Raising the Dead*, John Wiley & Sons, 2000.
8 La Valette (1494–1568) was Forty-eighth Grand Master of the Order of the Knights of St. John of Jerusalem.
9 Du Bellay op cit.
10 Ibid.

11 LP Vol 20, Pt 1, 1235.
12 Du Bellay op cit.
13 Ibid.
14 Ibid.
15 LP Vol 20, Pt 1, 1237. These were the same tactics that Drake was to employ against the Spanish Armada in 1588.
16 Ibid.
17 McKee, A, 'Henry VIII as Military Commander', *HT*, Vol 41, 1991.
18 Witherby, C T, *The Battle of Bonchurch*, published privately, 1962.
19 Ibid.
20 LP Vol 20, Pt 2, 16.
21 Ibid, 2.
22 Ibid, 26.
23 Ibid, 39.
24 Ibid, 5.
25 *State Papers of Henry VIII*, I (2) 136.
26 Quoted in Corbett, op cit.
27 Ibid.
28 Ibid.
29 LP Vol 20, Pt 2, 158.
30 Ibid, 1313.
31 D'Annebault, now in the role of ambassador.
32 LP Vol 20, Pt 2, 860.
33 Quoted in Barker, R A, *Fernando Oliviera: The English Episode, 1546–7*, Academia de Marinha, Lisbon, 1992.
34 Quoted in Bennell, J E G, 'English Oared Vessels of the Sixteenth Century', *MM*, Vol 60, 1974.
35 LP Vol 19, Pt 1, 512.
36 Bennell, J E G, op cit.
37 Nelson, A, *The Tudor Navy*, Conway Maritime Press, 2001.
38 The second ship to be named *Mary Rose* was built in Mary I's reign and converted to this new class in 1589.

Chapter 13

1 I am indebted to John Morgan of the Mary Rose Information Group for drawing my attention to this phenomenon.
2 Hooker, R, *The Lyffe of Sir Peter Carew*, 1575, published London, 1839.
3 The danger of adding decks to a ship not originally designed to carry them was illustrated recently with the capsize of a pleasure craft in Bahrain Harbour in 2006 with much loss of life. The weight and movement of passengers high up created the moment that led to her capsize.
4 *The Naval Tracts of Sir William Monson*, NRS Vol 22, 1902.
5 Anon, *The Complaynt of Scotland*, *c.*1550. Although anonymous, the work is widely believed to have been written by Robert Wedderburn, then Vicar of Dundee.
6 Hooker, op cit.
7 Guilmartin, J F, *Galleons and Galleys*, Cassell, 2002.
8 Rodger, N A M, 'The Development of Broadside Gunnery 1450–1650', *MM*, Vol 82 (3), 1996.
9 Strachan, M, 'Sampson's fight with Maltese Galleys, 1628', *MM*, Vol 55 (3).
10 *The Naval Tracts of Sir William Monson*, NRS Vol. 22, 1902.
11 Quoted in Wilson, D, *The World Encompassed*, Hamish Hamilton, 1977.
12 Quoted in McKee, A, *King Henry VIII's Mary Rose*, Souvenir, 1973.
13 Woodes, Rogers, *A Cruising Voyage Round the World*, London, 1712.
14 Cowper, William, 'On the Loss of the Royal George (written when the news arrived)', 1782.
15 Quoted in Weir, A, *Henry VIII, King and Court*, Cape, 2001.

Chapter 14

1 LMR 65.
2 *Jesus of Lubeck* had been seized by the Spaniards in 1568 at San Juan de Ulua during Hawkins's third voyage to the West Indies.
3 Suffolk to Paget, LMR 66.
4 LMR 72.
5 Ungerer, G, *Medieval and Renaissance Drama in England*, Vol 17, 2004.
6 'Toll for the Brave', by William Cowper written in 1782 to commemorate the tragic loss of the *Royal George.*
7 McKee A, *How We Found the Mary Rose*, Souvenir Press, 1982.
8 Ibid.
9 Young M, *Mary Rose – A Diver's View*, published privately, 2005.
10 These scaffolding poles were placed for the divers to hold on to while they worked to so that they would not raise clouds of fine silt to reduce further the visibility on the ever gloomy sea bed.
11 Stirland, A, *Raising the Dead*, John Wiley & Sons, 2000. Study of the DNA in the bones of a pig that was recovered led to a breakthrough in forensic science when it was proved that DNA could be extracted from old bones.
12 *The News.*
13 Ibid.
14 Ibid.
15 Ibid.
16 Ibid.
17 Ibid, 12 October 1981.
18 Ibid, 16 March 1982.
19 See AMR Vols 1 and 5.
20 *The News*, 2 October 1982.
21 Rule, Margaret, *The Mary Rose*, Windward, 1982.

Chapter 15

1 The *Vasa* was the Swedish warship that sank off Stockholm in 1628, minutes into her maiden voyage. She was raised almost complete in 1961.
2 A parrel is a collar of rope secured around the mast and attached to a yard enabling the latter to be hauled up and down. To reduce friction a number of wooden balls were fitted to run up and down the mast within the collar, thus acting as ball bearings.
3 This painting can now be seen in the Barber Surgeons' Hall in London.
4 The group consisted of Wilkinson Eyre, Pringle Brandon, Land Design, Gifford and Davis Langdon.

Index